T0383095

COLLECTED STUDIES SERIES

The Atlantic Frontier of the Thirteen American Colonies and States

Professor Jacob M. Price

Jacob M. Price

The Atlantic Frontier of the Thirteen American Colonies and States

Essays in Eighteenth Century
Commercial and Social History

VARIORUM
1996

This edition copyright © 1996 by Jacob M. Price.

Published by VARIORUM
Ashgate Publishing Limited
Gower House, Croft Road,
Aldershot, Hampshire GU11 3HR
Great Britain

Ashgate Publishing Company
Old Post Road,
Brookfield, Vermont 05036
USA

ISBN 0–86078–586–6

British Library CIP Data

Price, Jacob M. (Jacob Myron)
The Atlantic Frontier of the Thirteen American Colonies and States.
(Variorum Collected Studies Series; CS532).
1. United States–History–Colonial period, *ca.* 1600–1775. 2. Great
Britain–Colonies–America. I. Title.
973. 2

US Library of Congress CIP Data

Price, Jacob M.
The Atlantic Frontier of the Thirteen American Colonies and States / by
Jacob M. Price. – 1st ed. p. cm. – (Collected Studies Series; CS532).
Includes Index. (cloth: alk paper).
1. United States–Commerce–Great Britain–History–18th century.
2. Great Britain–Commerce–United States–History–18th century.
3. United States–Foreign economic relations–Great Britain. 4. Great
Britain–Foreign economic relations–United States. 5. Slave trade–
United States–History–18th century. 6. Slave trade–Great Britain–
History–18th century. I. Title. II. Series: Collected Studies Series; CS532.
HF3093. P75 1996   96–3758
382' . 097304–dc20   CIP

The paper used in this publication meets the minimum requirements of the
American National Standard for Information Sciences – Permanance of Paper
for Printed Library Materials, ANSI Z39.48–1984. ∞ ™

Printed by Galliard (Printers) Ltd, Great Yarmouth, Norfolk, Great Britain

COLLECTED STUDIES SERIES C532

CONTENTS

This volume contains xii + 270 pages

INTRODUCTION: FACING EAST

When Variorum expressed interest in republishing some of my articles, I naturally wondered about selection and arrangement. A single large volume might well have been too bulky and too expensive. It would also have shown relatively little thematic unity. Therefore we agreed that a substantial selection of my articles would be published in three separate volumes, each emphasizing somewhat different themes. The first, *Tobacco in Atlantic Trade* (published in December 1995) contained articles on the Atlantic tobacco trades and the colonial Chesapeake economy and social structure. The third, *Overseas Trade and Traders* will include papers more immediately relevant to British history. The present, the second volume, offers articles that 'face east', i.e., that are concerned with some of the external relations – commercial, political and cultural – of the thirteen North American colonies.

The wide variety of topics covered in the seven articles in this volume reflects to some degree my reluctance to decline invitations to what appear likely to prove interesting conferences. The first paper on 'The Transatlantic Economy' was prepared for a conference arranged by Professors Jack Greene and J.R. Pole at St Catherine's College, Oxford, in 1981. The second was written for the First Soviet-American Historical Colloquium held in Moscow in October 1972. At this conference, devoted to town studies, the United States was represented by Professors John Alexander, Bernard Bailyn, Leopold Haimson, Henry May and myself. The fifth paper – on credit in slave economies – was prepared for a conference organized by Barbara Solow on 'Slavery and the Rise of the Atlantic System' held at Harvard University in September 1988. The seventh was prepared in conjunction with a conference held at the Hall of Records in Annapolis in June 1975 to honor the retirement of Morris Radoff after thirty-five years as state archivist of Maryland. I was out of the country then and unable to attend the conference but was happy to contribute to the resulting volume honoring the creator of the Maryland archives. The sixth paper arose more indirectly from a conference held at Williamsburg in September 1985 on Anglo-American cultural history, *ca.* 1600–1820. Although I was not invited to the conference, I did accept a later invitation from the editors of its transactions to add a paper on the significance of the colonial connection for British society.

The papers in this volume are arranged not in chronological order but rather in a sequence proceeding roughly from the general to the particular. First comes a wide-ranging piece on 'The Transatlantic Economy'. It is not a report on research but a deliberately broad introduction to a big subject. In writing it, I imagined potential readers to include graduate students looking for a dissertation topic or approach. It introduces some of the principal types of sources available, and then the 'four dominant foci of attention for the study of colonial economic history: the empire, the colony, the community and the commodity'. Admitting my sympathy with the commodity approach, I also looked briefly at the familiar staple and population models for colonial development. Both help clarify the importance of market and other outside forces in the development of the major colonial export economies.

After the rather generalizing character of the first chapter come three more sharply focused papers. Chapter II examines at some length the comparative commercial, demographic and social character of the principal North American ports and tries to suggest some possible explanations for their differing success.[1]

Almost all investigations of likely early modern commercial or maritime topics soon run into the dead end of inadequate data. While the Public Record Office contains comprehensive national trade statistics for England from 1696 and for Scotland from 1755, those for the Thirteen Colonies cover only the years 1768–1772. But some other helpful accounts were prepared in the eighteenth century and have sometimes survived. The third article included in this volume discusses a document uncovered in the House of Lords Library which permits carrying back the Scottish and British foreign trade series to 1740.

The shipyards of colonial North America turned out vessels of every description, many destined for export sale. Maritime historians have long known about colonial shipbuilding, but there has been some disagreement about the exact tonnage launched and the value of vessels sold abroad. The third chapter attempts to review the question and to offer acceptable estimates about both colonial shipbuilding and the value of export sales *ca.* 1770.

Perhaps the most serious topic now under discussion in the economic and social history of the Atlantic world is the introduction and expansion of African slavery. The process was quite rapid with the black population of the British colonies in the West Indies and North America increasing over 50-fold between 1650 and 1770, and reaching about a million by the time of the American Revolution. How, one must wonder, was this great social upheaval managed and financed? Article V surveys the varieties of credit used to support the slave trade and the slave plantation economies.

An elusive and less frequently essayed aspect of Anglo-American history is the problem of the colonial impact on Britain. Features of this wide-ranging

---

[1] I have also written a paper, as yet unpublished, on some similar topics affecting competition between contemporary British ports. It was commissioned for a 1995 conference sponsored by the Spanish government.

questions are raised in Chapter VI, 'Who Cared About the the Colonies?' In 1924, Jay Barrett Botsford published a once well-known book entitled *English Society in the Eighteenth Century as Influenced from Overseas*. His research was based on printed materials suggesting the effects on English society of new commodities, new trades, new trading companies, and new or much expanded port towns that emerged to serve such trades and other overseas activities ranging from wars to missionary campaigns. Most researchers today would, I suspect, regard Botsford's ambitious scope as too vast for the limited research materials and techniques at hand. As a result, his rather literary approach appears impressionistic. By contrast, in writing Chapter VI, I tried to discern, as quantitatively as possible, what economic, social and geographic elements in Britain were privately or publicly interested in the colonies.

The seventh chapter, 'The Maryland Bank Stock Case', will appear much narrower in focus than most or all the above – even if its history stretches over three-quarters of a century. Maryland was a relatively conservative community and desired a trustworthy paper currency. To attract the desired confidence, in the 1730's, the colonial legislature established a trust fund in London to be built up by the proceeds of an export tax on the province's tobacco. The London merchants charged with the management of this trust were instructed to invest funds received in Bank of England shares which, it was expected, would secure the colony's paper money. All went well until the Revolution divided the interests of the new state and its trustees, necessitating after the war a generation of chancery suits and international diplomacy before the matter was finally settled in 1805. In the long run, perhaps the most interesting feature of the colonial Marylanders' experience was their ability to obtain relative monetary stability by tying their paper to the London stock market – another way in which a colony's economic life might 'face east'.

*   *   *

This volume is dedicated to Dr Lois Green Carr of Annapolis, an exemplar, guide and friend to all early modern researchers who come her way.

PUBLISHER'S NOTE

The articles in this volume, as in all others in the Collected Studies Series, have not been given a new, continuous pagination. In order to avoid confusion, and to facilitate their use where these same studies have been referred to elsewhere, the original pagination has been maintained wherever possible.

Each article has been given a Roman number in order of appearance, as listed in the Contents. This number is repeated in each page and is quoted in the index entries.

ACKNOWLEDGEMENTS

Grateful acknowledgement is made to the following institutions, and publishers for their kind permission to reprint the articles included in this volume: Johns Hopkins University Press (for articles I and VII); the President and Fellows of Harvard College (II); the Institute for Early American History and Culture, Williamsburg (III); Cambridge University Press (IV, V); the University of North Carolina Press (VI).

I

THE TRANSATLANTIC ECONOMY

INTRODUCTION

The external economy of British North America in the seventeenth and eighteenth centuries is a subject that has attracted a great deal of scholarly attention in the past century and might well merit a serious bibliographic review here. However, such a review would now be supererogatory, for exactly such a survey—and a superb one at that—has recently been conducted by two able scholars. In October 1980 a conference was held at Williamsburg, Virginia, on the economy of British America from 1607 to 1790. To that conference John J. McCusker and Russell R. Menard presented a 350-page report surveying current knowledge in the field with very comprehensive bibliographical apparatus. This report will soon be published in the Needs and Opportunities series of the Institute of Early American History and Culture. There is therefore no need for me to duplicate what they have done. Instead I propose to present some of my own ideas on the critical and interpretative problems that arise when one tries to look at the colonial economy from the outside, and suggest some areas where useful work remains to be done.

When confronted with the topic of external aspects of early American economic history, the average listener or reader will most likely be reminded of the modern concern with the relationship of foreign trade to economic growth. Ordinary historians, of course, have not usually been very rigorous in their use of the term "growth." Sometimes they are simply indulging in a common organic metaphor comparing a given polity to a plant or animal that "grows"; more often they mean little more than "increase," or the process that results in greater aggregates of whatever is being discussed. By contrast, when economists in recent decades have used the term "economic growth," they have meant something much more precise: usually the process of economic change resulting in higher income per head within a given polity or geographic unit. For all its clarity, this restrictive definition of economic growth can pose problems for the working historian. One can have the greatest admiration for the econometricians who prepare current national income estimates and for the scholars who carry these calculations back in time and yet be wary of a concentration of interest that may confine future historical research within the cul-de-sac of inadequate data. For when the best trained quantitative explorer reaches the eighteenth century, he begins to enter a wilderness so ill provided with his sort of data that he cannot proceed except with the most extraordinary caution.

Almost the only data available for income estimates are hard external trade figures and estimates of population. Most conceivable methods of estimating income therefore are likely to make the internal production of goods and services vary with the population and to leave external trade as the only independent variable (besides population), hence the one that has to bear the full burden of accounting for any changes in per capita income. This becomes less and less satisfactory as the growing complexity of the colonial economy over time leaves the external sector a progressively smaller part of the whole.

One could of course do a better job if one had better estimates of the value of the manufacturing and service sectors in the colonial period. I do not intend to discuss industrial production, which lies within Richard Sheridan's zone of responsibility. I am, however, optimistic enough to imagine the not too distant day when through careful censuses of colonial iron furnaces and forges, fulling mills, breweries, distilleries, and the like, as well as the output of shipyards, we shall be able to suggest rough estimates of colonial industrial production. These and rougher but improved estimates of the value of services should enable a future generation of talented quantifiers to construct significantly better estimates of gross national product, or "national income," for the colonial period. When that day comes, we may usefully begin to pose many questions of economic change in terms of economic growth strictly defined. We cannot do that yet, and therefore I must deny myself the pleasure of talking about "economic growth" and instead confine my remarks to the simple-minded aggregation of traditional historians.

SOURCES

Traditional historians have done a lot with simple aggregation of late, and they can do much more. The external sector of the colonial economy is particularly rich in its available quantitative and quantifiable materials. The various offices of inspectors general of exports and imports have left behind in the Public Record Office the series Customs 2 and 3 on English foreign trade, including that with the colonies; Customs 14, on Scottish trade from 1755, and Customs 16/1, on colonial trade from 1768 to 1772. In addition, there survive in the Colonial Office and Treasury records at the Public Record Office hundreds of quarterly reports from "naval officers" or inspectors of navigation in the North American and West Indian colonies from the late seventeenth century. British historians seemed almost totally oblivious to the value of this material even after the publication of Sir George Clark's handbook in the 1930s;[1] and it was not until the 1950s and 1960s, with the publication of Elizabeth Schumpeter's tables and two important articles by the late Ralph Davis,[2] that the possible value of these materials began to be dimly perceived by British economic historians. Significant breakthroughs came with the publication of B. R. Mitchell and Phyllis Deane's *British Historical Statistics* and Henry Hamilton's *Economic History of Scotland*.[3] American economic historians had been no more forward in using these resources, even though for two generations they had had Charles M. Andrews's *Guide*, pointing out exactly where the materials were to be found.[4]

When I first started working with such materials around 1950, I was unaware of any American economic historian—except my fellow student Richard Sheridan[5]—who had used or was using such data. My own work soon convinced me at least of the great utility of using both the English and the Scottish customs returns together, while the later work of James Shepherd and Gary Walton made very clear the value of the American series (Customs 16/1) and intelligent sampling of naval officers' reports.[6] Their work was based in part on the very ambitious collection of inspector general and naval officer accounts that Lawrence A. Harper had begun collecting in the 1930s and 1940s, a collection made possible by the introduction of microfilm in the late 1930s. Harper was also the chief mover behind the addition of chapter Z on colonial data to the 1960 edition of the *Historical Statistics of the United States*.[7] That was probably the most important single step in publicizing many of the materials available for the quantitative study of the early American economy—particularly its external aspects—and making such data available to students everywhere.

In the 1960s Harper started transferring his holdings into machine-readable, or computer, form.[8] This made it possible to ask new questions of the data. I understand that William Davisson, of Notre Dame University, has also put large amounts of naval officer material into machine-readable form. I should, however, like to question whether such private machine archives best serve the interests of the economic history profession. I am informed that Harper has been forced to remove part of his collections from his office to his home, and I hope that there is no danger that his valuable archive will be dispersed. I should like to suggest that there is a need for a strong machine archive on early American external trade and shipping based in an institution that will give it continuing support and open it to all interested users for a reasonable fee. Such an archive should not be confined to material already in summary forms (such as the reports in Customs 2, 3, 14, and 16) but should include the relatively undigested material both in the American naval officers' reports and in the English and Scottish port books. The English port books for the seventeenth century can help fill part of the great lacunae in American data. A patient individual can process a lot of such data with little more than a pencil and a desk calculator. But there are better ways.

The naval officers in the American ports sent their reports in quarterly. In even the best series there are no reports for some quarters. Where reports for only one quarter in a given year are missing in any series it should be possible to interpolate an estimated figure for that quarter based on other evidence available for that and the immediately preceding and following years. Where a colony—such as New York—has only a single port, such interpolations will be relatively risky; where a colony—such as Virginia—contains a good number of busy ports, the risk may be considerably reduced. With totals of each commodity and each port available in machine-readable form, it should be possible, with the advice of professional statisticians, to work out a system of limited interpolation that would minimize the risks of serious error. Ultimately I think that a single if substantial volume could be published containing all the most important data from the naval officers' reports and the port books. Time series of trade data could be arranged by commodity, port of shipment, port of destination, and, in some cases for the eighteenth century, merchant firms. Comparable series could be printed for shipping activity. Interpolated data could be indicated by italics. This presupposes a collective effort and financial support that may be difficult to obtain in the short run. However, much of the necessary work may already have been done by the teams of Harper, Davisson, and others, so that the costs may not be as great as imagined. Such a volume would be the greatest boon to the study of colonial trade since the publication of chapter Z in 1960.

Besides physical quantities, the most important data needed by early American economic historians are prices. An International Scientific Committee on Price History was set up in the 1920s. Under its auspices, many volumes were published giving price data for many parts of Europe and North America. The volumes of Arthur Cole and Anne Bezanson are well known.[9] Early American economic historians have also made some use of the volumes edited by Sir William Beveridge and N. W. Posthumus.[10] Not very much, however, has been done in the field of price publication in the past thirty years. This is rather unfortunate for students of early American economic history whose needs go far beyond Bezanson's Philadelphia series.

Ideally the best series are those based on printed price currents prepared by publicly recognized brokers. Unfortunately, none was printed in America in the colonial period, and those printed in London have not survived in usable numbers for the years 1715–75.[11] The situation is much better at Hamburg and Amsterdam, where additional price currents have come to light since Posthumus was published. Nor is it generally appreciated that Posthumus did not publish everything available of American interest; for example, he published only the price series for Virginia tobacco, although the Amsterdam price currents also contain a series for Maryland tobacco. It probably would be useful to publish a volume supplementary to Posthumus reporting more fully Amsterdam prices for commodities of American interest. Such a volume might also cover Hamburg.

On this side of the Atlantic, the absence of good printed price currents has forced economic historians to be much more ingenious in their development of price series. Bezanson and colleagues used both prices published in newspapers and prices obtained from merchants' accounts. Since their publications appeared, some interesting new price series have been developed from estate inventories.[12] Those who have made the greatest use of this source have checked it against other sources and report their confidence in the inventory prices. My own feeling is that such confidence may be justified in particular cases but that the validity of inventory prices needs constant checking against other sources, particularly merchants' accounts. Merchants' accounts from the seventeenth century are very few and far between, so that inventory data are likely to remain our chief source for price history. Merchants' accounts from the eighteenth century, however, are somewhat more plentiful, particularly in large commercial centers such as Philadelphia, New York, and Boston. For the Chesapeake and more southerly colonies they are fewer and more scattered, but they can make a valuable supplement to and check on the inventory data. Systematic work in price history would be considerably helped if one institution in each of the thirteen original states made itself responsible for preparing lists and collecting microfilm of seventeenth- and eighteenth-century merchants' accounts and other materials (originating in its state) rich in price data. These might eventually be the raw materials for the publication of series to supplement those in Cole and Bezanson.

INTERPRETATIONS AND FOCI

If the study of the internal American economy in the seventeenth and eighteenth centuries suffers from an absolute lack of data on many key points of production and distribution, the study of the external economy has been held back not so much by the absence of data (particularly in the eighteenth century) as by the bulk and intractability of much of the available material. If a beneficent foundation announced tomorrow that it was going to pay for the compilation and publication of all available quantitative data on colonial trade, shipping, and prices, the problems of bulk and intractability would be much closer to solution, but we would still have the problem of approach and interpretation.

There have been four dominant foci of attention for the study of colonial economic history: the empire, the colony, the community, and the commodity. The first and the last are essentially outward-looking, the second and the third more inward-looking. At the beginning of this century the imperial approach seemed very rewarding. The colonial economies were built, it seemed, if not precisely according to an imperial legislative blueprint, then at least within the protecting and restricting confines of an imperial trading "system." The weakness of the "imperial system" at the time and of the imperial approach in modern historiography is that both have tended to underrate the full influence of the market or of what Harold Innis called

I

"the penetrative powers of the price system" both on the supply side (as in the West Indies sugar and molasses trades) and on the demand side (as in the tobacco, wheat, and slave trades). A relatively small number of scholars are still cultivating the imperial garden, but except for a few articles on the costs of the navigation acts,[13] the impact of the imperial approach on the writing of early American economic history of late has not been impressive.

Antedating the imperial school, running parallel to it, and continuing strongly to the present has been the tradition of using the individual colony as the unit of scholarly focus in early American economic history as well as in political, institutional, and religious history. This approach makes perfect sense when one considers the logistics of research. Both manuscript sources and printed sources tend to be arranged by colonies. A project that is confined to one colony is logistically an efficient project. The colony is also a logical conceptual unit for framing problems in political, institutional, and religious history and for those aspects of economic history that are concerned with public policy. Even trade data are arranged by colonies, though the English inspectors general lumped together New England, the Chesapeake, and the Carolinas and ignored New Jersey and Delaware. However, the colony is probably a very unsatisfactory unit for the study of the external aspects of the economy. Most serious students of the sugar economy of the West Indies have preferred treating the British West Indies collectively as the appropriate unit of study, and John McCusker, like Richard Pares before him, considers the whole Antilles as the proper unit of investigation.[14]

For similar reasons, students of the external economy of the continental colonies may well find the individual province too confining a unit and prefer to think in the mode of a Harold Innis of a fur zone (from Hudson Bay to the Mississippi Valley), a fish zone (from Newfoundland to Massachusetts), a cereal zone (from New York or Connecticut to northwestern Virginia), a tobacco zone (from tidewater Maryland to north-central North Carolina), and a rice and indigo zone (extending from the lower Cape Fear River to Georgia). Other transcolonial divisions could be suggested.

Of late, however, much attention has turned from the colony to the community. Perhaps the most striking innovation of the last twenty years has been the success of a number of scholars in using the community (the town, parish, and county in particular) as the working unit for serious social and economic investigation. At this level of magnification, the study of the family and household becomes practical, and European techniques of family reconstitution can be fruitfully employed. For all their great successes, however, the community studies, even more than the provincial, have been inward-looking and have tended to isolate the community studied from the broader imperatives of the market. There have, of course, been effective exceptions— notably the work of Paul Clemens, Russell Menard, and Gloria Main on Maryland[15]—in which the greater outside world is ever-present through the penetrative powers of the price system.

Finally, there remains the commodity. There is nothing new about this approach, at least since Innis's day.[16] Freshmen and sophomores know all about staples, but serious scholars have done relatively little with them. If there have been popular or semipopular studies of the early modern trades in sugar, tea, coffee, and other exotic commodities,[17] "serious scholars" in English-speaking countries have been slow to follow the example of a Louis Dermigny or a Kristof Glamann and to organize their work on the acceptance of the integrity and utility of an internationally traded commodity as an effective unit for study.[18] We still await comprehensive international studies of most American commodities, particularly wheat, rice, and dyestuffs. Even the relatively well-studied iron and fish trades have yet to be put in their fullest international context. (Noel Deerr attempted this for sugar, but his important effort is only a beginning.)[19]

Part of the problem is that the commodity approach is too difficult. For example, a comprehensive study of the North Atlantic wheat trade in the second half of the eighteenth century must include, in addition to American production, exports, and prices, a discussion of European population trends, the subsistence policies of the principal western European states, and some appreciation of the significance of the Russian conquest of the southern Ukraine and the opening of the Black Sea to international trade. At the other extreme, it is all too easy to throw in a few sentences about "staples" or staple models and think that one has really placed an export trade in its international context.

Nevertheless, it seems likely that the most profitable coming work on the external economy of British North America will be based on either commodity/staple models or population models exploiting the skills of the community historians, but paying more attention to the weight of the market. Let us look at each in turn.

STAPLE AND/OR POPULATION MODELS

When the market price of any commodity rises relative to that of other commodities, there should be a tendency for some of the factors of production—land, labor, capital, and entrepreneurship—to be reallocated away from other uses towards the production of the now more attractive commodity. The staple thesis as usually understood describes the effect of such reallocation upon a country producing a raw material for export. In such a situation, the reallocation of resources may, if permitted, be international in scope and directed not only directly towards increased production of the commodity in question but also towards the provision of support facilities. (Today we think of pipelines and tankers; in the eighteenth century these support facilities may only have been dirt roads, wooden bridges, wagons, flats, coopers' shops, and vessels of two hundred tons or less.) The reallocation should stimulate other aspects of the affected economy; it should result

I

in the more efficient use of resources, and if it is substantial enough, it may result in true economic growth, that is, higher income per head in the territory affected. Whether this true growth is achieved will depend upon the relative importance of the commodity in question in the economy of that territory and upon its population trends.

When we try to carry the "staple model" back to the seventeenth and eighteenth centuries, we run into certain immediate difficulties with numbers. The staple model seems to work best in the very earliest years of settlement, when there was very little in the way of income or production (the base for subsequent calculations) and all resources except unimproved land were sadly lacking. In that dawn, any new resources could seemingly be productively and profitably employed, and slight increases might appear significant in percentage terms. In the era of large-scale indentured-servant trade, the reallocation of resources is not just a vague abstraction. However, when we come to the eighteenth century, we run into some problems in the application of full-blown staple theory. Tobacco, the most important export from North America then, provides an illuminating example. Between 1697–1702 and 1771–75, tobacco exports increased roughly threefold, while population in the tobacco colonies increased about 7.4-fold. Since there is no evidence of a decline in income per head, it is fairly obvious that a lot was going on in the Chesapeake besides growing tobacco. Eighteenth-century Virginia and Maryland in fact also exported many other commodities, including wheat, flour, provisions, naval stores, pig iron, and ships. The staple effect was still working—that is, external demand was encouraging the direction of further resources towards tobacco production—but the monocausal, single-commodity staple thesis is no longer very helpful.

With the conventional staple thesis, or model, more helpful for the seventeenth century than for the eighteenth, scholars working on the early American economy should consider models that better explain or help explain the evolution of the colonial economy. One of these may be a population, or mixed population-market, model. The staple thesis as already noted works best in the early days of settlement, when both labor and capital have to be attracted to the new colony by more or less rational market considerations.[20] However, at a certain stage—fairly early (the first generation) in New England, later in the Chesapeake—normal family life was established, and the primary determinant of the size of the labor force became not immigration but the natural growth of the population, both free and slave. With this more or less independent growth in population and the labor force went a growth in the productive capacity of the colony, although there may have been a transitional decline in income per head as a colony changed from a primarily adult community to a society supporting an exceptionally large number of children.

Less obvious is the proposition that this growing population could create its own capital almost automatically. The most obvious elements in the wealth of the colonies were land and slaves. The slave population tended to increase *pari passu* with the free population, considerably enhancing the wealth and productive resources of slaveholders. Land, too, tended to increase in value *pari passu* with the increase in population. If land beyond the frontier was almost worthless, land in settled areas varied in value with fertility, degree of improvement, and relative access to markets. The growth of population moved the frontier outwards and gave value to hitherto value-less land; the growth of population also created the labor force, both free and slave, to improve and render more valuable hitherto unimproved land. (In an economy where land is abundant and cheap, labor should be more productive than in an economy where land is scarce; thus a smaller proportion of the total labor force should be needed to provide for subsistence, leaving a larger proportion available for other employments, including land improvement and the creation of fixed and movable capital.) The increase in the value of his land or slaves increased the land- or slaveholder's ability to borrow (both from local and British sources), whether on mortgage or on his personal credit. This increased credit-worthiness may have been squandered on more luxurious consumption; it may have been used to buy more land and more slaves and to make agricultural improvements; or it may have been invested in industry (such as an ironworks) or trade. Some of the greatest fortunes in the plantation colonies were in fact made by those who combined landown-ing and trade. (Undeveloped land held for appreciation might still be valu-able enough to support some credit and thus indirectly be productive.)

If then the primary motive power in the expansion of the productive capacity of the colonial economies was the independent natural increase in population with the concomitant increase in aggregate wealth, the question still remains, How were these constantly increasing quanta of labor and capital to be employed? In the agricultural sector this was for most land-owners and even tenants a rational, market-oriented decision reflecting the quality and price of land available, transport costs to market, and the current market price of possible alternative productions. Limited migration was a real option, but only in exceptional periods such as that of the Seven Years' War was distant migration within the colonies anything but rare. For those determined to stay where they were, both soil quality and transport costs could be taken as fixed. (Soil exhaustion was compensated for by moving the area of cultivation within the plantation.) The only great variable in the short or medium term was the market.

Thus we return to where we started. Whether one thinks that the economic evolution of the colonies can best be explained by the elegantly simple staple model or by the somewhat sloppier mixed population-market model, one is forced to start with the market to explain much if not all of the short- and medium-term behavior of the colonial economy. A market is made by supply and demand. The writing of most early American economic history has concentrated upon supply. For many branches of the economy the great unexplored frontier may well be demand.

I

THE DEMAND SIDE OF COLONIAL ECONOMIC HISTORY

The principal commodities exported from British North America in the colonial period are relatively well known. In table 2.1 they are listed, in order of importance as of 1770, along with the proportions of each going to the principal destinations: Great Britain and Ireland; southern Europe; the West Indies and Africa. Some, the so-called enumerated commodities of the acts of trade and navigation, went almost exclusively to Great Britain: tobacco, rice, masts and yards, furs and skins, indigo, whale products, iron, potash and

Table 2.1

PRINCIPAL EXPORTS FROM THE BRITISH CONTINENTAL COLONIES (INCLUDING NEWFOUNDLAND, THE BAHAMAS, AND BERMUDA), 1770, AT OFFICIAL VALUES

Export Commodity	Value (£ sterling)	Destination		
		Great Britain and Ireland (%)	Southern Europe (%)	West Indies and Africa (%)
Tobacco[a]	£906,638	99.80%	0 %	0.20%
Bread and flour	504,553	8.37	40.34	51.28
Fish	397,945	3.24	61.73	35.03
Rice[b]	340,693	48.92	23.97	27.12
Wheat, oats, maize	176,086	11.95	56.64	31.41
Timber and wood products	171,737	—	—	—
Masts, yards, etc.[a]	*16,630*	99.90	0	0.01
Pine, oak, and cedar boards	*58,618*	14.84	1.14	84.03
Staves and heading	*61,619*	37.72	8.18	54.10
Furs and skins[a]	149,326	100.00	0	0
Indigo[a]	131,552	99.99	0	0.01
Whale oil and fins[a]	104,134	92.25	3.06	4.69
Horses and livestock	80,212	0	0	100.00
Iron[a]	70,250	96.55	0.12	3.33
Beef and pork	66,035	0	1.36	98.46
Potash and pearl ash[a]	64,661	100.00	0	0
Flaxseed	35,169	99.76	0.24	0.00
Tar, turpentine, etc.[a]	35,076	94.35	0	5.65
Other native produce[c]	122,094			
Total native produce	£3,356,160			
Re-exports	81,555			
Total exports	£3,437,715			

Source: U.S. Bureau of the Census, *Historical Statistics of the United States, Colonial Times to 1970*, 2 vols. (Washington, D.C., 1975), 2:1183–84.

Note: Italicized items represent subdivisions of the "timber and wood products" category.

[a] Enumerated commodities

[b] Enumerated, except for southern Europe

[c] New England rum, peas and beans, butter, cheese, copper and lead ores, among others.

pearl ash, tar and turpentine. Other products not needed in Great Britain and therefore not enumerated went both to the West Indies and to southern Europe: bread and flour, fish, cereals. Still other products went primarily to the West Indies: boards, horses and livestock, beef and pork. Only rice went in significant quantities to all three major market areas. The results of these diffuse trading patterns are summarized in table 2.2, covering the years 1768–72. In those five years some 52.7 percent of North American exports went to Great Britain; 25.7 percent went to the West Indies; and 17.9 percent went to southern Europe and the Wine Islands.

Britain of course, imported "colonial" goods not only from North America but from the West Indies as well. The value of English imports from both the American areas has been summarized for selected years over the eighteenth century in a well-known article by Ralph Davis (see table 2.3). Davis's data, of course, refer only to England. The omission of Scotland is more distorting for some trades than for others. Scotland's sugar imports add only 3.9 percent to England's (by value) in 1772–74, and her cotton imports add only 6.4 percent; but her tobacco imports add 87.9 percent to the value of South Britain's.[21] Even so, the preeminent place of sugar as the leading colonial import is unassailable. Strongly in second place (after Scotland is added in) was tobacco, followed after a significant gap by West Indian coffee and Carolina rice. Much further behind—in the £80,000–160,000 range—came West Indian spirits, dyestuffs, and cotton and North American timber products (masts, etc.), skins and hides, and whale products. Cereal imports from North America were important only in isolated years of bad harvests at home.

All in all, therefore, in 1772–74, on the eve of the American Revolution, Great Britain imported over £5.4 million worth of produce (almost all raw

Table 2.2

ESTIMATED VALUE OF TOTAL COMMODITY EXPORTS FROM BRITISH NORTH AMERICAN COLONIES BY DESTINATION, 1768–72 (IN THOUSANDS OF POUNDS STERLING)

Destination	1768	1769	1770	1771	1772	Annual Average
Great Britain	1,360	1,540	1,449	1,761	1,828	1,588 (52.7%)
Ireland	69	80	133	105	74	92 (3.1%)
Southern Europe and Wine Islands	378	604	565	557	592	539 (17.9%)
West Indies	583	699	815	813	964	775 (25.7%)
Africa	13	24	21	16	29	21 (0.7%)
Total	2,403	2,947	2,983	3,252	3,487	3,014

Source: James F. Shepherd and Gary M. Walton, *Shipping, Maritime Trade, and the Economic Development of Colonial North America* (Cambridge, 1972), 94–95.

I

Table 2.3

PRINCIPAL ENGLISH IMPORTS FROM NORTH AMERICA AND THE WEST
INDIES, 1699–1774 (IN THOUSANDS OF POUNDS STERLING)

Import Commodity	1699–1701	1722–24	1752–54	1772–74
Sugar	630	928	1,302	2,360
Spirits (rum)	0	6	70	163
Tobacco	249	263	560	518
Coffee	0	0	3	414
Rice	0	52	167	340
Dyestuffs	85	152	97	167
Timber	14	13	90	114
Skins and hides	23	34	46	111
Oil (whale, etc.)	19	26	43	93
Cotton	23	45	56	88
Drugs	6	22	55	55
Cereals	0	0	0	51
Iron and steel	0	0	5	10
Total	1,107	1,679	2,684	4,769

Source: Ralph Davis, "English Foreign Trade, 1700–1774," Economic History Review, 2d ser., 15
(1962): 300–301.

materials or semiprocessed goods) from her colonies in North America and
the West Indies. (Of this, £4.77 million came to England and £662,884 to
Scotland.)[22] A century and a half before, almost nothing had come from the
same area. Whence rose the demand in George III's subjects for so much that
their ancestors could do without? The simplest explanation would be the old,
dependable doctrine of comparative advantage taken by itself. That is, when
Englishmen, Irishmen, and Scotsmen settled in the American colonies, they
found that they could produce more economically in the colonies than at
home certain familiar products for which there was a known demand in
Europe. Therefore they set to work making these familiar products, and their
relatives at home, finding that these products could be more economically
obtained from the colonies, reduced production at home and turned their
attention to items in the production of which they had a comparative advantage. At both ends of the imperial system, people specialized in what they
could do best, to their mutual advantage and with higher ultimate income for
all. Or so we should expect.

   In fact, this rationalization happened only to a very limited extent. From
the beginning, emigrants to America brought with them the tools, skills,
breeding stock, and seed of north European agriculture, and from the beginning they used these to produce the arable and animal products they needed
for their own subsistence. In time, they found vents for their surplus production of these items (along with fish and forest products) in the West Indies
and southern Europe—but not in Britain itself. When they threatened to

send home products that would compete with the output of domestic agriculture, the home government sometimes prohibited the importation of such commodities—as did the British government in the case of colonial wheat and flour, and the French government in the case of colonial rum. For permanent and attractive markets at home the colonists had to turn to tropical products, which could not be produced at home, to forest products (masts, pitch, tar, and the like), in short supply at home, and to new products, such as tobacco, hitherto unknown at home. When it was discovered that tobacco could in fact be grown in northern Europe, its production was prohibited in both England and France, not so much to help colonial trade as to protect the king's revenue. This meant that Britain's (and France's) import trade from the East Indies and from the Americas in the seventeenth and eighteenth centuries developed around a congeries of new products (coffee, tea, chocolate, tobacco, tropical dyestuffs) or products hitherto imported indirectly and in very small quantities (sugar, pepper, silk, cotton).[23] In both cases substantial changes in consumption patterns were needed to create the effective demand that would support the volume of colonial and Asian trade achieved by the third quarter of the eighteenth century.

We are not talking about trifling quantities. Very often taxes had to be paid on the various colonial products imported, and the products underwent processing that added to their final cost to the consumer. The petty retail price was likely to be at least two or three times the wholesale value at importation. This wholesale value for all retained imports in 1765–74 was close to £12 million sterling,[24] of which perhaps a third was accounted for by products from America and the West Indies. If this American produce only doubled in value by the time it reached the consumer, then about £8 million per annum was spent by English consumers on transatlantic products, or something over £1 per head. If the American produce trebled in price by the time it reached retail sale, then the consumer expenditure on American produce would have been about £12 million, or near £1 13s. per head. A very optimistic estimate places per capita income at this time at about £18 per head;[25] even if it were only two-thirds as much, there was ample capacity to support this level of consumption. However, either way, there had been a significant reorientation of consumer demand towards colonial produce. How were consumers able to bear this?

There are two fairly obvious models that might explain this shift in consumer demand. One assumes that there was a more or less steady increase in income per head during the seventeenth and eighteenth centuries; the other starts from the premise that there was not. If there was an increase in income per head, then a very plausible explanation of the new consumption patterns is at hand: the English and later British consumer used part of the increase in his real income for colonial and other exotic products: tobacco, sugar, tea, coffee, rice, cottons, and all sorts of textiles dyed with the superior tropical or semitropical dyes. This explanation of the changed consumption patterns

I

may be simplistic and one-dimensional, but it is at least consistent. But where did the increased real income that in this model accounts for the changed consumption patterns come from? Part may have come from a slowing in the rate of population growth after 1660. Part may have come from increased productivity in the domestic economy, including agriculture. Part may have come from increased foreign demand for British manufactures—including colonial demand. Such increased demand would have permitted a more productive allocation of labor and other resources, particularly if one assumes a situation at the beginning of the seventeenth century characterized by substantial unemployment and underemployment of labor. However, there is no evidence that export markets for any major branch of British manufactures except woolens ever exceeded 20 percent of output before 1776. (In the small cotton industry it may have been as high as 25 percent.) Colonial markets only became an important part of export markets in the generation or two preceding 1776, and in the case of woolens the increase in the colonial market only compensated for decline in the European market.[26] It is of course possible to imagine a model in which higher income per head at home created an enhanced demand for colonial produce which in turn created increased colonial demand for British manufactures, engendering further increases in income per head at home; however, the small share of output taken by colonial markets, particularly during the first century of colonization, makes it improbable that colonial demand could have been the principal cause for any increase in real income per head that took place.

Pessimists may of course deny that there was any increase in real income per head for substantial stretches of the seventeenth or eighteenth centuries. Some would even argue that there was a decline in income per head during the decades 1600–1660 caused by rising population and prices and secular difficulties in traditional export industries. If such were the case, how could there have been a change in consumption patterns towards newer exotic and nonessential commodities? It can be argued that the new consumption was classbound. Even while the generality of the population was suffering a decline in real income per head, landlords and their hangers-on, officeholders, merchants, and some manufacturers of luxury products were gaining ground; they thus can be seen as the market for these new exotic imports.

Were, however, the new consumption patterns confined only to limited circles of the population? It is not unreasonable to suggest that even in a world of constant real incomes, significant shifts in consumption could take place. Do tea or coffee drinkers drink as much beer as those who drink only beer? Do those who take treacle with their bread need as much bread? Even in the seventeenth century men were aware that tobacco dulled the appetite and thus might substitute for some food or drink in the budgets of the poor. Thus, it is not inconceivable that, even with constant or declining incomes, the poorer sections of the population may have supported the newly acquired habits of tobacco, tea, sugar, and the like by consuming less beer, bread, or meat. (Increased cereal exports after 1690 and stagnant beer consumption give some credibility to this hypothesis.)[27] It was also alleged by late seventeenth-century and early eighteenth-century "moralists" that many obtained the wherewithal to purchase Indian calicoes by buying fewer woolen garments.[28]

It is not necessary to accept one explanation *in toto* and reject all others. Historians have always been good at syncretism. A pessimistic model may appear more useful for the early seventeenth century, while a more optimistic model may seem more applicable to the century after 1660. The historian of the colonial economy working on any one commodity is unlikely to get very far in his project if he insists on starting by first solving the problem of whether income per head in Britain was increasing or decreasing in each decade of the colonial period, any more than if he insists on starting by solving the same riddle for the colonies. He must, however, recognize that his story starts with the changing pattern of consumer preference in Europe or the changing demographic situation in Europe that creates the demand for the particular American product he is studying.

Tobacco was probably the most exotic new product introduced into Europe from America. Its strangeness accounts for the extreme slowness of its adoption. On the eve of the American Revolution, some two hundred years after its introduction into England, consumption was barely two pounds per head per annum. By contrast, annual consumption in many countries in the twentieth century is above five pounds per head of population. In most continental countries where there were monopolies, consumption was probably lower than in Britain. If the British consumer after 1685 paid an average price for small retail purchases of as much as 2s.6d. per pound, retail expenditure was at most 5s. per head of population per year; and in France it was unlikely to have been much more than 2s. per head. The student must always remember that the cultural penetration of tobacco, which probably reached its peak after the Second World War, had only gone a small part of the way by 1775. The incomplete cultural victory of tobacco combined with high taxation created a marked inelasticity of demand. Despite attendant low prices, the gluts created by periodic overproduction in the century before 1776 did not evoke compensating upsurges in demand and could only be worked off very slowly. Conversely, when supplies were sharply reduced, the same inelasticity could lead to very marked rises in wholesale prices: tenfold in the extreme case of the American Revolution.

Sugar was known in Europe long before tobacco, and its use was widespread, at least geographically. However, consumption per head remained very low until the seventeenth and eighteenth centuries. When cheaper, slave-grown sugar facilitated an increase in consumption in the seventeenth century, not all parts of Europe developed a sweet tooth at the same rate. English consumption of unrefined imports rose from 5.3 lb. per head per annum in 1699–1703 to 24 lb. per head in 1771–75 (at least 30 percent should be deducted to arrive at refined equivalents). By contrast, modern consumption is over 100 lb. per head. We need to know more about comparable consumption patterns in other European countries, particularly France, which appears to have reexported a higher percentage of its imports than did Britain, so that its consumption in 1783 was reportedly only 2 lb. per head.[29] Future work on sugar must start with all the new forms of demand, including the soft-drink revolution, which linked the fates of sugar, tea, chocolate, and coffee. Carolina rice is supposed to be particularly well suited and traditionally used for rice pudding. If all the Carolina rice retained in England around 1770 had been made into rice pudding, how many tons of sugar would have been used therein?

Given the extraordinary importance of the textile industries in Britain, I am surprised that more attention has not been given to the demand for American dyestuffs. Colonial historians are of course aware of the importance of indigo to South Carolina, but a wider perspective would find room for logwood, Brazil wood, cochineal, and others. How important were qualitative differences between different competing dyes? When we recall that the dying stage could sometimes double the value of a piece of cloth, we can perhaps appreciate the strategic importance of the dyestuffs trade for the hundreds of thousands of persons employed in the textile industries in Britain alone. Since such a study should ideally embrace the French, Spanish, and Portuguese colonies as well as the English, it is not recommended for anyone in a hurry.

LEGAL AND FISCAL BARRIERS

After the future economic historian of colonial trade has chosen his commodity and clearly established the character of the demand for it, he will have to ask what real market choices were open to merchants trying to meet that demand. This will of course bring him to "the old colonial system" so beloved of the imperial school of historians. After Beer and Andrews and Lawrence Harper, one would expect that little more can be said about the acts of trade and navigation and the directing role of the state. Yet I suspect that there are three aspects of the regulative apparatus that have not yet received all the attention that is their due: (1) the political, (2) the administrative/strategic, and (3) the fiscal.

First, English and British legislation rather obviously arose out of a process of competition and compromise between separate and sometimes conflicting interests. A slow but steady trickle of new works reminds us that we do not know all there is to know about the inner political history of most of the important legislative measures touching colonial trade. This trickle of new interpretation will undoubtedly continue.

Second, not all the interests involved were private. Some were state interests of great weight. One such was the need of the Royal Navy and the British merchant marine for a safe, dependable source of masts, ship timbers, naval stores, and flax and hemp for sails, cables, and cordage. To avoid a dangerous dependence on Russia and the Scandinavian countries, the British government in the eighteenth century encouraged by subsidies the importation of most of the key naval raw materials from North America. We know a good bit about this policy as far as it affected the New England mast and timber trade,[30] but much less about the Carolinas and the naval stores trade generally and the unsuccessful efforts to encourage the production of hemp and flax in America. A quite different state interest was the security of the food supply. If the British government in the eighteenth century normally left this to private enterprise, continental governments did not. We know next to nothing about the attitudes and activities of continental governments, including the French, towards the burgeoning North American wheat trade to southern Europe during the last decades preceding the Revolution.

And third, the most important thing about the fiscal interest of the state is that it almost always conflicted with the maximum development of colonial trade. But since governments need taxes, fiscal considerations often won out over other interests of state, including colonial. The extreme case was, of course, tobacco, which paid duties of several hundred percent in most European countries. The fiscal interest of the French state and the private interest of the French tobacco monopoly united to make France almost totally dependent on the British colonies for its tobacco between 1723 and 1775, even though it would have been possible—at a price—for the French colonies or France itself to supply all the tobacco France needed.[31] Other state monopolies, including the Spanish, also bought British tobacco. No other trade was as completely dominated by fiscal considerations, but other colonial products, including sugar and coffee, were taxed, though their fiscal history remains largely untouched.

Taxation inevitably requires regulation. To protect its revenues, the British government—like the French government—prescribed the ship and the package in which the tobacco could be imported. These regulations and the purely financial requirements of bonding and paying the duties are generally thought to have squeezed smaller firms out of the trade and to have encouraged its concentration in fewer hands. Since this same concentration can be detected in most colonial trades, it might be useful to investigate the restrictive and anticompetitive implications of both taxation and regulation in most such trades.

THE IMPORT TRADES

The bulk of this paper, like the bulk of the literature, has been devoted to staple exports and their problems. By contrast, the colonial import trades are much less studied than the export trades; hence, more attention to them may

I

prove profitable. We know too little about the quantities or qualities involved. A mere perusal of merchants' invoices or the ledgers of the inspector general of exports and imports suggests much about the quality of life in early America, and students of consumption could perhaps make fuller use of such sources.

Many but not all of British North America's imports were tropical, Asiatic, or luxury products that did not compete with goods manufactured or grown within the thirteen colonies. Included in this category would be unrefined sugar, molasses, coffee, tea, silks, fancier millinery and haberdashery, most books, and so on. There was, however, a large range of goods (woolens, linens, cottons, shoes and other leather goods, ironmongery) which competed with some colonial manufactures by 1775—although not in all qualities. If we had detailed breakdowns of imports by precise categories and by colonies, we could make some crude but interesting guesses about the relative progress of different manufactures in different colonies over time. Such material may be particularly suggestive if used in conjunction with censuses of colonial ironworks, fulling mills, distilleries, breweries, and the like.

I have the impression that colonial demand for imported manufactures was particularly pressing at the top and the bottom of the price range—at the top for quality goods not made in America; at the bottom for goods like inexpensive German linens, cheaper than anything obtainable in the colonies.[32] In the middle was a price range where some colonial products could compete. Only a very tedious analysis of the inspector general's ledgers—which contain price data—will indicate whether this is anything more than the optical illusion of tired eyes.

AN INTERDEPENDENT SYSTEM

The import trades of course included the trades in slaves and indentured servants, hardly neglected topics, least of all today, when we have a new journal devoted entirely to the history of slavery and emancipation. These will be even less neglected when we have digested David Galenson's new book[33] and have an opportunity to read Bernard Bailyn's promised major book on the peopling of America. However, for all the attention it has received, the slave trade still poses some big problems. I suspect that it was the single most important factor encouraging the descendants of eighteenth-century merchants to destroy their ancestors' papers or at least not to make them available to researchers. Some have suggested that there may still be large bodies of such papers in private possession.[34] Perhaps the attractive prices recently attained at manuscript auctions (by the Codrington Papers in particular) will draw some of these out of hiding. If so, we may be able to answer with a bit more assuredness than now some important questions about the profitability of the slave trade.[35]

One does not have to accept the full argument that the profits of the slave trade financed the industrial revolution[36] to see that in the final analysis we are not dealing only with a series of distinct economies producing commodities to be exported to Europe in bilateral exchange for European and Asian goods. Such a picture may in large part fit the tobacco, rice, indigo, masts, and naval stores trades but not others. Fish, flour, and wheat were exported to southern Europe, and the proceeds of sales were remitted to England to pay for goods to be sent thence to the northern fish- and wheat-producing colonies. Fish, flour, provisions, livestock, and forest products were exported to the West Indies, and the proceeds were either returned to North America in sugar, molasses, and other West Indian produce or remitted to Britain to pay for supplies needed thence.

If there had been no West Indies, how much trade would New England and the Middle Colonies have had? How many people then would have been content to emigrate to or reside in those areas? If there had been no slavery, would there have been any West Indies trade? What about Virginia and Maryland and the Carolinas? I detect a certain impatience with counterfactual propositions in much recent critical literature. These nevertheless are not unreasonable questions, even though we may never obtain answers to them that will give general satisfaction. I personally think that the Chesapeake and much of North Carolina would have developed almost but not quite the same productive capacity without slavery. Slavery was never necessary for the production of tobacco, even if it was necessary for the optimal exploitation of large landholdings. I am not so sure about coastal South Carolina and Georgia. There and in the West Indies, were nonslave economies conceivable? How high would the price of sugar have had to be to attract free labor to the West Indian cane fields? Under the medical conditions of the seventeenth and eighteenth centuries, could such a population have survived long enough to reproduce itself? These are some of the questions we must at least consider before we attempt to pass on the absolute indispensability of slavery. However, since such questions are uncongenial to most professional historians, most analysis will prefer to start with slavery and the slave trade as givens.

To speak of an interdependent multilateral trading system is to speak of a trading system requiring a complex multilateral payments mechanism. It had to be possible to realize anywhere in the system credits earned or held elsewhere in the system. In fact, such transfers could be made anywhere in the Atlantic world and most parts of Europe (and even India) through the general use by businessmen of the bill of exchange. Joseph Ernst has reminded us of the great importance of exchange rates,[37] and John McCusker's excellent handbook makes available for the first time the basic exchange data for the whole North Atlantic world.[38] We still need, however, to know more precisely how the system worked, particularly in the West Indies and between points in the thirteen colonies.

The international-payments mechanism provided by the bill of exchange supported armies abroad and could have handled such capital movements as took place. We know, though, very little about capital movements. Most of the debts owed by colonists to persons in Britain on the eve of the Revolution appear to have risen from normal commercial transactions and thus were simply unpaid balances on trading accounts rather than evidence of cash loans. Even sums owed on bonds and mortgages appear very often to have their origin in commercial transactions, though more work is needed on this topic. However, there was some direct British investment in America. Persons in Britain owned land in America—in a few cases plantations, in other cases unimproved land held speculatively. British firms not only owned stores in America but also held shares in nominally American firms. They had to invest as well in warehouses, wharves, and small craft in connection with their trading activities; some also invested in distilleries and ironworks. In addition to the post-1790 claims concerning unpaid prewar debts, there are also in the Public Record Office detailed records of the compensation paid by the British government around 1783–89 to persons who lost real estate in America as a result of the Revolution. Many of the claimants were loyalist émigrés, but there was a significant element of British investors claiming compensation for lost ironworks and the like. By separating out the records (claims and compensation) of this class, one could obtain a rough idea of direct British investment in American real estate and plant before the war. One would, however, have to allow something for underreporting, for when ironworks and the like were owned jointly by British and American residents, the Americans, if they accepted the Revolutionary government, were probably able to conceal the shares of their British partners. However, even a rough estimate would be helpful here.

I hope that my recent work on capital and credit in the Chesapeake trade will encourage those working in other trades to try to reconstruct more systematically what we can know of the origins and volume of the capital and credit employed in transatlantic trade.[39] How frequently did American merchants have British partners? Was the Chesapeake's "cargo trade," with its long credits, not characteristic of all branches of British-American commerce? Was most of the capital employed in the American trades accumulated out of the profits of the same trades, as Richard Pares suggested?[40] Were silent partners unknown outside of Glasgow? What about all those widows and orphans who lent money on bond to merchants trading to America, or to the wholesalers who supplied them? The study of the capital market in Britain has only just begun.

A SENSE OF SCALE

It is a truism in the social sciences that at some point in every process of growth quantitative change evokes qualitative change. A city is more than a

I

large village; a factory is more than a large workshop. Students working on the early American economy are very much aware of certain changes in scale—population, volume of exports, and so on—that may affect the structure as well as the aggregates of the colonial economies. Other changes in scale have gone relatively unobserved. One of these is the revolutionary change in scale of British firms trading to America and of indigenous American firms. To give a few examples from my own work, the two largest importers of tobacco in London in 1775 imported as much tobacco as the entire trade of more than a hundred firms in the 1660s.[41] At Glasgow, the largest single firm in 1775 imported more tobacco than the entire trade (ninety-one firms) in 1728–31.[42] Thus the world of the firm in 1775 is radically different from that of 50 or 100 years before. Though I do not have equivalent data, it is my impression that a comparable, if not as extreme, change of scale took place in the African, West Indian, and other North American trades.[43]

This change of scale and associated concentration was not the result of any conscious government policy and must reflect the survival of the fittest in a competitive market in which entry was easy but large firms had certain strategic advantages over smaller firms. These advantages probably included easier access to capital (both partners' "stock" and long-term loans on bond) and credit from banks and suppliers. The reputations of larger firms were more clearly established, so that their bills of exchange and acceptances also passed more readily from hand to hand and were easily discounted. The larger purchases of export goods by the greater firms must have attracted the most favorable terms either in price or in length of credit—even though smaller firms may have been able to select their export goods more carefully. In many trades these larger firms should also have been in a stronger negotiating position when selling to monopsonistic buyers like the French tobacco monopoly or oligopsonistic buyers like the relatively few sugar refineries in each outport. Finally, the larger firms had opportunities for the more economic utilization of shipping denied to smaller firms. A firm importing a quarter-shipload of sugar or tobacco had little room for maneuver and usually had to accept the added costs of long delays. The firm importing five or more shiploads of sugar or tobacco per year should have been and was able to utilize shipping more efficiently and to reduce freight charges in the final accounting.

Shepherd and Walton, among others, have already explained to us that the improved efficiency in the use of shipping is almost the only significant productivity improvement that we can definitely detect in the colonial period.[44] This improved efficiency was closely associated with the changing scale of the firm and with the increased availability of marine insurance. In the seventeenth century ships going out to the Americas characteristically carried "adventures" for a large number of relatively small firms. The individual firm, by dividing its ventures among many vessels, could in a sense

I

insure itself when external insurance was not available. However, such complex chartering commitments undoubtedly slowed down the loading of the ship, particularly at the American end, and contributed to the long "stays in the country" characteristic of the seventeenth century. The increased availability of insurance from the late seventeenth century reduced the risk of buying or chartering whole vessels and thus enabled the larger firms to obtain some economies of scale.

Even with the valued contribution of Shepherd and Walton and Ralph Davis, there is opportunity for further useful investigation of the economics of shipping in the colonial period. Equally necessary is serious attention to marine insurance on both sides of the Atlantic. Available scraps of evidence would suggest that lower insurance rates were one of the great advantages that the British had over the French in the eighteenth century—particularly in wartime. We need investigations that will go beyond the anecdotal histories of Lloyds of London and attempt the serious study of marine insurance and insurance rates. Outside of London, almost everything remains to be done on insurance in the English outports, Scotland, and the major North American ports.

Investigators must constantly be alert for signs that changes in scale opened the doors for other changes—that is, that the larger firm size was necessary before new institutional forms or new trades could be attempted. For example, the Glasgow store system in the Chesapeake would appear to have required larger capitalization both per firm and per unit of export or import than did the simpler consignment or earlier peddling trades. Similarly, the development of the wheat export trade to southern Europe very likely required the existence in Philadelphia and other wheat-exporting ports of firms larger than those common in the West Indian provision trade. Much work and much thought is needed on the ramifications of the relationship of scale to the institutional history of the various trades.

CONCLUSION

This paper reflects more the current state of my thinking about the early American external economy than it does the results of any systematic effort to catalog and evaluate all possible "significant" topics deserving attention. I have had to neglect some important subjects, including fishing and fish exports, shipbuilding,[45] and shipping earnings—though these have not been totally neglected in the existing literature. Much more could also be said on the internal organization of the firm.

In general in this paper I have been concerned as much with pointing out problems that need serious reflection as with marking topics that will make prize-winning dissertations. I hope that my weakness for intractable problems will not create the impression that early American economic history is just one dark dead end after another. If no one is likely to produce very soon a generally acceptable time series of per capita colonial income from 1607 to 1775, there are still numerous problems whose systematic investigation will produce interesting and illuminating results. The great success as always will go to those who combine disciplined imagination in defining problems with shrewdness in the choice of methodology and fearlessness in attacking the most forbidding sources. We are only now learning what secrets lay hidden so long in parish registers and inventories post-mortem. Who knows what treasures still lie buried in Admiralty, Chancery, or Exchequer? The best is yet to come.

NOTES

1. G. N. Clark, *Guide to English Commercial Statistics, 1696–1782*, Royal Historical Society Guides and Handbooks, No. 1 (London, 1938).

2. Elizabeth Boody Schumpeter, *English Overseas Trade Statistics, 1697–1808* (Oxford, 1960); Ralph Davis, "English Foreign Trade, 1660–1700," *Economic History Review*, 2d ser., 7 (1954–55): 150–66; idem, "English Foreign Trade, 1700–1774," ibid. 15 (1962): 285–303. Equally noteworthy is Davis's *The Industrial Revolution and British Overseas Trade* (Leicester, 1979).

3. B. R. Mitchell and Phyllis Deane, *Abstract of British Historical Statistics* (Cambridge, 1962); Henry Hamilton, *An Economic History of Scotland in the Eighteenth Century* (Oxford, 1963).

4. Charles McLean Andrews, *Guide to the Materials for American History to 1783 in the Public Record Office of Great Britain*, 2 vols. (Washington, D.C., 1912–14).

5. See Richard B. Sheridan, *Sugar and Slavery: An Economic History of the British West Indies, 1623–1775* (Baltimore, 1974), appendix.

6. See James F. Shepherd and Gary M. Walton, *Shipping, Maritime Trade, and the Economic Development of Colonial North America* (Cambridge, 1972).

7. Lawrence A. Harper, in U.S. Bureau of the Census, *Historical Statistics of the United States, Colonial Times to 1957* (Washington, D.C., 1960); the chapter was expanded in the 1976 edition.

8. See Lawrence A. Harper, "United We Stand; Divided We Fall: A Plea and a Plan for the Use of Modern Technology in Cooperative Research," in *Of Mother Country and Plantations: Proceedings of the Twenty-Seventh Conference in Early American History*, ed. Virginia Bever Platt and David Curtiss Skaggs (Bowling Green, Ohio, 1971), 71–127.

9. Arthur H. Cole, *Wholesale Commodity Prices in the United States, 1700–1861* (Cambridge, Mass., 1938); Anne Bezanson, Robert D. Gray, and Miriam Hussey, *Prices in Colonial Pennsylvania* (Philadelphia, 1935); idem, *Wholesale Prices in Philadelphia, 1784–1861*, 2 vols. (Philadelphia, 1936–37); Anne Bezanson, *Prices and Inflation during the American Revolution: Pennsylvania, 1770–1790* (Philadelphia, 1951).

10. William Henry Beveridge, *Prices and Wages in England from the 12th to the 19th Century* (London, 1939); Nicolaas Wilhelmus Posthumus, *Inquiry into the History of Prices in Holland*, 2 vols. (Leiden, 1946–64).

11. See Jacob M. Price, "Notes on Some London Price Currents," *Economic History Review*, 2d ser., 7 (1954–55): 240–50. John McCusker, of the University of Maryland, is now compiling a bibliography of all price currents and analogous materials published in Europe and America in the seventeenth and eighteenth centuries.

12. See, for example, Russell R. Menard, "Farm Prices of Maryland Tobacco, 1659–1710," *Maryland Historical Magazine* 68 (1973): 80–85; and idem, "A Note on Chesapeake Tobacco Prices, 1618–1660," *Virginia Magazine of History and Biography* 84 (1976): 401–10.

13. For example, Gary M. Walton, "The New Economic History and the Burdens of the

I

Navigation Acts," *Economic History Review*, 2d ser., 24 (1971): 533–42, which reviews earlier work by Peter D. McClelland, Robert P. Thomas, and Lawrence A. Harper. For further contributions by F.J.A. Broeze, McClelland, D. J. Loschky, and Walton see ibid. 26 (1973): 668–91.

14. For example, Sheridan, *Sugar and Slavery;* and Richard S. Dunn, *Sugar and Slaves: The Rise of the Planter Class in the English West Indies, 1624–1713* (Chapel Hill, 1972). See also Richard Pares, *War and Trade in the West Indies, 1739–1763* (Oxford, 1936).

15. See Paul G. E. Clemens, *The Atlantic Economy and Colonial Maryland's Eastern Shore: From Tobacco to Grain* (Ithaca, N.Y., 1980); Russell R. Menard, "Secular Trends in the Chesapeake Tobacco Industry, 1617–1710," *Working Papers from the Regional Economic History Research Center* 1 (1978): 1–34; idem, "The Tobacco Industry in the Chesapeake Colonies, 1617–1730: An Interpretation," *Research in Economic History* 5 (1980): 109–77; and Gloria L. Main, *Tobacco Colony: Life in Early Maryland, 1650–1720* (Princeton, 1983).

16. See Harold A. Innis, *The Fur Trade in Canada* (1930; reprint, New Haven, 1970); and idem, *The Cod Fisheries* (New Haven, 1940). See also E. E. Rich, "Russia and the Colonial Fur Trade," *Economic History Review*, 2d ser., 7 (1954–55): 307–28.

17. The vast literature on the new beverages is surveyed in A. W. Noling, *Beverage Literature: A Bibliography* (Metuchen, N.J., 1971).

18. See Louis Dermigny, *La Chine et l'occident: le commerce à Canton au XVIIIᵉ siècle, 1719–1833*, 4 vols. (Paris, 1964); and Kristof Glamann, *Dutch-Asiatic Trade, 1620–1740* (Copenhagen, 1958).

19. Noel Deerr, *The History of Sugar*, 2 vols. (London, 1949–50).

20. On the "rationality" of the indentured-servant trade see David W. Galenson, *White Servitude in Colonial America: An Economic Analysis* (Cambridge, 1981), esp. pts. 3 and 4.

21. For Scottish data see Hamilton, *Economic History of Scotland*, 412–13, 416, 419.

22. English totals are from table 2.3, Scottish totals are from the National Library of Scotland, Edinburgh, MS. 60.

23. Only for forest products and iron was import substitution important, imports from North America in the eighteenth century making it less necessary to depend on the northern countries.

24. Phyllis Deane and W. A. Cole, *British Economic Growth, 1688–1959* (Cambridge, 1962), 48.

25. Ibid., 156.

26. See Jacob M. Price, "Colonial Trade and British Economic Development," in *La Revolution américaine et l'Europe*, Colloques internationaux du Centre Nationale de la Recherche Scientifique, no. 577 (Paris, 1979), 221–42; an earlier version is in *Lex et scientia* 14 (1978): 106–26.

27. Peter Mathias, *The Brewing Industry in England, 1700–1830* (Cambridge, 1959), 542–43. Total output of taxed beer was no higher in 1771–73 than it had been in 1701–3, though population had increased in the interim.

28. Alfred P. Wadsworth and Julia de Lacy Mann, *The Cotton Trade and Industrial Lancashire, 1600–1780* (Manchester, 1931), 117, 132–34.

29. John Ramsay McCulloch, *A dictionary, practical, theoretical, and historical, of commerce and commercial navigation: illustrated with maps and plans*, 2d ed., 2 vols. (London, 1834), 2:1088.

30. See, for example, Joseph J. Malone, *Pine Trees and Politics: The Naval Stores and Forest Policy in Colonial New England, 1691–1775* (London, 1964).

31. See Jacob M. Price, *France and the Chesapeake: A History of the French Tobacco Monopoly, 1674–1791, and of Its Relationship to the British and American Tobacco Trades*, 2 vols. (Ann Arbor, 1973); and idem, "The Tobacco Trade and the Treasury: British Mercantilism in Its Fiscal Aspects" (Ph.D. diss., Harvard University, 1954).

32. "The Slaves are cloath'd with Cottons, Kerseys, Flannel & Coarse Linnen, all imported" (Board of Trade report on the colonies, Sept. 8, 1721, Cholmondeley Papers, Cambridge University Library).

33. See n. 20 above.

34. See F. E. Sanderson, "Liverpool and the Slave Trade: Guide to Sources," *Transactions of the Historic Society of Lancashire and Cheshire* 124 (1972): 154–76.

35. Much of the relevant literature is cited in J. E. Inikori, "Market Structure and the Profits of the British African Trade in the Late Eighteenth Century," *Journal of Economic History* 41 (1981): 745–76.

36. See Eric Williams, *Capitalism and Slavery* (New York, 1966).

37. Joseph Albert Ernst, *Money and Politics in America, 1755–1775: A Study in the Currency Act of 1764 and the Political Economy of Revolution* (Chapel Hill, 1973).

38. John J. McCusker, *Money and Exchange in Europe and America, 1600–1775: A Handbook* (Chapel Hill, 1978).

39. Jacob M. Price, *Capital and Credit in British Overseas Trade: The View from the Chesapeake, 1700–1776* (Cambridge, Mass., 1980).

40. Richard Pares, *Merchants and Planters*, Economic History Review supp. 4 (Cambridge, 1960).

41. *Joshua Johnson's Letterbook, 1771–1774*, ed. Jacob M. Price, London Record Society 15 (London, 1979), 158–59.

42. Northampton Record Office, Fitzwilliam-Burke MSS., A.xxv.74 (for 1775); PRO T.36/13 (for 1728–31).

43. On concentration in the British African slave trade see Inikori, "Market Structure," 748–53.

44. Shepherd and Walton, *Shipping, Maritime Trade and Economic Development*, chap. 5.

45. See Joseph A. Goldenberg, *Shipbuilding in Colonial America* (Charlottesville, 1976); and Jacob M. Price, "A Note on the Value of Colonial Exports of Shipping," *Journal of Economic History* 36 (1976): 704–24. No one has ever checked to see how complete is the coverage of *Lloyd's Register*. If it is incomplete to a significant degree, then colonial shipbuilding may have been larger than suggested in these works.

ADDENDA

On page 31 of chapter I, I suggested, 'there is no evidence that export markets for any major branch of British manufacture except woolens ever exceeded 20 percent of output before 1776. (In the small cotton industry, it may have been as high as 25 percent.)'. This represented my view of the state of the question as of 1980–81. Subsequent work, however, indicates that this view was probably too cautious.

In 1985, Nicholas Crafts reported his estimate that exports' share of 'gross industrial output' had risen from 24 percent in 1700 to 35 percent in 1760.[1] In a 1989 article, I noted that 'Craft's range fits in well with other scattered estimates of the export share of industrial production: 45 to 50 percent for woolens and worsteds, 25 to 50 percent for the rising cotton industry, but only 20 percent of English linens, 42 percent for bar and wrought iron, and 40 percent for the copper-brass group... [and that] in the special case of the Birmingham and Wolverhampton hardware trades and the West Riding woolen and worsted trade, contemporary estimates around 1760 to 1775 put the export share at 72 percent or more of production'.[2]

---

1. N.F.R. Crafts, *British Economic Growth During the Industrial Revolution* (Oxford, 1985), 132.

2. Jacob M. Price, 'What Did Merchants Do? Reflections on British Overseas Trade, 1660–1790', *Journal of Economic History*, XLIX (1989), 283. Davis calculated that as manufactured cotton outputs rose more rapidly than exports, the share of cotton production exported fell from 50 percent *ca.* 1760 to 15 percent in 1784–86 but recovered to 35 percent in 1794–96. Ralph Davis, *The Industrial Revolution and British Overseas Trade* (Leicester, 1979), 66. His Early data came from Phyllis Deane and W.A. Cole, *British Economic Growth 1688–1959* (Cambridge, 1962), 185. By my own rough calculations, in 1772–74, 19 percent of English cotton manufactures were exported.

II

ECONOMIC FUNCTION AND THE GROWTH OF AMERICAN PORT TOWNS IN THE EIGHTEENTH CENTURY

1. Introduction*

URBAN history is very much alive today as a field of serious research and intellectual interest in Britain and America. For students of the seventeenth and eighteenth centuries, however, the results do not seem as impressive as those for some earlier and later centuries. No city of the seventeenth and eighteenth centuries has received the continuing historiographic attention bestowed upon Renaissance Florence by historians since the days of Davidsohn.[1] Scholars approaching the great towns of these centuries have most often lacked a synthetic vision or an integrative model of process and have tended to work in conceptual isolation upon one or another aspect of town life: architecture and town planning; urban political institutions and political life; demography; social structure; economic activity. It is of course all too easy to criticize: frequently the lack of previous work on the

*This paper was originally presented to the First Soviet-American Historical Colloquium held in Moscow in October 1972. With this audience in mind, the author confined his footnote references to the more important and readily available printed materials. He deliberately excluded references to manuscript sources (except for statistics), particularly eighteenth-century mercantile records which he has been studying for more than twenty years and which constitute a general background to many of his observations on mercantile practice. He is particularly indebted to his colleague Professor John Shy for many helpful suggestions. For a comparable treatment of this subject in a later period, cf. David T. Gilchrist, ed., *The Growth of the Seaport Cities, 1790–1825* (Charlottesville, Va., 1967).

1. E.g., Robert Davidsohn, *Geschichte von Florenz*, 4 vols. (Berlin, 1896–1927); Gene A. Brucker, *Florentine Politics and Society, 1343–1378* (Princeton, 1962); Marvin B. Becker, *Florence in Transition*, 2 vols. (Baltimore, 1967–1968).

II

town or of useful models in works on comparable towns makes such isolated topical studies a most feasible way to start. One must begin somewhere.

There are of course other traditions. Sixty years ago, Werner Sombart in *Luxus und Kapitalismus*[2] suggested summarily and somewhat impressionistically a unified way of looking at the phenomenon of the great capital cities of the sixteenth to the eighteenth centuries. The combination of essentially agricultural economies, late feudal patterns of land ownership, and centralizing bureaucratic states produced the disproportionately large capital cities (Paris, Madrid, Naples) of the seventeenth and eighteenth centuries which are essentially centers of consumption not just for bureaucrats and courtiers, but for a much broader class of *rentiers* (noble, clerical, and bourgeois) with their attendant populations of purveyors, agents, and servants.

The approach of Sombart (even as developed by Weber) has not exactly founded a school. It finds echoes in Latin American studies in the broad integrative approach of Richard Morse[3] to the study of cities in colonial Latin America. James Scobie has shown that, even in the present century, comparable socio-economic circumstances can produce in Buenos Aires a city as "dominating" in the twentieth century as Naples was in the eighteenth.[4] In west European studies, examples of this approach are rarer. Perhaps the modern scholarly work which most fully explores the lines suggested by Sombart is Bartolomé Bennassar's valuable study of Valladolid, capital of Castile in the sixteenth century, a city with an "économie de consommation bien plus que de production."[5] (In-

2.Werner Sombart, *Luxus und Kapitalismus* (Leipzig, 1913); translated as *Luxury and Capitalism* (Ann Arbor, 1967), esp. pp. 21–38. The concept of the "consumer city" was subsequently (1921) given much wider currency by Max Weber in the papers published in the United States as *The City*, ed. and transl. by Don Martindale and Gertrud Neuwirth (Glencoe, Ill., 1958), esp. pp. 68–70. Weber, however, draws his examples from ancient and medieval cities, while Sombart refers specifically to the phenomenon of the seventeenth and eighteenth centuries.

3. Richard M. Morse, "Latin American Cities: Aspects of Function and Structure," *Comparative Studies in Society and History*, 4 (1962), 473–493.

4. James R. Scobie, *Argentina: A City and a Nation*, 2nd ed. (New York, 1971).

5. Bartolomé Bennassar, *Valladolid au siècle d'or* (Paris, 1967).

terestingly, there is no evidence that Bennassar ever read Sombart, but valuable ideas have lives of their own.)

In English-speaking countries, London, Dublin, and Edinburgh could all be approached in the Sombartian mode, but thus far have not been. There is a vast literature on each, including good studies of architecture and urban design, but, at the synthetic level, even the best modern work seems merely impressionistic. The literature on the smaller towns of England is rich but uneven. The older antiquarian literature fills libraries, but there is little to compare to the modern, French studies (ranging from Roupnel's older study of Dijon[6] to the more recent well-known studies of Beauvais,[7] Lyons, and Amiens[8]) in which the economic and social lives of the community are integrated with imagination, erudition, and quantitative precision. Perhaps the best-studied English town in this sense is Exeter, which has attracted modern work of considerable sophistication.[9] Like Beauvais and Amiens, Exeter has the advantage of being small enough to be handled by a single scholar. For the greater towns of France, cooperative studies now seem to be flourishing. For Marseilles, we have a narrowly commercial series;[10] for Bordeaux a less detailed but more broadly conceived series that attempts to cover (if not necessarily to integrate) economic, social, political, and demographic history.[11] For Paris, as for London, there are still only the antiquarian literature and the modern impressionistic studies. For both, the monographic work (surely a collective project) has yet to be done.

6. Gaston Roupnel, *La ville et la campagne au XVIIe siècle: Étude sur les populations du pays dijonnais*, new ed. (Paris 1955).

7. Pierre Goubert, *Beauvais et le Beauvaisis de 1600 à 1730*, 2 vols. (Paris, 1960).

8. Pierre Deyon, *Amiens capitale provinciale, étude sur la société urbaine au 17e siècle* (Paris, 1967); Maurice Garden, *Lyon et les Lyonnais au XVIIIe siècle* (Paris, 1970).

9. W. G. Hoskins, *Industry, Trade and People in Exeter, 1688–1800* (Manchester, 1935); Wallace T. MacCaffrey, *Exeter, 1540–1640* (Cambridge, 1958); W. B. Stephens, *Seventeenth-century Exeter* (Exeter, 1958); Robert Newton, *Victorian Exeter, 1837–1914* (Leicester, 1968).

10. *Histoire du commerce de Marseille*, ed. Gaston Rambert, 6+ vols. (Marseilles, 1949–). For a good example of current quantitative approaches to the study of port towns, cf. Pierre Dardel, *Navires et marchandises dans les ports de Rouen et du Havre* (Paris, 1963).

11. Charles Higounet, ed., *Histoire de Bordeaux*, planned in 7 vols. (Bordeaux, 1962–). See in particular vol. IV: Robert Boutruche, ed., *Bordeaux de 1453 à 1715* (1966); and vol. V: François-Georges Pariset, ed., *Bordeaux au XVIIIe siècle* (1968).

In this paper, I shall discuss the principal towns of the thirteen British colonies in North America in the eighteenth century, the colonies that were to become the United States. I have defined the subject as those towns having populations of 8,000 or more in the first federal census of 1790: Philadelphia and suburbs, 42,520; New York, 32,328; Boston, 18,038; Charleston, 16,359; Baltimore, 13,503. I shall also have something to say about Newport, Rhode Island, which had a population of over 9,000 on the eve of the Revolution, though this had fallen to 6,716 by 1790, as well as about Norfolk, Virginia, and some of the New England coastal towns from Salem to New Haven—all in the 3,000–8,000 range.[12] All of these were ports, as were all towns in the United States in 1790 with a population of more than 4,000. The port character of the principal towns of eighteenth-century America defines the two key problems with which we shall be concerned: (1) the characteristic occupational structure of the leading port towns; and (2) commercial factors influencing the growth or stagnation of these and lesser port towns.

The principal port towns of the thirteen colonies have not suffered from a neglected past. All the older towns of the United States have received a respectable body of attention from serious antiquarians and their vulgarizers. In addition, most (though not Boston) have received the attention of historians of commerce or the mercantile community. Unfortunately, most of these commercial histories seem to have been written under the spell of A. M. Schlesinger's famous work[13] on the role of the colonial merchants in the coming of the American Revolution, for they concentrate almost uniformly on the years immediately preceding the Revolution. Thus they do not convey a sense of process, of change over

12. United States Bureau of the Census, *A Century of Population Growth from the First Census of the United States to the Twelfth*, ed. W. S. Rossiter (Washington, D.C., 1909), pp. 11, 78. For a general discussion of population and other surviving eighteenth-century data, see Stella H. Sutherland, "Colonial Statistics," *Explorations in Entrepreneurial History*, 2d ser., 5 (1967), 59–107.

13. Arthur Meier Schlesinger, *The Colonial Merchants and the American Revolution 1763–1776* (New York, 1918). Cf. also Charles M. Andrews, "The Boston Merchants and the Non-importation Movement," *Publications of the Colonial Society of Massachusetts*, XIX (*Transactions, 1916–1917*), 159–259.

American Port Towns   127

time, in which the economy and life of the towns reflect changing conditions in the greater world about them. Most of these are also insufficiently quantitative in their approach: statistics are given in appendices; they are rarely integrated into the analysis. Nevertheless, such studies are useful in themselves and valuable beginnings.[14]

On quite a different level are the monumental works of Carl Bridenbaugh on the five principal colonial towns (Boston, Newport, New York, Philadelphia, and Charleston) from their beginnings until 1776.[15] Historiographically, Bridenbaugh is most important. He devoted twenty-five years to the study of the beginnings of town life in the United States long before urban studies were fashionable; he also pioneered "comparative studies" before that term had been invented. He brought to his work imagination and catholic interests that could find place for everything from drains to jails to theaters and a considerable erudition that absorbed all the printed sources plus the records of the towns investigated. It is unlikely that anyone else will soon attempt to do over what he has so thoroughly done. For our purposes, however, Bridenbaugh has not quite finished the job. First of all, he would himself, I think, be the first to admit that he is not particularly sympathetic toward the quantitative approach to history. If we compare Bridenbaugh's books with (for example) the Pariset volume on Bordeaux in the eighteenth century,[16] we can see what this means. The Pariset volume has the same broad focus as Bridenbaugh, with chapters on demography, intellectual, artistic, and religious life, as well as the expected politics and economics. However, when we look in particular at the elegant chapters on the port's trade by François Crouzet and on its demography by J. P. Poussou, we find not only sta-

14. Cf. Virginia D. Harrington, *The New York Merchant on the Eve of the Revolution* (New York, 1935), the best of the group with valuable statistics; Arthur L. Jensen, *The Maritime Commerce of Colonial Philadelphia* (Madison, 1963), despite its title heavily political; and Leila Sellers, *Charleston Business on the Eve of the American Revolution* (Chapel Hill, 1934).

15. Carl Bridenbaugh, *Cities in the Wilderness: The First Century of Urban Life in America 1625–1742* (New York, 1938), and *Cities in Revolt: Urban Life in America 1743–1776* (1955; 2d ed., New York, 1971). The second but not the first edition of the latter has a valuable bibliography.

16. See note 11.

tistical tables and charts but a solid quantitative substructure to the argument that is for the most part missing in Bridenbaugh. It seems likely that when young scholars in the future attempt to carry further the work of Bridenbaugh, they will, by attempting more precise quantification, find not only new materials but also new questions. Second, Bridenbaugh is essentially a social and institutional historian. He is interested in the public and private institutions of the city and how they worked, as well as in the colors, tones, sounds, and smells of the town, its layout, its buildings, the pulse of its daily life, its values, and its woes. For a social historian like Bridenbaugh, the economic foundations of a community tend to be a "given," something that is there like Mount Everest, to be described as one describes the topography and climate of the town. That approach, though justified when one is simply giving "background," leaves much unexplained. In more analytical or scientific studies, a more questioning approach may be needed. Just as the geologist sees in the earth process rather than fact, so the historians of towns must see in the economic base problems not preconditions.

ii. Function and Structure

THE basic problem facing the student of eighteenth-century American towns is why did the life of certain of the colonies produce relatively large towns and the life in others not. Why the relatively precocious town life of Boston, New York, and Philadelphia and the marked absence of significant towns before 1750 in the otherwise highly developed provinces of Maryland and Virginia—not to mention New Jersey and North Carolina? Why was Connecticut's pattern of several medium-sized towns so different from that of neighboring New York and Massachusetts? Why too was Boston's rapid growth stunted in the decades after 1740? Why did the Chesapeake, so bereft of towns in 1750, suddenly in the next generation produce two substantial towns (Baltimore and Norfolk) without any significant official assistance? To try to answer these questions, we must adopt a functional approach toward the life of the towns. What functions did the towns perform in their regional economies? Correlatively, what distinctive functions did the separate sections of the town's populations perform?

To many, these may not seem like real questions at all. There is a well-established tradition in international scholarship (in America associated with the name of C. H. Cooley[17]) that would explain the location and size of towns entirely in terms of the geography of production and markets and the technology of transportation. As goods move from the loci of production to markets and consumers, geography and transport technology require that they be transshipped at certain points. Around these points, towns developed; as the physical volume of production and exchange increased, so did the size of the towns affected. All this is correct, of course, to the point of being a truism. Yet to say this is not to explain everything. One must distinguish between necessary and sufficient causes. Access to feasible trade routes with appropriate volumes of activity is a necessary condition for the development of towns of various sizes. However, the mere existence of production and exchange and suitable geographic location are not conditions sufficient to guarantee that a town of any foreseeable size will develop in any given place. If New York and Philadelphia fit everyone's preconceptions, one must also consider the unexploited possibilities at the mouths of the Connecticut and Cape Fear (North Carolina) rivers and again the urban backwardness of the populous Chesapeake. Then too, certain towns historically have developed volumes of activity which transcend geography. The greatest mart towns (e.g., Amsterdam and London) seem to attract volumes of activity which exceed mere geographic convenience. On a much smaller scale, the activity of Boston, Newport, and even New York in the eighteenth century also seems to have exceeded what might have been geographically predictable. In short, while giving due weight to geography and to the physical volume of trade, we must also consider the *quality* of economic activity in explaining

17. Charles H. Cooley, *The Theory of Transportation* (Publications of the American Economic Association, IV, no. 3 [Baltimore, 1894]), pp. 90–100. Cooley drew heavily on Roscher.

urban growth: the nature of the commodities produced and exchanged, the marketing problems they create, the institutional and legal framework within which economic activity takes place.

Functionally, we may divide the roles of preindustrial towns (i.e., towns of the seventeenth and eighteenth centuries) as follows: (1) civil and ecclesiastical administration with their attendant "court life" and demimondes; (2) maritime transport and external commercial exchange; (3) industrial production; and (4) internal services. The first three can usually be described as independent variables, while the fourth is essentially a dependent variable. That is, the number of persons employed in a town in service functions (broadly conceived to include not just innkeepers, servants, tailors, dressmakers, barbers, and the like, but also petty retail shopkeepers, building trade workers, most teachers, ministers of religion, and other professionals) will vary roughly with the number of persons attracted to the town as residents or visitors by the other three functions.

It is not easy to find acceptable data that might enable one to construct functional profiles of colonial towns, measuring exactly the number of persons employed in each of the four sections just described. However, reasonable approximations can be made. Allan Kulikoff[18] has reported the number of adult males in each occupation recorded in the Boston tax records for 1790. I have reanalyzed his figures, classifying them according to the four "sectors" enumerated in the previous paragraph (Appendix C). For Philadelphia and its suburbs of Southwark and Northern Liberties, there are published and unpublished tax lists giving occupations. Sam B. Warner has supplied me with data for Philadelphia in 1774 (from tax and other official records) giving 3,793 occupations out of about 6,000 heads of household and single men listed.[19] I had

18. Allan Kulikoff, "The Progress of Inequality in Revolutionary Boston," *William and Mary Quarterly*, 3d ser., 28 (1971), 375–412, esp. 411–412. This is a valuable article, though marred by some errors in arithmetic and eighteenth-century commercial terminology.

19. For an explanation of the sources of these data (now stored in a machine archive at the Inter-University Consortium for Political Research, Ann Arbor), see Sam Bass Warner, Jr., *The Private City: Philadelphia in Three Periods of Its Growth* (Philadelphia, 1968), pp. 226–227.

earlier made a similar but less thorough calculation from the published tax lists of 1780 and 1783 giving the occupations of 3,265 adult males (also Appendix C). I have arranged these data in the same manner as I have Kulikoff's Boston data. (In both, "laborers" have been listed separately at the end as unclassified because they could not be assigned to a sector.) The results appear strikingly consistent, though there are far more unidentified people in the Philadelphia data.

I have not thus far been able to find equivalent data for other towns, but have located four possible substitutes for New York: (a) the printed admissions of freemen, which I have analyzed for the twenty-five years, 1746–1770; (b) the published New York wills of the eighteenth century;[20] (c) the New York City directories available from 1786 (I have chosen that of 1790 for analysis); and (d) the published record of all persons dying in New York City during the yellow fever epidemic of 1795, containing specific occupations for 258 men. Of the four, only the wills must be totally rejected, for an experimental analysis of those for the years 1771–1776 shows them to misrepresent grossly (as one might expect) the relative weight of the wealthier inhabitants of the city, particularly merchants. The other three (summarized in Appendix D) show less obvious bias and prove relatively consistent. The admissions of freemen have hitherto been deliberately neglected by historians because there was little effective compulsion to oblige residents to take up the freedom of the city. Even so, the political life of the community seems to have been lively enough to have drawn respectable numbers in that direction, from merchants and gentlemen to common laborers. The only possible distortions apparent are the paucity of clerks and the relatively large proportion of artisans in the industrial sector, considerably higher than that shown by our later (1790–1795) data for the city. It is possible, however, that New York City had a higher proportion of artisans in 1746–1770 than in 1790–1795; i.e., as the city's commerce and population

20. *Abstract of Wills on File in the Surrogate's Office, City of New York* [1665–1801], (*Collections of the New York Historical Society for the Year[s]* [1892–1908], XXV–XLI [New York, 1893–1909]).

grew, its industrial sector failed to grow with it and declined in relative importance. The 1790 directory (the fourth published) is remarkably full and detailed, even by London standards, but it suffers from one obvious blemish: no clerks are designated as such, though many clerks are undoubtedly concealed among the unidentified males. By contrast, the yellow fever list of 1795, though containing far fewer names than either the freemen's registers or the city directory, probably contains a more reasonable sample of New York's adult male population (women and children were more likely to have been out of town), and thus provides the best available picture of vocational distribution. Because of its less distorted measurement of nonhouseholders, including clerks, this 1795 death list is not only better than the other earlier and longer New York lists but also probably represents nonhouseholding elements in the population more clearly than do the Philadelphia data. Nevertheless, the sample is not perfect and has to be used with caution.

There is a further problem common to the data of all the towns. In assigning specific occupations to one or another of the sectors, certain difficult and somewhat arbitrary decisions have had to be made, for some occupations might rightly have fallen in more than one sector. Care must be taken to distribute such overlapping crafts so as not to favor any one sector. Thus, butchers and bakers (two numerous crafts) have been assigned to the service sector, where they are usually thought to belong, though many in those trades worked not for the local market alone but also for the export market and belong at least partly in the industrial sector. On the other hand, furniture makers and shoemakers (cordwainers), another numerous craft, have been placed in the industrial sector, for they made goods in job lots for external sale, but a good part of them also worked for local orders and could be put in the service sector. It is impossible, given present knowledge, to divide the totals employed in such crafts into fractions working for the local and external markets; however, it is more than likely that any overweighting caused by the assignment of certain crafts *in toto* to the external market (industrial sector) is balanced by the other overweighting caused by the assignment of other crafts *in toto* to the local market (service sector) so that the general proportions suggested by our sectoral totals are only minimally distorted.

With these data in hand, we may proceed to our sectoral analysis, starting with the service sector. Remembering the point made above that the number of service personnel (whether doctors or chimney sweeps) is ultimately dependent upon the other more independent activities in the town, the reader need not be unduly impressed by the proportions we find ascribable to this sector. From Kulikoff's data, it would appear that at least 45 percent of Boston's tax-inscribed adult males in 1790 were employed in the service sector. The equivalent figures are 48.93 to 49.29 percent for Philadelphia and 46.7 to 56.59 percent for New York. In general, it seems safe to say that, in all substantial colonial towns, the service sector broadly conceived accounted for around 50 percent of the employed adult male population. (The proportion would probably be even higher in the enumerated towns if we could get accurate information on slaves and women and on apprentices and other employees who resided on the premises of their employers.) Much rigorous quantification remains to be done, but the burden of proof lies on those who would claim that other towns might have had significantly different patterns. Of course, however finely measured, the impressive size of the service sector tells us nothing about the *raison d'être* of the town or of its ultimate proportions. To understand them, we must try to measure the more independent variables: the public, industrial, and commercial sectors.

In studying the American towns of the eighteenth century, we need not concern ourselves unduly with the first function or sector: governmental and ecclesiastical administration. The clergy were broadly dispersed among the general population. There were no bishops, cathedral chapters, or other types of salaried ecclesiastical administrators in any of the thirteen colonies. Most university colleges were of course church related or church controlled, but only two of them were in large towns (New York and Philadelphia) and could not have added as much as 1 percent to the population of those places. (In smaller towns, such as Cambridge or Princeton, the presence of a college had greater economic and demographic impact.) Nor was there much public employment created by royal, provincial, or local government. Boston, with a population of 18,000 in 1790, was the capital city of a state with a population of 378,500, yet it had only sixty-eight adult males on its tax rolls in 1790 who could be classified as "government officials," and not all of them occupied full-time remunerated positions. Our Philadelphia data are much less satisfactory than our Boston data; even so, the 2.85 percent shown in the public sector in the congressional capital of 1780–1783 is quite consistent with the 2.75 percent shown at Boston in 1790 (Appendix C), or with the 3.49 to 3.7 percent for New York, the capital in the 1790's. Even if we were to add to the public sector schoolmasters, lawyers, and notaries, we should still have a public sector of only 4.25 percent at Boston and 3.22 (1774) or 3.73 (1780–1783) at Philadelphia.[21] Military employment can also be ignored as a contributor to town growth in the eighteenth century. Except under the extraordinary conditions preceding the American Revolution, garrisons were not normally stationed in or near large towns.[22]

The industrial sector was quantitatively a much more important element in the structure and growth of the larger eighteenth-century towns, even though we are dealing with a primarily agricultural society. Historians have long been aware of this element, if only because persons styled "artisans" or "mechanics" were sometimes mentioned as active in mobs or revolutionary societies on the eve of the Revolution.[23] However, the precise composition of this artisan or "mechanic" element has received very little sys-

21. Appendices A–C.

22. For garrison policy, see John Shy, *Toward Lexington: The Role of the British Army in the Coming of the American Revolution* (Princeton, 1965), particularly chaps. i and ii. Some historians believe that military expenditures may have been important at New York, even without a garrison.

23. There is an enormous literature on the coming of the Revolution. For the most recent treatment (with a conscious social perspective, but little quantification), see Pauline Maier, *From Resistance to Revolution: Colonial Radicals and the Development of American Opposition to Britain, 1765–1776* (New York, 1972), esp. pp. 297–312. Cf. also Edmund S. Morgan and Helen M. Morgan, *The Stamp Act Crisis: Prologue to Revolution* (Chapel Hill, 1953), chap. x; Merrill Jensen, *The Founding of a Nation: A History of the American Revolution, 1763–1776* (New York, 1968); and Richard Walsh, *Charleston's Sons of Liberty: A Study of the Artisans* (Columbia, S.C., 1959).

tematic analysis. The Boston data for 1790 show that persons who can be considered to belong to the "industrial sector" constituted 26.6 percent of the tax-inscribed adult male population in 1790; our rough equivalent data for Philadelphia show 26.81 percent (1774) or 27.31 percent (1780–1783) in the same classification—not a significant difference, though Philadelphia has commonly been thought of as being much more "industrial" than Boston (Appendix C). However, when we look at the 664 individuals at Boston or the 1,017 at Philadelphia who constituted the "industrial" sector, we find them a rather disparate lot. Some of them, particularly the shoemakers, metal craftsmen, and cabinetmakers, must have been working for a predominantly local clientele and could arguably have been enrolled at least in part in the "service" sector. If the largest group in the industrial sector at Philadelphia were the leather workers processing the hides produced on the farms of Pennsylvania and New Jersey, the largest at Boston consisted of those in shipbuilding and shipfitting work. These last could with justice be ascribed in good part to the "commercial-maritime" sector, for much of their work consisted of building and repairing ships for Boston's own commercial fleet and fisheries; only a part of their output was for the market.[24] Were we to transfer from our "industrial sector" some shoemakers and the like to the service sector and some shipwrights, ropemakers, and such to the commercial sector, those left in the more strictly defined "industrial sector" (i.e., those making goods for outside markets) would be a smaller proportion of the whole—perhaps only 10 or 15 percent instead of the 26–27 percent originally shown.

At New York, the "industrial "sector appears to decline from 32 percent in the midcentury freemen's register to only 16.67 percent in the yellow fever sample of 1795, compared to the 26.6 to 27.3 percent for Boston and Philadelphia. This is the largest discrepancy produced by our sectoral comparisons. Other nonquantitative data suggest a large variety of crafts in mid-eighteenth-

24. For the structure of Boston's shipbuilding and shipowning at the beginning of the century, see Bernard Bailyn and Lotte Bailyn, *Massachusetts Shipping 1697–1714: A Statistical Study* (Cambridge, 1959).

century New York, consistent with the freemen's data.[25] At the same time there is reason to believe that the proportions inferred from the yellow fever data may be close to the truth for 1795. New York did not have the distilling or shipfitting activities of Boston or the leather and metal activity of Philadelphia. This is obviously another question on which much work remains to be done.

The data on the industrial sector contained in Appendices C and D permit us to scrutinize more critically some commonly accepted statements about colonial towns. We are sometimes told that Boston had lost much of its industry between 1740 and 1775 and on the eve of the Revolution was much more a "consumer" town (in the Weberian sense) and much less a productive town than New York, Philadelphia, or perhaps even Baltimore. Yet the data in Appendices C and D show the proportions of the male population engaged in the industrial sector just after the Revolution to be approximately equal at Boston and Philadelphia—and both considerably higher than at New York. If Philadelphia had a much higher proportion of its employment in the leather and fur-using trades, Boston still had proportionately more in shipbuilding and shipfitting: even if Philadelphia had more shipwrights[26] than Boston, the latter had a wider representation of ropemakers, sailmakers, and the like.

Finally, there remains that section of the leading towns' populations that was engaged in maritime commerce and fisheries. Our picture of them is relatively consistent: 25.64 percent of the studied population were so employed at Boston, 23.26 percent at New York (1795), and 22.73 percent (1774) or 20.61 percent (1780–1783) at Philadelphia. Although none of these figures can be taken too literally, the general picture is clear. The Philadelphia proportion for 1780–1783 is probably a little too low because of the war and be-

25. Newspaper notices of various arts and crafts have been reprinted in *The Arts and Crafts in New York 1726–1776: Advertisements and News Items from New York City Newspapers* (Collections of the New York Historical Society, LXIX, for 1936 [New York, 1938]).

26. For the social and political importance of the Philadelphia shipwrights, see James H. Hutson, "An Investigation of the Inarticulate: Philadelphia's White Oaks," *William and Mary Quarterly*, 3d ser., 27 (1971), 3–25. On Boston as a "consumer city," cf. Kulikoff, "The Progress of Inequality," pp. 376–379.

cause the Philadelphia data (all from tax records) probably failed to identify merchants' clerks to a greater degree than did the data used for Boston or even New York. (The clerks of course were not heads of firms and, usually being young, were infrequently heads of residential households.) However, even if we should triple the number of clerks in Philadelphia in 1780–1783 we should not raise the weight of this sector to much over 22 percent, suggesting that the maritime sector was indeed marginally less important at Philadelphia than at the somewhat smaller New York and Boston. At all three places, local employment data would tend to underrepresent grossly the number of sailors employed on the town's ships. Unless married and maintaining local households, they must have escaped the tax surveys almost completely.

In summary, then, our quite disparate and shaky data on the occupational distribution of the port towns suggest a pattern more remarkable for its consistencies than for its differences.

Table I

Sector	Boston (1790)	Philadelphia (1774)	Philadelphia (1780–1783)	New York (1795)
Governmental	2.75%	1.53%	2.85%	3.49%
Service	45.01%	48.93%	49.29%	56.59%
Industrial	26.60%	26.81%	27.31%	16.67%
Maritime	25.64%	22.73%	20.54%	23.26%

Transcending, however, this pattern of seeming consistency lies a dynamic of inconsistency. These towns did not grow at a uniform rate. As is well known, early in the nineteenth century New York was to pass Philadelphia and never look back. In the eighteenth century, both started out well behind Boston but caught up during the third quarter of the century. Boston, the first in the colonies almost from its founding (1630) until about 1755, stagnated from about 1740 until after 1790 (Appendix B). Why? As all our towns were port towns, we must turn for an answer to the structure and marketing conditions in the trades which animated their commercial lives.

II

III. Commercial Factors in the Growth of the Principal Port
Towns of British North America, Particularly before 1776

WHEN one talks of traders and trading towns even in an
early modern primarily agricultural society, one uses very
general terms to embrace a considerable variety of phenomena.
Traders range from petty hucksters doing a few shillings' worth of
business a day to great merchants trading for tens of thousands of
pounds sterling. At the lowest level were petty retailers, peddlers,
and hucksters (hawkers) who sold for cash or cash credit only.
They were of no great importance outside the few large towns. At
the next higher level were what I shall call the *primary traders* or
country storekeepers[27] who bought the goods produced by the agricultural sector and supplied farmers and planters with most of the
manufactured and foreign goods they required. At a slightly higher
level were *secondary traders* or wholesalers who, in addition to performing the same functions for farmers and planters, also acted as
wholesale suppliers to the primary traders, taking their agricultural
purchases in return. They traded over a larger area than the primary
traders and, when not themselves located in major ports, maintained
trading connections with one or more ports through which their
supplies might be obtained and their purchases marketed. They
might even order goods from Britain and pay for them with cash
or bills of exchange, but they did not really *trade* overseas, i.e., venture their wealth abroad; all their "effects" were "in the country."
These secondary traders might be styled "merchants" in America,
but were not strictly so in English usage. At a still higher level, we
find the *tertiary traders* or merchants proper, who, in the narrow
English usage of that term, had to be "traders by sea." They did
venture their effects abroad and thus took much greater risks for
themselves and those who advanced them credit. We may also

27. The terms "shop" and "store" are used almost interchangeably in the United States
today, if not in Great Britain. In the eighteenth century, however, the term "store" suggested something larger than a shop, a trading station where goods were bought as well
as sold.

distinguish between limited and general merchants, merchants who dealt with only one geographic area or commodity group and merchants who dealt with all areas and in all goods significant for the economies of their home regions. In America this distinction separated the smaller merchants who dealt only with the West Indies from their bigger confreres who traded to Europe.

This hierarchy of traders created a hierarchy of trading towns. Primary traders tended to scatter across the countryside where they would be accessible to their agricultural customers. Secondary traders, however, tended to congregate along main trading routes in places convenient for their customers, the primary traders, and with easy access to the major ports. Except for a few spots such as Lancaster, Pennsylvania, the seats of these secondary traders were almost entirely in riverine and coastal ports. While any hamlet or country crossroad or public warehouse in the Chesapeake might do for the site of the "store" of a primary trader, secondary traders tended to be found in towns and townlets of 1,500–4,000 population, which as ports and county seats often attracted more traffic than their modest size would suggest. Merchants properly so called tended to congregate in coastal or river ports which could handle ocean-going vessels, had easy access to the full variety of goods needed for their export trades, and were convenient to markets for their imported goods.[28]

Even so, not all the ports where mercantile activity took place performed the same functions. (1) Some were mere *shipping points*, where goods were loaded and unloaded, while others were *processing centers* where goods received some manufacture in transit. (2) Some merely received ships sent to them, but others were *shipping centers and markets* where ships could be built, outfitted, repaired, and bought, sold, or chartered, and sailors hired. (3) While some were only *limited marts*, where only the most restricted range of goods could be bought and sold, others were more *general marts* where a great variety of goods (by no means all of local produce)

28. For a related but different analytical system by a geographer, see James T. Lemon, "Urbanization and the Development of Eighteenth-Century Southeastern Pennsylvania and Adjacent Delaware," *William and Mary Quarterly*, 3d ser., 24 (1967), 501–542.

could be purchased and almost anything disposed of. (4) Some had only limited and indirect communication with the outside world, while others functioned as *communications centers*, with relatively easy communications to all the areas with which they traded. (It was no small boon to New York to be made the America terminus of the official mail packet boats from England.) (5) Finally, some gave little evidence of capital accumulation or sophisticated credit and other financial facilities, while others were more fully developed *financial centers* (relatively speaking) where capital could be raised for a wide variety and substantial scale of shipbuilding and trading ventures, where credit could be obtained for ventures overseas, where bills of exchange on a wide variety of places could be bought and sold, and where insurance could be obtained.

The degrees of functional development or underdevelopment in a port are not to be understood merely as *givens*, but were derivatives or reflections of the character of the trade of the port and of the institutional arrangements produced by the marketing requirements of the goods traded.

That Boston was the principal town and port of British North America until ca. 1755 is an historical fact but hardly a self-evident proposition. The capital of the province of Massachusetts Bay had some but not many natural advantages. Geography had endowed it with an excellent, deep, sheltered harbor with moderate tidal range. This excellent haven was not, however, particularly well situated to serve any obvious trade routes, lacking as it did any significant riverine connection with the interior of the continent. The immediate hinterland of Boston, its natural trading domain— the country for about forty miles around—was a land of forest and tidal marshes. There was some natural meadow and open land usable for unimproved pasture; hence grazing was an early profitable activity: horses and cattle, salted beef, pork, butter, and cheese were early exports. However, the soil of the region, as of almost all of eastern New England, was mediocre. This inadequate soil made the Boston region, as indeed all of New England except Connecticut, a net importer of cereals, reportedly even in the seventeenth century, but definitely and consistently in the eighteenth. By 1768–

1772 this dependence of Massachusetts, Rhode Island, and New Hampshire on cereal imports from New York, Pennsylvania, and Maryland had become quite marked.[29] Thus there were no agricultural riches for the infant town of Boston to exploit.

Yet Boston had another hinterland: the long strip of coastal settlements from Cape Cod in the south to the frontier of habitation in Maine on the north. This hinterland had two great natural endowments: fish and timber. The founders of Boston had not thought of themselves as coming three thousand miles across the ocean to found a fishing village; indeed they had the lowest opinion of the manners and morals of the fishermen they found already active on the coast of Massachusetts Bay. Yet necessity forced many in the Bay Colony to become fishermen, and its proudest houses were founded by traffickers in cod. It was not for nothing that a stuffed cod was placed ceremoniously over the speaker's chair in the Massachusetts legislature. Cod from off the colony's own coasts or from the Nova Scotia and Newfoundland banks[30] was the one locally available commodity which could be readily sold almost anywhere—in the colonies to the southward, in the West Indies (where the poorer grades could be sold for the use of the slaves), and in Spain and Portugal. Earnings from sales to the mainland colonies to the southward paid for the cereals and provisions needed in New England; sales to the West Indies paid for imports of sugar, molasses, and other tropical produce; sales to Spain and Portugal and their "Wine Islands" paid for imports of wine and the salt so vital to the fisheries; surplus earnings from the West Indies and Iberia could be remitted to England in commodities or bills of exchange to pay for the European and Asian produce and manu-

29. Public Record Office, London [hereafter PRO] Customs 16/1. This volume contains full data on intercolonial trade, 1768–1772. The data were rather fully analyzed by Max G. Schumacher in an unpublished thesis, "The Northern Farmer and His Markets During the Late Colonial Period" (University of California, Berkeley, 1948), particularly pp. 151–173. His work has been carried further in David Klingaman, "Food Surpluses and Deficits in the American Colonies, 1768–1772," *Journal of Economic History*, 31 (1971), 553–569.

30. In addition to the cod taken by their own fishermen, New England traders acquired much of the cod taken by fishermen resident in Newfoundland; this they usually sent directly to markets in southern Europe.

factures which all the colonies were obliged to buy only from the mother country whether or not they had anything to sell which the mother country wanted to buy.

The opportunities created by the fisheries called into existence at Boston almost from the beginning of settlement a shipbuilding industry, to supply fishing craft, then coastal craft, then sloops and schooners for the West Indies trade (important by the 1640's), and finally the larger brigantines, snows, and ships suitable for the trade to Spain and Portugal. The merchants of Massachusetts soon found that they could sell these larger vessels advantageously in Spain and Portugal and in Britain as well. While oak was expensive in England and the pine planks and deals for shipbuilding there had to be imported from Norway and the best masts from Riga, the shipbuilders of New England had close at hand inexpensive supplies of adequate oak and splendid pine for both planks and masts. Profits from the sale of ships in the ever fluctuating market in Europe constituted the most attractive "windfall profits" of the fish export trade and must have played an important part in capital accumulation among merchants and shipowners in the seventeenth century.[31]

Although dozens of seaside villages in Massachusetts, Maine, and New Hampshire participated in the fisheries, and Salem and Marblehead exported fish in quantity, only Boston developed the full panoply of trade based on the fishing-shipbuilding complex. There were economies of scale in these trades and the greater amounts of capital required for the longer voyages to Europe were probably not available at first in the lesser ports. But part of the concentration at Boston must be seen as arising from the very complexity of the trade. If the New England colonies' trade had been a simple bilateral trade with the mother country, it is possible that several Massachusetts havens might have participated as soon as volume justified. However, the complexity of the trade required a "comprehensive entrepôt" and not simply a "shipping point" for fish. Sloops going southward in the coastal trade carried not just fish but other New England produce (including some crude manufactures)

31. Cf. note 24 for data on shipbuilding in Massachusetts at the beginning of the century.

plus manufactures from Britain and salt from either Iberia or the
West Indies. Sloops in the West Indies trade carried fish, horses,
flour, and provisions (including some bought from the more southerly colonies) and manufactures and wine from Europe. To England went not only the furs and forest products (particularly turpentine) of New England[32] but sugar from the West Indies and
tobacco from the Chesapeake. With trade of this complexity, there
were advantages in concentration in a single mart town, or general
entrepôt, where one man's surplus could fill another's vessel, and
external economies of linkages be realized.

The earliest surviving shipping (naval officer's) accounts for
Boston, showing imports and exports on every vessel, date from
the 1680's.[33] By then, even before Philadelphia was founded, Boston was a general entrepôt, a miniature Amsterdam or London,
with a trade marked by extreme complexity if not necessarily great
volume by the standards either of what was to follow shortly or of
contemporary European ports. Boston was at the height of its relative importance in the small world of North American commerce
from the 1680's to the 1730's. As other colonies developed their
own agriculture and commercial activities, they might compete
with Boston in the West Indian trades, yet become markets for
Boston's fish, turpentine, rum, and European goods.

After 1740, however, Boston's population ceased to grow (Appendix B): from 1740 to 1775, it remained steady at ca. 15,000–
17,000 (and only reached 18,000 in 1790), while its principal rivals,
New York and Philadelphia, tripled and quadrupled in size. This
stagnation has long intrigued historians and its true character has
yet to be established—partly for lack of statistical data on Boston's
trade. While Boston stagnated, everything about it seemed to be
growing. The population of the future United States quadrupled
between 1740 and 1790, while that of Massachusetts (without
Maine) more than doubled (Appendix A). All commodity export

32. For the New England naval stores trade, see Joseph J. Malone, *Pine Trees and Politics: The Naval Stores and Forest Policy in Colonial New England 1691–1775* (London,
1964).

33. In PRO; I have used for Boston the extracts assembled by Prof. L. A. Harper at the
University of California, Berkeley.

indices show healthy rates of growth in these decades, though we lack a good series for fish and shipbuilding. English exports to the thirteen colonies were 4.6 times as much in 1772–1774 as they had been in 1737–1739, while those to New England alone had increased 3.73-fold (real values).[34] All indications are that the coastal trade of Massachusetts as a whole was growing throughout the century.[35] Yet, Boston's own commerce did not fully participate in this growth. Its tonnage cleared out in 1754–1755 was hardly higher than it had been in 1714–1717, though by 1772 it had increased about 60 percent over its 1754 level. (A more marked increase could be shown if we used the inward tonnage.)[36]

Paradoxically, then, while Boston's population stagnated after 1740, its commerce and that of Massachusetts Bay continued to grow, if somewhat irregularly. Whatever retardation Boston's seaborn commerce experienced in the 1740's and early 1750's was amply compensated for thereafter. Analytically, Boston seems to have been affected by a combination of temporary misfortunes and more lasting structural change. The start of the British-Spanish war in 1739 probably affected Massachusetts more than any other continental colony, for Spain was such an important market for New England fish. With the loss of this market, Boston's merchants would have lost part of the wherewithal to purchase European goods; at the same time, owing to the severe winters and bad harvests in western Europe in 1739–1741, the cereal-exporting colonies to the southward were earning unprecedentedly large balances in Europe and the means thereby to make their own purchases directly in Britain without going through Boston. Once the merchants of New York, Philadelphia, and elsewhere had expanded the connections necessary for acquiring goods directly in Britain, it was to prove almost impossible to force them to give up these efficient

---

34. John J. McCusker, "The Current Value of English Exports, 1697 to 1800," *William and Mary Quarterly*, 3d ser., 28 (1971), 624–625. The better-known official values (from Whitworth) can be found in U. S. Bureau of the Census, *Historical Statistics of the United States* (Washington, D.C., 1960), p. 757.

35. Klingaman, "Food Surpluses and Deficits," pp. 563–565.

36. *U. S. Historical Statistics*, p. 759.

channels of trade. Thus, in the 1740's, English exports to New England declined while those to all the other colonies increased.

Table II

ENGLISH EXPORTS TO NORTH AMERICA, 1737–1749

| | To New England | To All Colonies |
	(in thousands of pounds sterling)	
1737–1739	179 p.a.	583 p.a.
1740–1745	149	690
1740–1749	165	729

Though Boston's shipping activity resumed its growth in the generation 1755–1775, it was almost inevitable that Boston would lose its place as the leading American port, if only because wheat and flour passed fish as the leading export of the northern and middle colonies both generally and to southern Europe. In this, North American production was reacting to the expansion of population in Europe and the higher prices for cereals that characterized the last third of the eighteenth century. Thus, by 1765–1772, Philadelphia, which had long since passed Boston in population, also passed it marginally in shipping volume. The Philadelphia lead was most pronouneed in the trade to the West Indies and southern Europe, both of which took its flour, but Boston still led in the direct trade with Britain, suggesting that there was still life left in its old trade of reexporting goods from Britain to the other colonies.

Boston's problems were not confined to the rise of independent general entrepôts in New York and Philadelphia which could dispense with its services as intermediary. Within Massachusetts, its position in the simpler trades was also challenged by lesser ports which eventually seemed able to operate on a competitive scale at lower costs. The old bases of the area's ocean-borne commerce, fishing and shipbuilding, had never been Boston's monopoly. From the earliest days of settlement the lesser ports to the north and south of Boston had participated in these activities, though Boston marketed much of their fish and commissioned or bought much of the output of their shipbuilding yards.[37] Salem and (after 1717) Marblehead had long been major exporters of cod to Iberia but failed to develop much of an import trade from Britain.[38] By the third quarter of the eighteenth century most fishermen had long since deserted expensive Boston. Between 1771 and 1775, 121 vessels (14,020 tons) with 4,059 men were engaged in the Massachusetts whale fishery: of these, only five vessels (700 tons) with 260 men came from Boston.[39] During 1765–1775, 665 vessels (25,630 tons) with 4,405 men were engaged in the Massachusetts cod fishery: of these *none* were of Boston.[40] Marblehead and Gloucester to the north continued the great centers of the cod fishery, while Salem shared in its export trade. With the growing volume of the fishery, local traders had gradually been accumulating the capital and commercial knowledge which by the 1740's enabled them to act independently of their erstwhile great friends in Boston. By the 1760's these ports shipped all their cod directly to southern Europe and the West Indies (as Salem had been doing for a century) and not through Boston. What little cod the Boston port district did export must have come from the fishing villages to the southward or been purchased in Newfoundland. Boston merchants may have had an interest in these shipments from Gloucester and Marblehead and Salem, as they had in some from Newfoundland to Iberia, but this created little activity or employment at Boston.[41]

Boston's slippage was less marked in shipbuilding than in fishing. The Bailyns have analyzed the Boston shipping register of 1697–

37. Cf. note 24.

38. On Salem and vicinity, see William I. Davisson and Dennis J. Dugan, "Commerce in Seventeenth-Century Essex County, Massachusetts," *Essex Institute Historical Collections*, 107 (1971), 113–142.

39. Timothy Pitkin, *A Statistical View of the Commerce of the United States of America* (Hartford, Conn., 1816), pp. 78–79. By 1787–1789, employment in the Massachusetts whale fishery had declined to 1,611 men, of whom 78 served on Boston vessels. Appendix C shows only 37 fishermen on Boston's tax lists in 1790. They probably worked close by for the local market.

40. *Ibid.*, p. 74.

41. During 1768–1772 the customs district of Salem and Marblehead sent 103,700 quintals of dried fish p.a. to southern Europe, while Boston sent only 10,321; the former sent 87,904 qu. p.a. to the West Indies, while the latter sent only 58,193. The shipments from Boston came not from the town but from the fishing villages to the southward in the same customs district. PRO Customs 16/1.

1714: they show Massachusetts (without Maine) shipbuilding averaging 3,094 tons p.a. in 1697–1704 and 4,246 tons in 1705–1714.[42] By 1769–1771, Massachusetts shipbuilding averaged 7,667 tons p.a., an increase of about 150 percent since the beginning of the century (1697–1704).[43] This is not a very high rate of growth when we consider that Massachusetts' population increased by about 320 percent between 1700 and 1770. Yet in 1769–1771 Massachusetts accounted for about one-third of the tonnage built in the colonies. In all probability her share had been between half and two-thirds at the beginning of the century. A good example of the new competition Massachusetts had to face comes from our New Hampshire data. In 1697–1714 the Boston registry shows shipping built in New Hampshire of only 3,245 tons, or 4.75 percent of the 68,311 tons built in Massachusetts. (There was no separate registry in New Hampshire.)[44] By 1769–1771, shipping was being built in New Hampshire at the rate of 3,675 tons p.a. or about half the Massachusetts figure.[45] Within Massachusetts, shipbuilding had always been dispersed. The Bailyns reported that only 25 percent of the Massachusetts registered fleet of 1698 had been built in Boston. However, in succeeding years, Boston's shipbuilding activity increased so that 40 percent of all vessels registered through 1714 were built in Boston.[46] We lack accessible data at the present time (though the problem is not insoluble), but it seems unlikely that as much as 40 percent of the Bay Colony's shipbuilding remained in the confined and expensive site of Boston throughout the century.[47] The same cost-cutting forces that encouraged shipbuilding in New Hampshire would have encouraged it elsewhere in Massachusetts proper and in Maine (then part of Massachusetts). However, even if Boston's share of Massachusetts shipbuilding slipped somewhat from the 40 percent of 1674–1714, this would not have

42. Bailyn and Bailyn, *Massachusetts Shipping*, pp. 102–105.

43. John, Lord Sheffield, *Observations on the Commerce of the American States*, 6th ed. (London, 1784), p. 96.

44. Bailyn and Bailyn, *Massachusetts Shipping*, pp. 106–109.

45. See note 43.

46. Bailyn and Bailyn, *Massachusetts Shipping*, p. 50.

47. This problem could be solved by sampling the shipping records ("naval officers' reports") in the PRO.

meant any absolute decline, for the total volume of activity was increasing. Throughout the century a significant shipbuilding trade remained in Boston, probably specializing in larger vessels and leaving the fishing and coastal craft to the lesser ports. Some of these larger vessels were produced on order from merchants in Britain and others were sold in Britain or elsewhere in Europe after their first voyage. For example, of a group of 36 vessels of which we have information, carrying tobacco from Virginia to Britain in 1774, 13 were built in Massachusetts: 11 at Boston, 1 at Charlestown across the harbor, and 1 at Newbury on the Merrimack. All were registered, hence owned, at Glasgow.[48] By contrast, there were only one Philadelphia-, one Maryland-, and no New York–built ships in this trade. In short, it would appear that the Boston shipbuilding industry was very much alive and competitive in 1775, though it no longer accounted for as large a share of American shipbuilding as it had in the much smaller world of 1675. This would help to explain why in the previous section we found the shipbuilding group accounting for a somewhat larger share of the employed population in Boston than in Philadelphia or New York.

In shipping activity, Boston also came to share somewhat more with the lesser ports in Massachusetts. Between 1699 and 1714, the Bailyns report that Boston accounted for 83.8 percent of Massachusetts ship registrations by number and 89.7 percent by tonnage.[49] By the end of the century (1798), however, Boston accounted for only 37.5 percent of Massachusetts' registered tonnage.[50] This trend was probably of long standing for in 1768–1772 the port district of Salem and Marblehead already accounted for about 34 percent of the province's shipping activity, and it was to account for 34.6 percent of registration in 1798.[51] Before 1775 these home rivals had invaded all of Boston's trades except that to England.

48. Naval officers' (inspectors of navigation) accounts in PRO: T.1/506 ff. 1–2, 5, 7, 10, 13v; T.1/512 ff. 196, 198, 201v, 204, 207 (excluding Rappahannock as imprecise).

49. Bailyn and Bailyn, *Massachusetts Shipping*, p. 44.

50. Samuel Eliot Morison, *The Maritime History of Massachusetts 1783–1860* (Boston, 1921), p. 378.

51. *Ibid.*; PRO Customs 16/1.

To summarize, on the basis of an initially favorable position in fish and shipbuilding Boston had by the end of the seventeenth century an extensive and elaborate general entrepôt position touching all the colonies. In the eighteenth century, it lost the cod fishery and most of the fish export trade to lesser rivals within Massachusetts, and its relative position in shipbuilding declined, leaving it dependent on its rather artificial entrepôt trades. Except for the difficult years 1740–1755 these trades continued to grow down to the Revolution, though declining in relative importance as other ports, particularly New York and Philadelphia, through increased exports to the West Indies and southern Europe were increasingly able to finance their own imports from Britain without going through the Boston entrepôt. Boston's greatest weakness throughout remained the limitation of its immediate hinterland and the closeness of rival ports, which probably explains why its service sector and (except for shipbuilding and distilling) its manufacturing sectors were relatively less important than those of Philadelphia.

Newport's economy was a reduced and somewhat bizarre version of that of Boston. Located on the original island of Rhode Island, it too was endowed with an excellent harbor but only the most minimal natural hinterland in southern New England. It could, however, draw on the agricultural surpluses of the Connecticut River valley, but had to compete for them with New York and eventually with the petty Connecticut river and shore towns that also ventured into the West India trade. It did, however, have certain political advantages. In the seventeenth century, extreme religious toleration drew to it various Protestant sectarians who did not find easy toleration in the tight Calvinist-Congregationalist world of Massachusetts or Connecticut. Quakers and Jews were quite conspicuous there in the eighteenth century. By then, however, its most important political advantage was its virtually self-governing status. Alone of the colonies, Connecticut and Rhode Island chose their own governors and thus were effectively free of close imperial inspection. In practical terms this meant that it was easier to disregard imperial tax (customs) and trade regulations in Newport than in any other major commercial center. This perhaps explains why Newport more than any other colonial port seemed drawn to illicit trade—not simply trade to the Dutch and French islands, which was only technically illegal, but the smuggling in of European and Asian goods from the Dutch islands and from Holland itself. The more legitimate trade of Newport consisted of exporting fish, provisions, and local horses to the West Indies, and —rarely—to southern Europe. It was very much a busy entrepôt, for almost everything it exported it had to obtain from other colonies—fish from Newfoundland, flour and provisions from Connecticut and the colonies to the southward. Lacking natural endowments in its hinterland or any commercial imperative for its existence, Newport grew by pushing the most marginal trades, including the whale fishery. Its only significant industry was making whale-oil candles and distilling rum from the molasses it imported from the West Indies, much of it improperly. Most of this rum was sold in New England and to the southward, but Rhode Island also had the largest African trade of any of the colonies.[52] Rum purchased the slaves which in turn purchased the molasses and provisions needed by Newport. Newport could also supply all its own shipping, the Rhode Island shipbuilding industry being third among the colonies, after Massachusetts and New Hampshire. There was a significant surplus ship production available for sale in England, though small compared to that of Massachusetts. By the generation preceding the Revolution, Newport was earning enough sterling exchange on its West Indian and other trades to obtain its European goods directly from England (when it did not obtain them surreptitiously from Holland) rather than get them at second hand from Boston or New York.[53]

Though Newport was never again so prosperous as just before

52. PRO Customs 16/1. More than half of all rum exported from the colonies to Africa in 1769 came from Rhode Island. Only Boston was also active in this trade.

53. There is no full-scale study of Newport's commerce. The main lines can be derived from Bridenbaugh (note 15) or from the documents published in *Commerce of Rhode Island 1726–1800* (*Collections of the Massachusetts Historical Society*, 7th ser., IX [Boston, 1914]). The latter show, for example, Newport merchants in the 1770's sending ships to Philadelphia to purchase flour for shipment to Lisbon. This type of speculative activity is hard to trace in shipping records.

the American Revolution, its position was entirely artificial. Its trade was based upon no imperatives of geography but upon a series of historic accidents that brought together a trading population there and facilitated the accumulation of capital and entrepreneurial and technical skills. Even it in hour of prosperity, Newport's position was being undermined by the development of Providence at the head of Narragansett Bay on the mainland. Providence's trade to the West Indies and southern colonies inevitably intercepted much of Newport's trade from its very limited natural hinterland. The American Revolution dispersed the trading community at Newport and dissipated much of their capital, and the town was never again to be a serious commercial center. (Needless to say, it could not have, under the new federal government of 1789, the advantages of inefficient tax collection it had enjoyed when part of the British Empire.)

Philadelphia's position was as natural as that of Newport was artificial. While the New England commercial centers, starting with Boston and Newport, had trading hinterlands that hugged open coastlines and the valleys of navigable rivers and so were open to the intrusion of such rival, upstart port towns as Salem, Providence, and New London, the richest hinterland of Philadelphia lay inland from the town—to the west and northwest—and for long had access to no other large port town where its produce could be vended. Only after the zone of settlement in Pennsylvania expanded to the west of the Susquehanna River did the farmers and traders of central Pennsylvania have the option of sending their produce southward to the rival port of Baltimore. This alternative, however, became real only after the American Revolution.[54]

Between Philadelphia and the Susquehanna River lay a territory of superior soil, well suited to growing wheat. On this soil settlement became relatively thick in the eighteenth century, particularly that of German immigrants. In addition to raising wheat and hogs, they fattened cattle, including many driven in from the more outlying sections of Pennsylvania and up from the south along a drove

54. For the later story, see James Weston Livingood, *The Philadelphia-Baltimore Trade Rivalry 1780–1860* (Harrisburg, Pa., 1947).

road that extended from the interior of North Carolina through the valley of Virginia into Maryland and Pennsylvania. Closer to Philadelphia a large number of mills were set up along the streams flowing into the Delaware to grind the wheat into flour,[55] while the remarkably large number of bakers in Philadelphia (Appendix C) is some evidence of the important trade of baking this flour into biscuit for use on shipboard and in the West Indies. Similarly, the abnormally large number of butchers also shown in our occupational data for Philadelphia is evidence of the substantial trade there in slaughtering and packing beef and pork for exportation.

From the time of its foundation, in the 1680's, Philadelphia had an active trade, exporting its flour and provisions to the West Indies. This appears to have been a rather simple bilateral trade for the most part, supplemented by occasional shipments of wheat and flour to southern Europe as market conditions there justified. Although Philadelphia did supply West Indian and European goods to adjacent parts of New Jersey and Maryland, there is very little sign of a real entrepôt at Philadelphia in the first seventy years or so of its existence.[56] The volume of its imports from England was quite low[57] (Appendix E). This is not simply because Pennsylvania's population was still low (Appendix A), reflecting the later date of its foundation. (Pennsylvania did not pass Maryland in population until ca. 1760.) Although Pennsylvania passed New York in population in 1730, during the next thirty years New York regularly imported more goods from Britain than Pennsylvania did. This left no significant surplus for an entrepôt trade in European goods. Rather, Philadelphia appears to have continued to import such goods from Boston and other New England ports in payment for the provisions sold the New Englanders. This rather simple pattern of trade seems to have encouraged the development of a large community of small merchants in Philadelphia, big enough to trade to the West Indies but not very venturesome out-

55. Cf. Bridenbaugh, *Cities in Revolt*, pp. 50–51, 57, 75, 265, 268.
56. W. I. Davisson may not agree. Cf. his "The Philadelphia Trade," *Western Economic Journal*, 3 (1965), 310–311.
57. *U. S. Historical Statistics*, p. 757.

side those familiar waters, all too glad to sell wheat and flour and
provisions to New England craft that visited their haven in return
for fish and European goods, but not too inclined to send their
own craft to New England or Newfoundland and only rarely to
England.

Matters began to change in Philadelphia in the early 1750's,
about the time the young Robert Morris started in business. During the Seven Years' War (1756–1763), a substantial British military effort to drive the French out of Fort Duquesne (Pittsburgh)
led to considerable army expenditures in Pennsylvania on supplies.
This gave the merchants of Philadelphia unprecedentedly large
supplies of bills of exchange on London at the time when military
business was increasing the volume of direct sea traffic between
England and their port. (Part of this military business continued
after the peace of 1763.) During these same war years, cereal prices
in Europe began that secular upswing that was to last until ca. 1815.
A series of bad harvests in the late 1760's and early 1770's not only
greatly expanded markets for North American wheat and flour in
the familiar markets at Lisbon and Cadiz, but encouraged North
American ships to venture more frequently into the Mediterranean,
to Barcelona in particular, and even carried them to France ca.
1770.[58] Britain, a cereal exporter since ca. 1689, but now feeling the
pressure of rising population, was forced to open its harbors to
grain imports in the bad years of the late sixties and early seventies.
Philadelphia, as the principal flour exporter in North America,
profited particularly from these changes in the European markets.
Its flour exports increased almost sixfold between 1730–1731 and
1773–1774. Four times as many vessels went from Philadelphia to
the continent of Europe in 1768 as in 1733–1734 and six times as
many in 1769 and 1770. Tonnage to Britain in 1768 was 126 percent above that in 1765–1766.[59] Higher prices for cereals and flour
made overland transportation to Philadelphia economic from a

58. Ports inside the Mediterranean were long known to New England ships in the fish
trade. Cf. note 38.

59. *U. S. Historical Statistics*, pp. 759–760; Jensen, *Commerce of Philadelphia*, p. 292. Cf.
Donald Grove Barnes, *A History of the English Corn Laws from 1666–1846* (1931; New
York, 1961), pp. 38–43.

wider geographic area and greatly encouraged the settlement of the Pennsylvania frontier, made safe by the defeat of the French and their Indian allies.

At Philadelphia these same developments meant changes of scale and style for the mercantile community. The profits (often windfall profits) of the flour trade greatly facilitated the accumulation of capital. By the early 1770's Philadelphians were investing eleven times as much per annum in new shipping as they had in the 1720's and supplied almost all their shipping needs. The town's mercantile fleet was now worth about £500,000 sterling. The average ship sent to Britain or southern Europe in the 1770's was considerably larger than the average of those sent as recently as the 1750's.[60] With these developments went a change in scale of mercantile operations at Philadelphia and an articulation within the mercantile community. Larger firms emerged (of whom perhaps the best known is Willing and Morris) with correspondents in every major port between Barcelona and Amsterdam. In order to undertake very risky operations, these firms had to know the credit of great speculators in London who might send them purchase orders totaling tens of thousands of pounds sterling, as well as the creditworthiness of the houses at Lisbon, Barcelona, and Leghorn who would handle their flour sales and remit the proceeds to London. In many senses, the establishment of such liaisons by great merchants like Robert Morris was a commercial prerequisite of the American Revolution.

With such vastly increased earnings from military supplying and the flour trade, Philadelphia was able to multiply its imports from Britain and more than free itself from any dependence on New England. While the combined population of Pennsylvania and its dependency, Delaware, increased about 160 percent between 1740 and 1770, English exports to the same areas increased by more than a thousand percent. (In the same period, English exports to all the colonies increased by only 360 percent.) Philadelphia had by this

60. John J. McCusker, "Sources of Investment Capital in the Colonial Philadelphia Shipping Industry," *Journal of Economic History*, 32 (1973). 151–152. See also Jensen, *Commerce of Philadelphia*, p. 290.

time more than freed itself from dependence on Boston for any European supplies and was extending its own trading sphere southward into the backcountry of Maryland and Virginia. While the entrepôt trades of Boston and Newport show up very clearly in the records of ports up and down the coast, most of Philadelphia's went by wagon and has left less record. References in surviving mercantile correspondence leave no doubt, however, that by 1765–1776 merchants throughout Maryland and Virginia were much aware of the presence of Philadelphia. (The coastal export trade of Philadelphia with other colonies was largely in flour, West Indian sugar, and New England rum.)[61]

The "Conestoga" wagons and wagoners must have been a very important part of the life of Philadelphia. Bridenbaugh has vividly described the great files of these enormous wagons lumbering into Philadelphia along the Lancaster Road, sometimes a hundred or more a day.[62] In our discussion of the population structure of Philadelphia in the previous section, we noted that it had a somewhat larger service sector than Boston, and part of this must be ascribable to the wagon traffic. To move a given tonnage by wagon required a greater quantity of labor accompanying the goods than did moving the same tonnage by sailing vessels (perhaps ten times as much). Philadelphia at times must have been filled with wagoners, and despite Bridenbaugh's insistence on the thrift and abstinence of the "Pennsylvania Dutch" farmer-wagoners, this congregation must have created an enormous amount of business for innkeepers, tavernkeepers, harnessmakers, wheelwrights. Since the wagoners were often themselves farmers of the interior, they must have taken advantage of their stay in Philadelphia to make a wide variety of purchases for their families and neighbors at prices that of necessity were less than those charged by the country storekeepers (our primary traders) in their neighborhoods—even when they as carters were working for interior traders. Thus both the retail and wholesale trading areas of Philadelphia probably extended far deeper into

61. *U. S. Historical Statistics*, p. 757; Jensen, *Commerce of Philadelphia*, pp. 70–84.
62. Cf. note 55.

the interior than did that of any of its competing towns: hence the larger "service sector."

To compare Philadelphia and New York is to raise an obvious question. Early in the nineteenth century New York passed Philadelphia, to become the principal port and largest city in the United States. In the early eighteenth century New York was already larger and busier than Philadelphia but lost that edge by 1750 and did not recover it until early in the next century. Why did New York not grow as rapidly as Philadelphia in the decades after 1740? The answer probably lies in the difference between immediate and ultimate geographic advantage. In the long run New York had a more advantageous situation than Philadelphia, particularly before the construction of railroads, for the Hudson is more navigable than the Delaware and with its tributary the Mohawk opens up a larger and richer hinterland. This, however, was well in the future in 1740. The valley of the Mohawk and western New York were closed to significant European settlement by hostile Indians and their French allies. The valley of the Hudson south of Albany was safer but was geographically confined and had only limited agricultural possibilities. What counted in the 1740's was the immediate hinterland of the two ports, the areas within a fifty- or sixty-mile radius—and by this criterion Philadelphia was better endowed. In addition to the Hudson Valley, New York could draw on Long Island and adjacent parts of New Jersey and Connecticut (subject to competition from Newport) but this added up to less than Philadelphia's western breadbasket. Between 1730 and 1780 the population of New York province increased from 48,594 to 210,541 (333 percent) while Pennsylvania increased from 51,707 to 327,000 (533 percent). The slower growth of New York City is the slower growth of its region.

There may, however, be a slight pro-Philadelphia bias in accounts that compare the growth of Philadelphia with that of New York. Bridenbaugh (Appendix B1) suggests that Philadelphia in 1775 was 60 percent larger than New York City (40,000:25,000). However, in 1790 the first census (Appendix B2) showed Philadelphia only 28 percent larger than New York (42,444:33,131).

If, instead of using Bridenbaugh's figures for 1775, we use the older figures of Rossiter (Appendix B2), we find that Philadelphia's lead over New York in 1770 was only 33 percent (28,000:21,000). Recently, Warner has investigated the population of Philadelphia and calculated that it was only 23,739 in 1775. Part of this great difference is due to the previous use of high multipliers (ca. 6.3) when converting the number of houses into heads of population. Warner has calculated that the multiplier in the 1770's was only 4.44; hence his much lower population figure.[63] Although the last word has probably not been said on this subject, it is apparent that part of the supposed lead of Philadelphia over New York may be a statistical illusion.

At first glance, New York was very similar to Philadelphia in its commerce and population structure, though closer inspection reveals some marked similarities to Boston. Although it continued to count furs among its significant exports longer than any other northern colony—owing to the great Indian trade at Albany—its principal exports in the eighteenth century were, like Philadelphia's, flour and provisions. The general volume of its maritime activity was, however, less than that of any other major port.

Table III

AVERAGE SHIPPING TONNAGE
CLEARED OUTWARD P.A.
1768–1772

Philadelphia	42,790 tons
Boston	37,842
Charleston	31,075
New York	26,278

CF. *U. S. Historical Statistics*, pp. 759–760.

In value, all of New York's exports in 1769 were worth only £231,906 while Pennsylvania's, essentially Philadelphia's, were worth £410,757; its imports were valued at only £188,976, Penn-

63. Warner, *The Private City*, pp. 11–12, 225–226.

II

sylvania's at £399,821.[64] New York's trade to southern Europe was quite undeveloped relative to Philadelphia's. In a peak year for that trade, 1769, New York sent only 2,039 tons of flour and biscuit to southern Europe, Philadelphia 15,206 tons. (In addition, New York sent 79,565 bushels of wheat, while Philadelphia sent 165,-315.)[65] All of New York's exports to southern Europe that year were in one estimate valued at £52,199, Pennsylvania's at £204,-313: by a modern calculation they were worth only £37,810, Pennsylvania's £183,760.[66] New York's West Indian trade was also considerably smaller than that of Philadelphia or Boston.

Table IV

VALUES OF IMPORTS AND EXPORTS TO WEST INDIES, 1769

	Exports		Imports
Pennsylvania	£178,331	(123,557)	£180,592
Massachusetts	123,394	(101,569)	155,387
New York	66,325	(53,241)	97,420

NOTE: The figures in parentheses are Shepherd, "Commodity Exports," estimates.
SOURCE: U. S. Historical Statistics, p. 758; Shepherd, "Commodity Exports," pp. 32–33.

Yet, despite these relatively unsuccessful branches, New York by complicated entrepôt functions was able to send far more to Britain and Ireland than Pennsylvania and to maintain a favorable balance of trade with the mother country, something no other northern colony did. The £113,382 worth of goods which New York sent the British Isles in 1769[67] consisted of its own wheat, whale oil, flax-seed (in demand in Ireland), iron and ashes, plus Caribbean sugar, annatto (a cheese dye), logwood, and other dyes, Honduras

64. U. S. Historical Statistics, p. 758. For a full breakdown of colonial exports, 1768–1772, with somewhat different values, see the valuable long paper of James F. Shepherd, "Commodity Exports from the British North American Colonies to Overseas Areas, 1768–1772: Magnitudes and Patterns of Trade," Explorations in Economic History, 8 (1970) 5–76.
65. PRO Customs 16/1 (L. A. Harper's abstracts); Shepherd, "Commodity Exports," pp. 32–33.
66. U. S. Historical Statistics, p. 758; Shepherd, "Commodity Exports," pp. 32–33.
67. £65,016 before shipment, in a modern estimate. Ibid.

mahogany, and Carolina rice and naval stores.[68] In other words, because flour and provisions, "natural" endowments, were not available in sufficient quantities, even under the high prices prevailing ca. 1768–1774, New York was forced, much as was Boston, into a complex entrepôt trade. Its merchants were probably as adept as those of Boston; like those in Boston and Philadelphia, they had mastered, for example, the intricacies of underwriting marine insurance.[69] They enjoyed one marked advantage in having their port as the American terminus of the official British transatlantic packet boat. Getting mail early was no small commercial advantage. Although there was no Robert Morris in New York then, when the French government was forced—in the *pacte de famine* crisis of 1770—to purchase wheat and flour in North America, the French agents in London (Bourdieu & Chollet) chose to work through Wallace & Company of New York rather than through a Philadelphia house.

New York was significantly behind Boston and Philadelphia in one further respect; the shipbuilding of the province (essentially the town's) as of 1769–1771 was less than one-fifth that of Massachusetts and only 70 percent of Pennsylvania's, essentially Philadelphia's (Appendix F). New York's shipbuilding fell below that of less urban colonies such as New Hampshire, Rhode Island, Connecticut, Maryland, and Virginia. This is probably a significant explanation of why, as noted earlier (Appendix D), the manufacturing sector in the population of New York City, even if measured in 1795, was significantly below that of Boston and Philadelphia.

Before closing our discussion of the three great commercial centers of colonial America—Boston, New York, and Philadelphia—something ought to be said about the alleged independent character of their mercantile communities. Most people who write about

68. Harrington, *New York Merchant*, pp. 165–172. A more recent work confirming the "entrepôt" version of New York trade is William I. Davisson and Lawrence J. Bradley, "New York Maritime Trade: Ship Voyage Patterns, 1715–1765," *New York Historical Society Quarterly*, 55 (1971), 309–317.

69. It is noteworthy that ports as small as Boston, New York, and Philadelphia developed maritime insurance from the 1740's. Cf. Bridenbaugh, *Cities in Revolt*, pp. 93, 287. Even Charleston obtained an insurance office in 1761, though most of its insurance was made in London.

II

these three ports take it for granted that their trade was entirely in the hands of their own merchants on whose account (i.e., with whose capital and at whose risk) both exports and imports were made. There is evidence that, during the great boom in the wheat and flour trade in the 1760's and 1770's, big London grain speculators or French agents sent purchase orders to New York, Philadelphia, and perhaps Maryland. There is also better-known evidence (in standard accounts and unpublished sources) of British merchants sending goods to those centers on their own account to be sold on commission.[70] This means that, for a part of their business, the merchants of New York and Philadelphia and perhaps even Boston were acting as the agents or factors of metropolitan merchants to whom the risks and the profits belonged. If this was true in the 1760's and 1770's, might it not also have been true earlier? How did all those new houses in New York and Philadelphia get started between the 1720's and the 1760's? Finally, there is the matter of auctions. In the years after 1815 one of the characteristic institutions of British-American trade was the import auction, particularly at New York. British manufacturers who had surplus stocks or needed cash in a hurry bypassed the export merchants and sent their goods directly to New York to be auctioned on arrival, usually for cash. It is clear, however, from the monographic literature on the colonial period that similar auctions were being complained of in New York and Philadelphia in the 1760's and 1770's. But we are told nothing of the persons who sent such goods for auction—though we get tantalizing hints of direct contact with Manchester.[71] Then too we know all too little about the internal history of the businesses in these places. We have been told where the capital for their ships came from, but not the capital for the firms themselves. These are some of the problems that will have to be solved before we can understand fully the inner dynamics of the mercantile communities in those port towns.

70. E.g., Jensen, *Philadelphia Commerce*, pp. 17–19, 96–97; Harrington, *New York Merchant*, pp. 67–72.

71. Harrington, *New York Merchant*, pp. 92–93; Bridenbaugh, *Cities in Revolt*, pp. 78–79, 276–277; and, particularly, Jensen, *Philadelphia Commerce*, pp. 123–124.

The last of the great commercial centers of colonial America was
Charleston in South Carolina. At the beginning of the eighteenth
century it was important only for its Indian trade, though it enjoyed a small trade with the West Indies in forest products and
provisions. In the eighteenth century it developed two great agricultural staples: rice (after 1710) and later indigo, both grown by
slave labor in the coastal districts near Charleston. These trades
reached impressive proportions. In 1769, rice exports from the
thirteen colonies (83 percent originally from Charleston) were
worth £340,693, making this the fourth most valuable export of
British North America just after fish (tobacco and the wheat-flour
group being first and second). At the same time, indigo exports
from the same colonies (almost all originally from Charleston)
were worth £131,552, the fifth most valuable export from the
colonies.[72] More than half the rice went to Great Britain with a
large fraction also going to southern Europe and the West Indies
and lesser quantities to the other mainland colonies. (Large but
unknown quantities, were retained in South Carolina for local
consumption.) As provided by law, almost all the indigo went to
Britain, where it was valued for the textile industries.

One of the striking features of South Carolina colonial life was
the degree to which the single port of Charleston was able almost
to monopolize the import and export trade of that colony and even
of nearby Georgia. While New York and Pennsylvania really had
room for only one significant port at the mouth of each of their
great rivers, South Carolina had a number of river valleys and possible harbor sites. Nevertheless, river and coastal communication
was easy and a very high proportion of the external commerce of
South Carolina became concentrated in Charleston, which also
handled some of the trade that emanated from North Carolina and
Georgia. This pattern began in the first half century of settlement,
when the settled areas all lay close to Charleston, but persisted after

72. *U. S. Historical Statistics*, pp. 761–762, 767–768. For the five years, 1768–1772,
Shepherd ("Commodity Exports," p. 65) estimates annual average value of colonial
exports at: tobacco, £766,000; flour and biscuit, £412,000; rice, £312,000; dried fish,
£287,000; indigo, £117,000.

dispersion. From the early dangerous days down to midcentury, when relations with the Indians were not peaceful, many large planters chose to live in Charleston for safety's sake. This pattern persisted afterwards partly because the planting regions were unhealthy, partly because they were populated predominantly by slaves, and partly out of habit and convenience. This gave Charleston a significant population of resident gentry, a social phenomenon known in the West Indies but unusual in North America. With a significant number of planters spending at least part of the year in Charleston, it became the inevitable center of consumer handicrafts in the colony and of the import trade. That it also became a center of the export trade suggests that for its commodities, there were no ultimate economies in a more dispersed pattern. By concentrating export commodities in one place, larger vessels could be used and turn-around time for even large ships reduced.

Charleston never developed a significant shipbuilding industry. Its exports to England were generally carried in English-owned vessels employed in a bilateral service back and forth to England.[73] Charleston was also frequently visited by smaller craft from the northern colonies that may have carried a significant part of the colony's exports to the Caribbean. Shipping movements and rice exports to southern Europe fluctuated considerably from year to year depending upon the price of cereals in those parts. The picture is not clear. but British shipping probably also handled a good part of that trade. All of this added up to a considerable volume of activity. Charleston was a busier port than New York on the eve of the Revolution.

Despite this activity, Charleston did not have as large an autochthonous business community as the northern centers. In the early days many of her traders were factors sent there by firms in England. On the eve of the Revolution, we find some big firms in Charleston that are in effect branches of houses in London or Liverpool under the management of a local resident partner. There were of course locally based organizations as well but they never succeeded

73. Even after the Revolution, for a time the majority of vessels entering South Carolina ports were British.

in dominating trade as indigenous firms did in the northern ports. It was, of course, precisely because Charleston offered commodities desired in England (rice and indigo) that British merchants were attracted more toward this trade than toward that of the northern ports. This pattern tended to reduce Charleston to the level of a mere "shipping point" rather than a real "commercial center" or a "general entrepôt." Entrepreneurial decisions were made in Britain, capital was raised there, ships were built or chartered there and outfitted there, insurance was made there—all for the South Carolina trade. There was nothing conspiratorial in this, nor anything to be taken as evidence of the feckless character of the Charleston mercantile community. It was rather a rational adaptation to market conditions and comparative costs, given the commodities traded and the markets available to them. Nevertheless, this "colonial" character of Charleston's commercial life helps to explain why Charleston with a larger volume of tonnage and more valuable imports and exports than New York had only half the population of New York City in 1770.

The last remaining area to be discussed is perhaps the most paradoxical in colonial America: the Chesapeake Bay colonies of Virginia and Maryland. Virginia was the most populous continental colony, or state, from its foundation until passed by New York in 1820. Virginia and Maryland together accounted for over 30 percent of the population of the thirteen colonies in 1770. Their chief product, tobacco, was the most valuable export of North America for more than a century preceding the Revolution. In 1770, exports were estimated to be worth over £900,000 sterling. They were also major exporters of wheat. Yet down to 1750 or 1760 they had no town with a population of as much as 3,000. This was partly corrected in the years 1760–1775 by the rise of Baltimore and Norfolk, but on the eve of the Revolution the former had only 5,934 inhabitants and latter about 6,250. Williamsburg, the capital of Virginia (not a port but a *Residenzstadt* like Karlsruhe or Wolfenbüttel), then had a population of only 2,000 and Annapolis, the capital of Maryland, both a port and a capital, only 3,700.[74]

74. Bridenbaugh, *Cities in Revolt*, p. 217.

Without major centers almost to the eve of the Revolution, Virginia and Maryland were not without town life. The maps are filled with places that contemporaries considered towns. If most of the county seats (or "Court Houses") in Virginia were little more than hamlets, there were somewhat more substantial commercial towns at the mouths of rivers (Norfolk and Yorktown) and more characteristically at the limits of navigation of the principal rivers: Alexandria on the Potomac (population 2,748 in 1790), Fredericksburg on the Rappahannock (1,485 in 1790), Richmond on the James (under 2,000 in 1775), and Petersburg on the Appomattox (2,828 in 1790 but the most important tobacco shipping center), as well as Georgetown in Maryland. There were also even smaller but fairly busy little port towns along the rivers that handled local traffic and ships that could not or did not wish to venture up to the "heads" of navigation: Port Tobacco in Maryland, Dumfries on the Virginia side of the Potomac, Hobbs Hole on the Rappahannock. Busy or not, none of this latter group attracted very much of a population.

The failure of Virginia and Maryland to develop any large commercial centers before 1775 (or even any middling centers before 1750) has long perplexed historians and geographers. Moreover, it perplexed the people and leaders of the two colonies themselves in the seventeenth and eighteenth centuries. In general, royal policy favored town growth, and the legislatures of the two colonies passed numerous acts intended to encourage town growth, but all to very little effect.

The most common explanation for the lack of towns in the Chesapeake has been geographical. According to this explanation, towns did not develop in Virginia and Maryland because the area was so well endowed with waterways, the great Bay of Chesapeake itself, two hundred miles long, with the many rivers that flow into it, great and small, and the numerous tributaries of those rivers. Ships could come from Britain or other colonies and deliver goods and pick up tobacco at the wharf of the individual planter or country storekeeper. There was thus no need for a compulsory point of transshipment as at Philadelphia where wholesale dealers and greater

merchants might congregate and services usefully be centralized. I
have never been quite satisfied with this argument. (1) It seems to
place location before activity, saying that, if there had been towns
in Virginia, there would have been more merchants, wholesale
dealers, and manufacturing artisans. Is it not, however, sensible to
assume that, if there were merchants and wholesale traders and
artisans in the Chesapeake, they would have found some convenient place to settle? The relevant question then becomes, Why were
there not more merchants, traders, and artisans in the Chesapeake?
(2) Another assumption of the geographical argument is that ease
of transportation leads to population dispersal: thus because the
Chesapeake had the greatest ease of internal transportation it had
the most dispersed population. However, in studying other regions
and other times we are commonly told that ease of transportation
leads to greater urban concentration, that it allows a single town to
serve a larger area, to reach a larger market, that railroads in the
nineteenth century greatly encouraged the growth of large towns
by extending their trading areas. We have seen, even in the eighteenth century, how ease of coastal transport greatly extended the
trading areas of Boston and Charleston and helps to account for
much of their commercial success. Let us therefore recognize geography as an ever present element in any economic explanation,
but not make it into the single grand touchstone of analysis that
alone solves all problems.

If we are to analyze more exactly the factors retarding town
growth in the Chesapeake, we must look more closely at its economy. It was an agricultural economy dominated almost entirely
in the seventeenth and eighteenth centuries by a single commodity,
tobacco. After 1750, wheat exports were also increasingly important but never rivaled tobacco. In 1770, overseas wheat exports
from Virginia and Maryland were worth only £92,776 while tobacco shipments totaled £900,000.[75] By law, all tobacco in Vir-

75. PRO Customs 16/1; *U. S. Historical Statistics*, p. 761. Tobacco counted then for
27 percent of all native produce exported from the continental colonies. To the above
figure of wheat exports, about 37 percent should be added for exports to other colonies.
The wheat and Indian corn crops were, or course, much more valuable than suggested
here if one considers the amounts raised for local consumption. Cf. David Klingaman,

ginia (from 1730) and Maryland (from 1747) had to be sent to
public warehouses for inspection and storage. These were all located on navigable water. In the tidewater or low-country sections
of Virginia and Maryland, tobacco could often be sent to the warehouse by water or by road carriage of not more than ten miles
or so. From the inland areas of Virginia and North Carolina,
however, carriage to the warehouse often involved wagon trips of
fifty or seventy-five miles. The hogsheads were commonly sold
unopened in the warehouse by the transfer of warehouse receipts.
From the warehouse, the tobacco was generally taken in lighters or
other craft directly to ocean-going vessels lying in the river nearby
or some miles downstream. Tobacco was sufficiently bulky, with
hogsheads weighing about one thousand pounds in the 1770's, so
that all unnecessary handling was avoided. At the same time, tobacco was sufficiently valuable to make it worthwhile to keep ships
waiting while cargoes were assembled from a number of warehouses. The tobacco trade in the first instance was in the hands of
primary traders, rural storekeepers, scattered over the countryside,
who in return provided the planters with imported salt, sugar,
rum, tea, and European manufactures. Some of these storekeepers
were employees of British (particularly Scottish) firms; others were
indigenous independent traders. The latter obtained their imports
from and sold their tobacco to the Scottish stores, or dealt with
larger indigenous trader/merchants settled in the principal river
townlets (but relatively scattered for the convenience of their customers, the primary traders). These indigenous merchants or secondary traders carried on some Caribbean trade and ordered their
manufactures from Britain, which they generally paid for with
bills of exchange obtained from their West Indian trade and by
selling their tobacco to the Scots and others. Before the 1760's very
little tobacco arrived in Britain on the account of these native
"merchants," for they were characteristically short of capital and

"The Significance of Grain in the Development of the Tobacco Colonies," *Journal of Economic History*, 29 (1969), 273–274. For the five years, 1768–1772, Shepherd estimates that
Virginia and Maryland wheat exports were worth £84,085 compared to £756,129 for
tobacco. Shepherd, "Commodity Exports," tables I-III.

did not ship unless they could not dispose of their tobacco in any other way.

If any of these indigenous traders in the Chesapeake thought of going into the tobacco shipment business in a large way, they would immediately have run into a number of difficulties. The most obvious resulted from the effects of the English Acts of Trade and Navigation, which required that all tobacco had to be exported either to Great Britain or to other British colonies in America; in fact, over 99 percent was shipped to Great Britain. Demand for Chesapeake tobacco was quite limited in the Caribbean owing to the small populations there and to the availability of much-esteemed tobaccos and snuffs from Cuba, Venezuela, and Martinique, not to mention the substantial production of Brazil. Thus, small men in the Chesapeake area could not start out in tobacco exporting on a modest scale to the West Indies or southern Europe as small dealers in fish, flour, or provisions did elsewhere.

If the indigenous merchant in the Chesapeake thought of sending tobacco to Britain, the only available market, he would of course have to compete with British merchants already in the trade. This was most difficult for a variety of reasons. (1) When the tobacco got to Britain, about 15 percent—the best in quality—was retained for home consumption, while the remaining 85 percent was reexported, primarily to France, the Low Countries, and Germany. Before sale, the tobacco had to be carefully examined and graded according to type and quality; certain types and qualities could usefully be sold promptly for the ready cash that merchants always needed, others were best held back until the right buyer came along. These were difficult decisions to make three thousand miles away and left one uncomfortably dependent upon one's correspondent. (2) Tobacco was very heavily taxed in Britain—200 to 300 percent *ad valorem*. Even though tobacco reexported recovered the taxes after 1724, deposits had to be made and bond for the duties given. Giving and discharging bonds was a rather technical business and required finding others to sign one's bonds as sureties. All this created cash-flow and credit problems for new firms in the trade. (3) The goods sent out from Britain to America in return for the

II

tobacco were normally bought on long credit from middle men
(linendrapers, ironmongers) who obtained them from the manufacturers. These middle men were unlikely to supply such goods
on long credit to any firm that did not have a partner or agent resident in Britain who was of good credit and personally guaranteed
repayment. (4) Since there was a lot of competition in the Bay
area to get tobacco to fill ships, prices there tended to approach
European prices very closely and remittances of tobacco to Britain
were often made at a bookkeeping loss. The great profits of the
trade in Virginia and Maryland came not from sending tobacco to
Britain but from importing European goods which could be sold
at very great "advances." Thus when traders in the Bay did get
tobacco into their hands, they characteristically preferred to sell it
"in the country" and remit bills of exchange to London to pay for
European goods ordered. (5) Finally, there existed in both tobacco
colonies a class of middling and large planters who in varying degrees from year to year preferred not to sell their tobacco to nearby
stores but to remit it to London, Bristol, or Liverpool and have it
sold there by commission merchants who would pay them the
proceeds in cash (by accepting bills of exchange) or in goods purchased for them. Such consignments probably did not account for
more than one-fifth of the crop by the 1770's but they removed
some of the best tobacco from the grasp of the indigenous traders.

Putting all the bits of evidence together, one gains the impression
that the trade to Britain was not a very attractive proposition for
persons with money in the tobacco colonies. For the small man
with limited capital it was much easier to enter into the West Indian provision trade, just as it was for his sort in the northern colonies. For wealthier persons, there were the rival attractions of land
speculation or perhaps acting as sales agent for an English slave
dealer, or even iron making or shipbuilding. When Virginians or
Marylanders did build ships (and each colony built more than
New York did), they usually found it to their advantage to sell
their larger vessels after their first or second voyage to Britain
rather than try to keep them in what was obviously only a marginally attractive trade. Finally, when a Virginian or Marylander of

means decided despite all to go into the tobacco trade, more often than not he moved to London or sent a partner there. The trade could obviously be carried out much more efficiently from there.

Nevertheless, there were changes underway in the Chesapeake in the years from 1750 to 1775. The corps of indigenous traders was growing in both Virginia and Maryland. Some of them were not satisfied with the limited and highly competitive trade to the West Indies and sought entry to the vaster trade to Britain. Many were able to do so through the "cargo system" that flourished in the decade preceding the Revolution. Rich merchants in London, acting as factors (or agents on commission) for these smaller houses in the Chesapeake would buy "cargoes" of assorted goods for them from London middlemen on one year's credit and ship those goods out with the understanding that remittances would be made in tobacco or bills of exchange before the year's credit was up. These new indigenous houses were now indeed trading to Britain, but they were trading on other people's capital and credit and often in other people's ships. They were thus still closer to being "secondary traders" than real merchants. Nevertheless, much of the life in the new little towns of the interior of Virginia (Petersburg, Richmond, and the like) came from these new native firms trading precariously under the "cargo system." That those towns were not larger says something about the scale and nature of their operations.

Much more innovative in these years was the growth of Norfolk and Baltimore from mere hamlets to towns of about six thousand inhabitants and active commercial centers—larger than anything else in the Chesapeake. The important thing about them is that neither had very much to do with tobacco, that staple so little conducive to town growth. Norfolk, near the mouth of Chesapeake Bay, was in the southeastern corner of Virginia; its hinterland there and in the adjacent parts of North Carolina was a land of forest and swamp and marginal agriculture. It produced a limited amount of tobacco of no very great repute and abundant forest products (pitch, tar, and lumber) plus some Indian corn, pork, and beef suitable for the West Indies. With these endowments, Norfolk came to specialize in the West Indian trade. Because of the volume of this activity, Norfolk attracted a certain amount of the surplus provisions, etc., from elsewhere in Virginia though all the major rivers and havens of Virginia and Maryland continued to have their own West Indian trade, and New Englanders continued to bring West Indian produce into the Bay. Similarly, when traders elsewhere in the Bay were short of sugar, molasses, and rum, they knew they could always order some from Norfolk, where there were large distilleries.[76] Norfolk also became a major exporter of Virginia wheat to southern Europe though other districts also did their own wheat exporting.[77] The one thing that Norfolk did not handle very much of was tobacco.[78] With the surplus earnings of its sales to the West Indies, Norfolk imported manufactured goods from Britain, most of which were sold in its natural hinterland in southeast Virginia and adjacent North Carolina, but some of which were also sold elsewhere in Virginia.

In short, the not very impressive trade of Norfolk to the West Indies and southern Europe made possible a larger town than the infinitely more valuable tobacco export trade of the rest of Virginia did. Norfolk's size was consistent with that of other towns specializing in the West Indian trade, e.g., Providence, New London, New Haven. To be active in its trades, Norfolk had to be a smaller-scale Philadelphia, a city of mariners, shipwrights, small merchants, butchers, tanners, and shopkeepers.

The case of Baltimore is even clearer. Baltimore sits on a minor branch of the Patapsco River, one of the less important rivers flowing into the Chesapeake Bay, about two hundred miles north of Norfolk, and at the extreme northern limits of the tobacco producing zone. Nearby, on the main branch of the Patapsco River, was the hamlet of Elk Ridge where there was a public tobacco inspection warehouse—as there was at Balitmore. Elk Ridge tobacco

76. Thomas J. Wertenbaker, *Norfolk Historic Southern Port*, ed. Marvin W. Schlegel, 2d ed. (Durham, N.C., 1962), pp. 1–47.

77. PRO Customs 16/1.

78. *Ibid.*; for the years 1745–1756, see Edward D. Neill, *The Fairfaxes of England and America* (Albany, 1868), p. 225. Tobacco shipments from the Norfolk district may have risen significantly in the early 1770's, but still remained much less than that of any of the tobacco-producing districts.

had a very good reputation and often fetched a superior price. Tobacco growers round about preferred therefore to sent their tobacco to Elk Ridge and little came to Baltimore. In 1750 it was a
totally insignificant place. In the next quarter century, however, it
came alive. Baltimore sat near the geological line dividing lowland
or "tidewater" Maryland, the land of tobacco, from the upcountry
or "piedmont" region better suited to wheat. In fact, the back
country of western Maryland was an extension southward of the
wheat-producing lands of adjacent Pennsylvania. In the years after
1750, as wheat prices rose in Europe, there was a great incentive to
settle these areas, and Scotch-Irish and German farmers from Pennsylvania pushed southward to take up lands in hitherto neglected
western Maryland. Baltimore was most conveniently situated to
serve these new wheat-producing areas. Flour mills were established and soon Baltimore was attracting wheat shipments not only
from western Maryland but also from the adjacent parts of central
Pennsylvania west of the Susquehanna River. A distinct mercantile
community came into existence at Baltimore to handle wheat exports, for tobacco traders were not interested in a product whose
markets fluctuated radically from year to year and were quite different from their own. Shipyards were set up in and near Baltimore
to build the sloops, schooners, and ships needed to take Baltimore's
wheat, flour, and provisions to the West Indies and southern Europe. They also built some larger tobacco vessels for sale in Britain.
Her trade and occupational configuration were quite similar to
those of Philadelphia, and Baltimore was becoming Philadelphia's
keenest rival.[79] In the years after the American Revolution, Baltimore became much more of a general entrepôt, sending its wheat
to Britain and importing all sort of merchandise from there. The
tobacco regions of lowland Maryland which before the Revolution
had ignored Baltimore now began to feel its pull and sent their tobacco too for sale there. By then, of course, the Acts of Trade and
Navigation no longer affected American commerce, and Baltimore

79. Cf. Clarence P. Gould, "The Economic Causes of the Rise of Baltimore," *Essays in
Colonial History Presented to Charles McLean Andrews by His Students* (New Haven, 1931),
pp. 225–251.

merchants were free to send this tobacco to its best markets in the Low Countries and Germany.[80] But Baltimore's export trade consisted primarily of wheat and flour.

In short, most areas of Virginia and Maryland did not develop significant towns in the eighteenth century because they produced tobacco. Where alternative productions predominated, significant towns grew up—at Norfolk and Baltimore on the fringes of the tobacco regions but outside the grip of that staple trade. This was partly the result of the Navigation Acts. Because Britain had its own agriculture to protect, most of the products of North America were not affected by those acts. The exempted products included fish, some forest products, wheat, Indian corn, pork, beef, dairy products, and the like. Rice could be exported directly to southern Europe but, if destined for northern Europe, had to be landed in Britain first. Only tobacco and indigo of major North American produce definitely had to be landed in Britain. These two products could not, therefore, generate the flocks of small traders who appeared quite early at Philadelphia, Boston, and New York trading in small sloops to the West Indies and from whose numbers emerged the larger merchants of the next generation who traded in larger vessels to Europe and Africa.

However, too much should not be ascribed to the Navigation Acts. After the American Revolution, when those British laws no longer directed American commerce, the greater part of the tobacco of the Chesapeake still continued to find its way to Britain. And, as of 1790, the only two states that still had more British than American ships entering their harbors were South Carolina and Virginia—precisely those whose maritime economies had been most directed toward Britain and by British interests before the war. In other words, market forces strengthened the thrust of the Navigation Acts but had a life of their own that outlived these acts. Thus, the low degree of urbanization cannot be blamed simply on the Navigation Acts, any more than it could be blamed simply on geography, but represents the interaction of geography, legisla-

---

80. Cf. Stuart Weems Bruchey, *Robert Oliver, Merchant of Baltimore 1783–1819* (Baltimore, 1956).

tion, and forms of commercial organization rationally responsive to market conditions.

In summary, then, suitable geographic position was one necessary precondition for the development of a significant port town in eighteenth-century America as anywhere else. An appropriate volume of export trade was another. But these two preconditions were not sufficient in themselves to determine the size of a port town. Had they been, Charleston would not have been only half as big as New York, and Norfolk would have been bigger than Boston. When the entrepreneurial decision-making center of a trade was in a port, it necessitated the presence there of a population of sailors, shipwrights, sailmakers, ship chandlers, and the like, as well as specialist brokers, insurance underwriters, and often a manufacturing population to process goods in transit. Without such "entrepreneurial headquarters effect," the port need have been little more than a "shipping point" whose urban configuration would not reflect its shipping volume. With such entrepreneurial activity, the port could attract entrepôt business that enabled it to transcend the limits of the activity arising from its immediate hinterland. The precise locus of entrepreneurial activity was not primarily a cultural phenomenon (i.e., reflecting a different business ethos in different places), but represented to a considerable degree a rational adaptation to the availability of capital and other resources and the marketing problems of specific commodities.

The West Indian trade could apparently be carried on efficiently in towns in the 4,000–8,000 range: Providence, Rhode Island; the Connecticut towns, Norwich, New London, New Haven; and Norfolk. A significant export trade to Europe with substantial imports from Great Britain implied a size of 6,000–12,000 on the eve of the Revolution: Newport, Baltimore, Charleston. The functions of a "general entrepôt" went with a size of 15,000–30,000: Philadelphia, New York, Boston. Though we do not have all the data we need, the occupational/sectoral profiles of all the principal towns would appear to be similar, with the local service sector about twice the size of the maritime sector. The only variations that appear were in the manufacturing or industrial sector. Where the town was particularly active in shipbuilding (e.g., Boston) or in processing local products (e.g., Philadelphia's leather crafts), the industrial sector might appear slightly larger than elsewhere, but we do not have enough data to say with assurance what was normal.

APPENDIX A

Estimated Population of American Colonies, 1610–1780

Series No.	Colony	1780	1770	1760	1750	1740	1730	1720	1710	1700	1690	1680	1670	1660	1650	1640	1630
	WHITE AND NEGRO																
1	Total	2,780,369	2,148,076	1,593,625	1,170,760	905,563	629,445	466,185	331,711	250,888	210,372	151,507	111,935	75,058	50,368	26,634	4,646
2	Maine (counties)[1]	49,133	31,257												1,000	900	400
3	New Hampshire	87,802	62,396	39,093	27,505	23,256	10,755	9,375	5,681	4,958	4,164	2,047	1,805	1,555	1,305	1,055	500
4	Vermont	47,620	10,000														
5	Plymouth[2]										7,424	6,400	5,333	1,980	1,566	1,020	390
6	Massachusetts[1][2]	268,627	235,308	222,600	188,000	151,613	114,116	91,008	62,390	55,941	49,504	39,752	30,000	20,082	14,037	8,932	506
7	Rhode Island	52,946	58,196	45,471	33,226	25,255	16,950	11,680	7,573	5,894	4,224	3,017	2,155	1,539	785	300	
8	Connecticut	206,701	183,881	142,470	111,280	89,580	75,530	58,830	39,450	25,970	21,645	17,246	12,603	7,980	4,139	1,472	
9	New York	210,541	162,920	117,138	76,696	63,665	48,594	36,919	21,625	19,107	13,909	9,830	5,754	4,936	4,116	1,930	350
10	New Jersey	189,627	117,431	93,813	71,393	51,373	37,510	29,818	19,872	14,010	8,000	3,400	1,000				
11	Pennsylvania	327,305	240,057	183,703	119,666	85,637	51,707	30,962	24,450	17,950	11,450	680					
12	Delaware	45,385	35,496	33,250	28,704	19,870	9,170	5,385	3,645	2,470	1,482	1,005	700	540	185		
13	Maryland	245,474	202,599	162,267	141,073	116,093	91,113	66,133	42,741	29,604	24,024	17,904	13,226	8,426	4,504	583	
14	Virginia	538,004	447,016	339,726	231,033	180,440	114,000	87,757	78,281	58,560	53,046	43,596	35,309	27,020	18,731	10,442	2,500
15	North Carolina	270,133	197,200	110,442	72,984	51,760	30,000	21,270	15,120	10,720	7,600	5,430	3,850	1,000			
16	South Carolina	180,000	124,244	94,074	64,000	45,000	30,000	17,048	10,883	5,704	3,900	1,200	200				
17	Georgia	56,071	23,375	9,578	5,200	2,021											
18	Kentucky	45,000	15,700														
19	Tennessee	10,000	1,000														
	NEGRO																
1	Total	575,420	459,822	325,806	236,420	150,024	91,021	68,839	44,866	27,817	16,729	6,971	4,535	2,920	1,600	597	60
2	Maine (counties)[1]	458	475														
3	New Hampshire	541	654	600	550	500	200	170	150	130	100	75	65	50	40	30	
4	Vermont	50	25														
6	Massachusetts[1]	4,822	4,754	4,866	4,075	3,035	2,780	2,150	1,310	800	400	170	160	422	295	150	
7	Rhode Island	2,671	3,761	3,468	3,347	2,408	1,648	543	375	300	250	175	115	65	25		
8	Connecticut	5,885	5,698	3,783	3,010	2,598	1,490	1,093	750	450	200	50	35	25	20		
9	New York	21,054	19,112	16,340	11,014	8,996	6,956	5,740	2,811	2,256	1,670	1,200	690	600	500	232	10
10	New Jersey	10,460	8,220	6,567	5,354	4,366	3,008	2,385	1,332	840	450	200	60			15	
11	Pennsylvania	7,855	5,761	4,409	2,872	2,055	1,241	2,000	1,575	430	270	25					
12	Delaware	2,996	1,836	1,733	1,496	1,035	478	700	500	135	82	55	40	30	15		
13	Maryland	80,515	63,818	49,004	43,450	24,031	17,220	12,499	7,945	3,227	2,162	1,611	1,190	758	300	20	
14	Virginia	220,582	187,605	140,570	101,452	60,000	30,000	26,559	23,118	16,390	9,345	3,000	2,000	950	405	150	50
15	North Carolina	91,000	69,603	33,554	19,800	11,000	6,000	3,000	900	415	300	210	150	20			
16	South Carolina	97,000	75,178	57,334	39,000	30,000	20,000	12,000	4,100	2,444	1,500	200	30				
17	Georgia	20,831	10,625	3,578	1,000												
18	Kentucky	1,200															
19	Tennessee	1,600															

Series No.	Colony	WHITE AND NEGRO	
		1620	1610
5	Plymouth	102	
14	Virginia	2,200	350

[1] For 1660–1760, Maine Counties included with Massachusetts.   [3] Includes some Indians.
[2] Plymouth became a part of the Province of Massachusetts in 1691.   [4] Includes 20 Negroes.

SOURCE: United States Bureau of the Census, *Historical Statistics of the United States, Colonial Times to 1957* (Washington, D.C., 1960), p. 756.

APPENDIX B

Population of Eighteenth-Century American Towns

	Philadelphia	New York	Boston	Newport	Charleston	Baltimore
			(1. Bridenbaugh)			
1680	0	3,200	4,500	2,500	700	0
1685	2,500	—	—	—	900	0
1690	4,000	3,900	7,000	2,600	1,100	0
1700	5,000	5,000	6,700	2,600	2,000	0
1710	6,500	5,700	9,000	2,800	3,000	0
1720	10,000	7,000	12,000	3,800	? ⸳⸳0	0
1730	11,500	8,622	13,000	4,640	4,500	—
1740	—	—	17,000	—	—	—
1742	13,000	11,000	16,258	6,200	6,800	—
1760	23,750	18,000	15,631	7,500	8,000	—
1775	40,000	25,000	16,000	11,000	12,000	5,934
			(2. Rossiter)			
1700	4,400	ca. 4,900	6,700	—	—	0
1710	—	5,840 (1712)	9,000	2,203 (1708)	—	0
1720	—	7,248 (1723)	11,000	—	—	0
1730	8,500	8,500	13,000	4,640	—	—
1740	10,500	11,000	17,000	—	—	—
1750	13,400	11,300	15,731	6,508 (1748)	—	—
1760	18,756	14,000	15,631	6,753 (1755)	8,000	—
1770	28,000	21,000	15,520	9,000	10,863	—
ca. 1775	34,400	—	—	9,209 (1774)	12,000 (1773)	5,934
1780	30,000	18,000	10,000	5,530 (1782)	10,000	8,000
1790	42,444	33,131	18,038	6,716	16,359	13,503

(3. Population of other towns)

	Bridenbaugh	1790 census
New Haven, Conn. (1771)	8,295	4,487
Norwich, Conn. (1774)	7,032	—
Norfolk, Va. (1775)	ca. 6,250	2,959
New London, Conn. (1774)	5,366	—
Salem, Mass. (1776)	5,337	7,921
Lancaster, Pa. (1776)	ca. 5–6,000	3,762
Hartford, Conn. (1774)	4,881	4,072

	Bridenbaugh	*1790 census*
Middletown, Conn. (1775)	4,680	*5,298*
Portsmouth, N.H. (1775)	4,590	*4,720*
Marblehead, Mass. (1776)	4,386	*5,661*
Providence, R.I. (1774)	4,361	*6,380*
Albany, N.Y. (1776)	ca. 4,000	*3,498*
Annapolis, Md. (1775)	3,700	—
Savannah, Ga. (1771)	ca. 3,200	—

SOURCES: Bridenbaugh, *Cities in the Wilderness*, pp. 6, 143, 303; idem, *Cities in Revolt*, pp. 5, 216–217; Rossiter, *Century of Population Growth*, pp. 11, 78; *Return of the whole number of persons within the . . . United States* (Philadelphia, 1791), pp. 12, 23–24, 34, 37, 39, 45, 47, 50. For 1790, the last publication differs from Rossiter in giving 42,520 for Philadelphia and 32,328 for New York. Census-type data shown in italics; estimates in roman face.

APPENDIX C

A Sectoral Analysis of the [Tax-Assessed] Population
of Boston (1790) and Philadelphia (1774, 1780–1783)

	Boston (*1790*)	Philadelphia (*1774*)	Philadelphia (*1780–1783*)
I. Government	68 (2.75%)	58 (1.53%)	93 (2.85%)
A. Foreign diplomats	—	—	3
B. Federal or congressional	11	—	6+
C. State or provincial	13	23	16+
D. Local and law enforcement	44	34	15+
E. "Esquires" unidentified	—	—	34
F. Military	—	1	19
II. Service sector	1115 (45.01%)	1856 (48.93%)	1608 (49.29%)
A. Professional	102 (4.12%)	129 (3.4%)	94 (2.88%)
1. apothecary, druggist	17	10	10
2. architect	1	—	—
3. dentist	1	—	—
4. doctor, physician	26	38	41
4a. surgeon	—	2	2
4b. midwife	—	1	—
5. lawyer, attorney, conveyancer	21	17	13
5a. notary public	—	4	2

	Boston (1790)	Philadelphia (1774)	Philadelphia (1780–1783)
6. minister	20	13	8
7. schoolmaster	16	43	14
7a. schoolmistress	—	—	1
8. surveyor	—	1	3
B. Retailers and local wholesalers, etc.	243 (9.81%)	301 (7.94%)	336 (10.3%)
1. auctioneer, vendue cryer	7	7	1
2. bookseller	2	2	2
3. cyderman, cider cooper	—	1	1
4. grocer	33	17	93
5. hardware dealer, ironmonger, iron merchant	12	1	8
6. hosier	—	—	6
7. jeweler	3	3	2
8. lemon dealer, lime-seller	10	1	1
9. lumber merchant, board merchant	5	5	14
10. milkman	—	11	—
11. oysterman	—	1	1
12. peddler, huckster	10	39	8
13. retailer, shopkeeper, storekeeper	133	195	153
14. shoe dealer	6	—	—
15. slop-shop keeper	4	—	—
16. stationer	5	—	5
17. tallow chandler	—	11	8
18. trader, dealer, jobber	13	2	32
18a. horsedealer	—	1	—
19. wine cooper, liquor seller	—	1	1
19a. meadseller	—	3	—
C. "Retail" crafts	201 (8.11%)	495 (13.05%)	446 (13.67%)
1. bacon smoker	1	—	—
2. baker, biscuit baker	64	124	98
2a. gingerbread baker, pastry cook	2	1	—
3. butcher	10	121	89
4. confectioner	1	1	1
5. mustardmaker	—	1	—

	Boston (1790)	Philadelphia (1774)	Philadelphia (1780–1783)
6. bookbinder	3	9	2
7. furrier	3	—	—
8. tailor	100	190	207
8a. breechesmaker	—	26	17
8b. mantua-maker, muffmaker	—	2	—
9. tobacconist, snuffmaker	17	20	32
D. Building crafts	250 (10.09%)	428 (11.28%)	263 (8.06%)
1. carpenters, house carpenters	140	178	133
1a. fence-maker	—	—	2
1b. joiner	5	94	59
2. contractor, head builder	5	—	2
3. glazier	12	2	1
4. mason, bricklayer	44	70	31
5. millwright	—	—	1
6. painter	34	27	16
7. paver	—	1	2
8. plasterer	—	19	4
9. plumber	—	2	1
10. sawyer, woodsawyer, woodcutter	7	20	5
11. stonecutter, marble quarrier	3	13	4
12. wharfbuilder	—	2	2
E. Travel and transport services	187 (7.55%)	382 (10.07%)	385 (11.8%)
1. blacksmith, smith, farrier	59	125	116
2. carter, cartman, truckman	59	40	49
3. chaise-letter	3	—	—
4. coach-driver, coachman	6	6	5
5. drayman	—	—	2
6. drover	—	1	—
7. hack-driver	7	—	—
8. innkeeper, innholder, boarder-keeper	24	73	92
8a. lodging-house keeper	—	3	2
8b. waiter	—	—	2

	Boston (1790)	Philadelphia (1774)	Philadelphia (1780–1783)
9. stable-keeper, livery-stable-keeper	3	2	8
10. tavern-keeper, taverner, dram shop keeper	26	97	70
11. waterman, boatman, flatman	—	23	32
11a. ferryman	—	3	5
11b. shallopman	—	9	2
F. Other services	132 (5.33%)	121 (3.19%)	84 (2.58%)
1. barber, hairdresser	42	39	41
2. chimney sweeper	6	1	—
3. gravedigger	—	2	—
4. lightman	7	—	—
5. limner (portrait painter)	—	—	2
6. musician, fiddler	3	3	3
6a. dancing master	—	—	2
7. servant, porter	63	70	35
7a. overseer	—	2	—
8. sexton	11	1	1
9. razor grinder	—	2	—
10. washerwomen	—	1	—
III. Industrial	659 (26.6%)	1017 (26.81%)	891 (27.31%)
A. Textile trades	54 (2.18%)	110 (2.9%)	59 (1.81%)
1. calico printer	—	—	1
2. duckcloth maker	24	—	—
3. dyer, silkdyer, blue dyer	3	10	3
4. fuller	—	4	—
5. lacemaker	—	—	1
6. linen manufacturer, flax dresser	—	2	2
7. spinner	—	1	—
8. stocking weaver, stocking knitter, knitter	—	59	17
9. threadmaker	—	1	—
10. weaver	3	32	31
10a. clothier	—	—	1
11. woolcardmaker, card-maker	24	—	1
12. woolcomber	—	1	2

	Boston (1790)	Philadelphia (1774)	Philadelphia (1780–1783)
B. Leather and fur-using trades	136 (5.49%)	385 (10.15%)	349 (10.7%)
1. currier	—	6	4
2. glover	—	—	1
3. harnessmaker, whipmaker	—	9	4
4. hatter	29	72	57
5. leather dresser, skinner, skindresser	13	30	22
6. leather merchant	—	1	—
7. saddler, saddlemaker	6	32	20
8. shoemaker, cordwainer	78	198	206
9. tanner	10	37	35
C. Food and drink processing	59 (2.38%)	56 (1.48%)	35 (1.07%)
1. brewer, beer house	—	19	19
2. chocolate maker	—	3	3
3. distiller	47	17	7
4. miller, bran flourer, flour-maker	4	11	4
5. sugarboiler, refiner, sugarbaker	8	6	2
D. Shipbuilding and fitting crafts	213 (8.6%)	187 (4.93%)	169 (5.18%)
1. blockmaker	16	7	8
2. boatbuilder	—	13	16
3. caulker	14	14	7
4. mastmaker	7	5	2
5. oarmaker	1	—	—
6. pumpmaker	4	2	4
7. rigger	11	4	10
8. ropemaker	42	13	14
9. sailmaker	30	17	15
10. sea cooper	16	—	—
11. shipcarpenter, -joiner, -wright	72	112	93
E. Metal crafts (except blacksmiths)	80 (3.23%)	103 (2.72%)	118 (3.62%)
1. brassfounder, founder	15	4	6
2. bucklemaker, buttonmaker	—	1	2
3. clockmaker	—	8	2

	Boston (1790)	Philadelphia (1774)	Philadelphia (1780–1783)
4. coppersmith	4	9	10
5. cutler	—	10	6
6. file cutter	—	—	1
7. goldsmith	23	7	8
8. gunsmith	1	5	14
9. instrument maker	3	1	1
10. locksmith	—	3	1
11. nailor, nailsmith, nailmaker	—	7	6
12. pewterer	6	3	1
13. plane-maker, sawmaker	—	3	2
14. silversmith	5	15	28
15. tinner, tinker, tinman, whitesmith	15	20	21
16. watchmaker	8	7	8
16a. watchcase maker	—	—	1
F. Furniture trades	35 (1.41%)	34 (0.9%)	39 (1.19%)
1. cabinetmaker	15	—	2
2. carver	4	11	2
3. chairmaker	11	—	19
4. turner	1	17	15
5. upholsterer, upholder	4	6	1
G. Miscellaneous trades	82 (3.31%)	142 (3.74%)	122 (3.74%)
1. brickmaker	—	5	6
2. brushmaker	—	4	7
3. chaisemaker, coachmaker	16	29	13
4. paperstainer, papermaker	3	4	2
5. potter	—	24	23
6. printer, engraver	17	21	21
7. soapboiler, soap chandler	6	2	3
8. whalebonecutter, comb-maker, staysmaker	4	15	14
9. wheelwright	8	20	11
10. other trades	28	18	22
IV. Commerce (maritime) and fisheries	635 (25.64%)	862 (22.73%)	670 (20.9%)
A. Mariners	231 (9.33%)	331 (8.73%)	228 (6.99%)
1. sea captain, master mariner	114	83	71
2. mate	20	3	—
3. pilot	2	22	6
4. sailor, seaman, mariner	58	199	140
5. fisherman	37	24	11

	Boston (1790)	Philadelphia (1774)	Philadelphia (1780–1783)
B. Merchants and supporting personnel	404 (16.31%)	531 (14.00%)	442 (13.55%)
1. accountant	3	1	—
2. banker	1	—	—
3. broker, scrivener	16	6	10
4. chandler, ship chandler	17	15	13
5. clerk, scribe	66	34	28
6. cooper	70	142	56
7. corn dealer, flour merchant/seller	—	2	3
8. merchant	206	329	331
9. stevedore, trimmer	—	2	—
10. underwriter	1	—	—
11. wharfinger	24	—	1
I–IV TOTAL	2477	3793	3262
V. Unclassified			
A. Agricultural			
1. ditcher	—	1	—
2. farmer, yeoman	—	111	79
3. goat keeper	—	1	—
4. gardner	15	17	4
5. grazier	—	11	9
6. welldigger	—	2	—
B. Laborers (unassignable to sector)	157	614	371
C. Unemployed and retired (including gentlemen)	106	—	68
D. Women head of household without occupation			
1. widows	—	105	266
2. other	—	72	226
E. Males, without stated occupation	—	—	1332
1. married man	—	635	—
2. single man	—	612	—
F. Negro heads of household without stated occupation	—	—	28
G. Illegible and not indicated	—	40	—

APPENDIX D

Three Estimates of the Sectoral Distribution of the Employed Adult Population of New York City, 1746–1795

	Freemen Admitted 1746–1770[a]	Directory 1790[b]	Yellow Fever Deaths, 1795[c]
Government	0.7%	3.7%	3.49%
Service Sector	46.7%	59.9%	56.59%
Industrial Sector	32.0%	22.9%	16.67%
Maritime-mercantile Sector	20.6%	13.5%	23.26%

[a]"The Burghers of New Amsterdam and the Freemen of New York, 1675–1863," *Collections of the New York Historical Society, XVIII for 1885* (New York, 1886). Cf. Beverly McAnear, "The Place of the Freeman in Old New York," *New York History*, 21 (1940), 418–430.

[b]*The New York Directory and Register for the Year 1790* (New York, 1790): analysis based on 2,000+ names on pp. 1–70.

[c]New York Municipal Archives: MS, "Record of Persons who have died in the City of New York of the putrid bilious or Yellow Fever in 1795 as reported by Health Committee," printed, with the omission of some slaves and foreigners, as "New York Deaths," *New York Genealogical and Biographical Record*, 81 (1950), 146–155, 203–206.

APPENDIX E

A Sectoral Analysis from a Sample of New York City Population, 1795

I. Government		9 (3.49%)
A. Federal	4	
B. State	0	
C. Local	5	
II. Service Sector		146 (56.59%)
A. Professional	10	
B. Retailer	30	
C. Retail crafts	23	
D. Building crafts	39	
E. Travel and transport services	27	
F. Other services	17	
III. Industrial sector		43 (16.67%)
A. Textile	2	
B. Leather and fur trades	17	

C. Food and drink processing   1
D. Shipbuilding   12
E. Metal crafts   4
F. Furniture trades   2
G. Miscellaneous trades   5
IV. Commerce (maritime) and fisheries   60 (23.26%)
  A. Mariners, etc.   24
  B. Merchants and supporting service 36
            I–IV   258 (100%)
V. Other (occupation unknown)   427
  A. Men and boys   221
  B. Women and girls   206

APPENDIX F

Colonial Shipbuilding, 1769–1771

TS=top sail ships, snows, etc.
S+S=sloops and schooners

	1769 TS	S+S	tons	1770 TS	S+S	tons	1771 TS	S+S	tons
Newfoundland	0	1	30	0	0	0	0	4	50
Canada	0	1	60	0	1	15	4	3	233
Nova Scotia	0	3	110	1	2	200	1	3	140
New Hampshire	16	29	2,452	27	20	3,581	15	40	4,991
Massachusetts	40	97	8,013	31	118	7,274	42	83	7,704
Rhode Island	8	31	1,428	16	49	2,035	15	60	2,148
Connecticut	7	43	1,542	5	41	1,522	7	39	1,483
New York	5	14	955	8	10	960	9	28	1,698
New Jersey	1	3	83	0	0	0	0	2	70
Pennsylvania	14	8	1,469	18	8	2,354	15	6	1,307
Maryland	9	11	1,344	7	10	1,545	10	8	1,645
Virginia	6	21	1,269	6	15	1,105	10	9	1,678
North Carolina	3	9	607	0	5	125	0	8	241
South Carolina	4	8	789	0	3	52	3	4	560
Georgia	0	2	50	0	3	57	2	4	543

SOURCE: John Baker Holroyd, 1st earl of Sheffield, *Observations on the Commerce of the American States*, 6th ed. (London, 1784), p. 96.

APPENDIX G

Annual Averages of Values of American Colonial Exports
1768–1772 (Shepherd est.)

(1) by origin and destination

(in thousands of pounds sterling)

TO: FROM:	Great Britain	Ireland	S. Europe and Wine Islands	West Indies	Africa	TOTAL
Canada, etc.	36.8	4.8	133	12.2	0	186.8
New England	86.8	1.4	66.2	303.4	19.2	477
Middle Colonies	75	54.2	185	244.2	1	559.4
Virginia and Maryland	931.4	30.4	100.4	100	0	1,162.2
Carolina and Georgia	435	1.4	54.6	111.8	0.4	603.2
Florida, Bahamas, and Bermuda	22.6	0	0	3.2	0	25.8
TOTALS	1,587.6	92.2	539.2	774.8	20.6	3,014.4

(2) by commodities

tobacco	£766,000
bread and flour	412,000
rice	312,000
dried fish	287,000
indigo	117,000

SOURCE: adapted from James F. Shepherd, "Commodity Exports," pp. 55–56, 65.

III

New Time Series for Scotland's and Britain's Trade with the Thirteen Colonies and States, 1740 to 1791

THE most useful statistical material we have on British trade with the colonies before the American Revolution comes from the records of the Inspector-General of Exports and Imports.[1] This office, which began operations in 1696, kept quite detailed accounts of the quantities and estimated values of all commodities that England exported or imported. Despite the obvious utility of such records and the frequent references made to them by contemporaries, no equivalent office was set up for Scotland at the union of the two kingdoms in 1707—no doubt because the value of Scotland's trade did not at first seem high enough to merit burdening her customs with further overhead. Not until 1754-1755, as we shall see, was an Inspector-General of Exports and Imports for Scotland established at Edinburgh. His annual reports began in 1755.[2]

The Inspectors-General at both London and Edinburgh were on the customs establishment and subject to the immediate authority of the separate customs boards for England and Scotland. The annual accounts of the Inspectors-General appear to have been forwarded by customs only to the Treasury and Board of Trade.[3] In addition, usually on instructions from the Treasury, special reports giving a great variety of commercial statistics were prepared for the two houses of Parliament,[4] the Treasury itself, and the Board of Trade. Although the Treasury did not publish the annual reports and treated all information from the Inspectors-General as not available to the public,[5] the special reports made to either house

---

[1] See G. N. Clark, *Guide to English Commercial Statistics, 1696-1782* (London, 1938), 1-42.

[2] *Ibid.*, 14, 41, and above, pp. 310-312. On the low yields of Scottish customs after the Union see P. W. J. Riley, *The English Ministers and Scotland, 1707-1727* (London, 1964), 126-129.

[3] Based on annotation in surviving volumes of Customs 2 and 3, Public Record Office.

[4] The *Journals of the House of Commons* (London, 1803-   ) indicate that accounts were formally requested by and delivered to the House, but the destruction in 1834 of the House's records makes it impossible to determine whether other accounts may have come into the possession of committees by other routes.

[5] Sir William Keith, former customs official and governor of Pennsylvania, tried to get figures on colonial trade in Walpole's time, but "after a most assiduous and

of Parliament were beyond its control and as good as open to the public. Thus in 1776 Sir Charles Whitworth, M. P., a Kentish gentleman and minor politician with antiquarian tastes and literary ambitions, was able to publish a summary of English export and import data from 1696 to 1773 derived from the London Inspector-General's annual reports. As chairman of Ways and Means from 1768 until his death in 1778 and a most regular follower of Lord North, Whitworth was in a position to gain access to material in the custody of the clerk of Commons and perhaps to other records not generally open.[6] Although he entitled his book *State of the Trade of Great Britain in Its Imports and Exports Progressively from the Year 1697,* the tables he published covered only England. Arranging his data geographically, Whitworth presented a time series giving year-by-year figures for the *official* value of English exports to and imports from each foreign land and British colony. By "official value" one means a calculation of the monetary worth of exports and imports based on prices prevailing at the beginning of the eighteenth century. The use of prices of that period became routinized in the office of the Inspector-General, where little effort was made to keep up with price changes after about 1702.

For almost two hundred years Whitworth's has been the only published time series for English external trade in the eighteenth century. Its figures for trade with the thirteen continental colonies have been reprinted several times, most importantly by Lawrence A. Harper in the 1960 edition of the *Historical Statistics of the United States.*[7] Scholars have long recognized that there were two major shortcomings in these figures: (1) they were based on official values rather than on current market prices, and (2) they covered England only, although Scotland's share in Britain's foreign trade was becoming significant as the eighteenth century progressed. John McCusker recently made a most valuable con-

---

respectful application to the proper offices from whence these Accounts only can be had, it was told me, . . . That such things could not be granted without Orders from Above; which I had no Room to expect." Sir William Keith, *The History of the British Plantations in America* . . . Part I: *Containing the History of Virginia* . . . (London, 1738), "Preface," fol. A4v.

[6] On Whitworth see the *Dictionary of National Biography,* s.v. "Whitworth, Charles," and Sir Lewis Namier and John Brooke, eds., *The History of Parliament: The House of Commons, 1754-1790,* III (London, 1964), 632-634.

[7] U. S. Bureau of the Census, *Historical Statistics of the United States, Colonial Times to 1957* (Washington, D. C., 1960), 757. They were published earlier in Samuel Hazard, ed., *Hazard's United States Commercial and Statistical Register* . . . , I (Philadelphia, 1840), 4-5, and Emory R. Johnson *et al., History of Domestic and Foreign Commerce of the United States,* I (Washington, D. C., 1915), 120-121. Both Hazard and Johnson confuse "England" with "Great Britain." The most important modern extension of Whitworth is Elizabeth Boody Schumpeter, *English Overseas Trade Statistics, 1697-1808* (Oxford, 1960), giving much information on commodities but lumping the 13 colonies together.

III

tribution to correcting the first deficiency by publishing a new time series of his own calculation giving estimated current values, instead of official values, for English exports to the thirteen colonies (1697-1775) and the world (1697-1800).[8] The purpose of the present note is to make a partial step toward repairing the second deficiency by offering a series on Scotland's trade with the colonies from 1740. This should help to correct and avert some of the errors that arise from considering the colonies' trade with England only.

Although no Inspector-General of Exports and Imports was established for Scotland in 1707, elaborate record-keeping procedures were instituted in the new customs establishment for North Britain, and the customs board at Edinburgh was able to answer a great variety of requests—for commercial as well as revenue accounts—made by Parliament and Treasury in London.[9] The most important of these were the "quarter books" or quarterly "port books" prepared at each port for submission to the new Court of Exchequer at Edinburgh. These port books survive today from Michaelmas Quarter 1742 onward. The earlier ones are believed to have been destroyed by a fire in the Edinburgh Exchequer offices early in the nineteenth century.[10] In addition, in 1741 every port in Scotland was ordered to prepare and send to Edinburgh each quarter detailed accounts of all ships and goods arriving from America; these accounts were forwarded to the customs board in London.[11] After the passage of the Tobacco Act of 1751, the ports also had to submit most detailed accounts to the Assistant Register General of Tobacco for Scotland in Edinburgh.[12] Even before this, the collector of Glasgow

[8] John J. McCusker, "The Current Value of English Exports, 1697 to 1800," *William and Mary Quarterly*, 3d Ser., XXVIII (1971), 607-628. Note b to McCusker's Table IIB (p. 622) suggests that he used not Whitworth's figures, but the original data in Customs 2, 3, 14, and 17 as his basic source.

[9] For an idea of the variety of accounts requested from Scotland consult the Treasury's Out-Letter Book, North Britain, T. 17, P.R.O., or the minutes of the Scottish Customs Board (C.E. 1) in the Scottish Record Office, Edinburgh.

[10] From information supplied by Dr. Athol Murray of the S.R.O. One wonders whether the dating of the surviving port books (E. 504) from Michaelmas 1742 implies some procedural change associated with the reestablishment of a separate customs board for Scotland in August-September 1742. See also Port Glasgow, Index of Board's Orders, Nov. 24, 1757, June 30, 1730, C.E. 60/2/387, 1, 135, and Board Minutes, June 21, 1744, C.E. 1/6.

[11] Scottish Board Minutes, July 23, 1741, C.E. 1/6. Before the separate Scottish Board was reestablished in 1742, orders to the Edinburgh commissioners were routed through the London board of which they were a subcommittee. See Port Glasgow, Index of Board's Orders, Oct. 6, 1748, C.E. 60/2/387, 1, for a continuation of the orders for the colonial accounts. Another required account of colonial interest was the account of shipping belonging to each port sent each quarter to the Registers of Shipping at London and Edinburgh. See entries of May 3, 1774, Nov. 26, 1759, *ibid.*, 1, 3v. These reports have also been lost.

[12] Mar. 14, 1763, C.E. 60/2/387, 1.

had to send to Edinburgh each quarter seventeen different accounts or categories of documents.[13] This vast documentation in the customs houses at Edinburgh and London was lost in the nineteenth century by fire or other destruction or dispersal.[14]

Requests from London for trade or revenue accounts could theoretically be met from records available to the comptroller-general in Edinburgh, particularly the "quarter [or port] books." It was very tedious, however, to extract information from these completely nonaggregated records, and some of the lesser ports were often behind in getting in their quarter books. To circumvent such delays or because of special data requested, it sometimes was necessary to send a circular letter to every port in Scotland to procure the information requested by Parliament or Treasury.[15] Long delays were thus not unknown in answering London's requests for information.

In the years following the Scottish rebellion of 1745, much more attention was given in London to North British affairs, and the Treasury became more amenable to paying for a commercial accounts service in Edinburgh comparable to that in London. Early in 1754, shortly after the duke of Newcastle succeeded his brother Henry Pelham as First Lord of the Treasury, the Board of Trade suggested "the necessity of an Account being laid before them Yearly of the Exports and Imports to and from that part of Great Britain called Scotland in order to enable them to examine into the true State of the Trade of the Kingdom." The new Treasury Board concurred and orders were sent to the customs commissioners in Edinburgh on April 10, 1754, "to cause the s[ai]d Acco[un]ts to be made out, and Annually transmitted to the Lords for Trade and Plantations accordingly."[16] On April 27 the Scottish board replied, requesting a specimen of the ledgers prepared by the Inspector-General at London to serve as a model. On receipt of this example, and of the form of reports made by the English ports, the Scottish board on October 15 instructed the officers at the various ports to make the appropriate returns. These accounts were to be addressed to the secretary of the Edinburgh board, two of whose clerks were to prepare the annual summary for the Board of Trade. These clerks were promised extra remuneration when the size of the task became known.[17]

---

[13] Collector to Edinburgh Customs Board, Port Glasgow Letterbook, Nov. 4, 1749, C.E. 60/1/1.

[14] The minutes of the Scottish board were removed to London after the merger of the English, Scottish, and Irish boards in 1823. They have recently been returned to Edinburgh and deposited in the S.R.O.

[15] Board Minutes, Dec. 21, 1749, Apr. 5, 30, 1753, Dec. 31, 1754, C.E. 1/8.

[16] N. Hardinge to Scottish Board, Apr. 10, 1754, Treasury Out-Letters (North Britain), T. 17/16, 182.

[17] Board Minutes, Oct. 15, 1754, C.E. 1/8.

In the next few weeks the Scottish board had occasion to think further of the time likely to be required and decided that it was really too much for their secretary's clerks. On December 3, 1754, they sent a memorial to the Treasury in London suggesting that to prepare these reports the office of Inspector-General of Exports and Imports for Scotland be established at Edinburgh with duties similar to those of the Inspector-General at London.[18] The board suggested Archibald Campbell for this post, although not all the commissioners signed the recommendation. The Treasury authorized Campbell's appointment at an annual salary of £100 by warrant of December 13, 1754 (to take effect on January 5, 1755), but ordered the board to make no such nonunanimous recommendations in the future.[19]

The Inspector-General of Exports and Imports for Scotland, like his London counterpart, did not prepare his reports from the raw data of ship-by-ship cargo entries in the quarter or port books. He did not have the clerical staff for that. Instead, the collector at each port prepared an annual summary of the trade of his port on prescribed forms, distinguishing commodities and foreign lands of origin or destination. The job of the Inspector-General consisted mainly of adding up the reports from the separate ports, although he must have had much correspondence before all collectors understood the rubrics and measurements they were intended to use. The Inspector-General continued to receive requests from Parliament and elsewhere for accounts going back before the start of his office in 1755. To answer these, he had to circularize the collectors in all the ports. Such requests created a lot of paper work for the collectors, particularly in the busy ports. The collector at Port Glasgow complained as early as August 26, 1755, that since the beginning of the year he had sent the new Inspector-General nineteen separate accounts, including eight for linen going back twenty-five years. He requested an extra clerk both at Port Glasgow and at Greenock for this work.[20]

At first, the annual reports prepared by Campbell were sent only to the Board of Trade, although they were routed through the Treasury. However, in 1764, the more zealous Treasury of George Grenville requested that henceforth duplicates be sent to them. They were not pleased with the quality of those prepared by Campbell for 1755-1762, and in

---

[18] Ibid., Dec. 3, 1754. See also T. 17/19, 193-194.

[19] The recommendation of Campbell was another manifestation of the dominance of the Argyle patronage interest at this time, one of the customs commissioners then being Colin Campbell of the same interest. Board Minutes, Dec. 23, 31, 1754, Jan. 2, 14, 1755, C.E. 1/8; Treasury warrant, Dec. 13, 1754, T. 17/16, 278-279; West to Edinburgh Board, Dec. 20, 1754, ibid., 280, 281, 336; warrant reappointing Campbell, June 24, 1761, T. 17/17, 482-483.

[20] Port Glasgow Collector to Board, Aug. 26, 1755, C.E. 60/1/20; Collector to Archibald Campbell, Oct. 25, 1755, Mar. 18, 1756, ibid.

April 1764 he was removed to the collectorship at Prestonpans and replaced as Inspector-General by George Menzies.[21] The somewhat slapdash accounts prepared by Campbell (January 5, 1755–January 5, 1762) lump all the North American colonies together. The more careful accounts prepared by Menzies (1762 onward) distinguish each colony separately. This greater precision was to be useful now that Parliament was paying more attention to colonial affairs and requesting more accounts, including some distinguishing each colony.

These measures of 1754-1764 created a statistical service at the customs headquarters at Edinburgh that could handle orders for most information desired by Parliament or Treasury. Most requests for commercial data concerned a specific trade (linen or iron, for example). On occasion, however, the House of Commons asked for time series on the values of colonial or other foreign trade. An early instance occurred on March 15, 1750/1, when the House, while considering a London petition on colonial trade with the foreign West Indies, called for accounts of the value of goods exported to each of the continental and West Indian colonies from Christmas 1738 to Christmas 1748.[22] A circular letter had to be sent to all Scottish ports to assemble the required data.[23] On December 1, 1762, the House requested similar accounts covering imports from, as well as exports to, all the North American colonies from Christmas 1739 to Christmas 1760 or 1761.[24] As Parliament continued to consider American affairs more intensively, further requests from the House added to this time series. In January 1775 the last of such orders called for carrying the series down to Christmas 1773.[25] The House of Lords showed much less interest in commercial statistics, but, with the growing seriousness of the American problem, someone in the government apparently thought that that house too should have such accounts. On February 7, 1775, the Lords ordered "that the proper Officer do lay before this House 'An Account of the Values of Exports and Imports to and from *North America* and *England* [and Scotland], from *Christmas* 1739 to *Christmas* 1773, distinguishing each Colony and Year,'" together with similar accounts for the West Indies trade.[26] These dates were undoubt-

---

[21] Campbell and Menzies appointments, Apr. 14, 1764, T. 17/18, 48; T. Whately to Edinburgh Board, May 29, June 28, July 25, 1764, *ibid.*, 489, 496, 498. Menzies was allowed £70 per annum for two clerks, a favor denied Campbell. Memorial of Scottish Board, Feb. 21, 1765, T. 17/19, 193-195; Treasury warrant, Aug. 12, 1765, *ibid.* See also T. 17/20, 241.

[22] *Journals of the House of Commons*, XXVI, 131. See also 139, 166, 239.

[23] Board Minutes, Mar. 26, 1751, C.E. 1/8.

[24] *Journals of the House of Commons*, XXIX, 370, 392, 508.

[25] *Ibid.*, XXXV, 75, 80, 82, 95, 98, 113, 137. In 1765 the Treasury had ordered customs to keep this time series up to date. C. Lowndes to Scottish Board, Dec. 30, 1765, T. 17/19, 234-235.

[26] *Journals of the House of Lords*, XXXIV, 308.

edly chosen because comparable accounts for the same years had already been prepared or were then being prepared for the House of Commons. Even so, the reply of the Scottish Customs Board to the House of Lords was not made until June 13, 1775, and could not be presented until November 20 (although the last account requested by the House of Commons covering 1762-1773 was delivered as early as February 20).[27] Although the numerous accounts of American trade ordered by the House of Commons were lost in its great fire of 1834, the few prepared for the House of Lords, almost pro forma, have survived in its record office.[28]

The House of Lords' account of *English* trade with the colonies, 1739-1773, is of no special importance because equivalent information has survived in the Inspector-General's ledgers in the Public Record Office and in the summaries published by Whitworth. However, the account the House received from Scotland (which apparently survives only in the Lords Record Office original) contains the only continuous time series we have of the values of Scottish colonial trade from 1740, distinguishing each colony. (The Scottish Inspector-General's annual reports in the Public Record Office give a colony-by-colony breakdown only from 1762 and omit 1763 and 1769.[29]) The Scottish account thus surviving in the House of Lords was prepared much as were the English tables in Whitworth: for each year, the official values of Scottish exports to and imports from the individual colonies are given—and nothing more. As in Whitworth, bullion and specie movements are excluded. The Scottish account differs in one significant respect: it is slightly more precise geographically. While the English data have but a single entry for "Carolina" and for "Virginia and Maryland," the Scottish report, consistent with the practices of the Scottish Inspector-General's office from 1762, distinguished North Carolina from South Carolina, and Virginia from Maryland.

The data thus obtained (printed in Appendix I) are especially useful for the years before 1762 for which equivalent data are not available elsewhere. The series is not revolutionary in its import, for Scottish trade with the colonies was much less important than that of England.

[27] Scottish Board Minutes, Mar. 2, June 13, 1775, C.E. 1/14.
[28] Because records in the House of Lords Record Office are filed by the date of receipt, this account should be requested by its date: Main Papers, Nov. 20, 1775. For a general description of this repository see Maurice F. Bond, *Guide to the Records of Parliament* (London, 1971).
[29] For the official value of Scottish imports, exports, and reexports, 1755-1800 (totals only), see Henry Hamilton, *An Economic History of Scotland in the Eighteenth Century* (Oxford, 1963), 414-415. For official and current values of Scottish exports, 1755-1800 (totals only), see McCusker, "Current Value of English Exports," *WMQ*, 3d Ser., XXVIII (1971), 621-622. For "current or real value of goods exported to the thirteen colonies" (specified) from Scotland, 1762-1775, see Table III B, *ibid.*, 625.

In 1740-1744 Scottish exports to the thirteen colonies (official values) averaged £97,962 annually, only 10.99 percent of the British total (£891,778); by 1770-1774, Scottish exports to the colonies had risen to £298,922 annually, but were then only 9.77 percent of the British total (£3,061,027). But Scotland's share in the homeward trade was much more dynamic and important, her imports from the thirteen colonies rising from £92,656 per annum in 1740-1744 (10.77 percent of the British total of £860,309) to £524,318 in 1770-1774, or 29.2 percent of the British total (£1,795,711 per annum).[30]

The value of the Scottish data becomes greater, however, when we disaggregate the total for the thirteen colonies into figures for the separate provinces. The Scottish colonial trade was heavily concentrated on the two colonies of Virginia and Maryland. In 1740-1744 some 93.76 percent of Scottish imports from the thirteen colonies came from Virginia and Maryland alone (£86,762 out of £92,656 per annum, official values); the Chesapeake's share was still 90.05 percent of the much larger Scottish imports of 1770-1774 (£472,124 out of £524,318 per annum). Scotland's comparable exports were only slightly less concentrated, with 89.86 percent going to Virginia and Maryland in 1740-1744 (£88,030 out of £97,962) and 75.36 percent in the much larger trade of 1770-1774 (£225,257 out of £298,922). For Virginia and Maryland, Scottish trade thus accounted for a much higher percentage of trade with Britain than was true for the colonies as a whole. While Scotland's exports to the thirteen colonies were only 10.99 percent of the British total in 1740-1744 and 9.77 percent of the British total in 1770-1774, her exports to Virginia and Maryland were 24.4 percent of the British total in 1740-1744 (£88,030 out of £359,479 per annum) and 24.94 percent in 1770-1774 (£225,257 out of £903,189 per annum). For imports, the pattern was more complex and striking. In 1740-1744 Scotland accounted for only 10.77 percent of British imports from the thirteen colonies, but 15.84 percent of imports from Virginia and Maryland (£86,872 out of £548,353 annually). In 1770-1774 Scotland accounted for 29.2 percent of British imports from the thirteen colonies, but 46.25 percent of imports from Virginia and Maryland (£472,124 out of £1,020,760 annually). This means that while it may be relatively safe to ignore the Scottish data in discussing the economies of the other eleven colonies, it would be extremely imprudent to do so in discussing the situation of Virginia or Maryland.

A specific example may be useful. It has been generally understood that the thirteen colonies throughout their history characteristically experienced unfavorable balances in their bilateral recorded trade with Great Britain. The deficits were made up by sales of shipping (not in-

---

[30] See Appendix I, A and B.

TABLE I

OFFICIAL VALUES OF ENGLISH TRADE
WITH VIRGINIA AND MARYLAND, 1740 TO 1774
(annual averages)

	Imports from Va. and Md. £	Exports to Va. and Md. £	Balance for Va. and Md. £
1740-1744	461,481	271,449	+ 190,032
1745-1754	498,537	295,854	+ 202,683
1755-1764	463,484	458,363	+ 5,121
1765-1774	491,641	554,738	- 63,097
1770-1774	548,636	677,932	- 129,296

TABLE II

OFFICIAL VALUES OF BRITISH TRADE
WITH VIRGINIA AND MARYLAND, 1740 TO 1774
(annual averages)

	Imports from Va. and Md. £	Exports to Va. and Md. £	Balance for Va. and Md. £
1740-1744	548,353	359,479	+ 188,874
1745-1754	648,766	422,157	+ 226,609
1755-1764	718,283	587,593	+ 130,690
1765-1774	908,651	759,169	+ 149,482
1770-1774	1,020,760	903,189	+ 117,571

cluded in the ledgers of the Inspectors-General) and by remittances to London of surplus earnings on their trade with the West Indies and southern Europe.[31] It has been argued, however, that the case of Virginia and Maryland was different—that they had had a strongly favorable balance of trade in the 1740s, but that the balance had become unfavorable

[31] The most recent and best account is James F. Shepherd and Gary M. Walton, *Shipping, Maritime Trade, and the Economic Development of Colonial North America* (Cambridge, 1972), esp. Chap. 8.

by the 1770s.[32] This thesis seems substantiated when we look at the official values of trade between England and the Chesapeake colonies: a favorable balance for the tobacco colonies of £190,032 per annum in 1740-1744 or £202,683 in 1745-1754 had turned to an unfavorable balance of £63,097 per annum in 1765-1774 or £129,296 in 1770-1774 (see Table I). However, when we add the Scottish official figures to the English, this seeming change disappears, and the balance remains favorable for the Chesapeake throughout the period 1740-1775 (see Table II).

The explanation is quite simple. Scottish merchants imported vast quantities of tobacco from Virginia and Maryland, but could find in Scotland only part of the goods needed for their exports thither. The remaining goods (particularly German linens, tea and other groceries, Asian textiles, English woolens, and ironmongery) they had purchased and shipped for them from London and other English ports. A substantial part of the exports on Scottish account to Virginia and Maryland thus appear as exports from England and not from Scotland.

More serious, of course, is the question whether we should attempt to make any statements about something as tenuous as the balance of trade on the basis of the very artificial *official* figures. Tables I and II are therefore not designed to state the precise balance of trade, but simply to point out the danger of making certain kinds of calculations from English data alone.

What were Scottish "official" values? This is the key technical problem associated with the use of the data on Scottish trade with the thirteen colonies now published for the first time. We know that the English Inspector-General, when he started his "ledgers" in 1696, used current prices, but that after a few years his clerks ceased efforts to keep the prices up to date, so that the valuations continued to be made throughout the century with the prices of ca. 1700-1702 (the base years used by Mc-Cusker).[33] No literary evidence has yet been discovered on precisely what pricing policy was used by the Scottish Inspector-General in computing values of his imports and exports. One thing, however, is clear from an examination of the prices themselves. They were not identical with English prices. (Other procedures of Scottish customs record-keeping were not identical with English, including the handling of

[32] Joseph Albert Ernst, *Money and Politics in America, 1755-1775: A Study in the Currency Act of 1764 and the Political Economy of Revolution* (Chapel Hill, N. C., 1973), 13, 65. There seems to be a similar confusion in Ronald Hoffman, *A Spirit of Dissension: Economics, Politics, and the Revolution in Maryland* (Baltimore, 1973), 19-20.

[33] McCusker, "Current Value of English Exports," *WMQ*, 3d Ser., XXVIII (1971), 613-614; Clark, *Guide to English Commercial Statistics*, 9-12, 37-38.

Flanders and the distinction between Virginia and Maryland, and between North and South Carolina.) Like the English, however, the Scottish values seem not to fluctuate from year to year. The most likely hypothesis is that the Scottish values were drawn up when the Scottish series started in 1755 and represent prices of ca. 1754-1756 and not ca. 1700-1702. It seems wisest to proceed on this limited-risk hypothesis until evidence to the contrary comes to light.

Appendix I (A and B) presents the official values for Scottish trade with the thirteen colonies, 1740-1773, as they appear in the House of Lords manuscript mentioned above. From another source,[34] I have continued this series through 1791 to increase its utility for all persons interested in American foreign trade before the start of official federal statistics. In Appendix II (A and B) the previously available English data are combined with the new Scottish data to create a series for the official values of colonial and United States trade with all of Great Britain, 1740-1791.[35] This combined series is presented as a convenience to the researcher, but should be used with a little caution. I have already mentioned that the English series is based on prices prevailing ca. 1700, while the Scottish series would appear to be based on prices prevailing ca. 1755, so that they are not entirely compatible. However, even if one recalculated the Scottish values using the English official prices, it is unlikely that the final figures for British exports would be altered by more than 1 or 2 percent, Scottish exports to the thirteen colonies remaining only about 10 percent of the British total throughout. Although the Scottish share of British imports was much more important before 1776 (29.2 percent in 1770-1774), it consisted almost entirely of tobacco (85.25 percent in 1762 and 81.94 percent in 1772), for which English and Scottish prices were relatively close. (With Scotland accounting for 29.2 percent of British imports from the thirteen colonies and with 82 percent of Scottish imports from North America consisting of tobacco, the distortion in the final British import figures from a Scottish tobacco valuation 11 percent higher than the English valuation would be only about 2.63 percent.) However, researchers working specifically with Virginia and Maryland might, before attempting any minute calculations, consider the utility of reducing the figures for Scottish imports from those colonies by about 10 percent to bring the valuations into line with the English on the dominant commodity, tobacco.

---

[34] B.T. 6/185, 188v-204, P.R.O.

[35] The English series is that printed in *Historical Statistics*, 757, incorporating the necessary corrections for New York, 1763, and Virginia and Maryland, 1773, pointed out by McCusker, "Current Value of English Exports," *WMQ*, 3d Ser., XXVIII (1971), 612, n. 8.

APPENDIX IA

SCOTTISH IMPORTS FROM THE THIRTEEN COLONIES AND STATES, 1740 TO 1791
(official sterling values)

Year	N.E.	N.Y.	Pa.[a]	Md.	Va.	N.C.	S.C.	Ga.	Total
1740	2,301	0	595	9,910	38,125	1,215	0	0	52,146
1741	3,978	0	778	19,029	62,330	0	3	0	86,118
1742	1,988	0	564	15,611	79,575	1,710	2,277	0	101,725
1743	1,615	0	0	22,947	93,253	1,694	290	0	119,799
1744	2,419	0	0	16,186	77,392	789	6,708	0	103,494
1745	979	0	1,269	17,734	103,563	595	0	0	124,140
1746	2,477	0	0	10,924	75,734	0	10,846	0	99,981
1747	5,545	0	1,148	6,234	91,285	0	12,980	0	117,192
1748	2,703	0	0	18,105	128,049	0	13,820	0	162,677
1749	4,629	0	0	31,387	137,895	365	4,306	0	178,582
1750	3,205	0	896	26,246	128,804	349	1,297	0	160,797
1751	6,402	0	5	27,123	163,488	430	2,073	0	199,521
1752	5,975	2,019	1,217	20,928	154,814	281	1,777	0	187,011
1753	6,319	936	0	27,003	177,324	0	3,635	0	215,217
1754	7,055	1,357	1,395	25,414	130,237	1,473	550	0	167,481
1755	6,243	1,121	4,852	23,853	145,659	1,716	2,036	0	185,480
1756	14,418	1,630	2,390	40,239	95,006	0	8,468	0	162,151
1757	4,513	303	1,176	35,523	156,956	812	10,148	0	209,431
1758	71	286	0	68,485	221,320	4,343	20,449	1,016	315,970
1759	755	6,224	1,584	45,883	124,179	7,253	21,512	2,468	209,858
1760	2,006	13,241	92	84,288	270,299	1,938	17,530	0	389,394
1761	5,627	811	1,038	92,270	196,992	3,382	11,268	1,325	312,713
1762	9,103	2,981	616	59,535	242,057	1,086	10,669	0	326,347
1763	4,282	0	250	71,846	272,251	1,822	3,360	0	353,811
1764	9,104	8,197	6,440	56,625	244,723	6,849	6,024	0	337,962
1765	29,754	4,932	3,963	84,543	288,860	4,342	4,954	596	421,944

Year	N.E.	N.Y.	Pa.	Md.	Va.	N.C.	S.C.	Ga.	Total
1766	15,809	315	1,292	78,859	255,481	12,467	19,319	0	383,542
1767	19,309	3,072	5,022	94,908	237,156	12,247	5,096	0	376,810
1768	9,429	4,694	2,265	97,242	273,364	8,708	9,426	0	405,128
1769	13,422	39,916	2,001	98,353	299,715	11,312	6,588	0	471,307
1770	9,432	29,115	2,956	97,667	315,236	16,911	10,363	526	482,206
1771	12,542	19	20,042	125,424	423,105	16,458	8,874	0	606,464
1772	12,775	0	70	122,517	385,556	16,716	4,262	0	541,896
1773	7,454	2,304	0	91,232	374,243	24,586	3,563	14,572	517,954
1774	11,550	3,472	0	84,235	341,407	32,380	0	26	473,070
1775	11,587	9,204	758	140,644	348,041	25,878	0	0	536,112
1776	0	0	0	13,606	68,172	74	0	0	81,852
1777	0	3,161	0	0	830	0	0	0	3,991
1778	0	21,303	0	1,177	0	0	2,354	0	24,834
1779	0	33,599	216	0	0	0	0	0	33,815
1780	2,200	52,308	8,662	0	15,296	0	1,221	0	79,687
1781	0	32,866	0	0	0	0	11,057	387	44,310
1782	0	106,827	0	0	0	0	0	0	106,827
1783	176	19,366	801	0	11,175	991	2,161	0	34,670
1784	1,248	3,943	1,435	4,789	32,720	2,210	1,795	0	48,140
1785	0	4,828	1,722	5,362	88,097	7,283	8,559	1,854	117,705
1786	89	5,896	0	96	75,548	10,024	7,811	12	99,476
1787	297	6,429	0	2,976	76,142	7,200	17,186	2,961	113,191
1788	840	14,241	2,318	2,258	95,992	15,505	8,725	292	140,171
1789	1,904	19,030	0	293	92,519	19,984	23,087	77	156,894
1790	2,481	22,364	1,191	12,532	70,280	14,952	18,358	5,524	147,682
1791	3,464	12,901	0	20,070	104,846	19,606	18,362	3,617	182,866

Notes and Sources:
   [a] In this and the following tables, column heads are given as they appear in the original records. Pennsylvania includes Delaware. British customs reported no statistics for New Jersey. What little direct trade there may have been between New Jersey and Great Britain must have been classified in the figures for New York and Pennsylvania.
   1740-1773: House of Lords Record Office, Nov. 20, 1775.
   1774-1791: B.T. 6/185, 188v-204, P.R.O.

APPENDIX IB
SCOTTISH EXPORTS TO THE THIRTEEN COLONIES AND STATES, 1740 TO 1791
(official sterling values)

Year	N.E.	N.Y.	Pa.	Md.	Va.	N.C.	S.C.	Ga.	Total
1740	5,714	0	936	528	74,724	0	188	0	82,090
1741	4,380	0	735	2,449	70,204	838	345	0	78,951
1742	13,022	0	2,634	11,272	81,726	0	0	0	108,654
1743	7,003	0	0	8,237	112,550	460	2,210	0	130,460
1744	7,112	0	2,800	555	77,905	0	1,284	0	89,656
1745	5,601	0	1,658	4,640	82,033	0	3,275	0	97,207
1746	22,827	0	407	6,000	142,361	0	3,359	0	174,954
1747	18,259	2,787	5,157	16,211	146,337	0	1,809	0	190,560
1748	25,961	0	61	19,231	146,381	0	0	0	191,634
1749	11,370	1,466	1,521	9,109	85,144	576	5,633	0	114,819
1750	14,385	1,944	500	14,341	94,529	0	1,497	0	127,196
1751	21,242	1,417	2,214	17,550	113,449	2,713	5,620	0	164,205
1752	13,754	1,555	1,309	7,609	124,991	2,070	3,802	0	155,090
1753	12,386	3,767	2,547	6,046	120,901	173	11,722	0	157,542
1754	7,976	666	1,079	9,877	96,288	1,046	4,381	0	121,313
1755	6,218	1,024	2,001	8,493	91,002	431	917	0	110,086
1756	9,957	8,063	106	14,097	74,399	0	5,043	0	111,665
1757	7,841	10,174	641	16,615	85,676	1,484	1,363	0	123,794
1758	11,723	7,360	1,984	19,147	89,296	305	5,420	0	135,235
1759	22,715	13,789	4,626	15,858	96,381	460	6,715	0	160,544
1760	12,132	10,959	1,597	43,044	112,021	3,141	3,120	0	186,014
1761	4,245	3,774	0	45,664	86,514	400	3,923	0	144,520
1762	14,258	22,563	0	19,579	104,976	2,557	6,028	0	169,961
1763	20,405	17,698	11,913	20,923	175,112	4,843	10,049	0	260,943
1764	28,792	8,894	3,096	18,234	155,266	4,437	6,230	0	224,949
1765	17,404	4,996	5,653	27,012	108,642	7,408	4,696	0	175,811

Year	N.E.	N.Y.	Pa.	Md.	Va.	N.C.	S.C.	Ga.	Total
1766	9,773	2,088	6,854	37,790	109,391	7,063	4,707	0	177,666
1767	10,105	6,022	11,291	30,538	184,506	14,884	9,694	147	267,187
1768	11,010	7,743	9,722	40,774	152,795	6,330	4,727	0	233,101
1769	15,701	1,013	5,070	51,512	175,069	11,847	8,637	0	268,849
1770	22,243	4,229	4,753	54,458	224,917	17,968	4,259	3,137	335,964
1771	15,718	1,529	18,725	52,999	250,401	14,033	19,765	1,302	374,472
1772	19,592	5,494	18,032	50,747	170,913	18,562	11,481	3,267	298,088
1773	16,110	6,739	9,492	15,887	144,636	19,653	16,366	4,170	233,053
1774	14,175	21,701	19,973	24,454	136,874	28,491	5,859	1,505	253,032
1775	13,489	241	0	0	0	395	140	9,928	24,193
1776	905	0	0	0	0	0	0	0	905
1777	0	35,553	0	0	0	0	0	0	35,553
1778	0	28,693	6,517	0	0	0	0	0	35,210
1779	0	62,505	0	0	0	0	0	121	62,626
1780	0	73,705	0	0	0	0	69,519	28,093	171,317
1781	0	101,219	0	0	0	0	46,349	0	147,568
1782	0	44,324	0	0	0	0	0	0	44,324
1783	2,998	56,020	5,796	2,458	17,719	7,656	15,989	0	108,636
1784	4,818	56,040	35,813	11,521	161,043	30,611	19,758	0	319,604
1785	410	14,798	24,230	4,387	153,647	12,444	19,366	0	229,282
1786	1,705	22,008	7,722	7,919	115,068	6,643	11,146	0	172,211
1787	682	21,585	3,484	26,142	135,479	13,350	17,570	1,606	219,898
1788	946	28,743	9,109	30,241	79,363	9,668	17,560	594	176,224
1789	2,494	29,252	5,021	13,588	95,837	19,643	22,025	1,033	188,893
1790	1,189	34,428	3,383	11,302	85,748	15,665	21,009	818	173,542
1791	8,002	51,979	7,602	22,182	85,844	11,758	21,666	0	209,033

Sources:
 1740-1773: House of Lords Record Office, Nov. 20, 1775.
 1774-1791: B.T. 6/185, 188v-204, P.R.O.

Appendix IIA

British Imports from the Thirteen Colonies and States, 1740 to 1791
(official sterling values)

Year	N.E.	N.Y.	Pa.	Va. & Md.	Carolina	Ga.	Total
1740	74,690	21,498	15,643	390,032	267,775	924	770,562
1741	64,030	21,142	17,936	658,468	236,833	0	998,409
1742	55,154	13,536	9,091	522,955	158,594	1,622	760,952
1743	64,800	15,067	9,596	674,021	237,120	2	1,000,606
1744	52,667	14,527	7,446	496,287	200,091	0	771,018
1745	39,927	14,083	11,399	520,720	92,442	0	678,571
1746	41,089	8,841	15,779	506,029	87,743	0	659,481
1747	47,316	14,992	4,980	590,138	120,480	0	777,907
1748	32,451	12,358	12,363	641,006	181,125	0	879,303
1749	44,628	23,413	14,944	603,900	155,170	51	842,106
1750	51,660	35,634	29,087	663,989	193,253	1,942	975,565
1751	69,689	42,363	23,875	650,696	247,994	555	1,035,172
1752	80,288	42,667	31,195	745,195	290,322	1,526	1,191,193
1753	89,714	51,489	38,527	836,901	168,269	3,057	1,187,957
1754	73,593	28,020	32,044	729,086	309,261	3,236	1,175,240
1755	65,776	29,175	37,188	659,180	329,277	4,437	1,125,033
1756	61,777	25,703	22,485	473,004	231,383	7,155	821,507
1757	32,069	19,471	15,366	611,360	141,849	0	820,115
1758	30,275	14,546	21,383	744,167	175,303	1,016	986,690
1759	26,740	27,908	23,988	527,290	235,299	8,542	849,767
1760	39,808	34,366	22,846	859,038	182,237	12,198	1,150,493
1761	51,852	49,459	40,208	744,345	267,652	7,089	1,160,605
1762	51,136	61,863	38,707	717,301	193,450	6,522	1,068,979
1763	79,097	53,989	38,478	986,391	287,548	14,469	1,459,972
1764	97,261	61,894	42,698	860,756	354,600	31,325	1,448,534
1765	175,573	59,891	29,111	879,074	395,214	34,779	1,573,642

Year	N.E.	N.Y.	Pa.	Va. & Md.	Carolina	Ga.	Total
1766	157,542	67,335	28,143	796,033	325,373	53,074	1,427,500
1767	147,516	64,494	42,663	769,990	412,370	35,856	1,472,889
1768	157,804	91,809	61,671	776,654	526,242	42,402	1,656,582
1769	142,775	113,382	28,112	759,960	405,014	82,270	1,531,513
1770	157,443	98,997	31,065	847,997	306,181	56,058	1,497,741
1771	162,923	95,894	51,657	1,126,377	445,643	63,810	1,946,304
1772	139,040	82,707	29,203	1,036,477	446,901	66,083	1,800,411
1773	132,078	78,550	36,652	1,055,278	484,662	99,963	1,887,183
1774	123,798	83,480	69,611	1,037,672	464,682	67,673	1,846,916
1775	128,175	196,222	176,720	1,247,041	605,427	103,477	2,457,062
1776	762	2,318	1,421	155,004	13,742	12,569	185,816
1777	1,880	11,591	17	888	2,234	0	16,610
1778	372	37,495	56	1,177	3,428	0	42,528
1779	808	48,461	786	0	3,732	607	54,394
1780	2,232	67,840	8,699	15,296	1,929	2,251	98,247
1781	2,068	35,771	0	0	105,425	893	144,157
1782	0	114,517	0	0	14,182	6,804	135,503
1783	26,526	102,779	30,854	105,063	77,741	5,765	348,728
1784	51,079	47,303	70,263	390,251	167,545	22,889	749,330
1785	56,648	51,672	57,706	443,581	228,071	45,919	893,597
1786	45,392	75,293	22,834	451,671	216,289	31,641	843,120
1787	67,696	87,160	34,796	423,335	253,472	27,176	893,635
1788	67,146	111,848	32,807	504,672	282,259	25,057	1,023,789
1789	90,392	99,799	36,050	539,355	258,961	25,633	1,050,190
1790	100,864	119,971	51,731	566,774	286,332	65,399	1,191,071
1791	79,214	164,506	54,141	572,274	268,847	55,197	1,194,179

Sources:
Figures were obtained by adding Scottish data in Appendix IA to English data in U. S. Bureau of the Census, *Historical Statistics of the United States* (Washington, D. C., 1960), 757, and B.T. 6/185, 106-117v, P.R.O. See also n. 35.

Appendix IIB
British Exports to the Thirteen Colonies and States, 1740 to 1791
(official sterling values)

Year	N.E.	N.Y.	Pa.	Va. & Md.	Carolina	Ga.	Total
1740	176,795	118,777	57,687	356,680	182,009	3,524	895,472
1741	202,527	140,430	91,745	321,235	205,953	2,553	964,443
1742	161,921	167,591	77,929	357,184	127,063	17,018	908,706
1743	179,464	135,487	79,340	448,982	114,169	2,291	959,733
1744	151,094	119,920	65,014	313,315	80,425	769	730,537
1745	146,064	54,957	55,938	284,472	90,090	939	632,460
1746	232,004	86,712	74,106	430,906	106,168	984	930,880
1747	228,899	140,771	87,561	362,636	97,338	24	917,229
1748	223,643	143,311	75,391	418,236	160,172	1,314	1,022,067
1749	249,656	267,239	240,158	417,853	170,294	5	1,345,205
1750	358,044	269,074	218,213	458,289	134,534	2,125	1,440,279
1751	327,216	250,358	193,131	478,026	146,577	2,065	1,397,373
1752	287,094	195,585	202,975	457,751	156,649	3,163	1,303,217
1753	357,909	281,631	248,191	483,723	224,904	14,128	1,610,486
1754	337,409	128,163	245,726	429,678	154,642	1,974	1,297,592
1755	348,014	152,095	146,457	384,652	189,235	2,630	1,223,083
1756	394,328	258,488	200,275	423,393	186,823	536	1,463,843
1757	371,245	363,485	269,067	528,978	216,796	2,571	1,752,142
1758	477,417	363,915	262,937	546,914	186,727	10,212	1,848,122
1759	549,782	644,574	502,787	571,246	222,430	15,178	2,505,997
1760	611,779	491,065	709,595	760,947	224,392	0	2,797,778
1761	338,470	293,344	204,067	677,528	258,910	24,279	1,796,598
1762	261,643	310,609	206,199	542,154	202,755	23,761	1,547,121
1763	279,259	256,258	296,065	751,426	265,024	44,908	1,892,940
1764	488,557	524,310	438,287	688,692	316,475	18,338	2,474,659
1765	468,703	387,345	369,021	518,878	346,813	29,165	2,119,925

Year	N.E.	N.Y.	Pa.	Va. & Md.	Carolina	Ga.	Total
1766	419,415	332,917	334,168	519,729	308,502	67,268	1,981,999
1767	416,186	423,979	383,121	652,672	268,671	23,481	2,168,110
1768	430,807	490,673	441,829	669,523	300,925	56,562	2,390,319
1769	223,694	75,931	204,979	714,943	327,084	58,340	1,604,971
1770	416,694	480,220	139,631	997,157	168,500	59,330	2,261,535
1771	1,435,837	655,150	747,469	1,223,726	442,967	71,795	4,576,944
1772	844,422	349,464	525,941	1,015,570	479,653	95,673	3,310,723
1773	543,165	295,953	435,910	589,427	380,878	67,102	2,312,465
1774	576,651	459,638	645,625	690,066	412,466	59,023	2,843,469
1775	85,114	1,469	1,366	1,921	6,780	123,705	220,355
1776	55,955	0	365	0	0	0	56,320
1777	0	92,848	0	0	0	0	92,848
1778	0	55,142	14,054	0	0	0	69,196
1779	0	412,217	0	0	0	206	412,423
1780	0	570,307	0	0	306,460	119,981	996,748
1781	0	604,196	0	0	377,196	14,059	995,451
1782	0	230,566	0	0	69,743	340	300,649
1783	202,556	603,152	245,258	219,834	250,382	22,683	1,543,865
1784	526,561	709,548	689,491	1,272,346	492,834	47,231	3,738,011
1785	163,349	405,763	369,216	1,015,103	310,199	44,396	2,308,026
1786	126,833	226,293	211,592	824,821	199,199	14,728	1,603,466
1787	201,375	361,029	209,697	905,764	312,567	23,680	2,014,112
1788	233,690	330,675	212,503	766,282	318,657	24,345	1,886,152
1789	350,118	429,945	354,712	912,468	400,882	47,297	2,495,422
1790	339,973	532,127	731,822	1,389,257	396,266	42,335	3,431,780
1791	588,739	824,166	704,734	1,548,220	465,304	92,286	4,223,449

Sources:
Figures were obtained by adding Scottish data in Appendix 1B to English data in U. S. Bureau of the Census, *Historical Statistics of the United States* (Washington, D. C., 1960), 757, and B.T. 6/185, 106-117v, P.R.O. See also n. 35.

IV

A Note on the Value of Colonial Exports of Shipping

ASIDE from their studies of the iron industry, historians have given relatively little attention to the non-household manufacturing industries of colonial America—perhaps, many would say, for the very good reason that there was not much activity along these lines before the conjuncture of the American and the Industrial Revolutions. Yet there were manufactures that reached significant volumes for those times. One of these was the colonial shipbuilding industry which not only provided most of the vessels that carried North American commerce with the West Indies and the Old World but also provided the capital starved colonies with a significant export. In spite of its importance this trade has not received much attention from modern economic historians, including those who deal with the balance of payments. One reason is, perhaps, that the British government in the eighteenth century did not consider colonial built ships as foreign in any sense and did not regard their transfer to metropolitan ownership as "imports." Thus the values of such transfers were not included in the Inspector-General's accounts of imports from the colonies nor were any other records kept of them, except for the ship-by-ship entries in the Registries of Shipping (which for the most part have not survived).[1]

In a 1913 thesis on *American Shipping*, Hans Keiler touched only briefly on the colonial period, reproducing the figures given by Lord Sheffield on colonial shipbuilding, ca. 1769-1771.[2] Victor Clark's survey of early American manufacturing (published 1916-1929) mentioned foreign sales of colonial shipping but had little quantitative

---

[1] Cf. [Sir] G[eorge] N[orman] Clark, *Guide to English Commercial Statistics 1696-1782*, Royal Historical Society, Guides and Handbooks, no. 1 (London, 1938), 45-51; Rupert Jarvis, "Ship Registry to 1707," *Maritime History*, no. 1 (1971), 29-45.

[2] Hans Keiler, *American Shipping: its History and Economic Conditions*, Probleme der Weltwirtschaft: Schriften des Instituts für Seeverkehr und Weltwirtschaft an der Universität Kiel, 14 (Jena, 1913), 15.

data.[3] The really serious discussion of this subject began only with the work of Lawrence A. Harper in the 1930's. In an article of 1939, Harper surveyed the readily available information on colonial shipbuilding in an authoritative fashion, but he was on less firm ground in discussing colonial shipping exports. Lacking hard data, he tended to minimize the importance of colonial sales of shipping to Britain. Even if colonial shipbuilding reached 28,747 tons per annum before the Revolution (as the contemporary Champion alleged), the industry after the Revolution was to reach 29,606 tons in 1790 and 154,626 tons in 1815, without either a United Kingdom or a French market. The post-independence tonnage was almost entirely for the use of the American merchant navy, for American shipping exports averaged only 10,584 tons between 1815 and 1848. Harper implied that that was an impressive figure, all things considered—but, as we shall see, it was actually rather less than exports in the last years of the old empire.[4]

The question was left more or less as Harper formulated it until the 1960's. In 1962, Ralph Davis published his very useful book on English shipping in the seventeenth and eighteenth centuries. Davis's volume is concerned primarily with the operation of ships, rather than shipbuilding, but he has some valuable material on the sources of English shipping as well. Although the colonists were building vessels for their own use (both locally and in the West India trade) from the earliest days of settlement, sales to England appear to Davis to have been unimportant until the 1690's. During the long wars of 1689-1713, however, New Englanders took advantage of the war-induced demand for shipping in England to build for that market. "With the ending of the war, these English purchases dropped for a time to a lower level; but English-owned colonial-built ships were being used in some numbers in all the trades with the North American colonies, and to a small extent to the West Indies. On the whole, they were quite small ships; the great bulk-cargo carriers were not American products, and the advantages of American-built ships were not in cheap operation . . . but in cheap building." For all that,

---

[3] Victor S. Clark, *History of Manufactures in the United States*, Vol. 1, *1607-1860* (Washington, D. C., 1929), pp. 95, 98, 138, 147, 204, 206. The subject was ignored in Emory R. Johnson, "American Commerce to 1789" in E. R. Johnson et al., *History of Domestic and Foreign Commerce of the United States*, 2 vols., Carnegie Institution of Washington, publ. no. 215A (Washington, D. C., 1915), 1: 3-189.

[4] Lawrence A. Harper, "The Effect of the Navigation Acts on the Thirteen Colonies," in Richard B. Morris, ed., *The Era of the American Revolution: Studies Inscribed to Evarts Boutell Greene* (New York, 1939), 8-10.

colonial sales of ships to English operators were sufficiently numerous to elicit a protest to parliament from Thames shipbuilders in 1724. Davis realized that the greatest difficulties come in developing quantitative data, yet he offered the following restrained estimates. "Perhaps by 1730 one English ship in every six was American-built, and by 1760 one in four. In the late sixties, however, the pace of American shipbuilding quickened, and for a few years large ships as well as small poured out of the yards for English owners. Richard Champion stated in 1774 that nearly a third of British owned ships were American built (2,342 out of 7,694)."[5]

For all his venturesome aggregation, Davis was extremely wary about offering any estimates of the value of colonial shipping sales to England. The present writer, however, was less prudent. In 1964, I commented on Robert Paul Thomas' paper on quantitative measures of the effects of British colonial policy (given at the annual meeting of the Economic History Association). Thomas had not included any discussion of shipping sales in his paper, and I felt obliged to point out the significance of Davis's estimates of colonial shipping sales and to add: "If the average ship lasted 20 to 25 years, this suggests a sale of about 100 colonial ships yearly [on the eve of the Revolution], worth close to £100,000 exclusive of sails, cables, etc."[6] I was aware at the time that my estimate of £1,000 average sale price of the hull, exclusive of rigging, might be high if a substantial proportion of smaller vessels were included; but, on the other hand, my estimate that an average ship's life was 20-25 years (following Davis) was extremely conservative. The two biases tended to cancel each other out, and I thought that if anything I was erring on the side of caution. As with most such comments, I had no time for original research. I nevertheless thought it necessary to take some risks because an item of ca. £100,000 per annum in eighteenth-century trade was too important to be ignored.

The question remained in this less than satisfactory state until 1972, when James F. Shepherd and Gary M. Walton published their important book, *Shipping, Maritime Trade and the Economic Development of Colonial North America*. Appendix VI of this work is devoted to "Foreign Exchange Earnings from the sale of Ships to Overseas Buyers." Here they quote the figures first given by Lord Sheffield in 1784 (Table 1) for colonial shipbuilding in 1769-1771. To these ton-

---

[5] Ralph Davis, *The Rise of the English Shipping Industry in the Seventeenth and Eighteenth Centuries* (London, 1962), pp. 66-68, 374-75. All prices in this article are in sterling.
[6] Jacob M. Price, "Discussion," JOURNAL OF ECONOMIC HISTORY, 25 (1965), 656-57.

Colonial Exports 707

TABLE 1

SHIPBUILDING IN THE NORTH AMERICAN AND ADJOINING
COLONIES, 1769-1772

	1769			1770			1771			1772	
	TS[a]	S & S[b]	tons	TS	S & S	tons	TS	S & S	tons	TS	tons[c]
Nfld.	0	1	30	0	0	0	0	4	50	?	?
Canada	0	1	60	0	1	15	4	3	233	?	?
N. S.	0	3	110	1	2	200	1	3	140	?	?
B.N.A.	0	5	200	1	3	215	5	10	423	?	?
N. H.	16	29	2,452	27	20	3,581	15	40	4,991	?	?
Mass.	40	97	8,013	31	118	7,274	42	83	7,704	?	?
R. I.	8	31	1,428	16	49	2,035	15	60	2,148	?	?
Conn.	7	43	1,542	5	41	1,522	7	39	1,483	?	?
N. E.	71	200	13,435	79	228	14,412	79	222	16,326	123	18,149
N. Y.	5	14	955	8	10	960	9	28	1,698	15	1,640
N. J.	1	3	83	0	0	0	0	2	70	1	80
Pa.	14	8	1,469	18	8	2,354	15	6	1,307	18	2,897
Md.	9	11	1,344	7	10	1,545	10	8	1,645	8	1,626
Va.	6	21	1,269	6	15	1,105	10	9	1,678	7	933
N.C.	3	9	607	0	5	125	0	8	241	3	253
S.C.	4	8	789	0	3	52	3	4	560	2	213
Ga.	0	2	50	0	3	57	2	4	543	5	753
U.S.	113	276	20,001	118	282	20,610	128	291	24,068	182	26,544
W. Fla.	1	0	80	0	1	10	0	2	24	?	?
Bahamas	0	4	42	0	7	135	0	6	137	?	?
Bermuda	1	47	1,047	1	48	1,104	0	48	1,098	?	?
Total	115	332	21,370	120	341	22,074	133	357	25,750		

[a] TS = Topsails.

[b] S & S = Sloops and Schooners.

[c] TS only.

Source: (1769-1771) John Baker Holroyd, 1st earl of Sheffield, *Observations on the Commerce of the American States*, 6th ed. (London, 1784), p. 96; (1772) Rev. Andrew Burnaby, *Travels through the Middle Settlements in North America in the Years 1759 and 1760*, 3d ed. (London, 1798), p. 152. The addition in the total column in Lord Sheffield has been corrected. The chief error in Sheffield's table would appear to be in Newfoundland. Cf. also Appendix II.

nages, Shepherd and Walton applied the prices per measured ton for a ship of 200 tons in 1784, as reported by Davis:

New York, Philadelphia [and southern]	£6:8s. to £7:19s.
New England	£3:18s. to £5:9s.

Taking the mean of the range of prices indicated by Davis and applying it to the average production of the three years used by Sheffield (apparently adding 50 percent to convert registered into measured tonnage), Shepherd and Walton obtain a figure in the vicinity of £175,000 for the annual value of colonial shipbuilding ca. 1769-1771. This would allow for sales to Britain in the vicinity of

708

£100,000 (as suggested by the present writer) or £80,000 for the northern colonies only (as suggested by Curtis Nettels).

Shepherd and Walton were reluctant, however, to conclude that four-sevenths of the colonial tonnage constructed could have been sold 'abroad. For this reason, they suggested an alternative calculation. Without giving the original sources, they cited an estimate from the M.A. thesis of R. C. Berner, that the Massachusetts-owned fleet in the early 1770's was 59,000 tons. If Massachusetts vessels on the average lasted ten years, then the colony would need 5,900 tons of new construction each year or almost 77 percent of the 7,664 tons Sheffield reported as having been constructed there during 1769-1771; this would leave only 23 percent available for foreign sale. If, however, Massachusetts vessels lasted twenty years, then replacement would only require 2,950 tons per annum (38.5 percent of production), leaving 4,714 tons or 61.5 percent available for export sale. Shepherd and Walton do not attempt to answer the question of how long the lifespan of Massachusetts shipping actually was. They merely suggest that the average working life must have been somewhere between ten and twenty years, leaving something between ca. 25 percent and ca. 60 percent of the colony's shipbuilding available for export sale. Applying these two extremes to the reported output of all colonies, 1769-1771, they obtain low and high limits for the export sale of all the colonies:[7]

	From [i.e. 25%]	To [i.e. 60%]
New England	£26,000	£62,000
Middle Colonies	8,000	19,000
Upper South	8,000	18,000
Lower South	3,000	7,000
TOTAL	45,000	106,000

The method used by Shepherd and Walton is ingenious, but is it rigorous? Everything depends on (a) the unsolved average life of a vessel, (b) Davis's prices and (c) the figure of 59,000 tons for the Massachusetts fleet in the early 1770's. Turning first to point (c), I

[7] James F. Shepherd and Gary M. Walton, *Shipping, Maritime Trade and the Economic Development of Colonial North America* (Cambridge, 1972), 241-45. The thesis cited is Richard C. Berner, "The Means of Paying for Colonial New England's Imports" (M.A., University of California, Berkeley, 1950). Cf. also Davis, *English Shipping*, p. 375. On the need to add 50 percent to correct the tonnage, see John J. McCusker, "Colonial Tonnage Measurement: Five Philadelphia Merchant Ships as a Sample," JOURNAL OF ECONOMIC HISTORY, 27 (March 1967), 82-91; and Gary M. Walton, "Colonial Tonnage Measurements: a Comment," Ibid., pp. 392-97.

think we must reconsider the figure 59,000 tons. A large portion of Massachusetts' maritime effort at this time was accounted for by its fishing fleet: 665 vessels (25,630 tons) were involved in cod fishery alone between 1765 and 1775 (exclusive of the 14,020 tons involved in whale fishery).[8] Presumably these totals were included in the 59,000 tons. But the 7,664 tons of shipbuilding activity derived from Sheffield appear to cover registered vessels only. Do Sheffield's data cover all the fishing craft included in the estimate of the Massachusetts fleet? If not, the fleet figures and the shipbuilding figures are incompatible.

All this has a very speculative air about it—an unnecessarily speculative air, at that. Almost all our calculations hinge on Lord Sheffield's report on colonial shipbuilding and two or three other pieces of data. It might be useful if we stopped trying to dance any more complicated steps on the head of this very small pin and instead attempted to find further data on colonial shipbuilding and shipping sales to Britain.

The colonial shipbuilding industry had a dual aspect. From the earliest days of settlement, the colonists had a pressing need for small craft for river and coastal use and could most economically obtain these by local manufacture. As their trade to the West Indies developed, their shipbuilders inevitably expanded into the construction of the sloops, schooners, and other ships useful for this trade, vessels usually in the vicinity of 46-60 registered tons or 70-90 measured tons.[9] By contrast, the market in Britain was for larger craft, such as those used in the Chesapeake trade: ca. 135 registered tons in 1771, or 200 measured tons.[10] The transition from building the smaller to building the larger vessels, though technically not difficult, posed some financial and marketing problems. It was easy only when substantial merchants (found more commonly in Britain than in the colonies) placed firm orders and helped with the financing of construction.

As early as 1676, it was reported that it was not unusual for New England builders to receive orders for as many as thirty vessels a year from England. As we have seen, however, Ralph Davis ascribes the real breakthrough of American shipbuilding into the British market to

[8] Timothy Pitkin, *A Statistical View of the Commerce of the United States of America* (Hartford, Conn., 1816), pp. 74, 78.
[9] According to Shepherd and Walton, *Shipping*, p. 195, the average size of vessels trading in the port of Boston rose from 46.5 tons in 1688 to 61.4 tons in 1764/65. This would include a few ships trading to Europe which would raise the average slightly.

710

the war years, 1689-1713. New England may have taken the greatest advantage of this: between 1697 and 1714, Massachusetts sold 187 vessels of 20,601 tons to Britain, or an average of ten to eleven vessels per annum of 110 tons each. This was rather less than the reported orders of 1676, but many more were likely built for Caribbean sales. In 1712 Governor Dudley of Massachusetts reported that seventy vessels per year were built in that province for sale in Britain *and* the West Indies.[11] If the 110 ton average held, that would mean sales of 7,700 tons annually. Those sold in the West Indies were, however, undoubtedly of lesser tonnage than those sold in Britain. Massachusetts was not alone in this traffic. Three Virginians wrote in 1697 that their province "abounds also in Pitch, Tar, Rosin, Masts, and all Timbers for Shipping, which the *Bristol* Men being sensible of, make use of the Opportunity to build Ships there at very easy Rates."[12] This report of Bristol's pioneering role in the building of vessels in the colonies for the Chesapeake trade is confirmed in an account of 53 American-built ships (6,748 tons) carrying tobacco from Virginia to England, 1699-1702: almost half or 24 (3,127 tons) were owned in Bristol. Seven (980 tons) were owned in London and the rest scattered among a dozen or more ports. The account also reveals that while the 30 Virginia built ships averaged 147 registered tons, the 15 from New England averaged only 70 tons.[13] There was obviously much going on in the shipbuilding world of America at the beginning of the eighteenth century outside of, as well as in, New England.

The only contemporary author who discussed the whole question of colonial shipping sales to Britain is the unjustly neglected Alexander Clunie, a merchant with thirty years' experience who had visited almost all the North American colonies. In 1769 he published his description of the immediately preceding years.[14] According to Clunie, colonial shipping sales to Britain in an average year ca. 1763-1768 were:

---

[10] Based on 128 vessels carrying tobacco from Virginia to Britain in 1771; London, Public Record Office (henceforth PRO), C.O.5/1349, 1350.

[11] Bernard and Lotte Bailyn, *Massachusetts Shipping 1696-1714: A Statistical Study* (Cambridge, Mass., 1959), p. 53; Shepherd and Walton, *Shipping*, p. 241.

[12] Henry Hartwell, James Blair and Edward Chilton, *The Present State of Virginia and the College*, H. D. Farish, ed. (Williamsburg, Va., 1940), p. 6.

[13] Louis des Cognets, Jr., *English Duplicates of Lost Virginia Records* (Princeton, 1958), pp. 278-99. Although this is a nonprofessional publication, a check against the originals in PRO, C.O.5 shows it to be accurate, if not complete.

[14] [Alexander Cluny or Clunie], *The American Traveller: or, Observations on the Present State, Culture, and Commerce of the British Colonies in America* (London, 1769), pp. 8, 60-1, 75, 79, 82, 94.

New England	70 vessels	@ £700	£49,000
New York	20	@ 700	14,000
Pennsylvania	25	@ 700	17,500
Virginia and Maryland	30	@ 1,000	30,000
South Carolina	10	@ 600	6,000
[TOTAL	155	@ 751:12s.	116,500]

Clunie's figures were shortly afterwards reprinted by the anonymous author of *American Husbandry*,[15] and though that does not give them any additional guarantee of reliability, there is nothing about the figures themselves to arouse suspicion. The numbers are not unreasonable but may be a bit on the high side. If Massachusetts alone was selling 70 vessels to Britain and the West Indies in 1712, it is not impossible that all New England might have been selling 70 vessels to Britain alone in the 1760's. The value figures also seem reasonable (and considerably below the figure I rather rashly suggested in 1964). It is not clear, though, whether Cluny's sale price includes sails, rigging, ironwork, and so forth. According to William Douglass, writing ca. 1750, about one-third of the cost of a New England built vessel "fitted to sea" represented iron, cordage, sailcloth and small stores imported from Britain.[16] It is not clear, either, whether Cluny's values are costs in America or sale prices in Britain. In between lay the margin of profit. New England ships appear to have been built commonly on order from Britain, while those from the Chesapeake appear more frequently to have been constructed by local adventurers. When such ships were sent to Britain for speculative sale, there could in a good year be a profit of as much as £500 on a single vessel.[17] My own suspicion is that Cluny's prices are costs in America for ships built on British order rather than sale prices in Britain.

We can supplement these figures and those of Lord Sheffield by turning to George Chalmers, who had been a lawyer in Maryland before the Revolutionary War and returned to Britain to become a senior clerk at the Board of Trade.[18] Chalmers published an account

---

[15] Henry J. Carman, ed., *American Husbandry*, Columbia University Studies in the History of American Agriculture, 6 (New York, 1939), pp. 44, 91, 129, 182, 312.

[16] William Douglass, *A Summary, Historical and Political, of the First Planting, Progressive Improvements, and Present State of the British Settlements in North America*, 2 vols. (London, 1760), 2: 68.

[17] Jacob M. Price, "Joshua Johnson in London, 1771-1775," in Anne Whiteman et al., *Statesmen, Scholars and Merchants: Essays in Eighteenth-Century History Presented to Dame Lucy Sutherland* (Oxford, 1973), p. 169.

[18] John Baker Holroyd, 1st earl of Sheffield, *Observations on the Commerce of the American States*, 6th ed. (London, 1784), p. 96.

of all ships constructed and registered in the continental colonies, Bahamas, and Bermuda from 1768 to 1773 (Table 2).[19] Since Chalmers worked at the Board of Trade, he had access to the best available official data.

TABLE 2
AN ACCOUNT OF ALL SUCH VESSELS AS WERE
BUILT AND *REGISTERED* IN THE CONTINENTAL COLONIES,
WITH THE ISLANDS OF BAHAMAS AND BERMUDAS,
DURING SIX YEARS, DISTINGUISHING EACH YEAR, AND THE
TOP-SAIL VESSELS FROM THE SLOOPS AND SCHOONERS

When Registered	Topsails		Sloops & Schooners		Total	
	Nbr	Tonnage	Nbr	Tonnage	Nbr	Tonnage
1768	157	19,098	329	10,354	486	29,452
1769	114	11,247	336	10,213	450	21,460
1770	130	11,126	385	12,982	515	24,198
1771	131	14,695	347	10,580	478	25,275
1772	184	19,854	373	12,569	557	32,423
1773	212	24,500	426	13,529	638	38,029
Total	928	100,610	2,196	70,227	3,124	170,837
Average	115	16,768	366	11,705	520	28,473
Average (measured tons)	—	25,152	—	17,557	—	42,709

Source: George Chalmers, *Opinions on Interesting Subjects . . . arising from American Independence* (London, 1784), p. 105.

Chalmers' figures are most interesting. They show that the three years analyzed by the pessimistic Lord Sheffield were years of relative depression in the colonial shipbuilding industry. In these three years (1769-1771), shipbuilding in the area covered by Chalmers' data averaged only 23,644 tons per annum compared with 29,452 for 1768, and 35,226 for 1772-1773, or 28,473 for the whole six years, 1768-1773. This means that the figure of £175,000 given by Shepherd and Walton for the annual value of colonial shipbuilding may be significantly understated. If we can assume that shipbuilding in the Thirteen Colonies remained a constant proportion of shipbuilding in the slightly larger North American area reported on by Chalmers, then we can calculate (from the base provided by Shepherd and Walton) the annual value of ship construction in the Thirteen Colonies in the following periods:

[19] George Chalmers, *Opinions on Interesting Subjects . . . Arising from American Independence* (London, 1784), p. 105.

1768   £220,282
1769-1771 176,842 (rounded by them to £175,000)
1772-1773 263,468
1768-1773 212,960

These higher values would readily permit exports in the vicinity of £100,000, and, as we shall see, even make it possible to conceive of exports considerably above that figure.

Chalmers was not the only commoner to enter the great debate that Lord Sheffield opened on "the economic consequences of the peace." Nor were his official registration figures the only ones available on shipbuilding. The Society of Underwriters at Lloyd's compiled data on all insured vessels and printed them in their *Register*. From ca. 1760, the society published these *Registers* about once every two or three years. That for 1774, for example, appears to have covered 1772-1774, and that for 1776 covered 1775 and 1776. (Later the *Register* appeared annually.) Members were required to hand in their old *Registers* for destruction before receiving their new ones. It should not have been too difficult, however, for a well connected person to gain access to the file of *Registers* at the society, or to have a clerk employed there extract some data for him.[20] At least three publicists of the period appear to have done so.

The first of these was James Allen, secretary of the Committee of West India Planters and Merchants of London, whose work was published by the authority of the Committee. Since some underwriters at Lloyd's were also West India merchants, Allen should have been able to gain access to the Society's back-files of *Registers*. He clearly indicates that his information came from the 1772-1774 edition of *Lloyd's Register*, corrected into the early months of 1775. Drawing upon this source, Allen reported that some 37.16 percent of the empire-built shipping inspected for Lloyd's as of 1775 was built in "America":[21]

British built	3,908 vessels	(605,645 tons)
American built	2,311 vessels	(373,618 tons)
TOTAL	6,219 vessels	(979,263 tons)

The same figures are given in the previously mentioned work of

[20] *Annals of Lloyd's Register, being a Sketch of the Origin, Constitution and Progress of Lloyd's Register of British and Foreign Shipping* (London, 1884), pp. 3-10.
[21] James Allen, *Considerations on the Present State of the Intercourse Between His Majesty's Sugar Colonies and the Dominions of the United States of America* (London, 1784), pp. 52-3.

714

George Chalmers, who acknowledged getting them from Allen's work.[22]

Slightly different data are given in another contemporary tract by Richard Champion, former merchant and chinaware manufacturer of Bristol and briefly deputy paymaster-general. Champion reports 2,342 American-built vessels (30.4 percent) out of a total prewar British (that is, Lloyd's) merchant fleet of 7,694.[23] Although Davis[24] felt that Champion got his information somewhere other than Lloyd's, Champion explains in the introduction to the second edition of his work that his data came from the 1775-1776 edition of the *Register*. Champion's figures differ from those of Allen and Chalmers because he used the 1775-1776 edition of the *Register*[25] rather than that for 1772-1774 and because he included foreign-built ships in his summary of the place of construction of the vessels known to Lloyd's:[26]

	Vessels
North of England and Scotland	2,419
South of England [and Wales?]	1,311
Ireland	199
Loyal American Colonies	163
Thirteen Colonies (U.S.A.)	2,342
	6,434
Foreign Countries	1,260
Total Known to Lloyd's	7,694

Champion further pointed out that since the books were revised weekly, it was unlikely that any two computations from them would be exactly the same.[27]

Fortunately, we do not have to depend entirely on Allen's or Champion's arithmetic. In 1963, the Gregg Press Ltd. brought out a photo-offset edition of surviving copies of *Lloyd's Register*, and Joseph A. Goldenberg has recently published an analysis of the data in the

---

[22] Chalmers, *Opinions on . . . American Independence*, pp. 97-99.

[23] Richard Champion, *Considerations on the Present Situation of Great Britain and the United States of North America* (London, 1784), p. 14; 2nd ed. (London, 1784), p. 21.

[24] Davis, *English Shipping*, p. 68.

[25] Champion, *Considerations*, 2nd ed., pp. v, viii-x, and n.

[26] As in n. 23.

[27] Champion, *Considerations*, 2nd ed., p. xn. If we recalculate Champion's data in the way Allen's were presumably calculated, we get a total of 3,929 British and Irish vessels (compared with Allen's 3,908) or 61 percent, and 2,505 "American" (compared with Allen's 2,311), or 39 percent. We cannot, however, be sure that Allen included those built in the loyal colonies in his "American" total.

1775-1776 number of the *Register*. (That for 1772-1774 has not survived.) Goldenberg obtains figures slightly smaller than Champion's, but they show the same proportions. According to Goldenberg, the mercantile marine known to Lloyd's at the beginning of 1776 consisted of:[28]

British Built	3,464 vessels (49.2%)	561,563 tons (49.6%)
Br. American Built	2,246 vessels (31.9%)	361,435 tons (31.9%)
Foreign & Irish	1,333 vessels (18.9%)	209,519 tons (18.5%)
TOTAL	7,043 vessels	1,132,517 tons

The difference between the American percentage shown here (31.9%) and that given by Allen and Chalmers can be traced primarily to the omission of the foreign built by the latter authors. The difference in percentage between Goldenberg and Champion (30.4%) is almost trivial but is still surprising, considering that both used the 1775-1776 edition of the *Register*. The explanation is that Goldenberg used the surviving copy reproduced in the Gregg edition, which has three pages (75 ships) missing and few corrections beyond the early months of 1776. In addition, Goldenberg excluded all ships built in the fragment of 1776 covered by the *Register* as well as twenty vessels for which he had insufficient geographic information. By contrast, Champion used the official copy at Lloyd's, which was brought up-to-date weekly until the next edition came out in 1778. Furthermore, Goldenberg eliminated double entries, something which Champion may not have done. Thus, Champion's total (7,694 vessels) is significantly larger than Goldenberg's (7,043 vessels).

Goldenberg has further analyzed the 2,246 ships he shows built in the American colonies (Table 3): of them, 1,697 vessels (284,925 tons) definitely came from the Thirteen Colonies; while 383 others (56,100 tons) were shown as coming only from "America," they almost certainly were built in the Thirteen Colonies also. (The term America then did not in ordinary speech apply to the West Indies and rarely applied to Canada.) Together, they add up to 2,080 vessels (341,025 tons).

For our purposes the immediate problem presented by Goldenberg's data is that of estimating the proportion of the American-built ships in *Lloyd's Register* that had in fact been sold to persons resident outside the Thirteen Colonies. It was after all possible for colonials to build and own a ship even though it was inspected for Lloyd's when it

[28] Joseph A. Goldenberg, "An Analysis of Shipbuilding Sites in Lloyd's Register of 1776," *Mariner's Mirror*, 59 (1973), pp. 419-36. Cf. 422-23 for coverage.

TABLE 3
SHIPS BUILT IN AMERICA IN *LLOYD'S REGISTER* FOR 1775-1776

	Sloop	Schooner	Brig	Snow	Ship	Total
America	13 (975) 75.0	26 (1780) 68.5	219 (29095) 132.9	29 (4120) 142.1	96 (20130) 209.7	383 (56100) 146.5
Canada	7 (240) 34.3	8 (385) 48.1	70 (7550) 107.9	5 (870) 174.0	24 (5160) 215.0	114 (14205) 124.6
New England	25 (1910) 76.4	60 (4200) 70.0	503 (62335) 123.9	60 (8810) 146.8	378 (79482) 210.3	1026 (156737) 152.8
New York	9 (740) 82.2	4 (330) 82.5	42 (5770) 137.4	7 (1040) 148.6	50 (11775) 235.5	112 (19655) 175.5
Pennsylvania and New Jersey	2 (110) 55.0	1 (60) 60	50 (7080) 141.6	21 (3290) 156.7	132 (31125) 235.8	206 (41665) 202.3
Maryland and Virginia	3 (210) 70.0	14 (1110) 79.3	93 (12880) 138.5	29 (4480) 154.5	136 (33243) 244.4	275 (51923) 188.8
Carolinas and Georgia	—	2 (140) 70.0	33 (4370) 132.4	5 (650) 130.0	38 (9785) 257.5	78 (14945) 191.6
Bermuda	9 (735) 81.7	3 (260) 86.7	13 (1530) 117.7	3 (400) 133.3	9 (1720) 191.1	37 (4645) 125.5
West Indies	1 (70)	—	12 (1120) 93.3	1 (120)	1(250)	15 (1560) 104
Totals	69 (4990) 72.3	118 (8265) 70.0	1035 (131730) 127.3	160 (23780) 148.6	864 (192670) 223.0	2246 (361435) 160.9

Source: Joseph A. Goldenberg, "An Analysis of Shipbuilding Sites in Lloyd's Register of 1776," *Mariner's Mirror*, 59 (1973), p. 433.

visited British or Irish ports. I have examined all the North American-built ships under the sample letters A and N in *Lloyd's Register* for 1775-1776. Of these, 88 percent under A and 91 percent under N *appear* to have been sold to British or West Indian owners, but even with the use of directories, this work cannot be precise. For example, the firm of Wallace, Davidson & Johnson had partners in Maryland and London, while the firm of Eilbeck & Co. had partners in Virginia and Whitehaven—making classification very difficult. To be on the safe side, I concluded that only 85 percent of the ships in *Lloyd's Register* built in the Thirteen Colonies were definitely sold out of those colonies. This means that of Goldenberg's 2,080 vessels (341,025 tons) built in the Thirteen Colonies, we should assume that only 1,768 (289,871 tons) were so sold.

How do we convert this cumulative stock (1,768 vessels of 289,871 tons in 1775) into a figure for annual sale? Even in the eighteenth century, there was considerable difference of opinion about the longevity of colonial ships.[29] The ideal way of solving the problem is to take the total population of ships (for example, from *Lloyd's Register*) at two successive points in time, preferably only one year apart, and extract all vessels present in the earlier list which had dropped out of the later. With the date of construction known, it would be possible to calculate the age of one year's crop of terminated listings. This, however, is not possible because of the dozens of vessels with the same name, and the frequent change of name, ownership, and master which makes absolute identification impossible for a significant minority of our vessels. There are, however, other ways of calculating or estimating the longevity of ships.

Goldenberg tells us that over 90 percent of the colonial-built tonnage appearing in *Lloyd's Register* is accounted for by topsailed vessels (ships, snows, and brigs). It is probable that the bulk of colonial-built sloops and schooners were used only for the coastal and West Indies trades and were insured locally, if at all. By contrast, virtually all of colonial-built topsailed vessels must have visited British or Irish ports on occasion (if only because of the Navigation Acts) and thus have been known to *Lloyd's Register*, whether or not their owners chose to insure at Lloyd's. A combination of boldness and prudence suggests that we can use *Lloyd's Register* as a reliable record of topsailed vessels but not of sloops and schooners. Proceed-

[29] Cf. Marshall Smelser and William I. Davisson, "The Longevity of Colonial Ships," *American Neptune*, 33 (1973), pp. 16-19.

718

ing on this assumption, we can take the average number (Table 2) of topsailed craft built annually during 1768-1773 in British North America, the Bahamas, and Bermuda (155) and divide it into the total number of topsailed vessels built in the same area reported by Goldenberg (Table 3) as known to Lloyd's at the beginning of 1776 (2,059).[30] This yields the figure of 13.3 years for the life-expectancy of an average American-built topsailed ship ca. 1768-1776. Since topsailed vessels represented over 90 percent of the American-built tonnage in *Lloyd's Register*, we can safely apply this average lifespan to the whole American-built fleet known to Lloyd's.

Fortunately, this result is based upon the average figures for shipbuilding for six years, a fact that reduces the possibility of serious error. Since these six years lie rather close to the end of the period during which the ships covered by the 1776 list were being built, there is also a strong likelihood of downward bias (underrepresenting the average life of the vessels) if there was a marked tendency for shipbuilding to grow over time. Any such tendency was probably relatively modest, however, in the years 1763-1775. Cluny's figures suggest shipbuilding levels for pre-1768 that are very close to those we know about for 1768-1773 and there is other evidence that there was no distorting trend. A count of the year of construction of a sample of 500 American-built ships in *Lloyd's Register* for 1776 (ships whose names start with the letters A, F, N, and T) shows sharp annual fluctuations but no pronounced trend during 1764-1775: the number of listed ships built 1773-1775 is virtually the same as the listed number built 1764-1766. Only before 1764 do we find evidence of a probable upward trend. (The same inference can be drawn from the American data in Appendix II.)

The sample of 500 vessels gives us another tool for estimating the life-span of American-built vessels. The year of construction of these 500 ships indicates that they were an average of 8.4 years old in 1776. Assuming a static population model, this would suggest that the average lifespan of those vessels was 16.8 years. This figure (like the previous one) does not represent the physical duration of a vessel but merely its time on *Lloyd's Register*. Thus, a ship captured by the

---

[30] 1,035 brigs + 160 snows + 864 ships = 2,059. One could get even a shorter lifespan if one added 9.24 percent to Goldenberg's figures to bring them up to the level of Champion's, which are based on the same source. It could also be argued, however, that one should add something to the shipbuilding figures for 1768-1773 to reflect the higher level prevailing before 1768 suggested by Appendix 2. These two alterations would tend to cancel each other out. Neither correction would have the advantage of referring to top-sailed vessels only as do the data in the text.

Colonial Exports 719

French during the Seven Years' War would be as "dead" as any at the bottom of the ocean. These estimates—while certainly not perfect—suggest a possible range for a ship's effective life: that is, from 13.3 years by the first method to 16.8 by the second.

Before we can proceed to calculate the value of annual sales, however, we must settle two further problems involving tonnage and prices. Although Davis points out that in the course of the eighteenth century, the merchants' tons burthen came to approximate the ship-builders' measured tons, the actual tons registered were consistently less than the measured tons (primarily to save on tonnage duties).[31] McCusker and Walton have shown that in American ports registered tonnage fell consistently about one-third below measured, so that one must normally add fifty percent to registered to obtain measured tonnage.[32] Our basic tonnage is not registered tonnage, however, but is that appearing in *Lloyd's Register*. Neither the ship's owner nor the viewer for Lloyd's had any motive for underestimating the tonnage here. In a sample of 45 vessels in the Virginia trade in 1773-1775 which can be identified in both the Virginia naval officers' accounts and *Lloyd's Register* (1775-1776), it was found that the tonnages in the *Register* averaged 37.2 percent above those in the naval officers' accounts. It is thus only necessary to add 9.33 percent to the tonnages in the *Register* to bring them up to measured tonnage (150 percent of registered).[33]

Prices present a more difficult problem. Shepherd and Walton use some 1784 estimates given by Davis:[34]

Price of a ship of 200 tons (measure) per ton

London	£8:8s.	to	£9:9s.	(£8:18s.6d. mean)
Outports	7:5s.	to	8:8s.	(£7:16s.6d. mean)
New York, Philadelphia	6:8s.	to	7:19s.	(£7:3s.6d. mean)
New England	3:18s.	to	5:9s.	(£4:13s.6d. mean)

Shepherd and Walton assume that these prices are for a ship fully fitted out.[35] Other evidence indicates, however, that the English

---

[31] Davis, *English Shipping*, pp. 7n., 74. Cf. Allen, *Considerations*, pp. 52-53; Champion, *Considerations*, 1st ed., p. vi; 2nd ed., p. viii.

[32] Articles by McCusker and Walton in note 7. Chalmers suggested adding one-third (instead of one-half) to convert registered tonnage to measured. George Chalmers, *An Historical View of the Domestic Economy of Great Britain and Ireland*, new ed. (Edinburgh, 1812), p. xii; cf. also 1794 ed., p. cxxxvi.

[33] PRO, T.1/506, 512.

[34] Davis, *English Shipping*, p. 375.

[35] Shepherd and Walton, *Shipping*, p. 243.

prices can only refer to hulls, for fully fitted out vessels then cost ca. £12-14 per ton.[36] Since these are hull prices only, we must add 75 percent[37] to convert them into the prices of fully fitted-out vessels. But these are postwar prices, and all evidence suggests that prices were somewhat lower immediately before the war. In his second edition, Champion reports that before the war New Englanders could supply vessels fully fitted for sea at from six to seven guineas per ton (a minimum price that fits well with the £3:18s. shown above, plus 75 percent for fitting out); but Champion says that by 1784 the best that New Englanders could offer was £7:10s.[38] This implies that one should deduct 10 percent from postwar prices to get to the middle of the prewar range suggested by Champion or 15 percent to get to his prewar minimum. If we deduct 15 percent from Davis's 1784 prices to approximate prices of the prewar years, and then add 75 percent for fitting, we get the following prewar prices for American-built vessels fully fitted for sea:

New England	£6:19s.
Other Colonies	£10:13s.
Together	£8:16s.

These figures, though consistent with some of Champion's reports, are higher than any hitherto suggested in the literature. To avoid any unnecessary inflating of the results, I prefer not to use these indirectly deduced costs, but instead to use Champion's report of prewar New England costs for putting a vessel to sea (six to seven guineas) and John McCusker's recent account of similar costs at Philadelphia during 1765-1774 (£8:10s.),[39] which will serve for all other colonies.

[36] Davis (p. 378) gives the price of a sample prewar 250-ton ship in the Virginia trade, fully fitted out, as £11:8s. per ton. Two contemporary (postwar) writers estimate costs of fully fitted out vessels at £13 per ton: William Hutchinson, *The History of the County of Cumberland*, 2 vols. (Carlisle, 1794), 2:49; Champion, *Considerations*, 1st ed., p. 21; 2d ed., pp. 28-29. Hyde reports that the Liverpool firm of Fisher and Grayson's "ship books" show the average cost of ships built in the 1740's at £8 per ton for the hull and £6 for fitting out, totalling £14. Francis E. Hyde, *Liverpool and the Mersey: an Economic History of a Port 1700-1970* (Newton Abbott, 1971), pp. 14-15.

[37] Proportions suggested both by Hyde (*Liverpool and the Mersey*, pp. 14-15) and Davis (*Shipping Industry*, p. 378). Even higher proportional additions for fitting out are suggested by John J. McCusker, "Sources of Investment Capital in the Colonial Philadelphia Shipping Industry," JOURNAL OF ECONOMIC HISTORY, 32 (March 1972), 150.

[38] Champion, *Considerations*, 2nd ed., pp. 74, 196n.

[39] McCusker, "Sources of Investment," p. 150. McCusker's Philadelphia figure refers only to topsailed vessels (over 90 percent of the American total shown in *Lloyd's Register*) and could be reduced slightly to allow for the small fraction of sloops and schooners sold. It could, however, also be raised to allow for the more expensive vessels built to the southward, particularly in South Carolina. These two possible corrections would tend to cancel each other out. The price figure used is on the conservative or low side.

McCusker's figure falls almost exactly in the middle of the range suggested by Champion (seven to ten guineas). The resulting figure for New England (£6:16s.:6d.) is only 1s:6d. below that derived (above) from Davis's information, but for the other colonies, this calculation yields a more significant reduction in the estimate.

We can now calculate the value of annual foreign sales of ships built in the Thirteen Colonies (Table 4). Taking the totals for the Thirteen Colonies shown on *Lloyd's Register* as calculated by Goldenberg (Table 3), we prorate the tonnage designated only "America" among the Thirteen Colonies and add 9.33 percent to convert Lloyd's to measured tonnage (see line 1 of Table 4). We then multiply this

TABLE 4
ESTIMATES OF EXPORT SALES OF SHIPPING BUILT IN
THE THIRTEEN COLONIES AND APPEARING IN
LLOYD'S REGISTER (1776)

	New England	*Other Colonies*	*Total*
(1) 1776 measured tonnage	205,101	167,742	372,843
(2) × price (per ton)	£6:16:6	£8:10	
(3) gross cost	£1,399,814	£1,425,807	£2,825,621
(4) 85% sold	1,189,842	1,211,936	2,401,778
(5) annual sale: ÷ 13.3	89,462	91,123	180,585
(6) annual sale: ÷ 16.8	70,824	72,139	142,963
(7) annual sale: ÷ 20	59,492	60,597	120,089

estimate by the prewar prices (line 2) to obtain the historic gross cost of the American-built shipping known to Lloyd's (line 3). Since we have estimated above that perhaps 10 to 15 percent of the tonnage shown in the *Register* was still owned in the Thirteen Colonies, we must multiply by .85 (line 4). To convert this into the value of annual sales, we divide by the estimated duration of the vessels in *Lloyd's Register* (that is, before breaking up, sinking, transfer to trades not touching at British or Irish ports, or capture by the enemy). If we assume this to be 13.3 years, we obtain (line 5) an estimated annual sale of £180,585 sterling. If, however, we assume it to have been 16.8 years, we have (line 6) an annual sale of £142,963. It could be argued that both these estimates of ship's life are too low because they were calculated on the assumption of a static population and that even though shipping sales were at something of a plateau during 1764-1775, they most likely were rising earlier. I have, therefore, divided by twenty years for the average ship's life on the *Register* (surely the most extreme duration imaginable) to obtain (line 7) an average annual sale of £120,089.

722

Thus, instead of the range £46,000-105,000 suggested by Walton and Shepherd for the value of colonial shipping sales, we now have an estimate of £120-180,000, with a figure in the vicinity of £140,000 appealing most strongly to the present writer. The £140,000 estimate is distinctly on the conservative side. It makes no allowance for the value of North American smaller vessels (sloops and schooners) sold in the West Indies unless they visited British or Irish ports and were inspected for Lloyd's. Nor does it make any allowance for colonial-built vessels sold in Spain or Portugal or sold in London to non-British owners who employed them in trade that fell outside the network of Lloyd's inspectors.

Finally, let us return to the broader picture. If we take the average ship production of the British North American and West Indian colonies, 1768-1773 (Table 2) and multiply by £7:13s. or £7.65 (a rough average between the £6:16s.6d. used for the New England construction and the £8:10s. used for the other colonies), we obtain an average colonial ship production in these years of £326,724 sterling. Of this, 93.5 percent (derived from Table 1), that is 39,933 tons or £305,487 were produced in the future United States. Such a figure would allow ample room for foreign sales of £140,000 or even £180,000 and still leave a healthy margin for colonial use. If some official British figures underrepresent colonial shipbuilding, as Appendix II suggests, then the tolerance and margin would be even greater.

In short, if I were writing a paragraph in a textbook, I would say that ca. 1763-1775 shipbuilding in the Thirteen Colonies totalled about 40,000 measured tons annually and was worth about £300,000 sterling, of which at least 18,600 tons worth £140,000 were sold abroad. Given these estimates, American colonial shipbuilding, a neglected industry, does appear to have made a significant contribution to late colonial export earnings. Others, I hope, will investigate the question more fully and perhaps suggest other conclusions based on more extensive research and more sophisticated reasoning. Work is needed in particular on shipbuilding costs in the Thirteen Colonies and on the marketing arrangements for the export sale of colonial shipping. Until this work is done, the author of this paper hopes that he has at least suggested the likely proportions of the problem.

THE WORKING OF *LLOYD'S REGISTER*

To guard against imposition in insurances, a society of merchants and underwriters [i.e., the Society at Lloyd's Coffeehouse] have established surveyors at all the principal ports of the kingdom, who make weekly returns of every ship employed in foreign trade that enters the port; but take no cognizance of the coasting trade, upon which fewer insurances are made. Those returns state her name, tonnage and age, where built, who are the owners, her draft of water, her usual trade, and their opinion of her quality, both as to the hull and the rigging and outfit; and all these returns are posted weekly into books for the use of the subscribers. In the year 1775, the surveying ports were *London, Bristol, Liverpool, Lancaster, Whitehaven, Workington, Maryport, Leith, Tinmouth* [Teignmouth], *Hull, Whitby, Lynn, Yarmouth, Portsmouth, Cowes, Pool*[e], *Topsham, Exeter, Dartmouth, Biddeford, Barnstaple, Appledore, Dublin, Corke, Belfast, Newry,* and *Waterford;* . . .

—James Allen, *Considerations on the Present State of the Intercourse between His Majesty's Sugar Colonies and the . . . United States of America* (1784), 52-53.

IV

724

APPENDIX II
OTHER ACCOUNTS OF COLONIAL SHIPBUILDING, 1746-1775

	Virginia	Maryland	Pennsylvania
1746	—[a]	1	29 (1341 t.)
1747	—	2	28 (1404 t.)
1748	—	—	51 (3225 t.)
1749	—	3	30 (1749 t.)
1750	—	7	50 (2957 t.)
1751	—	6	43 (2264 t.)
1752	—	5	47 (2454 t.)
1753	—	9	27 (1630 t.)
1754	—	9	28 (1814 t.)
1755	—	10	24 (1275 t.)
1756	—	8	41 (1539 t.)
1757	—	11	24 (1706 t.)
1758	—	9	22 (1490 t.)
1759	—	21	33 (1831 t.)
1760	—	15	44 (2711 t.)
1761	—	18	36 (2187 t.)
1762	—	24	—
1763	31 (2785 t.)	27	—
1764	39 (2852 t.)	16	—
1765	47 (3880 t.)	18	45 (2554 t.)
1766	37 (3515 t.)	12	30 (1911 t.)
1767	33 (2474 t.)	22	27 (2025 t.)
1768	27 (2280 t.)	14	27 (1364 t.)
1769	26 (1480 t.)	19	31 (1775 t.)
1770	20 (1050 t.)	20	26 (2212 t.)
1771	37 (2454 t.)	21	30 (2233 t.)
1772	26 (1419 t.)	7	25 (2484 t.)
1773	30 (1797 t.)	20	40 (3645 t.)
1774	7 (475 t.)?	16	33 (3637 t.)
1775	—	7	25 (2985 t.)

[a] — means there is no data.

The above data may usefully be compared with the "official" accounts from Sheffield given in Table 1:

	Virginia	Maryland	Pennsylvania
1769-71 (above)	83 (4984)	60	87 (6220)
1769-71 (Sheffield)	67 (4052)	55	69 (5130)

The comparison seems to suggest that there may have been some basis for the charge made by Champion that the "official" statistics on American shipbuilding used by Lord Sheffield were incomplete. This is also suggested by a comparison of Sheffield's totals with those given by Chalmers in Table 2.

Source: William L. Kelso, "Shipbuilding in Virginia, 1763-1774," *Records of the Columbia Historical Society* (1971-72), 1-13; Paul H. Giddens, "Trade and Industry in Colonial Maryland, 1753-1769," *Journal of Economic and Business History*, 4 (1932), 535; Simeon J. Crowther, "The Shipbuilding Output of the Delaware Valley 1722-1776," *Proceedings of the American Philosophical Society*, 117 (1973), 93, with figures for West Jersey as well.

V

Credit in the slave trade and plantation economies

INTRODUCTION

A few years ago, I was invited to prepare for this conference a paper on credit in the slave trade. Over the years, I had accumulated some scraps of data on this topic, as well as bibliographic references to the vast and ever-growing library of scholarly books on slavery. After accepting this deceptively easy assignment, I proceeded through a very long shelf of publications on the slave trade – including many by those here today – only to discover that most of these erudite works had relatively little to say about credit. Thus, of necessity, this chapter is not a rich synthesis of existing scholarship but an exploratory essay suggesting some questions and answers hinted at by our still scrappy evidence.

We can perhaps usefully start with a generalized if simplified way of thinking about the problem of credit in the slave trade and slave economies. In the seventeenth and eighteenth centuries the dynamic areas of the slave economies, the principal destinations of the slave trade, were in most cases what can be described from a European perspective as initially frontier areas, underpopulated territories of new settlement. In such areas, land is characteristically abundant and cheap, whereas capital and labor are scarce and, by European standards, expensive. Such almost valueless land can be made productive and valuable – a process succinctly expressed is the French phrase *mettre en valeur* – only by the application of capital and labor. In those centuries, capital was generally slightly more mobile than labor. Thus, in such frontier areas with almost free land but a constraining shortage of labor, the successful entrepreneurial settler was likely to be one who could scrape together some capital to be used to obtain labor through the purchase of either indentured servants or slaves. In tropical and other areas unattractive to indentured servants, this usually meant slaves. A poor settler might acquire an indentured servant with the product of as little as one year of his own labor, but the product of several years' labor by a settler, servant, or slave would be needed to buy a slave. Thus the process of building up a labor force by reinvesting the yields of the labor of existing servants and slaves could be very slow. The prospects for the entrepreneurial agricultural settler with little capital were therefore not too attractive.

However, where credit was available, the linked processes of labor acquisition, capital investment, and land improvement could be speeded up significantly. Slaves bought on credit could not only pay for themselves but, provided that they lived long enough, by their labor could soon provide the wherewithal to purchase other slaves. Credit did not so much change the fundamental character of slave cultivation as accelerate the processes of initiation and expansion of slave systems.

Popular mythology associates credit and debt with the needs of the less advantaged competitors in the market. But in the early modern plantation world, credit was unlikely to benefit equally all would-be slave owners, least of all the poorest. Those in a position to lend money or sell on credit normally preferred to minimize their risks. Larger planters with more improved land, capital equipment, and bound labor should have appeared better risks for credit than their smaller competitors or beginners just starting out. Thus the readier availability of credit to the creditworthy should have tended to favor the growth of larger productive units and of social systems dominated by larger planters. Of course, these larger planters did not always have to buy on credit. But, for most of them, to buy four slaves on credit rather than one for cash appeared a rational and not unduly risky investment decision.

Cash, it should be remembered, did not necessarily mean coin. Most often, "cash purchases" were in fact paid for in colonial commodities or in bills of exchange. The bill, in turn, might be drawn against a credit balance of the planter with a metropolitan merchant but, more likely, was a claim against the anticipated value of commodities shipped to market but not yet sold or even landed when the bill was drawn. Only rarely was the bill a pure credit instrument drawn against nothing but the good will of the metropolitan merchant; such bills were more often returned unaccepted. Although any thrifty planter could expect some day to be able to buy a slave with the produce of his land, only the more substantial planter was likely to have a metropolitan correspondent who would accept and pay his bills of exchange. Thus, in cash as much as in credit purchases, the trading system favored the larger over the smaller planter.

Few areas remained frontiers indefinitely. But, on the terra firma of North or South America, as zones of initial settlement filled up, inland areas still worth settling retained the frontier characteristics of cheap land, scarce capital, and dear labor. If slavery was a viable option in such new frontier zones, then credit there too served to speed up both settlement and the development of slave plantation cultures. By contrast, in Barbados and other smaller islands, cheap land and underdevelopment very soon disappeared and with them the ostensible need for development credit. However, the slave populations in those islands did not reproduce themselves, and the importation of replacement slaves remained necessary down to the end of the slave trade. A well-managed plantation could perhaps be expected to finance the purchase of replacement slaves out of current earnings. But all plantations were not well managed in this sense, and so credit on slave purchases remained extremely useful to large and small planters down to the end of slavery.

Credit for slave purchases was not uniformly available over time. It was a market phenomenon whose availability and terms were governed by supply and demand conditions both in the slave trade and in the trade in the products produced by the slaves. When the prices of a slave-grown commodity (sugar, tobacco, coffee, indigo, rice, etc.) were high and the planters "in funds," then demand for slaves would be keen, resulting in higher prices and shorter credits. When those same commodity prices fell, planter demand for additional slaves would slacken and slave sellers would have to offer lower prices and easier credit terms, that is, longer delays before payment. Similarly, when the supply of slave imports was reduced, particularly by war, sellers could insist on higher prices and shorter credits. When, however, several consecutive years of peace facilitated cumulatively large slave imports in any particular area, the market might well become glutted and sellers who did not want to look elsewhere would have to offer lower prices and easier credit terms.

The length of credit offered to slave buyers was a significant cost and potential restriction of activity for those engaged in the slave trade. Where slaves could be sold for cash, commodities, or short-term bills of exchange, the venturers in that trade could expect to realize the returns for their venture in perhaps fifteen or eighteen months. Counting on this, they could move without too much imprudence from one year's ventures to the next. However, when slaves were sold on what amounted to two or three years' or longer credit, the turnover of risk capital was much slower. With much of their capital tied up in debts owed in remote plantation colonies, the slave traders had to plan on higher interest payments over time for the sums they may have borrowed, as well as on a more encumbered financial position that could make their dealings with their own suppliers and other creditors more difficult and probably more costly. As we shall see later, a strong preference for liquidity forced English slave traders in particular into rather complex and costly institutional experiments.

Although many of the conventions of purely mercantile credit appear to have been rendered relatively homogeneous across state boundaries by the "custom of merchants," the same does not appear equally true for credit arrangements that touch on the laws of landed and other property. Though no legal historian, I have tried in my reading to sort out the ways in which different legal systems facilitated or hindered the use of credit in slave sales. It may be useful to distinguish between two models describing the effect of the law on credit. In what I shall call the "Latin model," the law in the situations observed protected the integrity of the plantation as a working unit. Creditors could seize crops but could not use the courts to seize nonlanded accoutrements of the plantation or sugar mill – such as agricultural equipment, livestock, or slaves – and thus diminish its productive capacity. Opposed to this was an Anglo-Saxon or "creditor defense model." Where it prevailed, efforts by colonial legislatures to protect the productive integrity of the plantation were usually thwarted by the central or metropolitan government, which preferred to protect the interests of the creditor or credit seller.

Not all credit or debt was equally necessary to develop or maintain the productive capacity of a plantation. To clarify this distinction in a plantation economy, we may usefully distinguish between what I shall term "primary," "secondary," and "tertiary" credit or debt. "Primary" credit/debt refers to obligations incurred by the plantation to obtain replacement or additional labor, livestock, or tools and machinery absolutely necessary for its ongoing or expanding operations. "Secondary" credit/debt refers to the heavy obligations incurred, usually under a mortgage, when a plantation was sold by one owner to another. Such credit neither added to nor sustained the productive capacity of the plantation, but its availability undoubtedly encouraged investment in plantations. (An intelligent entrepreneur investing in the development of a plantation would take into consideration the degree to which the availability of mortgages would facilitate or enable him to sell out advantageously if and when he chose to do so.) "Tertiary" credit/debt refers to all other burdens assumed by the proprietors unrelated to either the ownership or productive capacity of the plantation (e.g., borrowing for dowries, family settlements, residential building, or luxury consumption).

BRAZILIAN ANTECEDENTS

In the main part of this chapter, I concentrate on the English and French colonies in the seventeenth and eighteenth centuries. It is useful, however, to start with a few remarks on Brazil, the first exemplar and seedbed in the Americas of the slave sugar system later transplanted to the British, French, Dutch, and Spanish colonies. When the Dutch invaded northeastern Brazil in the 1620s, they found in the areas they occupied a significant population of Portuguese planters using slave labor to produce sugar for export sale. This was the most productive sector of the local economy but depended on the continuing importation of slaves not just to expand but merely to sustain production, for there was a constant loss of slave labor through death and flight into the interior. Thus, the Dutch West India Company, after establishing itself in Brazil, was also obliged to seize many of the Portuguese stations on the Guinea and Angola coasts and enter into the slave trade systematically. Almost at once, the company found that the Brazilian planters were keen to acquire its slave imports but could do so in numbers only if assisted by credit such as they had received from their previous Portuguese suppliers. The Dutch company (and probably independent merchants as well) obliged with easy terms, and soon the Brazilian planters were reported to be heavily in debt to their slave suppliers. With earnings cut by bad weather and poor crops, the situation soon became so difficult that the Dutch West India Company in 1644 ordered its agents to cease slave sales on credit. The next year, 1645, the Brazilians rose in revolt against the Dutch. At least one contemporary Dutch observer thought that it was the desire to escape from the burden of debt that persuaded many Portuguese Brazilian planters to join the revolt. By 1654 the Dutch empire in Brazil was gone.[1]

With the departure of the Dutch, the Portuguese Brazilian sugar industry entered upon a half-century of only modest growth (down to ca. 1710) and of stagnation and decline thereafter. Much of the difficulty arose from the combination of stagnant or declining prices

[1] C. R. Boxer, *The Dutch in Brazil 1624–1654* (Oxford, 1957), pp. 81–4, 106–7, 138–9, 144, 164, 173; Ernst van den Boogaart and Peter C. Emmer, "The Dutch Participation in the Atlantic Slave Trade, 1596–1650," in Henry A. Gemery and Jan S. Hogendorn (eds.), *The Uncommon Market: Essays in the Economic History of the Atlantic Slave Trade* (New York, 1979), pp. 353–75, esp. pp. 358, 369–70.

for sugar and steadily rising prices for slaves, both ascribable in part to the development of slave sugar cultivation elsewhere in the Americas. Although the institutions of the Brazilian sugar industry are not within the scope of this chapter, I should like to emphasize one feature of those institutions noted in the recent work of Stuart Schwartz. As is well known, colonial Brazilian sugar production was characterized by the interdependence of the larger, heavily capitalized plantation with substantial investment in a sugar mill (*engenho*), slaves, and livestock and the smaller, dependent nearby plantations of the *lavradores* who did not have their own mills. The money for setting up a mill or *engenho* was frequently borrowed on mortgage from ecclesiastical and other lenders. For slaves, however, the owners of both the mills and lesser plantations were dependent on local merchants who conducted a largely bilateral slave trade with the Gulf of Guinea and Angola. The slaves were apparently sold to planters and mill owners on relatively short credit. Should the debtor not pay in time and the merchant attempt to recover what was owed him by seizing slaves or livestock, such action could interrupt the complex operation of the mill and the dependent plantations. To prevent this, the Portuguese authorities fairly early recognized what was termed earlier the Latin principle of the integrity of the plantation. A law of 1663 (frequently renewed) prohibited the "piecemeal attachment of parts of an *engenho*." Action could be taken only against the entire mill-plantation, and then only when the debt was roughly equal to the value of the whole. Otherwise, only the income (crops), and not the capital stock, could be attached. This protection was extended in 1723 to the holdings of the *lavrador* as well. As total Brazilian slave imports remained high throughout the eighteenth century, we can only speculate on the degree to which these restrictions on the rights of creditors may have diverted slave imports away from sugar toward other, less protected sectors of the Brazilian economy, particularly mining.[2]

THE ENGLISH COLONIES AND MONOPOLY

The Portuguese Brazilian planter revolt of 1645 led to the almost immediate suspension of Dutch slave sales in Brazil but not to the end of the Dutch slave trade. Almost at once the Dutch redirected part of their slave shipments toward the English colony of Barbados,

---

[2] Stuart B. Schwartz, *Sugar Plantations in the Formation of Brazilian Society: Bahia, 1550–1835* (Cambridge Latin American Studies, Vol. 52) (Cambridge, 1985), pp. 168, 186, 190, 192, 195–6, 204–12, 343; Philip D. Curtin, *The Atlantic Slave Trade: A Census* (Madison, Wis., 1969), pp. 207, 216.

where some Dutchmen had already been active in the introduction of Brazilian methods of sugar refining.[3] The Dutch traders helped develop this market, as Dalby Thomas pointed out, by giving "credit to those islanders, as well as they did to the Portugalls in Brasile, for black slaves, and all other necessaries for planting, taking as their crops throve, the sugar they made." But, as another contemporary pointed out, Dutch credit for slaves and the equipment of the sugar mill was restricted to the "most sober [i.e., substantial] inhabitants." These mandates of prudent credit help explain the emergence of the large sugar planters as the dominant social element in Barbados. The inability of the less "sober" inhabitants to get equivalent credit contributed to their decline in sugar-producing areas.[4]

After the restoration of Charles II in 1660, the implementation of the acts of trade and navigation eliminated the Dutch as suppliers of slaves to the English colonies. Their place was taken during 1660–72 by the monopoly Company of Royal Adventurers of England Trading into Africa and after 1672 by its successor, the Royal African Company. Almost from the start, the Royal Adventurers found that it could not supply as many slaves as the West Indian colonists wanted and was forced to license some "private traders" to supplement the flow. The Royal African Company had better luck defending its monopoly down at least to 1688, but thereafter lacked the effective legal powers to enforce its claims on the high seas. Thus, from 1689 the company had to share its trade with "interlopers" whose position was legalized from 1698 subject to the payment to the company of a 10% toll on goods exported to Africa. By the late 1720s the interlopers had in effect taken over the trade, though the Royal African Company wasn't formally wound up until 1750–2.[5] In his discussion of the failure of the company, David Galenson emphasizes its inability –

---

[3] For the Dutch role in the introduction of sugar cultivation in Barbados, see Richard S. Dunn, *Sugar and Slaves: The Rise of the Planter Class in the English West Indies, 1624–1713* (Chapel Hill, N.C., 1972), pp. 60–6.

[4] David Watts, *The West Indies: Patterns of Development, Culture and Environmental Change since 1492* (Cambridge Studies in Historical Geography, Vol. 8) (Cambridge, 1987), p. 188; William A. Green, "Supply versus Demand in the Barbadian Sugar Revolution," *Journal of Interdisciplinary History*, Vol. XVIII (1988), pp. 403–18, esp. pp. 416–17; [Sir Dalby Thomas], *An Historical Account of the Rise and Growth of the West-India Colonies . . .* (London, 1690), pp. 13–14, 36–7; Richard B. Sheridan, *Sugar and Slavery: An Economic History of the British West Indies 1623–1775* (Baltimore, 1973), pp. 272–3.

[5] For general accounts, see George F. Zook, "The Company of Royal Adventures of England Trading into Africa, 1660–1672," *Journal of Negro History*, Vol. IV (1919), pp. 134–231, esp. pp. 134–41 (also published separately); K. G. Davies, *The Royal African Company* (London, 1957); David W. Galenson, *Traders, Planters, and Slaves: Market Behavior in Early English America* (Cambridge and New York, 1986).

almost from the beginning – to enforce its monopoly.[6] K. G. Davies appears to attach somewhat more importance to the company's inability to collect with reasonable promptness the large sums owed it by the planters who bought its slaves on credit.[7]

The companies found credit a significant feature of the slave trade both in America and in parts of Africa. At the northern end of the slave trading coasts of West Africa, particularly in what is now termed Senegambia, the English and French companies frequently found it useful as early as the 1670s to make merchandise advances to African and Portuguese slave traders to be repaid in slaves at six months or so. Such arrangements made it easier to plan ahead and increase shipping efficiency by accumulating slaves at coastal shipping points before the arrival of the slaving vessels from Europe. In the earlier decades of the eighteenth century, this practice appears to have been geographically limited to Senegambia. However, by the second half of the century, there were a number of British merchants settled on the coast who also supplied slaves to the slave traders in arrangements that sometimes involved advances of trading goods. By the end of the century, a number of the largest British slave trading firms had established their own stations on the coast and very likely made credit advances to those who supplied them with slaves. However, there is no firm evidence to suggest that total credits outstanding on the coast from goods advanced were anything but a fraction of the sums outstanding in America from slave sales on credit.[8]

Almost from their start, the two English monopoly companies found it necessary, or at least commercially advisable, to sell slaves to the planters of Barbados and the other sugar islands on credit. The procedure worked out by the Royal African Company by the 1680s was built on the expectation that the sales would procure only a small fraction of their total value in cash or sugar or other goods. For the balance, the factors or commission agents of the company would take penalty bonds from the planter-buyers for payment in three, six, nine, or twelve months. The time allowed would carry the planter through

---

[6] Galenson, chap. 7.

[7] Davies, pp. 316–25, 335–43.

[8] Philip D. Curtin, *Economic Change in Precolonial Africa: Senegambia in the Era of the Slave Trade* (Madison, Wis., 1975), pp. 302–8; Davies, 216–18, 284–5. For credit advances to British traders on the coast, see J. H. Hodson, "The Letter Book of Robert Bostock, a Merchant in the Liverpool Slave Trade, 1789–1792," *Liverpool Libraries, Museums and Arts Committee, Bulletin*, Vol. III, Nos. 1 and 2 (1953), pp. 41, 53–5. For the trading station era, see J. E. Inikori, "Market Structure and the Profits of the British African Trade in the Late Eighteenth Century," *Journal of Economic History*, Vol. XLI (1981), pp. 745–76.

the next crop year. Most planters more or less paid when their bonds became due. But a substantial minority of them were very tardy in paying, and the agents of the company were reluctant to cut off the credit of substantial planters and good customers.[9] Sir Dalby Thomas, writing in 1690, argued that the debt problems of the slave buyers were exacerbated by changes in the market in recent decades. Since the 1660s, he reported, prices of slaves had risen considerably while prices of sugar had declined. West Indian planters had to buy replacement slaves, but the fall in sugar prices prevented them from paying.[10] Whatever the ultimate cause, the amounts owed the company in the West Indies kept rising, reaching £120,000 in 1680, £136,000 in 1684, and a peak of £170,000 in 1690. Though worrisome to the company, this rise in debt is not surprising, since the company's American deliveries grew steadily down to 1686–7.[11] To help carry these "accounts receivable" and the other requirements of its trading stock, the company itself had to borrow on bond in England. By 1708–10 its bonded debt was reported to be in the vicinity of £300,000–400,000.[12] This bonded debt is but one way in which the capital resources of the country were made available to the African slave trade by persons not otherwise involved therein.

The surge during the 1680s in the amounts owed the company in the West Indies occurred despite its frequent warnings to its factors against imprudent credit and neglect of collections. In some of the colonies the company could claim interest of up to 10% on these balances, but in others such interest was forbidden by law. Nor was the company satisfied ca. 1690 that its factors were doing all that they might to collect the interest permitted by law. Ultimately, in 1697, the company was forced to follow the lead of some interlopers and alter contractual arrangements with its factors. The latter's commissions were raised from 7 to 10% but they were made responsible for all credit extended to planters and "were obliged to undertake to remit to the company the entire proceeds of a cargo of slaves within twelve months." This was to be a crucial innovation for the institutional evolution of the trade in the next century. It was enforceable when introduced because the factors, like all senior employees and agents of the company, were required to give "security" and performance

---

[9] Davies, pp. 316–19; Galenson, p. 191.
[10] Thomas, pp. 38–40.
[11] Davies, pp. 319, 363.
[12] Elizabeth Donnan (ed.), *Documents Illustrative of the History of the Slave Trade to America*, 4 vols. (Washington, D.C., 1930–5), Vol. I, pp. 265 and n., 266n; Vol. II, pp. 89–90, 98, and n.

V

bonds countersigned by well-to-do figures, usually merchants in England.[13]

Because the Royal African Company had such difficulties in collecting the sums owed it in the West Indies for slave purchases by planters, it was interested during 1672–89 in experimenting with other sales arrangements, particularly contract deliveries tried earlier by the Royal Adventurers. A group or ad hoc syndicate of merchants in London would contract with the company in advance to purchase a number of slaves at a price of so much per head delivered. When the slaves were received in the colony specified or on the African coast, the local representative of the purchasing syndicate would give the agent of the company a bill or bills of exchange for the amount due drawn on a merchant in London designated by the syndicate. This system was used for the relatively few deliveries by the company to Virginia, where it did not attempt to sell slaves on its own before the 1690s. Syndicates of independent London merchants trading to Virginia were formed in the 1670s and 1680s, under the leadership of prominent merchants (such as John Jeffreys, his nephew Sir Jeffrey Jeffreys, Micajah Perry the elder, or Alderman Richard Booth), to contract with the company for the purchase on delivery in Virginia (or Africa) of about 100 slaves at a time. On such delivery, the agent of the syndicate would give the representative of the Royal African Company sets of bills of exchange drawn on the head of the London syndicate. One-third of the sale amount would usually be covered by a bill at "sixty days' sight" (payable sixty days after presentation to the addressee in London for acceptance), another third at four months' sight, and the final third at six months' sight. In such transactions, the Royal African Company accepted a smaller book profit per slave in return for an assured and not too prolonged schedule of payment. The syndicate, of course, most likely resold the slaves to Virginia or West Indian planters on credit, but the merchants in the syndicate had ongoing credit relationships with such planters, whose tobacco or sugar they marketed, and presumably were better able than the company to collect what was due from them.[14] The system

[13] Davies, pp. 296–7, 320–1; Galenson, 191. For registers of security bonds given to the Royal African Company, see PRO T.70/1428 and 1432. T.70/57 f. 127 (February 23, 1696–7) indicates that the company's 1697 innovations were based on practices used by the separate traders. See also ff. 127–9v, 132v–34.

[14] Davies, pp. 294–5; Donnan, 54–5; PRO T.70/269 (7 July 1676, 20 Aug. 1678); T.70/271 (16 Sept. 1684); T.70/273 (7 Sept. 1687). In the 1684 contract, John and Jeffrey Jeffreys took delivery on the African coast with payment in three- and six-month bills. See also Susan Westbury, "Slaves of Colonial Virginia: Where They Came

of staggered bills of exchange tried by the Royal African Company in the 1670s and 1680s was to become a marked feature of the slave trade in the next century.

Market conditions in the slave trade changed noticeably during the long wars of 1689–97 and 1702–13. The dangers of war and the rationing of sailors during the 1690s reduced the number of slaving vessels that could be sent to the African coast, and some of those that did depart were captured by enemy privateers and never reached the English colonies in America. These same wartime difficulties reduced the flow of sugar and tobacco from the colonies to England and led to significant increases in European prices.[15] Thus the inflow of slaves to the colonies[16] was reduced at the very time when higher European prices put more money or credit balances into the hands of consigning planters that they might well use for slave purchases. In these changed markets, sellers of slaves could be much less generous in offering credit. The Royal African Company was quick to sense the changed market conditions and in 1690 instructed its agents in the West Indies to sell only by auction and only "for money, Goods or Bills of Exchange with Securitie [endorsers or bonds] and not give further Creditt." These orders were repeated in 1691, but the next year the company found buyer resistance too strong and retreated, leaving the details of sales to the discretion of its factors. Even so, the balances owed the Royal African Company, which had been rising steadily in the 1680s, peaked at £170,000 in 1690, and declined in the ensuing decade to somewhere between £120,000 and £140,000 and in 1708, at £160,000, were still below their 1690, at peak. The private slave traders in the West Indies went further in the 1690s and were reported ca. 1698–1700 to be insisting on immediate payment (in cash or commodities) or offering only the most limited credit.[17] However, the very tight credit reported by our evidence for the 1690s does not appear to have persisted through the different market conditions of

From," *William and Mary Quarterly,* third series, Vol. XLII (1985), pp. 228–37, esp. pp. 229–30.

[15] For tobacco prices in Europe, see Nicolaas Wilhelmus Posthumus, *Inquiry into the History of Prices in Holland,* Vol. I, *Wholesale Prices at the Exchange of Amsterdam 1585–1914* (Leiden, 1946), pp. 199–206, and Jacob M. Price, *France and the Chesapeake: A History of the French Tobacco Monopoly, 1674–1791 . . . ,* 2 vols. (Ann Arbor, Mich., 1973), p. 852. For sugar prices in Europe, see Posthumus, pp. 119–46, and Sheridan, pp. 404–11, 496–7. For sugar and slave prices in the West Indies, see Davies, pp. 363–6; Galenson, pp. 63, 65.

[16] Davies, p. 363; PRO T.70/1205/A.43; C.O.388/10/H.105, H.108; Walter Minchinton, Celia King, and Peter Waite (eds.), *Virginia Slave-Trade Statistics 1698–1775* (Richmond, Va., 1984), pp. x–xiii.

[17] Davies, pp. 319, 325; Galenson, pp. 82, 84.

the later stages of the war of 1702–13. Despite reduced shipments, by 1710 both company and interloping sources report the return of longer credits in the West Indies.[18]

The 1690s saw a significant increase in the activity of interlopers or "separate traders" in the slave trade to the Chesapeake, as well as in the trade to the West Indies. From the records of an Exchequer lawsuit, we get a rather detailed picture of the activities of one of them, Thomas Starke of London. Starke had been trading to Virginia and Maryland as a conventional merchant in the 1670s and 1680s. Observing that no slaves had been imported into those colonies since the start of the European war in 1689, he and others applied to the Privy Council in 1692 for permission to send a slaving vessel to the Guinea Coast and Virginia. Permission was granted, though the number of sailors authorized was deducted from the wartime quotas allowed to the Virginia trade and the individual venturers. Starke remained active in both the slave and Chesapeake trades down to his death in 1706, with the slaves he sent to Virginia being entrusted at first to his chief factor there, Henry Fox of King and Queen County (York River). Fox apparently sold such slaves on credit, just as he did the other goods sent him. By 1696, Starke had become dissatisfied with the large balances owed him in the Chesapeake and decided to send his apprentice, John Sheffeild, to manage his affairs in Maryland and to take charge of any slaves sent to Virginia. Sheffeild found on arrival that it was then normal in the Chesapeake to pay for indentured servants in tobacco but to pay for slaves in bills of exchange. He appears to have been able to dispose of all the slaves Starke sent him during 1698–1702 for bills of exchange of rarely more than thirty days' duration (sight). This is consistent with what we read of the activities of the independent slave traders in the West Indies at that time and confirms the suggestion that during the wars of 1689–1713, longer credits on slave sales were much less necessary or common than they had been before 1689 and were to be again after 1713.[19]

We have thus seen that, before its role in the slave trade faded

---

[18] Donnan, Vol. II, pp. 132, 147. For activity during war down to 1708 see Davies, pp. 143, 363, and PRO C.O.388/11/I.8. For French privateering during war, see J. S. Bromley, "The French Privateering War, 1702–13," in H. E. Bell and R. L. Ollard (eds.), *Historical Essays 1600–1750 Presented to David Ogg* (London, 1963), pp. 203–31.

[19] Jacob M. Price, "Sheffeild v. Starke: Institutional Experimentation in the London–Maryland Trade, c. 1696–1706," *Business History*, Vol. XXVIII (July 1986), pp. 19–39, esp. pp. 27–8, 31–5; reprinted in R. P. T. Davenport-Hines and Jonathan Liebenau, *Business in the Age of Reason* (London, 1987), pp. 19–39. Based on original firm records in PRO E.219/446.

V

away, the Royal African Company had by 1700 evolved certain effective mechanisms for sale of slaves on credit: (1) Planters buying slaves on credit were expected to give bonds for payment at stated dates. (2) Merchants buying large shipments of slaves were expected to pay in bills of exchange, though these could be staggered, for example, with due dates in tranches of two, four, and six months after acceptance. (3) From 1697, the company's factors were made personally responsible for the collection of the proceeds of all slave sales on credit. (4) The last was enforceable because the factors had long been required to give the company security bonds for their right handling of the valuable property entrusted to them. Our evidence on the separate traders and their factors is much thinner, but, like Starke, most of them appear frequently to have had to let their factors sell on credit. During the war years 1689–1713, the separate traders, dealing on a smaller scale than the company, were at times able to restrict credit much more than the company. However, in the changed market conditions after 1713, the four credit practices developed by the company and the interlopers before 1700 were to be developed further by the separate traders and integrated by them into a coherent long-term credit system.

THE BRITISH SLAVE TRADE, 1713–75

In the years following their legalization in 1698, the separate traders steadily pulled ahead of the Royal African Company in the slave trade. Between June 24, 1698, and December 3, 1707, the private trade sent 376 vessels to Africa from London alone, whereas the company sent only 128.[20] In every colony for which we have data of any sort, the interlopers led the company: In Jamaica, for example, they imported 35,718 slaves in that same period, whereas the company imported only 6,854; in Virginia, the private trade accounted for 5,692 slave imports, whereas the company brought in only 679; in Maryland the total was 2,938 for the former and nil for the latter.[21] Conditions became even better for the separate traders de facto, if not de jure, when the legislation requiring them to pay a 10% toll on exports to Africa lapsed in 1710.

As they took over more and more of the trade, the burden of supporting its credit structure fell increasingly on the separate traders. Though they had boasted in 1711 of their "generosity" in this re-

[20] PRO C.O.388/11/I.8.
[21] PRO T.70/1205/A.43.

spect,[22] it would not appear that the burden of debt was too heavy in the years immediately following the war. These were years of good prices for growers of both sugar and tobacco,[23] and a good part of the higher disposable income of their estates went into the purchase of additional slaves. (These were the years of the triumph of the slave plantation in Virginia.) In South Carolina, the bounties paid by the British crown for imports of naval stores had the same stimulative effect on slave purchases.[24] Against this background of relative prosperity, we hear comparatively few complaints about the burden of debt.

Market conditions changed, however, in the late 1720s and 1730s, with falling and eventually abysmally low prices in Europe for both sugar and tobacco.[25] With their incomes thus reduced, slave owners understandably found it very difficult to support and clear the debt they had incurred for slave purchases. In such a trap, the planters inevitably turned for relief to the colonial legislatures they dominated. In colony after colony, bills were passed sheltering debtors, including debtor slave owners, from the claims of creditors.

In no colony did the legislature attempt to establish the full Latin principle of the integrity of the plantation that we saw recognized in Portuguese Brazil as early as the 1660s. But the trend was clearly if hesitatingly in that direction. As early as the 1660s, we find the Royal Adventurers complaining of the laws of Barbados, which made it almost impossible for them to sue for recovery of debts incurred by slave purchases.[26] K. G. Davies and Richard B. Sheridan have surveyed the legislative and other legal impediments to the collection of debts in the West Indian slave colonies. Typical legislative measures altered the ratio of the local money of account to the Spanish silver dollar, to the disadvantage of creditors, or required creditors to accept payment in commodities at more than their current market value. (An act to the latter effect was also passed in South Carolina in 1719.)[27]

---

[22] Donnan, Vol. II, p. 132.

[23] See footnote 15.

[24] Donnan, Vol. IV, pp. 265–6. Cf. Converse D. Clowse, *Economic Beginnings in Colonial South Carolina 1670–1730* (Columbia, S.C., 1971), pp. 129, 131–2, 203–4, 222, 230–1.

[25] See footnote 15. For the credit problems of the South Sea Company selling slaves in the Spanish colonies at this time, see Colin Palmer, *Human Cargoes: The British Slave Trade to Spanish America 1700–1739* (Urbana, Ill., 1981), pp. 126–7.

[26] Zook, p. 210; Donnan, Vol. I, pp. 165n–166n, 165–6. The Barbados legislature refused to make land liable for such debts. The most objectionable Barbados law was repealed in 1677.

[27] Davies, 319–23; Sheridan, 274–8; Donnan, Vol. IV, pp. 265–6 and n.; Richard Pares, *Merchants and Planters* (Economic History Review Supplements, 4) (Cambridge, 1960), pp. 45–7, 88–90.

V

These measures tended to affect all merchant creditors equally and were not specifically aimed at slave traders. In fact, a clause in one Antigua law specifically permitted creditors to recover slaves not paid for. However, the Royal African Company did not like the rest of the law, which, on their petition, was disallowed by the crown.[28]

Technical bills might have relevance to the slave trade that at first glance is not self-evident. In 1709–10 the merchants of London trading to Maryland obtained the disallowance by the crown of three measures passed by the Maryland legislature. One of these, "An Act for the Relief of Poor Debtors," would have exempted future earnings from the claims of current creditors (as is true of modern bankruptcy laws). The merchant creditors objected "Because the Merchants have given the Planters Credit to buy Negroes[,] to Cloath and Support their Familyes not upon any known or Supposed Stock they had, but [upon] their [sense of] Justice & [the] future Crops they should make." The law deprived the creditor of any claims upon "their future Labour . . . which alone was that foundation on which the Credit was solely given, & by which Credit those plantations have been supported & peopled & yᵉ trade itself sustained & without which it had been altogether Unable to have been Carried on & can't long without it be supported but by Credit." They also objected to the law reducing the penalty on protested bills of exchange from 15 to 10%. Since the bill of exchange was a common medium for paying for slaves, a planter anxious to get more slaves might well try paying for purchases with bills he knew would be refused acceptance and protested, calculating that 10% was not an excessive interest and penalty to pay to get the labor he needed.[29]

Tensions between creditors and debtors – and hence between debtor-dominated colonial legislatures and the creditor-influenced metropolitan government – so conspicuous during the price fall of ca. 1660–90 became pronounced again with the new fall in commodity prices in the late 1720s.[30] Many sugar and tobacco colonies experi-

[28] Davies, p. 320.
[29] PRO C.O.5/716/67; C.O.5/717/15; *Journal of the Commissioners of Trade and Plantations, 1704–1708/9*, pp. 36, 70, 75–6, 81, 82, 84, 96, 97, 181, 186. For protested bills in the slave trade, see Walter Minchinton, "The Virginia Letters of Isaac Hobhouse, Merchant of Bristol," *Virginia Magazine of History and Biography*, Vol. LXVI (1958), pp. 278–307.
[30] See the sources cited in footnote 14 and Jacob M. Price, "Glasgow, the Tobacco Trade, and the Scottish Customs, 1707–1730," *The Scottish Historical Review*, Vol. LXIII (1984), pp. 1–36, esp. pp. 34–5; and John M. Hemphill II, *Virginia and the English Commercial System 1689–1733: . . .* (New York, 1985), pp. 311–14 (for tobacco prices in Virginia).

enced this heightened tension but it was particularly apparent in Jamaica and Virginia, which merit our attention. In 1728 both houses of the Jamaica legislature passed a bill "to oblige creditors to accept of the produce of the Island in payment of their debts" at fixed prices. This was an oft-tried ploy (analogous to the South Carolina act of 1719) usually disallowed by the London authorities. This particular bill was strongly objected to by the merchants and traders of Kingston and at least one member of the council. Governor Hunter, on the advice of his council, decided that assenting would be contrary to his instructions and so referred the bill to the Board of Trade in London, where it died.[31]

In Virginia the legislative reaction to the decline in European prices for their commodity was more energetic. At first the legislature saw the problem as one of overproduction. In 1728, for the last time, they passed a stint act restricting production. That same year, they tried to discourage the growth of the labor force by introducing a bill taxing imports of slaves; this was disallowed by the Privy Council, as was a bill of 1726 prohibiting shipments of North Carolina tobacco through Virginia. More successful was the 1730 bill sponsored by Governor Gooch for the compulsory warehousing and inspection of all tobacco before shipment out of the colony. Tobacco that failed inspection was to be burned.[32] Inevitably, the Virginia legislature's attention was also drawn to the debt problem. When Gooch went out to Virginia in 1727, he received the standard instructions to ask the legislature for a bill enabling creditors to recover sums owed in Virginia to British bankrupts. The legislature did not think that such a bill was needed but, as a slight concession, passed a law in 1728 weakening previous legislation declaring slaves to be real property and thus unavailable to satisfy certain types of debt. The merchants of London now took the initiative and complained against a 1705 Virginia act setting time limits for legal actions for the recovery of sums owing by judgment, bond, bill, note, or open account. The Board of Trade, on the advice of counsel, recommended the disallowance of the 1705 act on the ground that it ran counter to an English act (21 James I) by which rights created by judgment or bond were unlimited in time. This disallow-

---

[31] *Calendar of State Papers Colonial: America and West Indies, 1728–1729*, pp. 167–9 (no. 344), 243 (no. 469); *Journal of the Commissioners of Trade and Plantations, 1722/3–1728*, p. 434.

[32] Jacob M. Price, "The Excise Affair Revisited: The Administrative and Colonial Dimensions of a Parliamentary Crisis," in Stephen B. Baxter (ed.), *England's Rise to Greatness, 1660–1763* (Berkeley, Calif., 1983), pp. 257–321, esp. pp. 272–3; Hemphill, pp. 150–73.

ance created new problems, for there were other clauses in the 1705 act useful to the merchants, including one by which a merchant creditor resident in Britain but party to a suit in Virginia could prove his accounts by swearing to them before the chief magistrate of his place of residence. Gooch tried to persuade the legislature to reenact the desirable clauses of the 1705 act, but the resultant bill did not include the clause for proving accounts in Britain.[33]

Concerned about their weakened legal position in litigation for debt collection, the merchants of London and Bristol trading to Virginia joined with their fellows trading to Jamaica to petition the crown for help. Their memorial complained not only of the Virginia laws just mentioned but of equivalent discriminatory legislation in Maryland, including one measure that also made it impossible there for British creditors or receivers to collect sums owed bankrupts, and of the laws of Jamaica and some other colonies by which lands and houses were not liable to pay ordinary debts, though by the laws of England "estates in the Plantations are deemed Chattel." The merchants' petition was referred to the Board of Trade, which reported that legislation would be necessary. The resulting Colonial Debts Act of 1732, supported by the active solicitation of merchants of London, Bristol, and Liverpool, met some of the merchants' complaints. A uniform system applying to all the colonies was established for proving accounts in Britain for use in colonial debt litigation. More sensitively, the act declared that the *lands, houses, chattels, and slaves* of debtors in the American colonies were liable for the satisfaction of debts "in the like Manner as Real Estates are by the Law of *England* liable to Satisfaction of Debts due by Bond or other Specialty."[34]

The Colonial Debts Act of 1732 was deeply offensive to many slave-owning planters in the West Indies and North America. Those in the

---

[33] Price, "Excise Affair," pp. 277–8; Leonard Woods Labaree (ed.), *Royal Instructions to British Colonial Governors 1670–1776*, 2 vols. (New York, 1935, 1967), Vol. I, p. 338; *Calendar of State Papers Colonial . . . 1728–1729*, nos. 45, 190, 241, 351, 593, 606, 614, 637, 722, 730–1; *1730*, no. 289; *1731*, no. 434iii; PRO C.O.5/1321/R.76; C.O.5/1337/75; William Waller Hening, comp., *The Statutes at Large; being a Collection of all the Laws of Virginia, from the First Session of the Legislature*, 13 vols. (Philadelphia, 1823; Charlottesville, Va., 1969), Vol. III, pp. 377–81 (4 Annae c. 34), Vol. IV, pp. 222–8 (1 Geo. I, c. 11); Hemphill, pp. 175–80.

[34] 5 Geo. II c. 7 (*Statutes at Large*, ed. Ruffhead, Vol. VI, pp. 74–5; Price, pp. 278–9; Bristol, Merchants Hall Archives, Minutes of Proceedings, V, 23 February 1730–1, 14 December 1731; *Calendar of State Papers Colonial . . . 1731*, nos. 367, 401, 406, 434, 473; *1732*, nos. 22, 24, 32, 36, 55, 136, 176, 196, 197; PRO C.O.5/1322 ff. 187–91v, 194–9v, 216–17v; Leo Francis Stock (ed.), *Proceedings and Debates of the British Parliament Respecting North America*, 5 vols. (Washington, D.C., 1924–41), Vol. IV, pp. 128, 130, 145, 150, 153–5, 160; Hemphill, 180–9.

Virginia legislature were so offended that they sought revenge against the merchants by petitioning for what became Walpole's abortive excise scheme.[35] However, planter wrath may have been misplaced. The act did not in fact hurt the slave trade or undermine the slave plantation system. It did, however, clear up many questions touching debts for slave purchases. In particular, it made a very effective legal instrument of the *bond* given by planters buying slaves on credit. With this legal protection in place, the credit-based slave trade in many colonies could and did expand significantly in the ensuing decades.[36]

If the 1732 act did not adversely affect slavery as an institution, the same cannot be said for its impact on slaves as individuals and members of families. Under the act, slaves could be seized and sold for the payment of certain classes of their owners' debts, separating them thereby from their friends and families. In the changed moral climate at the end of the century, such separations were no longer acceptable; Bryan Edwards was able to obtain an act of Parliament in 1797 abrogating so much of the 1732 act as made slaves "chattels for the payment of debts." But the slave trade was almost over by then. While it lasted unscathed, the act could "truly be called the Palladium of Colony credit, and the English Merchant's grand security".[37]

The first clear evidence of the reorientation of the trade following the act of 1732 comes from South Carolina. Planters there had been buying slaves for rice and giving bonds when credit was involved. As long as the law was weak on suing on such bonds, the merchant-factors in the colony were inclined to be lenient with overdue bonds, particularly as they could make such bonds with their penalties earn them 10% interest. After the 1732 act, however, the whole system was tightened up. Since the merchant-factors in the colony were now in a stronger position vis-à-vis the planters in collecting bonded debt, the English slave traders, in turn, sought to improve their position vis-à-vis the factors. They now insisted on formal contracts that obliged the factor to give security in England and to assume legal liability for the value of all slaves received and sold by him. Some contracts further obliged the factor to remit two-thirds of the sale

---

[35] Price, "Excise Affair," pp. 279, 284–8, 306–7.

[36] In Virginia, slave imports were quite buoyant in the years following the 1732 act, averaging 2,141 in 1733–7 compared with 173 in 1728–31 (Minchinton, King, and Waite, xv). The act was much less effective in facilitating debt recovery actions against land in Jamaica. See Edward Long, *The History of Jamaica*, 3 vols. (London, 1774), Vol. I, p. 546.

[37] 37 Geo. III c. CXIX (ed. Ruffhead, *Statutes at Large*, Vol. XVII, pp. 656–7); Sheridan, p. 289; [William Cobbett], *The Parliamentary History of England*, 36 vols. (London, 1806–20), Vol. XXXIII, pp. 261–3, 831–4.

proceeds within one year of the date of sale and the remainder within two years. To assume such contractual obligations, the factor had to be sure that he could collect from the planter. The initial sale was secured with credit of up to eighteen months; if the planter could not pay then, a new bond was taken for another year's credit with 10% interest or penalty.[38]

When Henry Laurens of the Charleston firm of Austin & Laurens entered the slave selling business ca. 1749, he approached a number of slave-trading firms in Bristol, Liverpool, and Lancaster, soliciting consignments. He proposed arrangements similar but not identical to those just enumerated, which had emerged in South Carolina in the 1730s. In return for a 10% commission, Laurens would give security in England and assume full responsibility for collecting all slave sale debts, but he insisted that he be given discretion in the length of credit and thus could not commit himself to remittance within any certain time limits – though he later claimed that he was usually able to remit in six to nine months in bills of exchange payable in England thirty or forty days after presentation (sight).[39] By 1755, however, some of the big slave traders in England were no longer satisfied with the uncertain timing of payment implied by such terms and transferred their consignments from Laurens's company to newer firms in Charleston that undertook *immediate remittance*, or what contemporaries called "bills in the bottom." That is, when a slave-trading vessel left the colony for home, it would carry whatever had been thus far received for the slave sales (commodities, specie, and planters' bills of exchange), with the balance (the greater part of the whole) covered by the factor's own bills of exchange on his surety (called the "guar-

[38] Donnan, Vol. IV, pp. 291–4, reprinted from *South Carolina Gazette* of March 9, 1738. For the use of bonds in slave sales in South Carolina before 1720, see ibid., Vol. IV, p. 266n. Advertisements for slave sales in the *South Carolina Gazette* in the 1730s sometimes mentioned credit of up to six months but at other times indicated that "Good Encouragement will be given ready Pay in Currency, Rice, Pitch and Tar." However, a merchant's letter of September 12, 1735, refers to the 2,400 slaves imported at Charleston that year, "which have sold very well tho' the greatest part upon Credit." Ibid., Vol. IV, pp. 276–80n (and pp. 302n, 311, for similar advertisements in 1749–52), 412n. The high rates of interest mentioned in the text were presumably based on the penalty clauses in the bonds and thus circumvented colonial usury laws.
[39] Ibid., Vol. IV, pp. 303, 317–18; Philip M. Hamer et al. (eds.), *The Papers of Henry Laurens*, 11+ vols. (Columbia, S.C., 1968–), Vol. I, pp. 202–6, 211–12, 226–7, 254–7. For the high frequency of three- to six-month credits in slave sales at Charleston, see Donnan, Vol. III, pp. 153–5, 161. Slaves were imported into North Carolina in smaller shipments from the West Indies, supported in part by six- to nine-month credits from West Indian slave dealers. North Carolina State Archives AB58/14 Hogg and Campbell invoice book.

antee") in England. These last were generally drawn in three or four tranches, or clusters payable – for example, at three, six, and nine months' "sight," that is, three, six, or nine months after presentation to the addressee or drawee in England for acceptance. The guarantee in England was prepared to accept these bills drawn on him because, if all went as arranged, he expected to receive remittances from the factor before the accepted bills became due for payment, and, if not, to be reimbursed for anything for which he was "out of pocket."[40]

How in fact were the guarantees reimbursed for both expenses and risks? In a letter in 1773 to a young slave factor in South Carolina, Henry Laurens, visiting England, wrote that, as far as he could find out, the guarantee received only the usual 0.5% commission both on bills accepted (and paid) by him and on bills sent him for collection. If he did not receive remittances in time and had to use his own funds to pay the bills he had accepted, he was entitled to charge interest at 5% per annum.[41] (As the guarantees were substantial merchants, they should have been able to borrow for less than 5% in peacetime, and so should have made from 0.5 to 1% on such interest charges.)[42] Richard Pares could not find any hint in the records of Lascelles &

[40] In 1755–6, Laurens lost the sale of at least two slave ships to Charles Mayne, who undertook to return bills in the bottom. On one occasion, Richard Oswald & Company of London was prepared to consign a shipload of slaves to Laurens without security in England. Laurens's principal correspondent in England was Devonsheir, Reeve & Lloyd, of Bristol. When a London guarantee was needed, he could use Augustus & John Boyd & Company, for which he bought rice for shipment to the West Indies. The Charleston supply of bills of exchange on England was created by rice sales. With the advent of war, discouraging to the rice trade, and the new payment system, Austen & Laurens withdrew from slave selling in 1756: Hamer et al., Vol. II, pp. 37, 42–7, 169–70, 185–6, 239–43, 294–5, 451, 522. See also Vol. I, pp. 257–9, 269–76; Vol. II, pp. 47–50, 169, 217–19, 283; Donnan, Vol. IV, pp. 319–22, 334–5, 348–9. See also Donnan, Vol. III, p. 161, for the length of credit (six-nine months) of a consignment of sixty-three slaves sold in Charleston for a Rhode Island firm. On the share of the guarantee, see the following discussion in text. In exceptional cases, it was possible for the guarantee to reside in America. In such cases, he had a correspondent in England accept the bills. Hamer et al., Vol. VII, p. 503. For the continuation of the immediate remittance system in South Carolina during 1763–75, see Donnan, Vol. III, pp. 268–9; Vol. IV, pp. 391–4, 399, 414, 424–6, 431–2, 440, 451–2, 457–8, 460–2, 469; Hamer et al., Vol. VI, pp. 87–91. Around 1772 there appears to have been an effort to reduce the time of the planter-buyer's credit: Donnan, Vol. IV, pp. 446–9, 451–2. See also S. G. Checkland, "Finance for the West Indies, 1780–1815," *Economic History Review*, second series, Vol. X (1958), pp. 461–9, esp. pp. 466–7; Leila Sellers, *Charleston Business on the Eve of the Revolution* (Chapel Hill, N.C., 1934), chap. VII, esp. pp. 138–42, 145–6; Elizabeth Donnan, "The Slave Trade into South Carolina before the Revolution," *American Historical Review*, Vol. XXXIII (1928), pp. 804–28, esp. pp. 812–13.

[41] Hamer et al., Vol. VIII, pp. 638–9.

[42] Cf. Jacob M. Price, *Capital and Credit in British Overseas Trade: The View from the Chesapeake, 1700–1776* (Cambridge, Mass., 1980), Chap. 4.

Maxwell, which accepted bills for West Indian slave factors, that they received any more.[43] However, George Buchanan, a Glasgow merchant, wrote to his Maryland correspondent, George Maxwell, that he understood that "the Suretys in Britain generally gett one half" of the 10% commission earned by the slave-selling factor in America.[44] I have found only one confirmatory example – in Maryland in 1718 – of a slave-selling factor sharing half his commission, but it is probable that others in that line had to offer some sort of special consideration to get solid people to act as guarantees. Of course, in most cases the guarantees were firms trading to America as commission houses (like Lascelles & Maxwell) and were willing to help the slave-selling factors in America because they received other remunerative business from them.[45]

The immediate remittance or bills in the bottom system that was introduced into South Carolina ca. 1755 was almost certainly developed first in the West Indies, whence it was imported into Charleston. There were, however, significant differences in the system in the two areas. At Charleston in the generation before the American Revolu-

---

[43] Richard Pares, "A London West-India Merchant House 1740–1769," in Richard Pares and A. J. P. Taylor (eds.), *Essays Presented to Sir Lewis Namier* (London, 1956), pp. 75–107, esp. pp. 103–4. I am not sure that what Pares wrote about contracted prices represented normal practice in the trade. The records of this firm were largely destroyed by bombing in 1940.

[44] Scottish Record Office, C.S.96/507 pp. 47–9, G. Buchanan to G. Maxwell, 6 December 1761.

[45] Henry Laurens arranged for the London firm of Bourdieu & Chollet to act as a guarantee for his protégé, John Lewis Gervais, in Charleston. This was a firm with activities all over the Atlantic world but was only beginning in the Charleston trade when approached. On them, see Price, *France and the Chesapeake*, Vol. II, pp. 687–8 and index. In the papers of James Rogers, a Bristol slave trader, there are a number of letters of credit from British merchants guaranteeing acceptance and payment of bills of exchange drawn by factors in the West Indies to remit the proceeds of the sale of Rogers' slaves. See, e.g., PRO C.107/7(i) Bridgman, Combe & Bridgman (London, 1 Jan. 1793); Alex. Houstoun & Company (Glasgow, 19 Apr. 1787); C.107/7(ii) Thomas Daniel & Son (Bristol, 19 July 1788); C.107/9 Lindo Aguilar & Dias (London, 19 Feb. 1789); C. 107/10 Turner Gammell & Company (London, 16 Feb. 1792); John Campbell Sr. & Company (Glasgow, 30 July 1792). For the correspondence of a Bristol guarantee, see Kenneth Morgan (ed.), "Calendar of Correspondence from William Miles to John Tharp 1770–1789" in Patrick McGrath (ed.), *A Bristol Miscellany* (Bristol Records Society's Publications, Vol. XXXVII) (Bristol, 1985), pp. 84–121. There are also references to letters of credit from guarantees in Richard Pares's transcripts from the (destroyed) Lascelles & Maxwell letterbook (Bodleian Library), boxes I and IV. On the relations between the slave-selling factors in the West Indies and their merchant correspondents/guarantees in London, see Richard B. Sheridan, "The Commercial and Financial Organization of the British Slave Trade, 1750–1807," *Economic History Review*, second series, Vol. XI (1958), pp. 249–63, esp. pp. 260–3. The 1718 example is in Georgetown University Library, James Carroll letter book, fo. 97, with at least one of the sharers living in Maryland.

tion, merchant buyers of rice and indigo (regardless of whom they were buying for) normally paid with bills of exchange on London. This created a regular if not always adequate supply of London bills that planters could use to help pay for their slave purchases when due and that the slave-selling factors could acquire for the necessary remittances to their guarantees in England. In the West Indies, by contrast, the larger planters did not normally sell their sugar locally but shipped it to consignment merchants in England to be sold on commission. They then could draw bills against these consignment earnings but ran the risk of nonacceptance and "protest" if they drew too much without permission. Charleston bills normally drawn by merchants were therefore less likely to be protested than West Indian bills drawn by planters.[46] This was a particularly sensitive point, for West Indian planters buying slaves, instead of giving buyer's bonds, sometimes paid at purchase with long bills on London payable up to eighteen months after acceptance. Through the immediate remittance system, however, the risk of such long bills fell not on the English slave traders but on the West Indian factor and his guarantee.[47] Even the new Liverpool intruders after 1750 found it wiser, therefore, to sell through factors (with sureties) rather than through their ship captains, as before.[48] Some Liverpool firms went even further and tried to get the factors to guarantee them in advance a minimum sale price – but there is no evidence that this became a common practice.[49]

At the beginning of the American Revolution, though, when the North American market was cut off, something of a slave glut appears to have developed in the West Indies, and the factors reportedly could sell the slaves they received only by giving planters up to five years' credit secured by bond, instead of taking the previously normal twelve- to eighteen-month bills of exchange. Such bonds, unlike the

[46] For the nonacceptance of planters' bills, see Donnan, *Documents*, Vol. III, pp. 248–9, 297–8.

[47] Ibid., Vol. III, pp. 248–9, 255, 259, 272n–273, 291–2, 295–302; Vol. IV, p. 418.

[48] Francis E. Hyde, Bradbury B. Parkinson, and Sheila Marriner, "The Nature and Profitability of the Liverpool Slave Trade," *Economic History Review*, second series, Vol. V (1953), pp. 368–77, esp. p. 369n.

[49] Gomer Williams, *History of the Liverpool Privateers and Letters of Marque with an Account of the Liverpool Slave Trade* (London, 1897), pp. 486–8, 550. With the threat of war in 1775, some smaller-scale Rhode Island slave traders attempted to sell a whole cargo at a flat price per head. We do not know how common this attempt was; at other times, the Rhode Islanders also used the bills in the bottom system. Jay Coughtry, *The Notorious Triangle: Rhode Island and the African Slave Trade 1700–1807* (Philadelphia, 1981), pp. 180–2; Virginia Bever Platt, "'And Don't Forget the Guinea Voyage': The Slave Trade of Aaron Lopez of Newport," *William and Mary Quarterly*, third series, Vol. XXXII (1975), pp. 601–18, esp. p. 613.

previous bills, were not negotiable in England, and this sudden loss of liquidity forced some English firms into bankruptcy.[50] In the 1790s another glut developed (perhaps reflecting the loss of the St. Dominguè market); the length of credit on slave sales in the West Indies is reported to have been distinctly longer than before 1776, with the factors' bills on their guarantees allegedly averaging three years' sight, but still fully acceptable for discount or circulation on the credit of the signatures of the acceptors and endorsers. Planters needing longer credit were reportedly giving bonds then at 6% with such interest retained by the factor and available to reimburse the guarantee in case he did not get returns in time to cover his acceptances.[51]

In summary, the immediate remittance system had two major features that must be clearly understood: (1) It involved two separate streams of bill of exchange operations. The first stream was bills drawn by slave-selling factors on their guarantees in England and remitted to the slave traders immediately after the American sale as returns on their ventures. The second stream consisted of bills drawn by sugar planters or rice-purchasing agents on their correspondents in England, acquired by the slave-selling factors and remitted by them to their guarantees in England to reimburse the latter for accepting and paying the bills in the first stream. (2) The first stream of bills drawn by the factors on their guarantees were long bills normally drawn in three or four tranches, with intervals between the payment dates of at least three months. The timing of the tranches changed over time with market conditions. At first, we read of three tranches at three, six, and nine months' sight. Later we read of durations of up to eighteen and twenty-four months and longer.[52] Whatever their lengths, to serve their remittance function the bills had to be negotiable, that is, acceptable for discount or circulation. That is what the English slave traders meant when they "said that Bills in the bottom kept the wheel in motion."[53]

---

[50] Donnan, *Documents*, Vol. II, p. 553n.
[51] Ibid., Vol. II, pp. 625–9. In the Rogers papers, the maximum length of bills drawn in the West Indies in the late 1780s and early 1790s appears to have been thirty months. PRO C.107/8, 9, 10, 12.
[52] For three-, six-, and nine-month tranches, see Hamer et al., Vol. II, pp. 47–8, Vol. VI, pp. 87–91; Donnan, *Documents*, Vol. III, p. 286, Vol. IV, p. 399. For twelve- to fifteen-month tranches, see Hamer et al., Vol. II, pp. 46–7, Vol. VI, pp. 87–91, Vol. VIII, pp. 636, 637; Donnan, *Documents*, Vol. III, 298–302, Vol. IV, pp. 391–4, 424–6. For eighteen-month tranches, see Donnan, *Documents*, Vol. III, pp. 295–6, 305. For twenty-four-month tranches, see Donnan, *Documents*, Vol. III, p. 305; James A. Rawley, *The Transatlantic Slave Trade: A History* (New York, 1981), p. 188; PRO C.107/8, 9, 10, 12.
[53] Hamer et al., Vol. VI, pp. 89–90.

V

316

The immediate remittance system thus understood was particularly suited to the needs of the Liverpool slave traders who increasingly dominated the trade from the 1740s. In London, Bristol, or Glasgow, local bills of exchange with two months or less to run before maturity could be discounted at local banks or passed in some branches of trade. (Glasgow or Bristol merchants receiving bills on London would send them to their correspondents in the capital, where they also could be discounted within two months of maturity.) Accepted bills of longer maturities, however, normally had to be kept until they were within two or so months of payment, when they became negotiable.[54] However, in South Lancashire a local practice had developed of passing longer bills in trade with an appropriate discount. (These were normally accepted bills on London.) This was of special use to the Liverpool slave traders, who could use the bills they received from the West Indies of whatever length to pay for their export goods (purchased on about twelve months' credit) and some of their ships' gear.[55] David Richardson's analysis of the accounts of the slave-trading firm of William Davenport of Liverpool shows that almost all the bills of exchange received (90% of total returns) were disposed of before maturity with a discount.[56] There would thus appear to have

[54] For normal practice, cf. Price, *Capital and Credit*, chap. 5, esp. pp. 89–95. The "bill book" of Buchanan & Simson of Glasgow makes it clear that longer local bills (up to one year's sight) were normally kept in the firm's strong box but that bills with less than sixty days to maturity could be discounted or passed in trade. Scottish Record Office, C.S.96/508.

[55] Alfred P. Wadsworth and Julia de Lacy Mann, *The Cotton Trade and Industrial Lancashire 1600–1780* (Manchester, 1931), pp. 96, 249; L. S. Pressnell, *Country Banking in the Industrial Revolution* (Oxford, 1956), pp. 19–20, 77, 170–3; T. S. Ashton, *An Economic History of England: The 18th Century* (London, 1955), pp. 185–8; Henry Thornton, *An Enquiry into the Nature and Effects of the Paper Credit of Great Britain (1802)*, ed. F. A. Hayek (London, 1939), p. 94n; B. L. Anderson, "Financial Institutions and the Capital Market on Merseyside in the Eighteenth and Nineteenth Centuries," in B. L. Anderson and P. J. M. Stoney (eds.), *Commerce, Industry and Transport: Studies in Economic Change on Merseyside* (Liverpool, 1983), pp. 26–59. For other contemporary references to the circulation (at discount) of slave factors' bills on their sureties, see Donnan, *Documents*, Vol. II, p. 629, Vol. IV, pp. 418, 457–8.

[56] David Richardson, "Profits in the Liverpool Slave Trade: The Accounts of William Davenport, 1757–1784," in Roger Anstey and P. E. H. Hair (eds.), *Liverpool, the African Slave Trade, and Abolition* . . . (Historic Society of Lancashire and Cheshire, Occasional Papers, Vol. 2) (s.l., 1976), pp. 72–3; idem., "Profitability in the Bristol–Liverpool Slave Trade," in *La Traite des Noirs par l'Atlantique: Nouvelles approches* (Bibliothèque d'Histoire d'Outremer, Nouvelle Série, Etudes, 4) (Paris, 1976), pp. 301–8, esp. pp. 304–5. See also B. L. Anderson, "The Lancashire Bill System and Its Liverpool Practitioners . . . ," in W. H. Chaloner and Barrie M. Ratcliffe (eds.), *Trade and Transport: Essays . . . in Honour of T. S. Willan* (Manchester, 1977), pp. 59–77; and [James Wallace], *A General and Descriptive History of the Ancient and Present State of . . . Liverpool* (Liverpool, 1795), pp. 232–3.

been a most singular organic connection between the South Lancashire bill circulation system and the rise of Liverpool as a slave-trading
port from the 1740s. Every businessman in that area who sold export
goods on long credit or who received and passed American bills of
exchange was in a sense helping to finance the slave trade.

However, in seeking to comprehend the handling of the very long
bills of exchange produced by the slave trade, one should be wary of
overemphasizing the importance of the Lancashire bill system to the
relative neglect of the London and other money markets. Davenport's
bill book of the 1770s shows that only 21% (by value) of bills received
from the West Indies were disposed of in Liverpool and vicinity; 75%
were sent to London to a rather large group of merchants with whom
Davenport dealt.[57] Some of these were clearly merchants from whom
Davenport purchased textiles, ironmongery, and other goods for his
African voyages. Thus West Indian bills could be passed (with an
appropriate discount) to pay at first hand for goods purchased. Other
bills, however, may have been sent to London for discount in what
were essentially financial as distinct from commercial transactions.
Since we do not have Davenport's correspondence, we cannot be absolutely sure of the underlying character of his London bill transactions.[58]

We are fortunate, however, in having a considerable surviving correspondence dating from the 1780s and 1790s of the Bristol slave trader
James Rogers. As a return of the proceeds of the sale of his slaves,
he also received from his factors in the West Indies the familiar "sets"
of bills in tranches of twelve, eighteen, and twenty-four months, or
some variant thereof. He does not appear to have passed these bills
to his suppliers in the reputed Lancashire fashion but instead sought
to get cash for them. His London bankers, including the Quaker firm
of Smith, Wright & Gray, and its successor, Sir James Esdaile & Company, would discount bills sent them when within two months of
maturity, but this did not help with the longer bills.[59] Rogers was,

---

[57] Keele University Library, William Davenport bill-book, 1769–85, omitting the atypical
war years, 1776–82.

[58] An earlier bill and letterbook of Davenport at Keele shows that in the early 1750s
he sent bills to his London banker, Hoare & Company, for collection and deposit.
It is not possible to tell from this source or from an examination of Davenport's
account in the ledgers of Messrs. Hoare & Company, Fleet Street, whether or not
they discounted for him.

[59] PRO C.107/3 to Smith, Wright & Gray, 2 Oct. 1790, 3, 13 June 1792; C.107/9 from
same (many letters). Rogers was informed that "nothing is discountable here [Lon-
don] that has more than 2 Months to Run." C. 107/10 from John Hallett, 10 Mar.
1785.

however, in touch with a number of West Country provincial bankers (particularly in Bath) who would take bills at four months from maturity and give him in exchange two-month bills, charging him two months' discount for the time saved. He could send these shorter bills to London for immediate discount at his bankers.[60] For the much longer bills characteristic of the slave trade, Rogers had to make private discount arrangements. There were men in Bristol (most likely retired merchants) who would discount them, but Rogers, his correspondence would suggest, most often went outside. In at least two cases, the London merchants or guarantees who had accepted some of his West Indian bills agreed to discount or prepay their own acceptances. This was a very safe way for a semiretired merchant to earn the best market interest on his capital.[61] In other cases, country bankers with idle cash at places such as Bradford (Wilts), Chepstow (Monmouth), and Worcester discounted Rogers's long bills. These slave paper discountings were large transactions, sometime £3,000–5,000 at a time.[62] Rogers's varied experience suggests that each active slave trader had to develop his own circle of affluent acquaintances with available liquid resources who would help him with large, longer-term discounts as needed. Through such discounting, remote pockets of capital were made available to the slave trade.

In Virginia there was nothing strictly comparable to the immediate remittance system characteristic of the slave trade in the West Indies and South Carolina after 1750. However, Chesapeake factors were expected to give sureties too, and the same results (speedy and secure remittances) were achieved by slightly different practices. Remittances for slave purchases in Virginia had commonly been made in bills of exchange from the late seventeenth century.[63] The sale of slaves for credit secured by bonds was known there before 1732,[64] but we have no way of determining how widespread the practice was. However,

---

[60] PRO C.107/10 from Atwood Abraham & Company, Bath, 1791.

[61] The two semiretired merchants were Robert Cooper Lee and Robert Shedden, both of whom lived in or near Bedford Square, not a neighborhood for active businesses. See PRO C.107/9 from R. C. Lee, 5 June 1789, 16 Oct., 3 Nov., 16, 18 Dec. 1790; C.107/10 from R. Shedden, 2 Feb. 1792; from R. C. Lee, 25 Mar. 1791.

[62] PRO C.107/3 to Glover, Embury & Cross, Worcester, 17 Nov. 1789; C.107/10 from D. Clutterbuck, Bradford (Wilts), 12 Dec. 1785, 2 Jan., 10 Feb. 1786; from Lewis, Stoughton & Company, Chepstow, 5 Dec. 1791.

[63] For problems arising from the nonacceptance of planters' bills in England, see Minchinton, "Isaac Hobhouse," *Virginia Magazine of History and Biography*, Vol. LXVI (1958), pp. 278–307. For earlier attempts to get Virginia slave selling factors to assume collection responsibility without English surety, see Bank of England Archives, B48 (H. Morice Papers) invoice and instructions for Anne-Galley, 25 Mar. 1725.

[64] Donnan, *Documents*, Vol. IV, pp. 94–5.

after the passage of the Colonial Debts Act, the use of bonds in such transactions became almost universal. There was an active local market in the colony for the sale of Virginia-born slaves by owners, executors, administrators, receivers, or trustees. An examination of several dozen advertisements for such sales published in the *Virginia Gazette* in 1772 shows that, where terms were specified, these almost always included credit (for ca. six to twelve months) secured by bond with security. That is, the bond had to bear the signature not only of the debtor (slave buyer) but also of one or two cosigners who stood surety for him.

However, when slaves newly imported from Africa were advertised for sale in the *Virginia Gazette*, different modes of settlement might be demanded. Five notices of such sale appeared there in 1772: One of these gave no terms, and another specified only that credit would be given with security, probably meaning that bonds would be taken; the other three announced that payment was to be made in "merchants' notes" payable at the next "merchants' meeting."[65] In Virginia before the Revolution, the principal merchants (and managers for British firms) met four times a year at Williamsburg at the time of the regular meetings of the province's General Court (April and October) and Oyer and Terminer Court (June and December). At these meetings they settled accounts among themselves after agreeing on a rate of exchange on London for that session. At such meetings, holders of merchants' notes could therefore expect to receive payment, if desired, in the form of bills of exchange on London at the agreed-upon rate.[66] Where slaves were sold for merchants' notes only, purchases could be effected only by merchants or by the substantial planter who could get such notes as needed. Merchants who bought slaves at such sales undoubtedly planned to resell them on credit to

[65] The first mentioned in the text was the *Prince of Wales*, with 400 slaves (*Gazette*, 24 Sept.); the second was the *Thomas*, with 200 slaves (30 July); the last three were the *Polly*, with 430 slaves (4 June), the *Nancy*, with 250 (9 July), and the *Union*, with 280 (20 Aug.). Cf. also Donnan, *Documents*, Vol. IV, p. 160; Minchinton, King, and Waite, p. 185. Payments were not necessarily punctual where bonds were taken. Advertisements also appeared reminding slave buyers at specific sales that their bonds were overdue. See *Virginia Gazette*, March 20 and October 1, 1772. It is possible that *merchants' notes* came to be insisted on in Virginia because an unacceptable proportion of the planters' bills of exchange were refused acceptance and returned protested. Cf. Donnan, *Documents*, Vol. IV, pp. 147–8. In Maryland, sales seem to have been handled by slave factors on a system comparable to that described by H. Laurens for South Carolina in 1749–55. Planters' bills of exchange were accepted as cash. Ibid., Vol. IV, pp. 26, 38–40, 43.

[66] On merchants' meetings, see James H. Soltow, "The Role of Williamsburg in the Virginia Economy," *William and Mary Quarterly*, third series, Vol. XV (1958), pp. 467–82.

V

320

planters at a profit, presumably taking bonds for the security of the credit. From the standpoint of the English slave traders, sales by factors for merchants' notes meant a slightly slower return than expected under the immediate remittance system but should have been just as secure. And they didn't have to worry about the nonacceptance of planters' bills.

The slave sale advertisements in the 1772 *Virginia Gazette* include one instructive shipload for which no mode of payment was specified. In September 1772 there was entered in the Upper District of the James River the ship *Prince of Wales,* containing 400 African slaves consigned by John Powell & Company of Bristol to their local agents, John Wayles and Colonel Richard Randolph.[67] Wayles was a successful lawyer (and planter) with extensive experience representing British firms, including Farell & Jones of Bristol.[68] Richard Randolph of Curles came from a distinguished Virginia family – his father had been treasurer of the colony earlier in the century – and represented Henrico County in the House of Burgesses from 1766 to 1772. (The fact that he was unseated on petition in 1772 suggests, however, that all was not absolutely well with his affairs.) He also had a Bristol connection, his cousin William Randolph being a partner in Stephenson, Randolph & Cheston, a merchant firm there.[69] Wayles's friends, Farell & Jones, were the guarantees enabling Wayles and Randolph to get this consignment. Neither Wayles nor Randolph was a professional merchant, but leading people in Virginia – including Governor Spotswood – were more than interested in receiving such consignments, both for the 10% commissions and for the air of importance they gave.

The immediate remittance system did not normally operate in Virginia, but, to get their consignment from Powells, Wayles and Randolph undertook – with Farell & Jones guaranteeing their performance – to remit half the proceeds of the sale in six months and the balance in twelve months. Their slave cargo was advertised for sale in the *Virginia Gazette* of September 24, rather late in the year for such business, as planters ordinarily preferred to buy slaves early in the summer so that their new hands could do some work and be "seasoned"

---

[67] *Virginia Gazette,* September 21, 1772; Minchinton, King, and Waite, 185.

[68] John M. Hemphill II, "John Wayles Rates His Neighbours," *Virginia Magazine of History and Biography,* Vol. LXVI (1958), pp. 302–6.

[69] Cynthia Miller Leonard, comp., *The General Assembly of Virginia . . . A Bicentennial Register of Members* (Richmond, Va., 1978), pp. 95, 97, 100, 103; William G. Stanard, "The Randolph Family," *William and Mary Quarterly,* first series, Vol. VII (1898–9), pp. 122–4, 195–7, Vol. VIII (1899–1900), pp. 119–22, 263–5, Vol. IX (1900–1), pp. 182–3, 250–2; *Sketchley's Bristol Directory* (Bristol, 1775).

before the advent of cold weather. With not enough planters coming forward, large lots of these slaves had to be sold to merchants intending to resell them. No terms of sale were given in the advertisement but, in the light of what happened subsequently, they were likely to have been fairly generous, explainable in part by the lateness of the season, by the previous arrival of four other slave ships that year, and perhaps by Randolph's desire to do favors to rebuild his local political position. Had they insisted on merchants' notes in payment – as did at least three other slave ships that summer – Wayles and Randolph would have had no difficulty meeting their obligations to Powell & Company. But they obviously did not and missed both their remittance deadlines, forcing their sureties, Farell & Jones, to pay for them. Wayles died in 1773, leaving an estate estimated at £30,000. In a codicil to his will, he directed that his executors (his three sons-in-law) not distribute his effects to his heirs until his slave accounts with Farell & Jones were cleared. But the sons-in-law (including Thomas Jefferson) ignored this provision and in 1774 divided the estate among the heirs (mostly their wives and themselves). Since Randolph, the surviving partner, could not pay by himself, Farell & Jones could only seek redress at law, but the closing of the courts in 1774–5 and the Revolution obstructed this course for many years. Although the peace treaty of 1783 and the Jay Treaty of 1794 recognized the validity of claims for such prewar debts, the heirs of Farell & Jones were unable to recover much until Jefferson's administration, when, in accordance with a bilateral convention of 1802, the United States paid the British government £600,000 sterling to be quit of claims against it relating to the treaty provisions on prewar debts. The British government turned this money over to a commission, which in 1811 paid the estates of Farell & Jones about 46% of their claim (without interest) after almost forty years. The case is interesting not only because it involved Jefferson but also because it gives some indication of the strategic role of the guarantees in financing the trade and suggests some of the risks they ran.[70]

---

[70] Price, *Capital and Credit*, 138; Farell & Jones claim, PRO T.79/9 and 30; Somerset Record Office, DD/GC 62. The slaves were sold for £8,537, of which £6,017 (without interest) was still owing in 1783. For an analogous case of 1733 in which Lyde and Cooper, another Bristol firm of guarantees, was forced to pay when the slave-selling factor, Henry Darnall, Jr., defaulted, see Maryland State Archives, Chancery Records, Vol. 8, ff. 9–75. For British debt claims after the war and the compensation of 1802–11, see Jacob M. Price, "One Family's Empire: the Russell–Lee–Clerk Connection in Maryland, Britain and India, 1707–1857," *Maryland Historical Magazine*, Vol. LXXII (1977), pp. 165–225, esp. pp. 201–14; idem., "The Maryland Bank Stock Case: British–American Financial and Political Relations Before and After the American

V

The planned credit emphasis of this chapter should not, of course, mislead the reader into thinking that *all* slave sales were for credit. In every colony there were a few well-to-do planters and merchants who could buy for cash but who expected substantial reductions in price in return for their coin, notes, or bills. The seller needed much skill to steer between the Scylla of reassuring "cash" sales at unacceptably low prices and the Charybdis of easier sales at strikingly higher prices with unacceptably long credits and attendant risks. In a letter of 1773 to a young man starting out as a slave seller in Charleston, Henry Laurens advised:

> ... I would by no means encourage you to give Credit to every Man who may offer to deal with you merely for the Sake of a high price & a flaunting Average, which must end in the prejudice of your Constituents & your own Ruin. Yet on the other hand if you Consult only your own Safety by Selling to Monied Men who are always careful to obtain full abatement for Cash, you will depreciate your prices to Such a degree as will Injure your Friends, the Owners of Cargoes consigned to you . . . & greatly undervalue your Own Credit & Reputation.[71]

It is not within the scope of this chapter to explore at length the North American slave trade after the American Revolution. Published work does, however, suggest that there was some continuity in credit arrangements. Perhaps the single most significant interstate slave trade affecting the United States after the abolition of the import trade in 1807 was the coastal trade from the Chesapeake to New Orleans. The newspaper advertisements published by Bancroft indicate that professional slave buyers in Virginia had to offer hard cash for their purchases. However, at the New Orleans end, the advertisements on the eve of the Civil War announce that these same traffickers would sell for "good town bills," that is, accepted bills of exchange on mer-

Revolution," in Aubrey C. Land, Lois Green Carr, and Edward C. Papenfuse (eds.), *Law, Society, and Politics in Early Maryland* (Baltimore, 1977), pp. 3–40. For the sale of slaves to merchants in lots of ten to thirty-one, see Virginia State Library, *Jones, Surviving Partner of Farell and Jones v. Wayles exors*, 1797 Circuit Court Cases, as cited in Michael L. Nicholls, "Competition, Credit, and Crisis: Merchant–Planter Relations in Southside Virginia" (unpublished paper presented at the Conference on Merchant Credit and Labour Strategies in the Staple Economies of North America, Memorial University of Newfoundland, August 1987), p. 6.

[71] Hamer et al., Vol. VIII, pp. 671–2. In an earlier letter on the same subject, Laurens advised young Gervais to "take Collateral Security from every Person whose Circumstances are doubtful" (ibid., p. 637). Comparable advice was given by Samuel and William Vernon, Rhode Island slave traders, to their captain in the West Indies in 1771–3 (Donnan, *Documents*, Vol. III, pp 248, 272).

chants in New Orleans.[72] In this way, the sellers gave several months' credit to buyers, whether planters or inland dealers, without running the risk and burden of collecting such debts. This is functionally just what the sellers in prerevolutionary Virginia achieved by demanding merchants' notes.

In summary, the English slave trade started in the seventeenth century without any clearly established credit conventions of its own. Slaves were sold to planters more or less like any other trade goods. But planters were hungrier for slaves than they were for almost any other conceivable purchase and pushed the existing system of agricultural credit to its limits in their greedy effort to get as many slaves as possible. The slave traders thus found it much easier to sell slaves on credit than to collect debts – and the planter-dominated colonial courts and legislatures were not much help. By the end of the seventeenth century, both the Royal African Company and the separate traders normally found it necessary to require their factors to assume responsibility for the payment of all their credit sales. The factors could undertake such commitments only if they could, in turn, require planter-buyers to give bond or equivalent security. The credit control practices introduced in the last quarter of the seventeenth century were further developed by the private traders in the opening decades of the new century, with the planter's bond becoming a much more effective debt instrument after the passage of the Colonial Debts Act of 1732. Thus, by the 1730s and 1740s, English slave traders were fairly certain of eventually receiving the proceeds of credit sales, but they still were not certain about *when* they would see their money. As such uncertainty could be fatal for a business, in the 1750s slave traders to both the West Indies and South Carolina turned increasingly to the immediate remittance system by which their factors were required to send back on the slave-importing vessel the total net receipt of the slave sales, most of it in the form of bills of long maturity drawn by the factors on their guarantees in England. Since such bills could often be discounted or passed into circulation in England, the slave traders gained substantially in liquidity. This arrangement made the factors' guarantees, or sureties, the linchpins of the trade's credit structure. In this, the guarantees were in effect performing a role anticipating that of the Victorian "accepting house."

---

[72] Frederic Bancroft, *Slave Trading in the Old South* (New York, 1959). For offers to buy for cash, see pp. 22, 24, 25, 28n et passim; for the New Orleans sale, see facing p. 316. The New Orleans *Picayune* slave sale advertisements show the use of other credit merchanisms, including bonds, in earlier years.

THE PROBLEM OF MORTGAGES

Thus far, we have been discussing what is essentially short- and medium-term credit – but important credit nevertheless. At the level of the planter buying a slave, the extent of credit was set by the market. There may not have always been as much credit available as ambitious planters would have wished, but there was always enough to sell all slaves. The development of the immediate remittance or bills in the bottom system shifted the burden of carrying this credit from the slave trader to the factor and his guarantee, with the slave trader receiving full remittance on sales (in the form of discountable bills) on the return of his vessel, normally within eighteen months of departure. By the 1790s, we are told, the average length of the bills accepted was three years. With bills of this duration, the guarantees would have had acceptances (obligations) outstanding that far exceeded the average annual return from the trade. Even if the average acceptance was only two years, they would very likely have been at least equal to the annual returns.

But was there no long-term credit? What about the mortgages that loom so large in some popular accounts of the plantation economy of the West Indies? In considering such questions, we can usefully start with the last work of Richard Pares, who, with a few others, laid the foundations of the post–World War II study of the slave economy of the West Indies. For the purposes of this chapter Pares made several major points: (1) Except for the relatively modest sums that some emigrants brought with them, there was (*pace* Adam Smith) no significant long-term movement of capital from the mother country to the colonies. (2) The credit that was available from the mother country was largely short-term commercial credit. As the West India houses of London and Bristol prospered, they reinvested part of their profits in further advances to their planter and merchant correspondents in the Caribbean, so that their outstanding balances grew at least as fast as their capital. (3) The great fortunes we find in the West Indies were built up by reinvesting profits and utilizing to the fullest available commercial credit. (In a few cases, profits of office also helped.) (4) Where we do find mortgages, they are unlikely to represent independent capital movements and are more likely to be only the last stage in the ontogeny of debt: book debt, bond, judgment, mortgage. In his dealings with a merchant (in the colony or in Britain), a planter ran up a debt on the trader's books too large to be cleared by the next crop or two. To assuage the merchant and gain more time, the planter entered into a bond for the debt. When the bond was not cleared in the time specified, the merchant or his representative went to court and obtained a judgment against the planter. To forestall action on the judgment, the planter gained more time by giving the merchant a mortgage on some or all of his real estate and slaves.[73]

Although I tend to agree with the main thrust of Pares's generalizations, I do not find them equally applicable to all the slave economies in the old or Atlantic British Empire at all stages of their existence. Pares's formulation is probably truer of the continental colonies before 1776 than it is of the West Indian colonies if we carry their story down to 1833. Although we have only vague estimates of West Indian debt, we have quite precise information about preindependence debt in the thirteen colonies. Much of it wasn't repaid because of the Revolution and caused considerable legal and diplomatic difficulties thereafter that have left a useful subsidence in the archives.

British merchants trading to the thirteen colonies in the generation before 1776 generally operated in one (or more) of three modes: (1) They were factors acting on commission for planters in the Chesapeake who consigned them tobacco for sale and ordered goods for them to purchase. These arrangements were very similar to those connecting West Indian sugar planters to commission houses in London or Bristol. (2) They corresponded in normal merchant fashion with independent merchant houses in the colonies, north and south, with each side buying and selling for the other as requested, charging the usual commissions. (3) They operated "stores" (a new word) in the interior of Maryland, Virginia, and North Carolina, serving small and middling planters in particular. Although the first mode has attracted the most attention in writings on the Chesapeake, it was probably the least important by the 1770s where debts were concerned.

So far, I have been able to discover the balance sheets of only two English firms trading to the Chesapeake in the generation before the Revolution: James Buchanan & Company and John Norton & Son(s). Both dealt with American merchants and planters, though planters were slightly more important in Norton's business than in Buchanan's. Dealings with American merchants were generally in the mode then called the "cargo trade." The American merchant ordered a "cargo" of goods (possibly worth £5,000 or more), which his London or Bristol correspondent purchased for him on one year's credit from

[73] Pares, pp. 45–50.

the great wholesalers in those ports, the American correspondent undertaking to remit goods or bills of exchange to pay for the same before the year's credit had expired. In 1768, the peak year for Buchanan & Company, about 60% of the amount owing the firm in Virginia was from merchants and only 38% was from planters. Despite their greater involvement with planters, Norton's debt figures for 1773 were not too different: 54% owed by merchants and other traders and 42% owed by planters.[74] In the stores run by Glasgow, Whitehaven, and other firms, we should expect naturally to find a higher percentage of planter debt, but even there some large wholesale transactions with local merchants appear.[75]

The total commercial debt owed by the thirteen colonies to Britain tended to rise in the century along with the rise in population and trade, reaching a peak of ca. £6 million sterling in 1774. As the American Revolution approached and imports from Britain were stopped in 1775, the debt outstanding was cut back by perhaps one-half. One merchant claimed that during 1775 merchant-to-merchant debt (as in the cargo trade) was cut by at least two-thirds. However, net collections were much less impressive from the small and middling planters who patronized the stores in the interior of Virginia, Maryland, and North Carolina. Hence, with the peace, prewar debts outstanding were disproportionately those of the southern colonies (84.1%), particularly Virginia and Maryland (57.7%).[76]

However, in the mass of paper left behind by the debt problem,

---

[74] Jacob M. Price, "The Last Phase of the Virginia–London Consignment Trade: James Buchanan & Co., 1758–1768," *William and Mary Quarterly*, third series, Vol. XLIII (1986), pp. 64–98, esp. p. 91; Price, *Capital and Credit*, chap. 6; on Nortons, see also Frances Norton Mason, *John Norton & Sons, Merchants of London and Virginia . . . 1750 to 1795*, new ed. (Newton Abbot, 1968), with an introduction by Samuel M. Rosenblatt.

[75] For examples of local merchants owing substantial amounts to the local stores of Glasgow firms, see PRO T.79/24, Cuming, Mackenzie & Company's Nansemond store; T.79/25 Archibald & John Hamilton & Company (Virginia and North Carolina).

[76] Price, *Capital and Credit*, chap. 1. For the reduction in merchant-to-merchant debt, see Richard Champion, *Considerations on the Present Situation of Great Britain and the United States of America*, 2nd ed. (London, 1784), p. 269n. The planter debt reduction was much less in the Chesapeake and North Carolina during the nonimportation year, 1775. There was some collection of debts during that year, but new debts were created by the sale of merchandise in the stores at the beginning of the year. Thus the British firms' total effects (merchandise and debts) in those colonies may have been reduced by as much as a third, although total debts remained much as before. The Alston accounts in PRO T.79/33(10) show no reduction in debts owed at four North Carolina stores between August 1774 and August 1775. At the Nomony store (in Virginia) of John Ballantine, the net total investment of the company was reduced 40% between September 1774 and August 1775, whereas the customer debt was reduced only 11.7%. PRO T.79/31.

we find mortgages appearing less frequently than we should expect. There are, of course, conspicuous examples: On the eve of the war in 1774–6, Daniel Dulany had entered into two mortgages (totalling £12,121) to Osgood Hanbury & Company of London to cover debts owed that firm by his late father, Walter Dulany.[77] This is a classic example of what I have termed Pares's "ontogeny of debt." We can find the same process at work among the smaller planters of Southside Virginia in the depressed years 1772–4, when many were obliged to give mortgages to appease their creditors. Michael Nicholls has shown that mortgages and deeds of trust recorded in seven Southside Virginia counties increased from 31.3 per annum in 1768–70 to 145.3 per annum in 1771–3 as tobacco prices fell. However, the total amounts involved were small, with the total recorded for the seven counties in the peak year 1772 being only £22,117 in Virginia currency (ca. £17,700 sterling), or less than the estate of John Wayles.[78] The infrequent mention of mortgages in the postwar debt claims would seem to reinforce the impression that in the thirteen colonies mortgages were, at most, a tactic to collect old debts and not a vehicle for independent transatlantic capital movements. The planters of Virginia and Maryland could avoid the worst pitfalls of debt because they did not have to buy replacement slaves as urgently as did their West Indian counterparts. Their slaves, by contrast, tended to grow more numerous over time, even without new purchases. With both their speculative landholdings and their slaveholdings growing steadily more valuable, they could, in a pinch, get out of serious debt by selling land or slaves – or so the advertisements in the *Virginia Gazette* would suggest – and thus normally avoid the threatening grasp of the mortgage.

In the West Indies, the mortgage situation tended to become markedly different, particularly after 1763. Even there, Pares's paradigm of the ontogeny of debt would appear to hold true for the older settled areas. However, Richard Sheridan has pointed out that after 1763 there was an increased demand for new credit associated with buying and developing estates in the islands ceded by France, as well as with improving the as yet undeveloped areas of Jamaica and Demerara.[79] This demand came to the surface in the pressures behind two acts of

---

[77] Price, "The Maryland Bank Stock Case," pp. 16–18.
[78] Nicholls, pp. 20–1. Nicholls's aggregation does not distinguish British from local creditors or primary obligations from obligations protecting cosigners to bonds, etc. Nicholls's paper has been published in Rosemary E. Ommer, ed., *Merchant Credit and Labour Strategies in Historical Perspective* (Fredericton, Canada, 1990).
[79] Sheridan, "Commercial and Financial Organization," p. 258.

Parliament on colonial mortgages passed in the early 1770s. The first (1773) recognized the right of Dutch and other foreigners to lend money on mortgage in the British West Indian colonies at the British legal maximum interest rate of 5% – provided only that, in case of foreclosures, the land so seized was to be sold at auction and not retained by the foreigner.[80] The second act (1774) regularized the legal standing of persons resident in Britain (where the legal maximum interest rate was 5%) who had been lending large sums on mortgage in Ireland and the colonies at the 6% rate permitted in those jurisdictions.[81]

In the debate on the bills in the House of Commons, it was asserted that the first measure was opposed by those interested in the fully developed, smaller island colonies but pushed by those desiring to develop the ceded islands and the undeveloped sections of the larger colonies. Although the legal rate of interest in most of the colonies was then 6%, it was alleged without explanation that it was impossible to borrow in the islands for less than 8% – a rate considered prohibitive for many improvements. Outside mortgage money at lower rates was therefore desired to encourage the development of the more backward areas of the colonies.[82]

Of special interest in the debates is the leading role in steering both acts through the House of Commons played by William Pulteney (né Johnstone), a private member. William Johnstone, who took his wife's family name on marrying the heiress to the vast Pulteney fortune, was one of the four remarkably adventurous (in the eighteenth-century sense) Johnstone brothers of Westerhall, Dumfriesshire, Scotland. One of his brothers, John, was a survivor of the Black Hole of Calcutta; another, George, was a naval officer and governor of West Florida from 1763 to 1767. From brother George, Pulteney could have found out some of the difficulties of developing newly acquired lands in or near the Caribbean. More relevant, perhaps, were Pulteney's close connections with the Alexander brothers of Edinburgh, who had bought large plantations on Grenada and Tobago from their former French owners but were having trouble paying for their purchases in the difficult aftermath of the crash of 1772. The Alexanders were

---

[80] 13 Geo. III c. 14 (*Statutes at Large*, ed. Danby Pickering, Vol. XXX, pp. 22–6). Jamaica subsequently permitted 6 percent interest on such mortgages. Long, Vol. I, pp. 556–7, 577n, 578n.

[81] 14 Geo. III c. 79 (*Statutes at Large*, ed. Pickering, Vol. XXX, pp. 542–5).

[82] Cobbett, *The Parliamentary History of England*, Vol. XVII, pp. 482–3, 642, 686–8, 690. On interest rates, see Pares, p. 44; Long, Vol. I, pp. 555–6; *Considerations on the State of the Sugar Islands, and on the policy of enabling foreigners to lend money on real security in those colonies . . . by a West Indian Planter* (London, 1773).

V

Credit in the slave plantation economies 329

interested in getting a Dutch or other mortgage on their West Indian estates, and Pulteney, in pushing his bills, most likely had in mind their needs, as well as those of broader interests.[83]

One wonders, though, whether Pulteney's success in getting these bills through with relatively little trouble was due solely to the support of those interested in developing new areas in the West Indies. By the 1770s, the absentee West Indian plantation owner had become a conspicuous feature of British social life. There were thirteen "West Indians" in the house that passed the acts of 1773–4.[84] Many others in Parliament must have been connected to West Indians by blood, marriage, or friendship. Most should have known that it wasn't easy to manage a West Indian estate from afar for very many years. One solution was to sell the estate if one could find a buyer who could pay an attractive price. But such buyers were rare, particularly when large fresh mortgages (as distinct from mortgages converted from older debts) were needed but difficult to obtain in the islands or at home. For many an absentee, fearing that no mortgage meant no sale, the acts opened new possibilities.

In the longer run, what difference did the mortgage acts of 1773–4 make? The 6% rate should have been attractive in peacetime, when the yield on the government "funds" in Britain hovered around 3.5 percent, but less so in wartime, when yields on the funds and British mortgages were around 5%.[85] One therefore wonders whether the colonies were entirely wise in setting their maximum rates of interest as low as 6%.[86] One picks up chance references to the Dutch lending on mortgages in both the British and French islands after this time, but it is difficult to assess the weight of such lending. Van de Voort has studied Dutch mortgage records but does not distinguish between the periods before and after 1773; his data show, however, that during 1753–94, the British islands received only 4.9% of Dutch mortgage loans to the West Indies.[87] In the British islands, we are told, mortgage lending from all sources increased substantially both in the prosper-

---

[83] All four Johnstone brothers were in Parliament at one time or another between 1768 and 1805. Sir Lewis Namier and John Brooke, *The History of Parliament: The House of Commons 1754–1790*, 3 vols. (Oxford and New York, 1964), Vol. II, pp. 683–7, Vol. III, pp. 341–3. On the Alexander–Pulteney connection and the Alexanders' interest in the West Indies, see Price, *France and the Chesapeake*, Vol. II, pp. 693–700.

[84] Namier and Brooke, Vol. I, p. 157.

[85] T. S. Ashton, *Economic Fluctuations in England 1700–1800* (Oxford, 1959), pp. 85–8, 187.

[86] On interest rates, see footnote 82.

[87] J. P. Van de Voort, "Dutch Capital in the West Indies During the Eighteenth Century," *The Low Countries History Yearbook: Acta Historiae Neerlandicae*, Vol. XIV (1981), pp. 85–105, esp. p. 105.

V

ous times following the return of peace in 1783 and the removal of
St. Domingue competition after 1790 and in the distressed times following the ending of the slave trade in 1807 and the decline of sugar
prices after 1815. We have already noted the process by which merchant advances to planters had to be protected by bonds and judgments and, ultimately, mortgages. The final step came when the
mortgage was foreclosed and the merchant house became the plantation owner. To gain some liquidity, the merchants, in turn, sometimes had to take out a new mortgage in Britain on the estate.[88]

What did it all add up to? When St. Lucia changed from French to
English land law, more than £1 million in 2,000 unrecorded mortgages
had to be registered ca. 1833.[89] Sheridan and others suggest that when
slavery was abolished after 1833, much of the £20 million sterling in
compensation paid to the former slave owners had to be repaid by
them to clear their mortgages.[90] But I have as yet seen no hard data
on the total burden of such mortgages ca. 1830, and wonder whether
anyone has gone through the registries of deeds in the various West
Indian islands and analyzed the registered mortgages. Until this is
done, we can only speculate on the relative importance of local, British, and European lenders, or on what changes, if any, are noticeable
after the mortgage acts of the 1770s or the abolition of the slave trade
in 1807. On the financial side, at least, much still needs to be done
in historical research on the economics of the West Indian slave
plantation.

The pre-1807 slave trade, of course, was normally financed by short-
term and not by long-term credit secured by mortgage or otherwise.
However, the need for replacement slaves could push the running
debt of a plantation so high that a first or additional mortgage became
inevitable, just as could a plantation owner's desire for large numbers
of new slaves to open up hitherto undeveloped lands. Thus, the
difference between short-term and long-term debt may be clearer as

[88] Richard B. Sheridan, "The West India Sugar Crisis and British Slave Emancipation,
1830–1833," *Journal of Economic History*, Vol. XXXI (1961), pp. 539–51; Pares, pp. 48–
9. On the difficulty of obtaining outside mortgages in the 1820s, see Lowell Joseph
Ragatz, *The Fall of the Planter Class in the British West Indies: A Study in Social and
Economic History* (New York, 1928), pp. 381–2. On mortgages from merchant houses,
see also Michael Craton and James Walton, *A Jamaican Plantation: The History of Worthy
Park 1670–1970* (Toronto and Buffalo, 1970), pp. 119, 159. On bank mortgages, see
L. S. Pressnell, *Country Banking in the Industrial Revolution* (Oxford, 1956), pp.
307–8.
[89] Ragatz, p. 382.
[90] Sheridan, "West India Sugar Crisis," pp. 547–9; Pares, p. 49.

abstractions than as realities in the demanding world of tropical agriculture.

THE FRENCH ANTILLES:
A COMPARATIVE APPROACH

I propose to discuss the slave trade in the French Antilles rather briefly, emphasizing those key features of the credit system that can be compared or contrasted with those prevailing in the British West Indies. There is a rich body of erudite modern scholarship on the French slave trade.[91] Unfortunately, little of it concentrates on the specific questions I raised earlier in this chapter. However, Father Dieudonné Rinchon has published several volumes of documents that furnish some valuable clues to the precise commercial practices facilitating the use of credit in France's slave trade.[92] His important publications enable us at least to ask of the French record some of the questions raised by British experience – though the answers often prove different.

At the beginning of this chapter, I suggested two models describing the attitude of the law toward the availability of plantation slaves to satisfy creditors' claims against a plantation owner. On the one hand, there was the Latin model, which placed great emphasis on protecting the functioning integrity of a plantation and made it almost impossible for a creditor to seize slaves, livestock, or equipment. On the other hand, there was the Anglo-Saxon model, giving primacy to the rights of creditors, particularly when reinforced by bond or judgment. We have seen the Latin model at work in Portuguese Brazil and the Anglo-Saxon model at work both in the Board of Trade's review of colonial legislation and in the Colonial Debts Act of 1732.

In the French colonies, policy was at first ambiguous, with one colony giving primacy to the integrity of the plantation and another

---

[91] See in particular the valuable bibliographies in Robert Louis Stein, *The French Slave Trade in the Eighteenth Century: An Old Regime Business* (Madison, Wis., 1979); Jean Meyer, *L'Armement nantais dans la deuxième moitié du XVIIIᵉ siècle* (Ports-Routes-Trafics, Vol. XXVIII) (Paris, 1969); and P. Dieudonné Rinchon, *Les armements négriers au XVIIIᵉ siècle d'après la correspondance et la comptabilité des armateurs et des capitaines nantais* (Académie royale des sciences coloniales, Classe des sciences morales et politiques, Mémoires, Vol. VII, 3) (Brussels, 1956).

[92] See P. Dieudonné Rinchon, *Le trafic négrier, d'aprè les livres de commerce du capitaine gantois Pierre Ignace Liévin van Alstein* (Bruxelles, 1938); idem., *Pierre-Ignace-Liévin van Alstein, capitaine négrier* (Memoires de l'Institut Français d'Afrique Noire, 71) (Dakar, 1964), and his work cited in the previous footnote.

332

paying more attention to the rights of creditors. This ambiguity even crept into the *Code Noir* of 1685, the legal foundation of the slave system in the French colonies for the next century and more. Articles 44 and 46 of the code declared slaves to be *meubles*, personal property or chattels, hence divisible among heirs and as subject to seizure as any other personal property. However, article 47 declared that in seizures and sales, slave "wives" were not to be separated from their "husbands" or small children (under age seven, in practice) from their mothers; article 48 provided further that slaves aged fourteen to sixty working on sugar, indigo, or other plantations could not be seized for debts unless the whole plantation or farm was seized. However, within this exception, a further exception was made to permit the recovery of recently sold slaves if the price of their purchase had not been paid. This last concession does not appear to have been much used and, in practice, the integrity of the plantation was respected in the French colonies as much as in Brazil. This meant that creditors could seize crops but could not seize anything that would diminish the productive capacity of a plantation.[93] Thus, although French law knew documents (*contrats d'obligation*) analogous to an English bond, in practice these did not give the recourse against slaves that British bonds enjoyed under the Colonial Debts Act of 1732. Persons selling slaves for credit were thus ordinarily in a weaker legal position in the French colonies than in the English ones.

In the British colonies, the general tendency in the late seventeenth and eighteenth centuries was for the proceeds from the sale of slaves to be remitted with increasing frequency in bills of exchange rather than in commodities. French slave traders had also experimented with bills of exchange (*lettres de change*) but found a discouraging proportion of nonacceptances in France of bills drawn by planters and therefore tended, with some exceptions, to avoid using bills.[94] English slave traders also had troubles with the nonacceptance of planters' bills and therefore preferred bills drawn by merchants and factors, such as

---

[93] Lucien Peytraud, *L'esclavage aux Antilles Francaises avant 1789* (Paris, 1897), pp. 160, 164, 245, and n, 247–65. See also Alain Buffon, *Monnaie et crédit en économie coloniale: Contribution à l'histoire économique de la Guadeloupe 1675–1919* (Basse-Terre, 1979); Louis-Philippe May, *Histoire économique de la Martinique (1635–1763)* (Paris, 1930), pp. 264–6; Adrien Dessalles, *Histoire générale des Antilles*, 5 vols. (Paris, 1847–8), Vol. III, pp. 243–9; [Michel René Hilliard d'Auberteuil], *Considérations sur l'état présent de la colonie française de Saint-Domingue*, 2 vols. (Paris, 1776), Vol. I, pp. 111–29.

[94] Gaston Martin, *Nantes au XVIIIᵉ Siècle: L'ère des négriers (1714–1774)* (Paris, 1931), p. 133. For an exception in which 226,498 livres were remitted in twenty-one bills of exchange by the Cap Français (St. Domingue) firm of de Russy, Gauget & Cie to the Nantes slave trader François Deguer, see Rinchon, *Les armements négriers*, p. 64.

they obtained in the immediate remittance system. There does not appear to have been anything precisely corresponding to this system in the French slave trade, even though eighteenth-century France was familiar with the assignment of bills of exchange by endorsement and with discounting. The chief difficulty may have been in finding rich merchants and bankers at home who could be persuaded to act as guarantees for trustworthy slave-selling factors in the West Indies and to accept their long bills. French firms appear to have had difficulty finding strong, independent correspondents in the West Indies and, when they needed factors there, often found it necessary to set up branches (*succursales*) under junior partners or client firms in which they retained a major interest (*sociétés en commandite*). Since such branches or client firms could draw heavily only on their partners in France, such drawing would hardly have been a useful channel for their remission of the proceeds of slave sales to those same partners.[95]

There are, of course, always exceptions or partial exceptions. In a letter of 1770, François Deguer, a big Nantes slave trader, described the existence of certain large houses in Le Cap (St. Domingue) who, for the high commission of 12%, would agree to guarantee all collections on credit sales of slaves and would send back in the slave ship the proceeds of the sale paid for then or payable within six months. The proceeds of credit sales payable beyond six months would be remitted as received.[96] This is little more than Henry Laurens of Charleston offered to do for a 10% commission in 1749. It differed from the Liverpool immediate remittance system in that the French slave trader had no guarantee or even firm knowledge of when he was going to get remittances for sales with more than six months' credit. Though Deguer and a few others may have experimented with such guaranteed sales through the big merchants of Le Cap, the existing literature would seem to suggest that most French slave traders stayed with more traditional methods.

British slave traders, we have seen, preferred selling through factors

---

[95] For example, four-fifths of the capital of the Saint-Marc (St. Domingue) firm of Reynaud Frères & Cie was held by the partners in the Bordeaux slave-trading and West Indies firm of Henry Romberg, Bapst & Cie, which they represented in the colony. Françoise Thésée, *Négociants bordelais et colons de Saint-Domingue: . . . la maison Henry Romberg, Bapst et C*^{ie} *1783–1793* (Bibliothèque d'Histoire d'Outre-mer, Nouvelle Série, Travaux, 1) (Paris, 1972), pp. 29–32. For the use of bills of exchange in France then, see Charles Carrière, *Négociants marseillais au XVIIIe siècle*, 2 vols. (Marseille, 1973), Vol. II, pp. 845–74; Charles Carrière et al., *Banque et capitalisme commercial: La lettre de change au XVIIIe siècle* (Marseille, 1976). For the mercantile community in the French Antilles, cf. Dessalles, Vol. IV, p. 592; May, pp. 208–9.

[96] Rinchon, *Les armements négriers*, p. 53.

V

334

rather than ship captains even in the late seventeenth century. Where captains were sometimes used, especially in the West Indies, there was a tendency to change to factors by the mid-eighteenth century.[97] By contrast, many French slave traders appear to have continued to make heavy (though not exclusive) use of ship captains in slave sales throughout the eighteenth century. A typical large French slave trade vessel (with 250 to 400 slaves) would be staffed with two captains. As soon as the slaves were disposed of and return cargo taken on board, the ship would depart for France under the command of the second captain, with the first remaining in the islands for up to a year to collect the debts arising from the slave sale. The first captain had a strong interest in staying behind because he collected a substantial commission (5 to 7%) on the slave sales he completed.[98] If on departure he had had to leave the collection of some debts in the hands of a firm in the island, he would have had to share his commission with it.

A substantial portion (10–35%) of French slaves sales were paid in *comptant*, or current effects. These took the form of the worn Spanish coins that circulated in the islands for more than their intrinsic worth, or *mandats* (drafts or sight bills) on local traders, or promissory notes (*billets*) from the buyer given with the understanding that they would be almost immediately converted into commodity deliveries. In whatever form, the *comptant* were speedily converted into commodities for the slave vessel's return cargo. The unpaid balances earned by the slave sales were acknowledged by the buyers' personal notes (*billets*) payable ordinarily at two to twelve months, but sometimes at up to eighteen or twenty-four months. These notes were usually paid off in commodities at the current market price. The commodities so acquired were freighted back to the slave-trading firm in France in whatever vessels were available. After about twelve months, when most but not all the *billets* had been redeemed by the slave purchasers, the captain returned to France, leaving any unsettled notes in the hands of his employer's factor for collection. Substantially the same procedures were followed when the sales were made by factors.[99]

Contemporary commentators and modern scholars agree that the

---

[97] Hyde et al., pp. 368–77, esp. p. 369n.
[98] Rinchon, *Van Alstein*, pp. 120, 212–13.
[99] Ibid., pp. 89–92, 114–15, 120, 194–7, 200–1, 203–5, 215, 217, 243–4, 282 passim; idem., *Le trafic négrier*, pp. 129–30, 222–23; idem., *Les armements négriers*, pp. 67, 93–4, 101, 107, 109, 116. It is possible that because the Van Alstein papers are those of a ship captain, they exaggerate the relative importance of sales by captains. In *Les armements négriers*, Rinchon gives more details of sales through factors. See also Paul Butel, *Les Négociants bordelais, l'Europe et les îles au XVIII* siècle (Paris, 1974), pp. 222–35.

chief weakness of the French system was that buyers of slaves (particularly planter buyers) did not clear their notes at the times promised. (Here the difference between the French and British debt laws are relevant.) We regularly find indications of ventures taking five and six years to be settled, and some reportedly took up to ten years.[100] As a result, many slave-trading firms accumulated large balances owed them in the Antilles. In 1785, eight large firms in Nantes were owed over 8 million livres in the islands.[101] (If these were *livres tournois*, they would have been the equivalent of ca. £333,445 sterling.) On collections, therefore, the French slave traders were working under a significant disadvantage compared with the Liverpool slavers, who after 1750 usually received the product of their American sales "in the bottom" on the return of their vessels, either in goods or in negotiable bills.

We need not, however, be overly concerned about the balance sheets of French slave traders, nor ought we to take too seriously the tales of their great losses from uncollectable debts. Whatever misfortunes may have befallen individual slave traders, the great growth of the French slave trade in the eighteenth century[102] can only mean that the trade as a whole was most attractive. The profit margins of the French slave traders had to be large enough to absorb the costs, delays, and losses of debt collections.

CONCLUSION: THE ECONOMIES AND COSTS OF CREDIT

Credit, with all its difficulties, was just one of the necessary transaction costs that the slave trade could support and still be attractive. We can conceive of a slave trade conducted entirely for cash, but it

---

[100] Rinchon, *Les armements négriers*, pp. 62–3, 72, 92, 101–2, 110, 124–6; Martin, pp. 131, 375–6; Meyer, pp. 227–231; Thésée, pp. 85–6, 96–7, 101; Perry Viles, "The Slaving Interest in the Atlantic Ports, 1763–1792," *French Historical Studies*, Vol. VII (1972), pp. 529–43, esp. p. 532; Stein, 113–16, 149–50; H[ervé] du Halgouet, *Au temps de Saint-Domingue et de la Martinique d'après la correspondance des trafiquants maritimes* (Rennes, 1941), pp. 63–84.

[101] Rinchon, *Van Alstein*, p. 215. At the time of the Seven Years War, it was estimated that all the Nantes slave traders had 10 million livres owed them in St. Domingue, alone. Martin, pp. 131, 309. Even so, the share of their total indebtedness owed by Antilles planters to merchants, local and metropolitan, was less (40%) than the share (53%) owed to other West Indians for land purchases and family settlements. Christian Schnakenbourg, *Les sucreries de la Guadeloupe dans la second moitié du XVIIIe siècle (1760–1790)* (Thèse pour le doctorat d'état, Paris II, 1973), pp. 146–56; Alain Buffon, *Monnaie et crédit en économie coloniale: Contributiion à l'histoire économique de la Guadeloupe 1635–1919* (Basse-Terre, 1979), p. 111.

[102] Stein, pp. 207–11.

would undoubtedly have been a much smaller trade: With markedly less effective demand, profit margins on sales should have been significantly lower, and in the aggregate such a trade should have been less profitable.

We must therefore take credit into account when we calculate the profitability of the trade. Since I have been able to examine the original business records used by only a few of the scholars who have attempted to make such calculations, I refrain from commenting on their individual works and instead confine myself to some general remarks on the problem of the relationship of credit to profits.

Slave traders in both Britain and France tended to keep separate records for each "adventure"; this was necessary in part because the adventure was sometimes an ad hoc association of persons who were not otherwise partners. In their accounts they debited the adventure with all charges relating to the *mise-hors* or "outfit" and cargo of the venture (cost of buying or chartering the vessel, expenditure for sails, cables, and repairs, trading goods, provisions, wages of crew, etc.) and credited it with net receipts realized from the remittances for the slave sales. Such calculations showed whether or not the individual venture was profitable, but not the return on capital invested, inasmuch as the outfit and cargo were not necessarily identical to the capital ventured by the adventurers.

Between 1741 and 1810, approximately 61,000 slaves were transported annually from Africa to the American plantations of the various European colonial powers. If over these years the outset and cargo expenditure of the slave ventures in peacetime had averaged £20 per slave landed, the annual ventures would have been about £1,220,000 sterling. The total at risk would have been perhaps double this figure, since the returns for one year's venture would not in most cases have come home before it was time to send out the next year's venture (except in Brazil). Where did these large sums come from? Slave traders did not usually start out as rich men and had therefore to act together to mobilize the resources necessary for their speculations. Their ventures could be conducted by ongoing partnerships but were often, as noted, an activity of ad hoc and temporary groups of co-venturers. In England, the participants in any given venture were usually recruited from the same port, though we find evidence of nonlocal participation (e.g., Glasgow merchants taking shares in Liverpool slaving ventures).[103] Outside money (particularly from Paris)

---

[103] Price, "Buchanan & Simson," pp. 29–31; Curtin, *Atlantic Slave Trade*, p. 216. The £20 figure is a crude and arbitrary estimate, given the fluctuations in costs over this

was more in evidence in French slave trading ventures, a mobilization facilitated by the French limited partnership (*société en commandite*). Merchant firms in Britain frequently supplemented their capital by medium- or long-term borrowing on bond from persons with money who wanted a better rate of return than they could get from the public funds.[104] I know less about practices in France but find evidence of a slaving firm in Bordeaux borrowing on *contrats d'obligation* (bonds) both from its own inactive partners (*commanditaires*) and from other merchants in its port.[105] References also occur to slaving firms or syndicates borrowing on bottomry bonds (*contrats à la grosse aventure*), a practice more likely exceptional rather than routine. French slave traders are also reported to have obtained substantial advances from Paris bankers. English slave traders rarely got much help from banks (almost unknown in the outports before 1750) except in the discounting and collecting of short-term bills of exchange. (The Bank of England normally did not discount bills of more than sixty days' duration, and private banks were only slightly more helpful.)[106] All borrowing – including discounting – reduced, of course, the amount that the participants had to put "up front".

A further level of credit appears in the terms on which the outward-bound trading goods were purchased. David Richardson reports that, in the outport firm records he has examined, 40 to 50% of such goods were normally purchased on credit.[107] However, we must distinguish between expenditures for trading cargo and expenditures for the ship's outfit or "outset." For the outset, some cash was needed for advances on sailors' wages and certain port charges and services. Other outset items, including victuals and drink for the ship and some ship's supplies, such as sailcloth, could only be purchased for cash or very short credit. By contrast, most cargo items could be purchased

---

long period. It is close to the figure given in Rinchon, *Armements négriers*, p. 52, and not inconsistent with the data given by Richardson (footnote 56), though higher figures are suggested by Stein, pp. 137, 140, 144. At the other extreme, Brazilian outsets should have been much lower than French.

[104] Price, *Capital and Credit*, chap. 4.

[105] Thésée, pp. 86–7.

[106] Stein, 148–9; Sir John Clapham, *The Bank of England: A History*, 2 vols. (Cambridge, 1966), Vol. I, pp. 124–5; Bank of England Archives, Court Minutes, passim; Price, *Capital and Credit*, chap. 5. On bottomry loans, see Butel, 196–7. In a *bottomry bond*, the master or owner of a vessel gave security for a loan made to him by pledging the keel or hull of his vessel. If the vessel was lost at sea within the time contracted, the bond was voided. Analogous was the *respondentia bond* secured against all or part of the cargo of a vessel.

[107] David Richardson, "West African Consumption Patterns and Their Influence on the Eighteenth Century Slave Trade," in Gemery and Hogendorn, pp. 303–30, esp. p. 315n.

on long credit. (The big exceptions were beads and guns.) The usual export credit in Britain, particularly on textiles and hardware, was twelve months, but many suppliers would by the 1780s grant up to eighteen months to the African trade.[108] Of course, since sellers allowed a discount or rebate calculated at up to 10% per annum for early payment, firms in funds also had a strong incentive to repay export credits early. These long credits were a distinctive British institution that did not exist in Holland, where almost all trade goods were sold for payment within six weeks and the buyers were left to arrange their own financing.[109] Long credits were known in France, but I do not know whether they were available in all export trades. Three to six months may have been more typical in French ports.[110] The relevant point here is that if the slave-trading firm did not have to pay cash for its outbound trading goods, the capital requirements of the trade were somewhat reduced, with *possibly* beneficial effects on profits expressed as returns on venture capital.[111] Such credit was,

---

[108] Price, *Capital and Credit*, pp. 101–18, 156–7. The Rogers papers are filled with letters, particularly from London and Manchester, offering goods on credits of twelve to eighteen months. PRO C.107/3, 7(i), 7(ii), 9, 15. But the cargo notes in C.107/10 show shorter credits for perishables and sailcloth. The Davenport ship accounts (Keele University Library) show that on outfit expenditures, cash disbursements always exceeded credit notes by a good margin, but that on cargo items there was greater irregularity. Presumably, when cash was tight, Davenport took full advantage of credits on purchases, but when cash was easy, he used cash obtainable at no more than 5 percent to obtain discounts of 10 percent and up on his purchases.

[109] Price, *Capital and Credit*, p. 119.

[110] Cf. Butel, pp. 258–9, C. F. Gaignat de L'Aulnais, *Guide du Commerce* (Paris, 1791), pp. 27, 368–84.

[111] A careful examination of surviving accounts and correspondence reveals several ways in which payment mechanisms reduced the amount of cash that slave trade adventurers had to advance or "put up front". Humphry Morice's journal (Bank of England Archives B19) suggests that about 1710, shares in slaving voyages were paid to the managing partner in cash. However, the William Davenport papers (Keele University Library) show that by midcentury, participants in his ventures did not pay their full subscriptions in cash. Instead, Davenport of Liverpool, as manager, divided most (not all) of the bills or "shopnotes" that came in from suppliers among the individual participant-adventurers according to their shares. Each was thereby free to take full advantage either of credit or of discounts for early payment on his share of the bills. A different but equivalent system is revealed by the papers relating to the ventures managed in the 1780s by James Rogers of Bristol, who obtained most of his textiles from London. Shortly before the year's credit on purchases had expired, the London credit seller would sometimes write Davenport for the "divisions" (shares of the several venturers) so that he could send out a bill for his share to each venturer. Since this practice was not general, it presumably was a technique by which some big London textile houses sought to get more of the slave trade business. See, e.g., PRO C.107/7(ii) from Ludlam Parry & Son, London, 16 July 1788; C.107/8 from Sargent, Chambers & Co., 15 Oct. 1785. However, whether or not such divisions were made, the long credit offered by suppliers

of course, expensive, as the firms recognized when they repaid their suppliers early to save on interest.

However, the most important effect of credit on the profitability of the slave trade arose from the length of credit with which slaves were sold. Jean Meyer has pointed out that profits impressive at first glance could waste away to less than ordinary interest if the adventurers had to wait too many years to collect the proceeds of their slave sales.[112] The Liverpool slave traders escaped from this dilemma by insisting on immediate remittances, which ideally would have enabled them to close their books on an adventure in eighteen to twenty-four months – though at the cost of higher commissions to their factors and substantial discounts on the bills remitted. The French slave traders, who did not have this institutional option, had to wait for returns. To get a sharper picture of the profitability of the slave trade, we must also consider the opportunity costs of the capital tied up in that trade for such long but varying periods of time.

Despite individual cases of planter mortgages foreclosed, slaves seized, and slave trader bankruptcies, we have been dealing with a system that, in its own narrow bookkeeping terms, worked. Through various credit mechanisms, the external resources of bankers, bill negotiators, accepting/guaranteeing houses, merchant and manufacturer suppliers, and lenders on mortgages and bonds were in varying ways added to those of slave traders and planters to make possible the continuous expansion of the British and French slave plantation economies from the 1660s to 1790 or 1807. As a Liverpool slave trader put it, the right sort of credit "made the wheel turn."

reduced the amount of cash participants had to advance at the beginning of an adventure.
[112] Meyer, pp. 227–34.

VI

Who Cared about the Colonies?
The Impact of the Thirteen Colonies on British Society and Politics, circa 1714–1775

From the settlement of Jamestown to the onset of the Revolution, the thirteen colonies were part of the English (later British) imperium, subject to the British crown and Parliament and to British laws and very much part of the British market system and the British religious-cultural world. A vast library exists purporting to explain what this connection meant for the thirteen colonies, but relatively little has been written to explain or explore what it meant for England and Scotland. This essay attempts a foray into, if not a full-scale exploration of, the latter question: the backward influence of the colonies on Britain.

In 1924 Jay Barrett Botsford published a well-received book (originally a Columbia thesis) entitled *English Society in the Eighteenth Century as Influenced from Overseas*.[1] Botsford cast his net rather wide: in addition to such obvious topics as trade and trading companies, missionary societies, and the like, he included the rise of port cities and urban civilization, the increased importance of the middle class, new urban patterns of consumption (particularly tea, coffee, sugar, and tobacco), new facilities for social intercourse (such as coffeehouses), and new scientific interests. Botsford's book is based heavily on travelers' accounts and literary texts and tends in a rather journalistic style to regard all phenomena as equally important. For him, too, "overseas" meant the whole world outside Europe, so that he can skip in one paragraph from America to Asia and back again. Botsford's work is interesting in conception, though I suspect that few dissertation students today would attempt to emulate either his world scope or methodology.

Here, I essay a much more limited investigation of the impact of the colonies on Britain, focusing on concern in Britain for the thirteen colonies in the years between the accession of the House of Hanover in 1714

---

1. Jay Barrett Botsford, *English Society in the Eighteenth Century as Influenced from Overseas* (New York, 1924).

VI

396

and the end of the old empire in 1775. I shall not pay too much attention to such epiphenomena as the consumption of snuff made from Virginia tobacco or of pudding made from Carolina rice, but shall instead be looking for evidence of the ability of the colonies to involve the interests and command the attention and concern of people in Britain, from the politically eminent to those in trade and to the nation at large.

Those on High

Lance Davis and Robert Huttenback have analyzed the costs and benefits of the Victorian and Edwardian empire. They demonstrate quite convincingly that, while the empire meant careers for some and opportunities for advantageous investment for others, fiscally it was disadvantageous for the United Kingdom as a whole, creating a significant burden for most British taxpayers, especially those unable to draw private benefit from the overseas dependencies.[2] However, this British Empire of 1857–1914 differed greatly from the thirteen colonies of 1714–1775. Before the Peace of Paris in 1763, the British government spent very little on the civil administration of its North American colonies, leaving responsibility for most expenses to local assemblies and local taxes. Even defense expenditures before 1755 were minimal—except in wartime. Although questions of colonial expenditures and taxation assumed the highest political importance from 1763 and although even earlier the expenses connected with the French wars of 1744–1748 and 1756–1763 were substantial, the negligible *peacetime* expenditures before 1763 meant that the British taxpayer qua taxpayer had little reason then to think much about the colonies. Moreover, because both expenditures and establishments in North America were normally so modest, there could not have been very many people in Britain who had experience in North America or anticipation of appointments there. Aside from the customs establishment and the governorships, there was only a scattering of positions in the North American colonies likely to attract any of the well-connected or the hungry in Britain.[3]

2. Lance E. Davis and Robert A. Huttenback, *Mammon and the Pursuit of Empire: The Political Economy of British Imperialism, 1860–1912* (Cambridge, 1986), esp. chaps. 8, 11.
3. On British expenditures in North America, see Julian Gwyn, "British Government Spending and the North American Colonies, 1740–1775," *Journal of Imperial and Commonwealth History*, VIII (1980), 74–84. On the military arrangements in the thirteen colonies before 1760, see John Shy, *Toward Lexington: The Role of the British Army in the Coming of the American Revolution* (Princeton, N.J., 1965), chap. 1; and Stanley McCrory Pargellis, *Lord Loudoun in North America* (New Haven, Conn., 1933), chaps. 1–4.

VI

Some readers will wonder at this point whether the importance of colonial patronage is not being sloughed off too unthinkingly. They should reflect that its alleged importance is in good part a matter of perspective. For the student of the individual colony, royal or proprietary, patronage frequently emerges as a central problem in that colony's corporate history.[4] Politically active or involved colonists were, naturally, concerned about the naming of a governor, attorney general, naval officer, or customs collector. However, from the standpoint of London, such positions are just details in the grand schema of British patronage. One can get some idea of the relative weight of colonial offices in this schema by looking at some of the manuals of officeholders published circa 1750–1775. In those published in the 1750s or 1760s we find only 2 or 3 pages devoted to colonial posts (in volumes of 225–250 pages), though, with heightened interest, this rises to about 5 pages in the 1770s (in volumes of 250–300 pages). When we deduct from the totals all the pages in these books devoted to Parliament, baronets, dignitaries of the established church and universities, army and navy officers, lords lieutenant of counties and all places not in crown patronage (officers of municipalities, companies, charities, and so forth) and thus reduce our coverage to crown civil patronage only, we find the colonial posts still come to only 3–4 percent of this reduced total in the 1760s and about 6 percent in the 1770s. If we put back the higher offices in the armed forces and the church, the share of colonial posts shrinks even more. The duke of Newcastle and colleagues thus had reams of other patronage matters to fuss with, even after surrendering colonial patronage to the Board of Trade in 1752.[5]

There were, to be sure, people in Britain who had substantial politico-economic interests in America not dependent on royal office, starting with the owners of proprietary colonies. In the seventeenth century, persons of the greatest political importance had been included among those to whom the Carolinas and Jerseys were granted—persons as important as George

---

On the customs establishment, see Thomas C. Barrow, *Trade and Empire: The British Customs Service in Colonial America, 1660–1775* (Cambridge, Mass., 1967). On the general character of the pre-1763 administration, see James A. Henretta, *"Salutary Neglect": Colonial Administration under the Duke of Newcastle* (Princeton, N.J., 1972). On officeholding in the colonies, see Bruce C. Daniels, ed., *Power and Status: Officeholding in Colonial America* (Middletown, Conn., 1986).

4. For the patronage problem as seen from the perspective of the individual colony, see Stanley Nider Katz, *Newcastle's New York: Anglo-American Politics, 1732–1753* (Cambridge, Mass., 1968); Donnell MacClure Owings, *His Lordship's Patronage: Offices of Profit in Colonial Maryland*, Studies in Maryland History, no. 1 (Baltimore, 1953).

5. Based on a more detailed examination of *The Court and City Register* (1764, 1772); *The St. James Register; or, Royal Annual Kalendar* (1765); *The Court and City Kalendar* (1769); and *The Royal Kalendar* (1774). For the duke's role in colonial patronage before 1752, see Henretta, *"Salutary Neglect,"* esp. 306–318.

VI

Monck, duke of Albemarle, Edward Hyde, earl of Clarendon, and Anthony
Ashley Cooper, earl of Shaftesbury. However, this phase had more or less
ended by the time of the surrender of the Carolinas in the 1720s. The
remaining governing proprietors, the Penns in Pennsylvania and the lords
Baltimore in Maryland, were, particularly after 1689, primarily concerned
with retaining their proprietorships. (In fact, the lords Baltimore temporarily
lost theirs from 1689 to 1715.) At least as limited and defensive were the
aspirations of the nongoverning proprietors of the Jerseys and the Northern
Neck of Virginia. Such restricted ambitions were appropriate to proprietors
whose political importance gave them little expectation of being able to
influence colonial policy more generally.[6]

A few apparent and temporary exceptions during the ascendancy of Robert Walpole and Henry Pelham (1721–1754) merely proved the rule in the
long run. Charles Calvert, fifth Lord Baltimore, proprietor of Maryland, was
an active parliamentary politician in the 1740s, attaching himself to the
group around Frederick, Prince of Wales. That foray led nowhere, for both
the prince and Lord Baltimore died in 1751.[7] A more important figure in the
same circle about the prince was John Perceval, second earl of Egmont, son
of one of the founders of the Georgia Society, of which he also was a trustee.
In the 1760s Egmont was to hold the position of first lord of the Admiralty,
among other places. However, the second earl's involvement in Georgia was
quite minimal: he became a trustee only on the death of his father in 1748
and, in effect, joined only in time to help with the winding up. He was not
otherwise meaningfully involved in American affairs.[8]

Among others who were politically important there is even less evidence of
significant interest in the colonies. Curious Britons did visit the colonies
from time to time, and some of them left travel accounts, but no member of
the royal family or inner cabinet appears to have visited the thirteen colonies
between 1714 and 1775. Nor did many other prominent people become
involved as individuals in matters American in these years, except for the

6. Charles M. Andrews, *The Colonial Period of American History*, 4 vols. (New
Haven, Conn., 1934–1938), II, chaps. 8–9, III, chaps. 5–7; J. M. Sosin, *English
America and the Revolution of 1688: Royal Administration and the Structure of
Provincial Government* (Lincoln, Nebr., 1982), chaps. 8, 12, 13; Sosin, *English
America and Imperial Inconstancy: The Rise of Provincial Autonomy, 1696–1715*
(Lincoln, Nebr., 1985), chaps. 6–8. There were, of course, partial exceptions, such as
Paul Docminique, a Jersey proprietor and member of the Board of Trade, 1714–
1735.
7. Romney Sedgwick, *The House of Commons, 1715–1754*, 2 vols., The History
of Parliament (London, 1970), I, 518–519; John B. Owen, *The Rise of the Pelhams*
(London, 1957).
8. Sedgwick, *House of Commons, 1715–1754*, II, 339–340; Owen, *Pelhams*, s.v.
Perceval; Allen D. Candler, ed., *The Colonial Records of the State of Georgia*, I
(Atlanta, 1904), 27–30. For key literature on the trustee period in Georgia, see
Kenneth Coleman, *Colonial Georgia: A History* (New York, 1976).

aforementioned service by a few as trustees of Georgia before 1752 or the membership by a larger number in the Society for the Propagation of the Gospel in Foreign Parts. That most respectable organization was heavily clerical in membership, with only a few and very senior politicians moved to join.[9]

Within the home government, there were, of necessity, a handful of permanent or semipermanent officials who were paid to know something about the colonies: undersecretaries of state and functionaries at the Board of Trade. Most of this small set were quite knowledgeable about American affairs, and they generally knew how to get more information when they needed it, even if their channels of communication were, of necessity, limited. The most obvious, if somewhat suspect, of these channels were the London agents of the several colonies. In the generation before the Revolution, six of those representing the North American colonies were also, as we shall see, members of Parliament.[10] Earlier the agents had tended to be more obscure people, though men quite obscure to us may have had channels of influence whose extent we can scarcely guess at. For example, Peter Leheup, who was at various times agent for Virginia, Barbados, New Jersey, and New York, was a pluralist Treasury clerk and deputy to Horatio Walpole, auditor general of American revenues, to whom he was also connected by marriage. Leheup's influence extended to legislation.[11]

Undersecretaries, legal counsel, and senior clerks could only advise; they

9. For published accounts of British travelers in colonial America, see Thomas D. Clark *et al.*, eds., *Travels in the Old South: A Bibliography*, 3 vols. (Norman, Okla., 1956–1959), esp. vol. I; and Frank Freidel, ed., *Harvard Guide to American History*, rev. ed., 2 vols. (Cambridge, Mass., 1974), I, 139–141. Lord Adam Gordon, an army officer, member of Parliament, and son of the duke of Gordon, would appear to be the only (nonproprietary) visitor of the highest social status.

The membership lists of the Society can be found appended to the published annual commemoration sermons. In the outer cabinet, at least four first lords of the Admiralty—Wager, Anson, Saunders, and Hawke—had some experience of America while naval officers on sea duty, but only Anson and perhaps Hawke had any significant exposure to the society of the thirteen colonies.

10. Franklin B. Wickwire, *British Subministers and Colonial America, 1763–1783* (Princeton, N.J., 1966); Ella Lonn, *The Colonial Agents of the Southern Colonies* (Chapel Hill, N.C., 1945); Dame Lillian M[argery] Penson, *The Colonial Agents of the British West Indies: A Study in Colonial Administration in the Eighteenth Century* (London, 1924); Edward P. Lilly, "The Colonial Agents of New York and New Jersey" (Ph.D. diss., Catholic University of America, 1936). Cf. also Jack M. Sosin, *Agents and Merchants: British Colonial Policy and the Origins of the American Revolution* (Lincoln, Nebr., 1965), chap. 1; and Michael G. Kammen, *A Rope of Sand: The Colonial Agents, British Politics, and the American Revolution* (Ithaca, N.Y., 1968), esp. chap. 1.

11. On Leheup, see Jacob M. Price, "The Excise Affair Revisited: The Administrative and Colonial Dimensions of a Parliamentary Crisis," in Stephen B. Baxter, ed., *England's Rise to Greatness, 1660–1763* (Berkeley, Calif., 1983), 274–276.

did not make policy. Colonial agents could hope to influence policy only if they could reach people of policy-making responsibility either directly or via the undersecretaries and others at that level. The body that was formally charged with advising the crown on colonial affairs (via the Privy Council or the secretaries of state) was the Board of Trade. In its earliest days following its foundation in 1696, it was quite active both in administration and policy formation, but became progressively less energetic and influential in the eighteenth century. By the time of the Pelham ascendancy (1743–1762), membership was too frequently viewed as a sinecure. During the presidency of the second earl of Halifax (1749–1761), the board reasserted some—not total—control over patronage but did not otherwise change its character or effect real control over policy. For service on such a board, interest in or even knowledge of the colonies was desirable but hardly a prerequisite. Of the seventy-five men who served on the board between 1696 and 1775, only five had any conspicuous connection with the Americas: three with the West Indies only; one, Paul Docminique, with the Jerseys; and one, Martin Bladen, with both the West Indies and North America. Bladen, whose wife had inherited a sugar plantation on Nevis, was a director of the Royal African Company (1717–1726) and a prominent spokesman for the West India interest. His brother William Bladen (1670–1718) had in the 1690s emigrated to Maryland, where he became, inter alia, clerk to the provincial council (1698–1716), commissary general (1708–1718), secretary of the colony (1701–1718), and attorney general (1704–1718). William's son Thomas moved to England on his father's death and became a member of Parliament, but returned to Maryland for a time as deputy governor (1742–1746). However, one swallow doesn't make a spring, and one Bladen doesn't constitute an American interest on the Board of Trade.[12]

12. On Martin and Thomas Bladen, see Sedgwick, *House of Commons, 1715–1754.* On William Bladen, see *Dictionary of American Biography*; and Edward C. Papenfuse *et al.*, eds., *A Biographical Dictionary of the Maryland Legislature, 1635–1789,* 2 vols. (Baltimore, 1979, 1985), I, 136. Another rather insignificant member of the Board of Trade, William Sloper (1756–1761) was the son of an original Georgia trustee of the same name. For membership of the Board of Trade, see J. C. Sainty, *Officials of the Boards of Trade, 1660–1870,* Office-Holders in Modern Britain, III (London, 1974). See also Ian K. Steele, *Politics of Colonial Policy: The Board of Trade in Colonial Administration, 1696–1720* (Oxford, 1968); Oliver Morton Dickerson, *American Colonial Government, 1696–1765: A Study of the British Board of Trade* (New York, 1912); Arthur Herbert Basye, *The Lords Commissioners of Trade and Plantations: Commonly Known as the Board of Trade, 1748–1782* (New Haven, Conn., 1925), esp. 71–84, 220–232.

Others on the Board of Trade may have had different sorts of connections with the American colonies, even though they had neither experience nor property interests there. The sixth earl of Westmorland, first lord, 1719–1735, was the head of the aristocratic Fane family, a cadet branch of which resided near Bristol, where they had intermarried with local merchant families (with American trade connections), including the Swymmers and the Scropes (the family also of the secretary of the Treasury).

Paradoxically, the very thinness of American experience on the Board of Trade meant that any lone commissioner who did attend and read the papers—most noticeably Halifax or Charles Townshend—could quickly acquire the reputation of an expert and exert a disproportionate influence on his colleagues. Realistically, too, it meant that senior members of the board's staff and colonial governors trusted by this activist board minority could also have an influence on policy greater than their rank would suggest. However, here we are not concerned with how specific individuals influenced specific policy decisions, but, rather, with the relations of broader strata—within and without the political nation—to American questions.

Below the level of statesmen and significant placemen lay the several thousand knights of the shire and burgesses who between 1715 and 1775 sat in the House of Commons, the very heart of the political nation. We may usefully divide this corps into those serving in the relatively quiet years (from a North American perspective) down to the death of Pelham in 1754, and those entering Parliament only in the more turbulent ensuing generation. In the first period (1715–1754) there was at least one conspicuous group in the House of Commons associated with North America: the Georgia trustees. Approximately three-fourths of the colony's lay trustees between 1732 and 1752 (some 47 individuals) were members of either the British House of Commons (44) or House of Lords (3). However, only a handful—most noticeably, James Oglethorpe and Lord Egmont—were seriously involved in the affairs of the trust. For the rest this American activity was largely eleemosynary and passive.[13]

We can legitimately look for other and possibly more intense American interests in the House of Commons among three occupational groups: navy officers, army officers, and merchants.

Between 1715 and 1754, 54 naval officers served in the House of Commons. The naval war of 1739–1748 helped swell the number from an average of 12 in the parliaments of 1715–1741 to 20 in the parliaments of 1741–1754. It is difficult to ascertain readily the full details of the professional postings of naval officers, but the information on those elected to the Commons assembled by Romney Sedgwick suggests that at least 21 of the 54 served in the West Indies or Newfoundland but that only 2 had any noticeable experience of the thirteen colonies. Matthew Norris, of a naval family,

---

Such connections go far in explaining how Francis Fane of Bristol became counsel to the Board of Trade. The connections by blood and marriage between aristocratic and mercantile families are well known but have not been systematically studied. See also Alison G. Olson, "The Board of Trade and London-American Interest Groups in the Eighteenth Century," *Jour. Imperial and Commonwealth Hist.*, VIII (1980), 33–50.

13. Candler, *Records of Georgia*, I, 27–30; Sedgwick, *House of Commons, 1715–1754*.

VI

was in New York long enough to marry a daughter of Lewis Morris of Morrisania, sometime governor of New Jersey. Sir Peter Warren was also in those waters long enough not only to marry a De Lancey but also to acquire substantial landholdings in New York and South Carolina.[14]

In part because the military was a less technical service preferred by the landed classes, army officers were more numerous (182) than naval officers in the House of Commons during 1715–1754. However, American experience was no more common. Of the 182, only 3 appear to have had experience in the thirteen colonies before 1755: James Oglethorpe and two governors of New York, James Montgomerie and the Honorable John West. A few others of this pre-1754 contingent served in the West Indies or in Canada, or later in the thirteen colonies during the Seven Years' War. However, the New York governors and those serving after 1755 saw North America after their years in the House of Commons. They thus had no American experience to draw upon while in Parliament. In effect, among the army officers in the House of Commons before 1755, only Oglethorpe could call on prior North American experience.[15]

In the same parliaments of 1715–1754, there were 169 merchants and 12 bankers. Inasmuch as merchants frequently traded to more than one area, one cannot be absolutely sure that one has classified them comprehensively. Even so, it is noteworthy that only 14 of the 169 can definitely be identified as trading to the thirteen colonies: 12 to Virginia and Maryland and 2 elsewhere.[16]

In the next generation, 1754–1776, the American connection in the House of Commons became much more conspicuous. America, it should be remembered, was not a constant. While the population of England and Wales was increasing by only 27 percent between 1701 and 1771 (from about 5.1 million to about 6.4 million), that of the thirteen colonies increased by something like 756 percent between 1700 and 1770, or from about 250,000 in 1700 to about 2.1 million in 1770 and 2.5 million in 1775. This much bigger satellite had a much stronger pull upon the tides of interest in the mother country, observable even in the House of Commons. In this last generation we find some new types there, such as the four or five members born in the thirteen colonies and six colonial agents: James Aber-

---

14. Sedgwick, *House of Commons, 1715–1754*, I, 144–145, 155, II, 299, 522–523; Julian Gwyn, *The Enterprising Admiral: The Personal Fortune of Admiral Sir Peter Warren* (Montreal, 1974).

15. Sedgwick, *House of Commons, 1715–1754*, I, 142–144.

16. *Ibid.*, 148–150, utilizing also my own file of merchants trading to America. Those with interests in Virginia and Maryland: Thomas Benson, Robert Bristow, Neil Buchanan, John Buck, John Burridge, Daniel Campbell, Sir William Daines, Abraham Elton the younger, Richard Gildart, Sir Thomas Johnson, Micajah Perry, Edward Tucker; elsewhere in North America: William Baker, John Sargent. Many of those interested in Virginia and Maryland also had interests in other colonies.

cromby (Virginia), Edmund Burke and John Sargent (New York), Charles
Garth (South Carolina and Maryland), John Thomlinson and Barlow Trecothick (New Hampshire). We also begin to find for the first time a small group
in the Commons who had American interests without any usual career or
professional involvement.[17] More striking was the great new speculative
interest in the North American lands either ceded by France and Spain in
1763 or newly secured for settlement. Dozens of members of Parliament,
peers, and other prominent people applied for and received extensive land
grants in East Florida, though only five members had actually secured such
grants by settlement before 1776. Equally impressive was the large number—five great peers and seventeen members—who were persuaded to subscribe for shares in the Grand Ohio (or Walpole) Company, which was
striving, circa 1768–1772, to obtain royal confirmation to their title to more
than two million acres acquired from Indians by the Treaty of Fort Stanwix.[18] However, as in the earlier period, the overwhelming majority of

17. E. A. Wrigley and R. S. Schofield, *The Population History of England, 1541–
1871: A Reconstruction* (Cambridge, Mass., 1981), 208–209; U.S. Bureau of the
Census, *Historical Statistics of the United States: Colonial Times to 1970* (Washington, D.C., 1975), II, 1168; Sir Lewis Namier and John Brooke, *The House of
Commons, 1754–1790*, 3 vols., The History of Parliament (London, 1964), I, 159–
162.
    Lauchlin Macleane (member of Parliament, 1768–1771) had been a civil and
military surgeon in Pennsylvania (1756–1763). Among other American posts,
Thomas Pownall (member, 1767–1780) had been governor of Massachusetts Bay
(1757–1760). Denys Rolle (member, 1761–1774) had worked hard to attract settlers
to his land grant in East Florida. All particulars on individual army and navy officers
among the members can be found in Namier and Brooke, *House of Commons,
1754–1790*, II–III.
    The subject of the American interest in the House of Commons on the eve of the
Revolution has been dealt with most interestingly in Sir Lewis Namier, *England in
the Age of the American Revolution*, 2d ed. (London, 1961), chap. 4. My compressed
handling of the topic here covers a different block of years and is somewhat more
quantitative.
    18. The five members "who settled their land before 1776" were John Tucker,
Peter Taylor, Admiral Sir Edward Hawke, Denys Rolle, and Henry Strachey. For the
others, see Charles Loch Mowat, *East Florida as a British Province, 1763–1784*,
University of California Publications in History, XXXIII (Berkeley, Calif., 1943),
58–61. Two other members, Lord Adam Gordon and Staats Long Morris, acquired
large land grants in New York and Canada, respectively. See also Wilbur Henry
Siebert, *Loyalists in East Florida, 1774 to 1785*, 2 vols., Publications of the Florida
State Historical Society, 9 (Deland, Fla., 1929), II, 307–308, which shows that other
important people had acquired land claims in Florida by 1783, including lords
Arden, Brownlow, Loughborough, and Moira and members of Parliament Robert
Barker and Jacob Wilkinson.
    Of those subscribing for shares, the peers (all earls) were Hertford, lord chamber-
lain; Camden, lord chancellor; Rochford, secretary of state; Gower, lord president of
the council; and Temple, head of the Grenville clan. The members of Parliament were
Thomas Bradshaw, junior secretary of the Treasury; Sir George Colebrooke, bart.;
General Henry Seymour Conway, secretary of state; Grey Cooper, secretary of the

VI

404

members with American interests belonged to the three big occupational groups: navy officers, army officers, and merchants.

The Seven Years' War should have noticeably expanded the Western Hemisphere experience of many navy and army officers. In the case of the navy, however, the American experience of most naval members of Parliament was in the West Indies or as governors of Newfoundland or, in this war, in the Quebec campaign. The number of naval officers in the Commons with evident experience in the thirteen colonies proper rose from two in 1715–1754 to four in 1754–1776. The situation was rather different among army officers serving in the Commons during those same years, owing particularly to the extensive military operations on the North American frontiers. Thus, in place of one member with military experience in the colonies in the parliaments of 1715–1754, we find eleven in the ensuing generation of 1754–1776.[19]

This expanded army–American service element in the Commons was but one manifestation of the impact of the Seven Years' War on British public life. The period between the start of the war in 1755–1756 and the end of the American Revolutionary war is marked by the extreme prominence of government remittance and supply contractors in the House of Commons, where they all too obviously used their political influence to obtain bigger and better contracts for themselves. Their activities became so notorious that their eligibility to sit in the house was removed by Clerke's Act of 1782. In the generation 1754–1776 the House of Commons included 29 merchant members with some sort of connection with the thirteen colonies (compared with 14 during 1715–1754). Six of these were interested only in remittance

---

Treasury; Sir Matthew Fetherstonehaugh, bart.; George Grenville, former prime minister; Richard Jackson; Lauchlin Macleane; Thomas Pitt; Thomas Pownall; John Robinson, later junior secretary of the Treasury; John Sargent; William Strahan; Richard Walpole; Thomas Walpole; Robert Wood. Clarence Walworth Alvord, *The Mississippi Valley in British Politics*, 2 vols. (Cleveland, Ohio, 1917), II, 96–101, 127, 179n; Jack M. Sosin, *Whitehall and the Wilderness: The Middle West in British Colonial Policy, 1760–1775* (Lincoln, Nebr., 1961), chap. 8; J. A. Cannon, "Hon. Thomas Walpole," in Namier and Brooke, *History of Parliament, 1754–1790*, III, 598–602; Peter Marshall, "Lord Hillsborough, Samuel Wharton, and the Ohio Grant, 1769–1775," *English Historical Review*, LXXX (1965), 717–739.

19. Naval officers: Hon. George Clinton and Sir Charles Hardy, governors of New York; Lord William Campbell, governor of South Carolina; and Hon. Augustus Keppel, naval commander in chief in North America, 1754–1756.

Army officers: James Cuninghame, Sir Charles Davers (?), Simon Fraser, Francis Grant, James Grant, Hon. William Hervey, Hon. Robert Monckton (governor of New York, 1761–1765), Hon. Archibald Montgomerie, Staats Long Morris, James Murray, John Stanwix. Others, particularly Isaac Barré and William Howe, appear to have served in the Quebec campaign but not in the thirteen colonies.

or supply contracts and do not appear to have had other involvement in those colonies. The remaining 23 had more conventional, continuing interests in the colonies, including New England (5), Virginia and Maryland (5), South Carolina and Georgia (4), New York (2), New Jersey and Pennsylvania (1 each), and North America generally (5).[20]

Though the number of army officers and merchants with American interests or experience had increased markedly in the period 1754–1776, when compared with the previous period, persons with such interest or experience were still a tiny minority in the Commons, and few expected that many officers interested in promotion or merchants interested in contracts would take an independent line in debate—though some merchants without contracts did so most energetically. All in all, though, as Isaac Barré pointed out at the time, "there are very few [in the House of Commons] who know the circumstances of North America."[21]

Those in Trade

So much for Parliament. What about the political nation out-of-doors—that section of the British populace that participated in parliamentary elections, served on grand juries, or were members of bodies corporate of some dignity and weight? And the wider community beyond them? Did elements in either have much observable knowledge of or concern for the North American colonies? This is an almost impossible question to answer precisely. One could, perhaps, start by examining the thousands of names on petitions, but too many motives might be involved in signing a petition, including both

20. For the contractors during the American Revolutionary war, see Norman Baker, *Government and Contractors: The British Treasury and War Supplies, 1775–1783* (London, 1971), esp. chap. 9. Remittance and supply contracts: Sir George Colebrooke, James Colebrooke, Adam Drummond, Henry Drummond, Hon. Thomas Harley, and Arnold Nesbitt (Nesbitt was active in the West India trade). Conventional interests: New England: John Henniker, John Huske, John Thomlinson, Chauncey Townsend, B. Trecothick; Maryland and Virginia: William Alexander, Anthony Bacon, Robert Bristow, Ellis Cunliffe, John Hardman; South Carolina and Georgia: Sir William Baker, Brice Fisher, Nicholas Linwood, Charles Ogilvie; New York: H. Cruger, Sir Samuel Fludyer; New Jersey: Henry Drummond; Pennsylvania: D. Moore; North America generally: G. R. Aufrere, P. Cust, G. Hayley, John Sargent, S. Touchet.
21. Namier and Brooke, *House of Commons, 1754–1790*, I, 161. For other expressions of similar opinions at the time, see Paul Langford, "The First Rockingham Ministry and the Repeal of the Stamp Act: The Role of the Commercial Lobby and Economic Pressures," in Walter H. Conser, Jr., *et al.*, eds., *Resistance, Politics, and the American Struggle for Independence, 1765–1775* (Boulder, Colo., 1986), 102–103.

political commitment and deference.[22] I think it preferable to start with a simpler and more neutral record of concern.

One such type of evidence not hitherto used can be found in the subscription lists printed in books. These vary in purpose and character. An expensive book with many plates depicting antiquities or flora and fauna might need advance subscriptions to help pay the costs of engraving the plates. Royal and noble names among the subscribers would, one might expect, give the book a definite éclat.[23] At the other extreme, a modest, utilitarian textbook of accounting would benefit from subscriptions from the proprietors of well-known private academies of bookkeeping. For our purposes the most useful are the extraordinarily long subscription lists included in the successive editions of John Wright's *American Negotiator* (1761–1765), a reference work on the varieties of coins and moneys of account used in the various American colonies.[24] Its three editions together contain the names of almost thirty-seven hundred people sufficiently interested in the American colonies to pay 2s. 6d. (about a day's pay for a junior clerk) for this information.

We do not know how Wright collected his subscriptions (probably through booksellers), but the contents of the successive lists suggest great ingenuity and application.[25] (No other known lists are remotely as long as his.) The fullest list, that in the first edition, consists almost entirely of names from London (1,998) and Bristol (185). In the second edition names were

22. For good use of the names on petitions, see James E. Bradley, *Popular Politics and the American Revolution in England: Petitions, the Crown, and Public Opinion* (Macon, Ga., 1986).

23. On subscription lists, cf. F.J.G. Robinson and P. J. Wallis, *Book Subscription Lists: A Revised Guide* (Newcastle upon Tyne, 1975). For an example of American interest, see Griffith Hughes, *The Natural History of Barbados* (London, 1750). The subscribers to this included the king of France; the Prince and Princess of Wales; the royal duke of Cumberland; 3 German princes; 9 English dukes; the archbishops of Canterbury, York, and Armagh; and the prime minister, Henry Pelham; and 33 persons from Virginia. By contrast, the subscribers to Patrick Browne, *The Civil and Natural History of Jamaica* (London, 1756), contained only 1 peer.

24. John Wright, *The American Negotiator; or, The Various Currencies of the British Colonies in America . . .*, 1st ed. (London, 1761), 2d ed. (London, 1763), 3d ed. (London, 1765). Numerous examples of accounting textbooks can be found in Robinson and Wallis, *Book Subscription Lists*. Particularly interesting are Thomas Harper, *The Accomptant's Companion . . .* (London, 1761); and Peter Hudson, *A New Introduction to Trade and Business . . .* (London, 1767). For a more advanced Scottish example, with subscriptions by eminent merchants, see William Stevenson, *Book-keeping by Double Entry . . .* (Edinburgh, 1762).

25. For the collection of subscriptions through provincial booksellers, see John Feather, *The Provincial Book Trade in Eighteenth-Century England* (Cambridge, 1985), 51–53; Marjorie Plant, *The English Book Trade: An Economic History of the Making and Sale of Books*, 3d ed. (London, 1974), 227–232.

added from southern England, the Liverpool-Manchester-Chester area, the London suburbs, and the maze of riverside hamlets and quarters along both sides of the Thames below London Bridge. The third edition noticeably adds names from Yorkshire and the east coast, northwest England, and southern Scotland. Residents of 144 different places in England and Scotland subscribed for copies, or 120 if we delete 24 Thames-side hamlets and quarters. With the exception of 3 subscribers from Dublin, there are no names from Ireland or Wales. We do find subscribers from all the coastal counties of England except Cornwall and Suffolk. Also unrepresented were 13 inland English counties embracing a great swath of territory from Hertfordshire and Bedfordshire in the Home Counties to the Welsh border and including all the Midlands except for the industrial towns of Birmingham, Coventry, and Nottingham.[26] The inland omitted areas were primarily agricultural. Their rural industries were not insignificant but, as we shall see, were unlikely to be in direct commercial communication with the North American colonies. In Scotland almost all the subscribers were located about Edinburgh in the Lothians or along the southwest coast between Glasgow and Dumfries.[27]

There are some rather odd features to the list of places. There were no subscribers from Oxford and only 1 from Cambridge, but there were a respectable number from Canterbury (22) and York (24) as well as from ten other English cathedral towns including the unexpected Rochester, Chichester, Salisbury, and Wells. Cathedral towns would, of course, have had booksellers, and the inclusion of such places suggests that in the south of England at least it was quite easy to subscribe.

The geographic distribution of subscriptions is summarized in Table 1, specifying places with 20 or more subscribers. The first thing that strikes one is that 62 percent of the subscriptions came from the greater London commercial (as distinct from fashionable) area. This is not unexpected when we reflect that Wright's book was published in London and subscriptions were undoubtedly easiest to procure there. Nor is it unexpected when we

26. The omission of Cornwall undoubtedly owes more to the organization of the book trade than to the lack of American awareness. The packet boats from New York terminated at Falmouth, where many vessels to and from America stopped for mail and instructions. Of Cornish ports with even minimal American trade circa 1750–1775, Falmouth and Truro had only one bookshop each. H. R. Plomer *et al.*, *A Dictionary of the Printers and Booksellers Who Were at Work in England, Scotland, and Ireland from 1726 to 1775* (Oxford, 1932), 4, 188.

The other omitted counties in England were Bedford, Bucks, Derby, Hereford, Herts, Huntingdon, Monmouth, Northampton, Oxford, Rutland, Shropshire, Stafford, and Worcester.

27. In Scotland, a few subscriptions were received from inland manufacturing centers including Paisley (6) and Kilmarnock (7).

remember that, at this time, from half to two-thirds of England's foreign trade was handled by the port of London.[28] The careful reader will also have noted that, of the 17 provincial centers responsible for 20 or more subscriptions each, a good number were ports trading to America: Bristol, Liverpool, Glasgow, Edinburgh-Leith, Lancaster, Portsmouth, Whitehaven, Hull, Poole, and Yarmouth. (Of the ports listed, only Chester and Preston then had no known direct trade with the American colonies.) If we add the subscriptions of the 10 ports just mentioned to those of the port of London, the share of ports trading to North America rises to more than 80 percent of subscriptions. The impressiveness of this share should not, however, lead us to disregard the remaining 20 percent of subscriptions that came from some 665 individuals in 105 other places, inland and coastal. These ranged from major manufacturing centers such as Manchester and Birmingham, with 60 and 48 subscriptions, to numerous minor places with only 1 or 2. Together they remind us both of the wide diffusion of interest in the American colonies and of the concentration or intensity of such interest in major marketing centers serving export industries.

The subscription lists to the three editions of John Wright's *American Negotiator* differ from most other such lists in a further important respect: they contain the occupations of most subscribers. Of the 3,694 subscribers, only 179 showed no occupation: of these, 10 were blank, the others being described only by a title of distinction (lord, baronet, knight, esquire, gentleman) or of an unpaid, honorific public office (mayor, provost, alderman) normally distinct from the holder's occupation. In addition to the 73 identified only as esquire, there were a substantial number of other esquires also described by an occupation (merchant, brewer, and so forth). These appear for the most part to have been businessmen who combined with their regular trades a distinguishing position, such as director of the Bank of England, the East India Company, an insurance company, or the like. We have classified these by their primary occupation (for example, merchant), as we have also done for knights and baronets for whom an occupation was given.

After deducting the 179 for whom we have no occupational information, we find the remaining 3,515 subscribers scattered among roughly 282 occupations. (Since many occupational descriptions overlap, the enumeration can be only approximate.) Given the function of Wright's book, it will not come as a surprise that 1,103 (31 percent) of the subscribers were merchants (Table 2). But what of the remaining 69 percent? We see that a prominent place was occupied by the mostly wholesale traders who supplied merchants with export goods on credit: such as warehousemen, woolen-drapers, linendrapers, haberdashers, hosiers, mercers, ironmongers, and grocers. Even

28. Cf. Ralph Davis, "English Foreign Trade, 1660–1700," *Economic History Review*, 2d Ser., VII (1954–1955), 160.

Table 1. Places in Great Britain with Twenty or More Subscribers to
John Wright's *American Negotiator*

Places	Number (Share) of Subscribers
Greater London	
London	2,106
Thames-side hamlets (24)[a]	163
Southwark	17
Total	2,286 (62.0%)
Major provincial subscription towns	
Bristol	193
Liverpool	181
Glasgow and Port Glasgow	78
Manchester	60
Edinburgh and Leith	55
Birmingham	48
Chester	44
Lancaster	38
Portsmouth	36
Preston	36
Whitehaven	33
Hull	27
Norwich	24
York	24
Poole	23
Yarmouth	22
Canterbury	22
Total	944 (25.6%)
Lesser places in England (89)	385 (10.4%)
Lesser places in Scotland (10)	71 (2.0%)
British total (144)	3,686 (100.0%)

Note: Table omits Dublin (3) and overseas (5), which would yield a worldwide total of 3,694.

[a] Places on north side of Thames from Tower to Blackwall and River Lea; on south side of Thames from Southwark's eastern boundary to River Pool, stopping short of Greenwich.

brewers and bakers belonged partly in this category, for they supplied beer and biscuit (hardtack) both as ship's stores and as export goods. Besides the major occupations (Table 2), there were among the subscribers more than 250 other callings both familiar and unfamiliar. For example, at Birmingham we find among them specialist makers of hinges, watch chains, spoons, awl blades, edge tools, and buckles. Dozens of more exotic specialties could be cited, suggesting at the very least the wide ramifications of American interest in eighteenth-century Britain.

The printed lists also contain evidence of further distribution beyond the 3,694 printed names. The lists in the second and third editions identify subscribers who ordered more than 1 copy: anywhere from 2 to 100 each. For example, the Board of Trade in 1764–1765 ordered 18 individual copies for named commissioners and senior clerks plus an unexplained bloc of 50 copies in the name of its secretary. (Some of these were perhaps to be distributed to colonial officials.) There were also multiple orders from ship captains and ship chandlers. The captains could have used theirs as gifts or as trading goods; the ship chandlers, all in the Thames-side hamlets, were obviously supplying customers in areas without bookstores. Most of the multiple copies, however, went to professional booksellers in London (24), the English provinces (48), and Scotland (34). The provincial and Scottish booksellers generally ordered from 6 to 12 copies each while those in London commonly took from 12 to 25, with one taking 100. These multiple-copy orders raise the total sales revealed by the second and third edition subscription lists by 80 percent (from 1,506 to 2,713). If the first edition list (which does not specify quantities) had had multiple sales in the same proportion, sales for the three editions together would have been in the vicinity of 6,650. However, adding the extra copies sold does not change the general picture of the market for Wright's book (Table 1), for the booksellers were distributed geographically much as were the ordinary subscribers.

Wright's subscription lists, it must be remembered, are not a census, but only a sample of persons interested in the colonies—but a very big sample. Other samples available are smaller and weaker in coverage than Wright's, but they confirm at least the outlines of the picture derivable from his lists: interest in the colonies widely diffused but disproportionately concentrated in the bigger ports and the important inland marketing centers for manufactures. One example arises from the difficulties British businessmen trading to America experienced after the Revolutionary war in attempting to collect their substantial prewar debts. In 1790–1791 a committee of these British creditors drew up a list of such debts still outstanding. Although the sums claimed were swollen by interest, some prewar debts had been paid since the peace; thus, the account does not represent the exact prewar weight of debt. Nor are the values shown likely to be proportionate to what the prewar debts totaled in 1776, for different centers employed different trading methods

Table 2. Occupations Furnishing Twenty-five or More Subscribers to Wright's *American Negotiator*

Occupation	Subscribers
Attorney-at-law	26
Baker	61
Bookseller	130
Brewer	42
Broker (every sort)	43
Captain (of merchant ships)	41
Cheesemonger	54
Coachmaker	33
Cooper	29
Distiller	55
Druggist	31
Goldsmith	30
Grocer	173
Haberdasher	54
Hosier	33
Ironmonger	57
Linen-draper	106
Mercer	49
Merchant	1,103
Oilman	53
Schoolmaster	49
Silversmith	35
Stationer	33
Sugar refiner	28
Tallow chandler	61
Warehouseman	32
Watchmaker	41
Weaver	37
Woolen-draper, draper	38

and organization and had different success in collecting their debts after the war. Glasgow, of course, was heavily involved in retail trade with planters in Maryland, Virginia, and North Carolina and had greater difficulty than other centers in realizing its claims. Even so, there is an air of familiarity about the geographic distribution of the 1790 claims (Table 3). All the major ports producing the most numerous subscriptions to Wright's book (Table 1) reappear here. (Although the list in Table 3 covers only ten places, those ten

Table 3. Unpaid American Commercial Debts (Including Interest)
Claimed by British Creditors, February 1791

Place	Number of Claims	Value Claimed (Sterling)		
London	67	£2,324,652	11s.	8d.
Glasgow	96	£2,178,442	7	1
Liverpool	6	127,566	2	4
Bristol	4	104,583	12	10
Leeds	7	92,758	12	4
Chester	2	71,031	17	10
Greenock	2	34,501	7	10
Whitehaven	8	28,396	7	3
Kilmarnock	4	20,809	16	6
Workington	1	1,912	10	0
Total	197	£4,984,655	5s.	8d.

Source: PRO, PRO 30/8/343, fols. 167–169

accounted for 77 percent of the subscriptions for Wright's book received
from 144 places in England and Scotland.)

Similarly consistent is the evidence from pro-American petitions to the
House of Commons between 1766 and 1775. When the Rockingham administration decided to proceed with the repeal of the Stamp Act, Barlow
Trecothick, member of Parliament for London, with ministerial encouragement, organized an influx of petitions from twenty-five trading towns depicting the commercial and industrial distress caused by the decline in exports to North America and asking for relief, that is, repeal. Among the
twenty-five were sixteen major trading centers accounting for more than 80
percent of the subscribers to Wright's book. The nine other places, which do
not appear in Wright's subscription lists, were mostly smaller manufacturing
centers in the west, which most likely were not canvassed by or for Wright
and which most probably did not have direct trading links with America
even though the goods they manufactured found their way eventually to
markets in the thirteen colonies.[29]

29. *Journal of the House of Commons* (London, 1801–), XXX, 462–465, 478–
479, 484, 489, 499, 501, 503, 601–602, 611; R. C. Simmons and P.D.G. Thomas,
eds., *Proceedings and Debates of the British Parliaments respecting North America,
1754–1783* (Millwood, White Plains, N.Y., 1982–), II, 95–97, 100–101, 103–104,
106–108, 115, 305 (omitting Nottingham and Worcester). See also P.D.G. Thomas,
*British Politics and the Stamp Act Crisis: The First Phase of the American Revolu-
tion, 1763–1767* (Oxford, 1975), 187–190; Paul Langford, "The First Rockingham
Ministry," in Conser *et al.*, eds., *Resistance, Politics,* 97–111; and John Money,

This lack of direct connection between some smaller manufacturing centers and their American markets can perhaps be better understood if we look at the marketing arrangements in the West Country woolen trade. Putting-out manufacturers and others in Somerset and Wiltshire (which included four of the eight omitted places alluded to above) commonly sent their cloth for sale to Blackwell Hall factors in London, who sold the same on commission to wholesale woolen-drapers; they in turn resold the cloth on long credit to export merchants who bought for their own speculative shipments or on commission for overseas correspondents. Similarly, in places like Birmingham and Wolverhampton there were few or no merchants who traded overseas. Instead, local factors acting for wholesale ironmongers in London and Bristol bought the nails and other hardware from small masters, paying them with cash obtained by selling short bills of exchange on their principals in London or Bristol. Those big ironmongers in turn sold to export merchants much as did the big drapers. The manufacturers and other traders in both the cloth and ironware manufacturing areas thus usually had no direct correspondence with the American colonies, though the factors with whom they dealt (and the wholesalers behind them) kept them informed about market conditions there and changing demand.[30]

Of comparable interest are the petitions to the House of Commons in early 1775 from trading centers complaining of the interruption of trade with the thirteen colonies and asking for relief—which in the context could mean only conciliation. By the beginning of the year the nonimportation in America had gone into effect, and news was arriving both of the deteriorating situation in Massachusetts and of the adoption by the Continental Congress of nonexportation. (In one striking case, this news soon doubled the

Experience and Identity: Birmingham and the West Midlands, 1760–1800 (Montreal, 1977), 161–166.

The 16 subscribing: London, Bristol, Liverpool, Halifax, Leeds, Lancaster, Manchester, Leicester, Bradford (?), Birmingham, Coventry, Chester, Taunton, Glasgow, Nottingham, and Sheffield.

The 9 not subscribing: Worcestershire: Stourbridge, Dudley, Worcester; Somerset: Frome, Minehead; Wiltshire: Chippenham, Melksham; Staffordshire: Wolverhampton; Oxfordshire: Witney. For the availability of bookstores, see Plomer *et al.*, *Dictionary of Printers*.

30. Cf. Jacob M. Price, *Capital and Credit in British Overseas Trade: The View from the Chesapeake, 1700–1776* (Cambridge, Mass., 1980), chap. 6; J. de L. Mann, *The Cloth Industry in the West of England from 1640 to 1880* (Oxford, 1971), 63–85; Jacob M. Price, ed., *Joshua Johnson's Letterbook, 1771–1774: Letters from a Merchant in London to His Partners in Maryland*, London Record Society, Publications, XV (London, 1979), xiii–xiv, nos. 35a, 41c, 47a. Some Birmingham firms traded to Europe but not to America; see Eric Robinson, "Boulton and Fothergill, 1762–1782, and the Birmingham Export of Hardware," *University of Birmingham Historical Journal*, VII (1959–1960), 60–79.

export price of tobacco in Britain.) If word of the disturbances in New England propelled the government toward further measures of repression, the commercial news from Congress stirred some merchants toward a new effort at conciliation, similar to that of 1766, but this time without the encouragement of the government. A petition from the merchants and traders of London was soon followed by sixteen comparable relief (conciliatory) petitions from eighteen places.[31] Although not everyone in the towns concerned agreed with the petitioning activity, in only three areas (Birmingham, Nottingham, and the West Riding) were there opposing loyalist petitions calling for the maintenance of British law. In Birmingham, the loyal petition appears to have reflected some local fear of the growth of iron and steel manufacturing in the northern colonies.[32] In other places, the petitioning of early 1775 still seems to have been commercial and relatively nonpartisan, after the mode of 1766. By contrast, the much more heavily solicited and canvassed petitioning in late 1775—after news had arrived of serious fighting in America and a state of rebellion had been proclaimed—was much more political and noncommercial, with both repressive (progovernment) and conciliatory (antigovernment) petitions coming from almost every significant commercial center. As political statements, the autumn petitions attracted many more signatures than those of the previous winter: for example, in London in October 1775, 941 for the loyal petition and 1,029–1,100

31. For general situation, see Ian R. Christie, "The British Ministers, Massachusetts, and the Continental Association, 1774–1775," in Conser et al., eds., Resistance, Politics, 325–357; Paul Langford, "The British Business Community and the Later Nonimportation Movements, 1768–1776," in Conser et al., eds., Resistance, Politics, 278–324; and Bradley, Popular Politics, chap. 1. For the jump in tobacco prices, see Jacob M. Price, France and the Chesapeake: A History of the French Tobacco Monopoly, 1674–1791 . . . , 2 vols. (Ann Arbor, Mich., 1973), I, 646–647, 676, II, 683.

The 18 places and their petitions include a combined petition from the Yorkshire woolen towns of Wakefield, Halifax, Bradford, and Huddersfield; 2 petitions from Bristol (1 from Society of Merchant Venturers, 1 from the traders); and individual petitions from Glasgow, Norwich, Dudley (Worcestershire), Birmingham, Manchester, Wolverhampton, Liverpool, Newcastle (Staffordshire), the pottery towns (Staffordshire), Leeds, Nottingham, Bridport (Dorset), and Whitehaven. In addition there were relief petitions from Belfast and Waterford in Ireland and a further London petition from the West India interest. Journal of the House of Commons, XXXV, 71–72, 74, 77–78, 80–83, 86–87, 89–92, 99, 108, 123–124, 139, 141, 171, 186; see also Simmons and Thomas, eds., Proceedings and Debates, V, 261–266, 287–328, 338–344, 405–406, 425–426, 517–519; and Bradley, Popular Politics, chap. 1.

32. Two conciliatory petitions from (1) Leeds and (2) Wakefield, Halifax, Bradford, and Huddersfield were balanced by two loyal petitions from (1) Leeds, Wakefield, Halifax, and Bradford and (2) Huddersfield. Journal of the House of Commons, XXXV, 89, 90, 124, 186. There are a few minor slips in the table in Bradley, Popular Politics, 22. For the complexities of the situation in Birmingham, see Money, Experience and Identity, 197–201.

for the conciliatory. Yet the increase in signatures does not imply any extension of the geographic area concerned with America. The winter 1775 petitions came from places accounting for 80 percent of the subscribers to Wright's handbook, whereas the petitions of the following October involved only 70 percent.[33]

Unlike those of 1766, the petitions of January–February 1775 were unwelcome to the government, which was determined not to be diverted by them. On January 19, Lord North had presented to the Commons 149 documents on the American situation preparing the way for later legislative action. These were immediately referred to a committee of the whole. When the London relief (or conciliatory) petition was presented on January 23, its supporters wanted it referred to the aforesaid committee of the whole on the American papers, but the government used its substantial majority to refer it instead to another, separate committee of the whole. As each additional relief petition was presented, it too was, after a division, referred to the committee considering the London petition.[34] Because the American merchants of London refused to testify before the latter committee, its meetings were continually postponed; the first committee (on the American papers) meanwhile proceeded expeditiously with the work that led to the legislation against the commerce, navigation, and fisheries of Massachusetts and other New England colonies.[35] Only after the Massachusetts Bay bill had passed its third reading in the house on March 8 did the other committee of the whole on the London and similar petitions meet and hear a few witnesses from the West Indian trade.[36]

As already noted, the petitions submitted by the merchants of London and the other commercial centers were all drafted along common lines similar to

---

33. Bradley, *Popular Politics*, chaps. 2, 3, esp. pp. 65, 67. Sainsbury has been able to identify 504 of the 1,100 signatories of an October 1775 pro-American petition to the king, though his categories are not helpful. He reports that they included only 7 company directors while contemporary loyal petitions included at least 50 such. This suggests the degree to which the petitioning had become politicized but is not in itself too surprising, since there were very few American merchants then among the directors of the major companies, circa 1775. John Sainsbury, "The Pro-Americans of London, 1769 to 1782," *William and Mary Quarterly*, 3d Ser., XXXV (1978), 447.

34. *Journal of the House of Commons*, XXXV, 71–124 passim (see n. 31, above).

35. The Commons did, however, receive two further petitions from the merchants and corporation of London against the Massachusetts Bay bill. These were considered when the Commons went into committee on that bill, at which time London witnesses against the bill were heard. *Journal of the House of Commons*, XXXV, 112, 129, 144, 151, 152, 163–164, 166, 182; Simmons and Thomas, eds., *Proceedings and Debates*, V, 322–323, 481–497, 501–503, 555–577.

36. *Journal of the House of Commons*, XXXV, 183, 197, 200, 202, 208, 232; Simmons and Thomas, eds., *Proceedings and Debates*, V, 534–536, 555–577, 581–583. The printed committee transactions in March were concerned mainly with effects upon the West Indies. It is not clear what other evidence was heard.

those used in the 1766 petitions. Each locality complained that its trade and manufactures were languishing because of the American nonimportation agreements and that serious unemployment threatened; it then prayed the house for relief. All constitutional or political argument was eschewed. Such tactics had been successful in 1766 but were not to work as well in 1775– 1776, a situation forcing some of the petitioners to venture into more turbulent waters. When the merchants of London realized that their petition of January 23, 1775, would not be considered by the committee of the whole on the American papers, they submitted a second petition to the House of Commons on the twenty-sixth. This more radical document attacked the principle of dividing the American question between two committees—the principle that one could separate the American political problem from British-American trade. They insisted, on the contrary, "that the Connection be[tween] *Great Britain* and *America* originally was, and ought to be, of a commercial Kind, and that the Benefits derived therefrom, to the Mother Country are of the same Nature; . . . [so] that the fundamental Policy of those Laws of which they complain, and the Propriety of enforcing, relaxing, or amending the same, are Questions inseparably united with the Commerce between *Great Britain* and *America*; and consequently that the Consideration of the one cannot be entered on, without a full Discussion of the other."[37] This argument was not to impress George III or Lord North or the majority of the House of Commons in 1775.

Were the merchants of London engaging in the hyperbole of special pleading when they placed the commercial nexus at the heart of the whole imperial system? Such hyperbole came easily to them and to some historians of later centuries. But underneath the hyperbole lay at least one important truth: the American trades were extremely dynamic in an age when most branches of the British economy were relatively static. Precise measurement is impossible, but most scholarship now agrees that British (or English) national income per capita was either stagnant or increasing very slowly (about .3–.45 percent per annum) in the first two-thirds of the eighteenth century.[38] The most notable exception was foreign trade. For the political leadership the most important, or at least sensitive, aspect of foreign trade was traditionally the export market for home manufactures, so important for employment.

Very rough calculations suggest that as early as 1688 something like 33 percent of English national income could be ascribed to industry (including manufacturing, mining, and building) and commerce (including transportation). Another estimate, for 1770, ascribes to these two sectors 37 percent of

37. *Journal of the House of Commons*, XXXV, 80.
38. N.F.R. Crafts, *British Economic Growth during the Industrial Revolution* (Oxford, 1985), chap. 2, esp. p. 45.

national income. Much of this industrial and commercial activity was, of course, directed toward purely domestic demand. But exports were still impressive. Calculations by Nicholas Crafts show English exports rising between 1700 and 1760 from 24 percent to 35 percent of "gross industrial output."[39]

However measured, the export sector was the most dynamic sector of the English economy in the first three quarters of the eighteenth century. While total real output in England is estimated to have grown by 44 percent between 1700 and 1770, the product of the export industries grew by 156 percent; by contrast, purely home industries grew by only 14 percent and agricultural output by only 17 percent.[40] However, of particular relevance to our problem is the observation that, within the general pattern of dynamism, there were striking shifts of geographical direction. About 1700, more than 80 percent of English domestic exports went to the unprotected markets of Europe (exclusive of Ireland). By the early 1770s, the share of these markets had declined to only 40 percent. By contrast, the share of exports taken by the more protected markets of Ireland, the Americas, West Africa, and the East Indies had risen from less than 20 percent to 60 percent. Within this protected sphere, the share of North America had risen from 5.7 percent of all domestic exports at the beginning of the century to 25.3 percent in 1772–1773—even without counting the peak shipments of 1771 after the removal of most of the Townshend duties and the collapse of the nonimportation agreements. No other market for English exports had grown as much in those seven decades. (The addition of Scotland does not change the picture significantly.)[41]

39. Phyllis Deane and W. A. Cole, *British Economic Growth, 1688–1959: Trends and Structure*, University of Cambridge, Department of Applied Economics, Monograph no. 8 (Cambridge, 1962), 156; Crafts, *British Economic Growth during Industrial Revolution*, 132.

40. Deane and Cole, *British Economic Growth, 1688–1959*, 78.

41. *Ibid.*, 87; Ralph Davis, "English Foreign Trade, 1700–1774," *Econ. Hist. Rev.*, 2d Ser., XV (1962–1963), 302–303; B. R. Mitchell and Phyllis Deane, *Abstract of British Historical Statistics* (Cambridge, 1962), 312.

The addition of Scottish data to English data for 1772–1774 raises total imports by 9.2% and total exports by 9.7%; English data from Davis and Scottish data from Henry Hamilton, *An Economic History of Scotland in the Eighteenth Century* (Oxford, 1963), 414–415. However, when we add Scottish data to English for trade with the thirteen colonies, 1772–1774, we find that exports are raised by 10.2%, but *imports* are raised 38.3%! The difference is ascribable to the large transit trade in tobacco in Scotland. For Scottish trade with the thirteen colonies, see Jacob M. Price, "New Time Series for Scotland's and Britain's Trade with the Thirteen Colonies and States, 1740 to 1791," *WMQ*, 3d Ser., XXXII (1975), 318–321; for English trade with same, see U.S. Bureau of the Census, *Historical Statistics of the United States*, 1176–1177. (There is a typographical error in the column headings of series Z227–244 for Scotland, reversing the designations "imports" and "exports.")

If we add reexports to domestic exports, the change over the seven decades is not quite so striking: the European markets still took almost half of England's combined exports and reexports in the 1770s (instead of 40 percent for domestic exports alone) while the protected markets then took slightly more than half (instead of 60 percent). In other words the European market (in particular) for reexports was growing impressively down to 1776 even while the market there for English (or British) produce grew slowly or stagnated under the double burden of continental protectionism and sharp price competition.[42] Yet, the reexport of American produce to the Continent had a strategic implication that is often neglected. By the eighteenth century, almost all branches of British industry were dependent on imported raw materials to a greater or lesser degree. This was most noticeable in shipbuilding (where imports included masts, ship timbers, pitch, tar, and hemp and flax for sails, cables, and cordage), but it was true also of metallurgy (where a substantial proportion of the iron needed by British industry had to be imported) and textiles (where the same held true for raw and thrown silk, cotton, flax, and linen yarn). Even the woolen industry required significant imports of Irish wool and yarn. This dependence created payments problems for needed imports of raw materials, particularly from northern Europe. All English exports there (Russia, Scandinavia, and the Baltic littoral) covered only 19 percent of English imports thence. Of course, it wasn't necessary for individual trades to be balanced, since British earnings on exports to other areas in Europe, particularly Holland (the United Provinces) and Germany could be used to pay for imports from the Baltic via bills of exchange drawn on Hamburg or Amsterdam. Even so, combined English exports to northern Europe and northwestern Europe (Germany, Holland, Flanders, and France) covered only 62 percent of English imports from those areas. The difference was more than made up, though, by English reexports of overseas products, particularly calicoes and silks from the East Indies, coffee and dyestuffs from the West Indies, and tobacco and rice from North America. Reexports of the North American items (tobacco and rice) alone were enough to balance English trade with northern and northwestern Europe. These were, of course, not necessarily the richest imports from overseas. Sugar, in fact, was the most valuable import from any source and tea the most valuable from Asia, but both these commodities were consumed almost entirely in Britain and Ireland—or, in the case of tea, partly reexported to the American colo-

42. From 1756 to 1776, in Scotland reexports exceeded domestic exports in value by a considerable margin (Hamilton, *Economic History*, 414). For England in 1772–1774, reexports to the world were only 59% of domestic in value, but in those same years in the trade to northern Europe, northwest Europe, Ireland, and the Channel Islands, reexports exceeded domestic exports in value. Davis, "Foreign Trade, 1700–1774," *Econ. Hist. Rev.*, 2d Ser., XV (1962–1963), 302–303.

Table 4. English and Scottish Exports (and Reexports)
to the Thirteen Colonies

Measure	1699–1701	1772–1774
Population of colonies (estimated)	251,000 (1700)	2,320,000 (1773)
Annual English exports (official value)	£364,000	£2,561,000
Per head of colonial population	£1.45	£1.10
Annual English exports (current value)	£364,000	£2,682,000
Per head of colonial population	£1.45	£1.16
Annual British exports (official value)		£2,822,000
Per head of colonial population		£1.22
Annual British exports (current value)		£2,954,000
Per head of colonial population		£1.27

Sources: U.S. Bureau of the Census, *Historical Statistics of the United States: Colonial Times to 1970* (Washington, D.C., 1975), II, 116; Jacob M. Price, "New Time Series for Scotland's and Britain's Trade with the Thirteen Colonies and States, 1740 to 1791," *William and Mary Quarterly*, 3d Ser., XXXII, (1975) 325; John J. McCusker, "The Current Value of English Exports, 1697 to 1800," *WMQ*, 3d Ser., XXVIII (1971), 623–626.

nies—and thus did not provide significant reexports to the European continent.[43]

The fecundity of the North American population was the key to the dynamism of Britain's trade thither. Increased population meant an increased labor force to produce exports and an increased market for British and other foreign goods. The seven- or eightfold expansion of English (or later British) exports to those colonies between the periods 1699–1701 and 1772–1774 was based almost exclusively on the more than ninefold increase in the colonial population during the same decades. In fact, neither English nor British exports thither increased as much as colonial population, so there was actually a slight decline in exports per head of colonial population, whether calculated in official or current prices (Table 4).[44] But to contemporaries it was the growth in aggregate trade that impressed.

43. Davis, "Foreign Trade, 1700–1774," *Econ. Hist. Rev.*, 2d Ser., XV (1962–1963), 300–303. For the Irish yarn trade, see L. M. Cullen, *Anglo-Irish Trade, 1660–1800* (Manchester, 1968), 55. For the settling of English trade deficits with northern Europe by bills of exchange drawn on Amsterdam or Hamburg, see Jacob M. Price, "Multilateralism and / or Bilateralism: The Settlement of British Trade Balances with 'The North,' c. 1700," *Econ. Hist. Rev.*, 2d Ser., XIV (1961–1962), 254–274.

44. A somewhat different picture is evident in the data presented in John J. McCusker and Russell R. Menard, *The Economy of British America, 1607–1789* (Chapel Hill, N.C., 1985), 280. They show British exports to the thirteen colonies

From the perspective of the total British economy, the North American trades in the eighteenth century may now appear to have been of only moderate significance. Yet at the time they were of vital importance to many businessmen and should have impressed statesmen as worthy objects of concern on both their export and their import sides. We have just noted the rapid growth of the North American market, a particularly important vent for a number of British and Irish manufactures, particularly woolens, linens, and hardware.[45] Imports from both North America and the West Indies freed Britain from dependence on foreign suppliers (to the benefit of the trade balance); and, in the case of wheat, they could be helpful during crises of poor harvests, such as in fact occurred in the late 1760s and early 1770s.[46] Imports from North America, particularly tobacco and rice, also provided valuable reexports to areas of Europe with which Britain's trade would otherwise have been unbalanced and from which Britain obtained much-needed raw materials.

The impact of the burgeoning American trades was not felt evenly throughout Britain, not even among the ports. In the seventeenth century, when there were very few great merchants in the new American trades, numerous petty traders with bits of capital found it possible to enter the trades both to the West Indies and to North America. They traded from a wide range of ports, large and small. In the eighteenth century, the more substantial merchants, with access to easier credit, found it possible to expand their share of the trades. As a consequence, in the last quarter of the seventeenth century and throughout the eighteenth century, there was a gradual increase in firm size and a reduction in the number of firms in the principal branches of the American trades. The number of firms or individuals in the London tobacco import trade, for example, was reduced from 573 in 1676 to 56 in 1775 while the average annual importation per firm increased at least thirty-five-fold. At Glasgow, the average firm's annual im-

---

per head of colonial population increasing from £.90 in 1699–1704 to £1.20 in 1767–1774. Their figure for the earlier period is depressed by the inclusion of three war years, 1702–1704, when exports were artificially discouraged. The peace years 1699–1701 (also used by Ralph Davis) would appear to be less distorted.

45. The data given by McCusker and Menard, *British America*, 284, show that the American markets in 1770 took more than 50% of total English exports of wrought copper, wrought iron and nails, beaver hats, cordage, linen, printed cotton and linen, wrought silk, and "Spanish cloths." Their account is based on Elizabeth Boody Schumpeter, *English Overseas Trade Statistics, 1697–1808* (Oxford, 1960), 63–69. The year 1770, chosen by Schumpeter, probably underestimates the importance of the North American market, as some element of nonimportation was then being observed.

46. For the suspension of the corn laws to permit imports of colonial wheat, see Donald Grove Barnes, *A History of the English Corn Laws from 1660–1846* (New York, 1930; rpt., 1961), 31–32, 37–45.

VI

portation in the 1770s was ten times as much as in the 1720s. In the sugar trade at Bristol, the number of importers was reduced by almost three-fourths between 1672 and 1789 while the average annual importation per firm increased about twenty-six-fold.[47]

At the same time, the number of ports involved in the American trades was significantly reduced. At the beginning of the century, London and Bristol had to share the English trades to America with a great range of havens, including the western ports of Whitehaven, Lancaster, Liverpool, Barnstaple, and Bideford; the south coast ports of Falmouth, Penryn, Fowey, Looe, Plymouth, Dartmouth, Exeter, Lyme Regis, Weymouth, Poole, Cowes, Portsmouth, and Dover; and the east coast ports of Hull and Newcastle. In Scotland, Glasgow (Port Glasgow and Greenock) in the first generation after the Union had to share part of the American trade with about thirty lesser ports, particularly Bo'ness, Dumfries, Kirkcaldy, and Montrose. By the generation of the American Revolution, however, the trade with North America and the West Indies had become concentrated in a much smaller group of ports: in effect, five key ports (London, Glasgow, Whitehaven, Liverpool, and Bristol) with minor shares (the equivalent of one or two ships a year) to a few other places (Lancaster, Hull, Penryn, Aberdeen, and Ayr). The three or four largest ports might easily dominate 80 or 90 percent of one of the American trades.[48]

This meant, of course, that traders in the smaller ports lost their close connections with and probably even their interest in the American colonies. They had, therefore, no pressing motive to petition in 1775, even if their ports were parliamentary boroughs. Among the places *not* petitioning then were the following ports and parliamentary boroughs, which had lost their North American trade entirely or seen it shrink radically since the beginning of the century: Fowey, Truro, Looe, Plymouth, Dartmouth, Barnstaple, Exeter, Lyme Regis, Weymouth, Portsmouth, and Dover. In such places, there likely were good local political reasons for not petitioning that reinforced the lack of economic interest. Several of them were for parliamentary elections considered in whole or in part Admiralty or Treasury boroughs (Plymouth,

47. Jacob M. Price and Paul G. E. Clemens, "A Revolution of Scale in Overseas Trade: British Firms in the Chesapeake Trade, 1675–1775," *Journal of Economic History*, XLVII (1987), 1–43.

48. *Ibid.*, 39–40. For data on lesser English ports, see PRO, T 1/278/30; T 1/345, fol. 5; T 38/363; T 64/276B/327; and PRO 30/8/297, fol. 150. For Scottish ports, see PRO, CO 390/5/13; T 1/139/29; T 1/282/23; T 1/329, fol. 128; T 36/13; BL Add. MS 8133B, fols. 366–367. A similar concentration had taken place in the English Newfoundland fishery, which earlier had attracted vessels from dozens of havens between Bristol and Southampton. By the 1760s, however, it had become concentrated in a smaller number of ports, particularly Bristol, Dartmouth, Teignmouth, Topsham, and Poole. Ralph Greenlee Lounsbury, *The British Fishery at Newfoundland, 1634–1763* (New Haven, Conn., 1934), 314.

Dartmouth, Portsmouth, Dover) while others were controlled by local families that most often preferred a proadministration stance (Fowey; Truro; Looe; Lyme Regis; and Weymouth and Melcombe Regis).[49]

Once the fighting started in America, there were very apparent *political* reasons for joining in prowar or antiwar petitions, whether or not one had connections of any sort with the colonies. Before the start of hostilities, however, when the political atmosphere was less tense, purely commercial concerns could express themselves more uninhibitedly.

Yet one would be wrong to assume that the commercial were the only concerns creating in such Britons interest in or even sympathy for the American colonies and colonists. There were also significant, long-established religious connections, particularly for the nonconformists, for whom so many of the colonists were simply "congregations of brethren beyond the seas." The keenness of such interests and the warmth of such sympathies showed themselves at the time of the American Revolution, when "most of the leaders of Old Dissent, Congregationalists and Baptists no less than rational Dissenters, supported their co-religionists on the other side of the Atlantic." Only John Wesley publicly supported the government uncompromisingly, even while privately hoping for conciliation and compromise.[50]

It does not necessarily follow, however, that these noteworthy religious connections were totally distinct from commercial links. The Church of England had, we know, formal connections with the colonial Anglican churches through the authority of the bishop of London and his commissaries in the colonies. Anglican missionary work in the colonies fell primarily to the Society for the Propagation of the Gospel in Foreign Parts, whose membership was heavily clerical. Relatively few politicians and businessmen—even merchants trading to North America—turn up among its members. Each dissenting denomination for its part had to design its own links with its brethren in North America. The nonconformists taken as a whole were more urban, hence more commercial, than the general English population.[51] Their

49. Namier and Brooke, *House of Commons, 1754–1790*, I, 227–228, 232–233, 241–242, 250–253, 257–258, 266–267, 272–273, 297–299, 445–446.

50. Namier, *England in the Age of the American Revolution*, 39; Michael R. Watts, *The Dissenters: From the Reformation to the French Revolution* (Oxford, 1978), 479–480. The attitudes of articulate, published dissenting leaders on the colonies after the start of hostilities are discussed in C. C. Bonwick, "English Dissenters and the American Revolution," in H. C. Allen and Roger Thompson, eds., *Contrast and Connection: Bicentennial Essays in Anglo-American History* (London, 1976), 88–112. Bonwick omits the Quakers, who, in any event, had little recourse to the self-publicizing activities of his "dissenters." See also Bernard Semmel, *The Methodist Revolution* (New York, 1973), 63–71; William T. Whitley, *A History of British Baptists* (London, 1923), 233–235, 238–239, 255–257.

51. Watts, *Dissenters*, 285. The membership lists of the Society were printed as appendixes to the annual commemoration sermon. The only merchants trading to North America noted in the lists for 1756 and 1766 were Thomas Harley (member

members were thus rather more likely than others to have private concerns in and correspondence with North America. Such private commercial links could facilitate noncommercial communication between coreligionists on both sides of the Atlantic.

The Society of Friends tended to have a higher proportion of merchants than other denominations and was probably the nonconformist group with the most continuous and intense links to America. The key central bodies for English Quakers were the London Yearly Meeting and the standing Meeting for Sufferings, which had a subcommittee for the American colonies. The latter included correspondents appointed to keep these London bodies in touch with Friends in different parts of the British Isles and the American colonies. A conspicuous, indeed a leading place among the correspondents was taken by prominent London merchants and others trading regularly to the colonies (see Table 5). In such cases, the Quakers' network of correspondence and the merchants' commercial networks substantially overlapped.[52]

The relations of the other nonconformist groups to America are more diffuse than those of the Quakers and harder to measure. Perhaps a good sample of them is to be found in the history of the missionary New England Company. Its membership was diverse geographically and socially and difficult to delineate exactly. Yet it is clear that merchants trading to America occupied a prominent place in its leadership in the eighteenth century, when it was an overwhelmingly nonconformist body. For many years a most prominent place in the company was occupied by the Ashurst family, merchants of London. Alderman Henry Ashurst (died 1680) was treasurer of the company (1659–1680); his son, Alderman Sir William Ashurst (died 1720), a director of the Bank of England, was also treasurer (1681–1696) and then became governor of the company (1696–1720), to be succeeded in turn as governor by his son Robert (1720–1726). Sir William Ashurst was particularly active as a merchant trading to Massachusetts and served the colony as agent.[53] A comparably prominent place in the company was after 1748

---

of Parliament), Stephen Theodore Janssen (member), John Thomlinson, Sr., John Thomlinson, Jr. (member), Chauncey Townsend (member), and Barlow Trecothick (member).

52. Many of these Quaker merchant-correspondents are discussed in Jacob M. Price, "The Great Quaker Business Families of Eighteenth-Century London: The Rise and Fall of a Sectarian Patriciate," in Richard S. Dunn and Mary Maples Dunn, eds., *The World of William Penn* (Philadelphia, 1986), 363–399. For a fuller discussion, see Anne Thomas Gary (afterwards Pannell), *The Political and Economic Relations of English and American Quakers, 1750–85* (D.Phil. thesis, Oxford, 1935).

53. William Kellaway, *The New England Company, 1649–1776: Missionary Society to the American Indians* (London, 1961), for both a general treatment of the society and for a list of its members and officers (in index). For Ashursts, see *ibid.*; J. R. Woodhead, *The Rulers of London, 1660–1689* . . . (London, 1965), 19; Bernard

Table 5. Prominent London Merchants and Others Serving
as Correspondents with the North American Colonies
for the Society of Friends, 1725–1775

Name	Occupation	Address	Colonies
Samuel Arnold	[merchant]	Gracechurch St.	South Carolina
Silvanus Bevan	apothecary	Lombard St.	New England
Timothy Bevan	apothecary	Lombard St.	New York
James Beesley	merchant	Paternoster Row	Maryland
John Bell	merchant	Lombard St.	North and South Carolina, Maryland
Elias Bland	merchant	Tower Hill	New England
John Bland	merchant	Lime St.	Virginia
James Collinson	mercer and merchant	Gracechurch St.	Maryland
Peter Collinson	mercer and merchant	Gracechurch St.	New York, Maryland
Philip Eliot	merchant	Bucklersbury	South Carolina
John Falconar	merchant	—	Maryland
Joseph Freame	goldsmith-banker	Lombard St.	North Carolina
John Gopsill	merchant	St. Saviours, Southwark	Maryland
Jacob Hagen	merchant	Mill St., Southwark	New York, Pennsylvania
John Hanbury	merchant	Tower St.	Virginia
Jeremiah Harman	merchant	St. Martin's Lane, Cannon St.	Maryland
John Hunt	merchant	Leadenhall St.	Pennsylvania, Maryland, Virginia, North Carolina
Thomas Hyam	merchant	Philpot Lane, Fenchurch St.	Virginia
John Midford	merchant	—	South Carolina
Daniel Mildred	merchant	Broad St. Buildings	New York, Pennsylvania
Richard Partridge	merchant	Water Lane, Tower St.	Pennsylvania, North and South Carolina
Thomas Plumstead	ironmonger	Gracechurch St.	Pennsylvania, New Jersey
John Roberts	merchant	Fenchurch St.	New England

Table 5 *(continued)*

Jonathan Scarth	merchant	Liberty of the Tower	Virginia
Peter Williams	warehouseman	Lombard St.	South Carolina

Source: Yearly Meeting Minutes, vols. VI–XIV, Friends House Library, London.
Note: The colonies shown are those for which each correspondent was responsible. He may have traded to other places as well. Where nonmerchants are shown, it is known or believed that they also traded abroad in merchant style. The list does not claim to be complete; only those readily identifiable have been included. Retailers and brewers in London have been excluded.

occupied by the Mauduit brothers and their firm Mauduit, Wright and Company. Jasper and Israel Mauduit, sons of a nonconformist minister, and Jasper's son-in-law, Thomas Wright, started as "warehousemen," or wholesalers, selling woolens to merchants exporting to America. They also had correspondents of their own in the colonies and in later years were described in the directories as merchants. Jasper (who died in 1772) was treasurer of the New England Company (1748–1765) and governor (1765–1772). Wright succeeded Jasper as treasurer (1765–1773), and Israel later became governor in 1787 just before his death.[54] On Jasper's death, his place as governor from 1772 to 1780 had been taken by William Bowden (died 1780), a director of the Bank of England and Virginia merchant. The leadership of the New England Company also had close links with the board of Deputies of the Protestant Dissenters, of which both Jasper Mauduit and William Bowden were chairmen, as was another member of the company, Nathaniel Polhill, a Southwark tobacco manufacturer and merchant and later banker.[55] There is no accessible information on all the callings of the ordinary members of the New England Company, but more than a dozen of them can be identified as merchants trading to the North American colo-

---

Bailyn, *The New England Merchants in the Seventeenth Century* (Cambridge, Mass., 1955), 183.

54. On the Mauduits and Wright, see Kellaway, *New England Company*, index; Price, ed., *Joshua Johnson's Letterbook*. Other examples of their dealings with the American trade can be found in the Norton cash-book, Virginia State Library, Richmond; and Robert Carter correspondence, Virginia Historical Society, Richmond.

55. Kellaway, *New England Company*, index. On Polhill, see Namier and Brooke, *House of Commons, 1754–1790*, III, 306; on Bowden, see W. Marston Acres, "Directors of the Bank of England," *Notes and Queries*, CLXXIX (1940), 116.

nies.[56] A smaller number of such American merchants can be identified as members of the Anglican Society for the Propagation of the Gospel in Foreign Parts, but I have found nothing to suggest that they were leaders in that clerically dominated society.[57]

Our evidence would therefore suggest a considerable overlap between the commercial networks linking the British and colonial economies and the less material networks linking at least dissenters in Britain and the thirteen colonies.

America and the British Nation

In the first part of this essay, we were concerned with the very limited experience of and interest in the American colonies among the ruling strata of Britain. In the second part we looked into the much greater concern with America among some limited sections of the population engaged in trade and manufactures. What about the British nation as a whole? This is a most difficult question. An assessment of the longer-term impact of the growing American colonies on Britain, circa 1700–1775, must include three important areas in which British society then was in varying degrees affected by the American connection: emigration, trade, and the military, civil, and fiscal burdens of empire.

Emigration

Between 1630 and 1700, it is estimated that 378,000 people left the British Isles (primarily England) for overseas. This was large enough to help cause a decline in total English population in the period 1650–1689. These high levels were interrupted during the wars of 1689–1713; and when emigration resumed in the next half-century, 1713–1763, it was to be at levels well below those of the seventeenth century. During this last span, emigration from England was partly balanced by immigration from Wales, Scotland, and Ireland, so that the net loss from emigration was not high enough to prevent the total population of England from rising along with that of Scotland and of Ireland.[58] This rise in population, associated with parallel

56. Trading to or connected with New England: Alexander Champion, John Lane, Thomas Lane; New York: Nathaniel Paice; Pennsylvania: Richard Neave; Virginia: Latham Arnold, Robert Bristow, Edward Hunt, Thomas Hunt, Sir Lyonel Lyde, bart., Nathaniel Polhill, Samuel Waterman. I am indebted to Mrs. Katherine Kellock for help on this point.

57. See n. 51, above.

58. Henry A. Gemery, "Emigration from the British Isles to the New World, 1630–1700: Inferences from Colonial Populations," *Research in Economic History*, V (1980), 179–231; Wrigley and Schofield, *Population History of England*, 185–187,

rises in other European countries, helps explain the higher prices for food and other agricultural products, which led gradually to higher rents throughout the British Isles. While larger and more efficient, progressive farmers could afford to pay these higher rents, tenants on very small holdings or on poorer lands could find the new rents more burdensome, particularly in parts of Ireland and Scotland where the new terms were part of a transition from customary (nonmarket) to market relationships.[59] The resulting difficulties are reported to have helped persuade some tenants to emigrate at a time when many artisans and others were pushed in the same direction by the higher cost of living. Between 1763 and 1775, emigration to North America took about 30,000 people from England, 40,000 from Scotland, and 55,000 from northern Ireland. Since the weight of the English emigration (less than 1 percent of the 1760 population) was much less than that of the Scottish and Irish (3 percent and 2.3 percent, respectively) and since emigrants were not evenly distributed among the population of any of the countries, the effects of the emigration would not have been uniformly felt. Abstractly, these departures should have reduced pressure on resources, thus improving real wages and reducing the upward trend of rents. But such tenuous benefits have left little trace in the records.[60] Instead, we find the complaints of landlords and employers at the loss of tenants and workers.

Trade and Manufactures

If British industry may have suffered a bit from the emigration of labor to America in the years immediately preceding the American Revolution, it benefited much more from the growth of population and markets in the thirteen colonies over the preceding century. As already noted, the seven- or eightfold expansion of English (later British) exports to those colonies be-

---

219–228; J. Potter, "The Growth of Population in America, 1700–1860," in D. V. Glass and D.E.C. Eversley, *Population in History: Essays in Historical Demography* (London, 1965), 642–646. Potter (p. 645) makes a rough guess of 350,000 for nonslave immigration to the United States, 1700–1790, from Europe as well as the British Isles. See also David W. Galenson, *White Servitude in Colonial America: An Economic Analysis* (Cambridge, 1981), 216–217. Gemery discusses the difficulties of estimating post-1700 American immigration in "European Emigration to North America, 1700–1820: Numbers and Quasi-Numbers," *Perspectives in American History*, n.s., I (1984), 283–342. For increases in Scottish and Irish population, see Mitchell and Deane, *Abstract of British Historical Statistics*, 5–6.

59. Jan de Vries, *The Economy of Europe in an Age of Crisis, 1600–1750* (Cambridge, 1976), 5; Deane and Cole, *British Economic Growth*, 91; J. D. Chambers and G. E. Mingay, *The Agricultural Revolution, 1750–1880* (New York, 1966), 109–112. On burden of rents, cf., for example, T. C. Smout, *A History of the Scottish People, 1560–1830* (New York, 1969), 340–351.

60. Bernard Bailyn, *Voyagers to the West: A Passage in the Peopling of America on the Eve of the Revolution* (New York, 1986), 24–66, esp. 26.

VI

tween the periods 1699–1701 and 1772–1774 was based almost exclusively
on the more than ninefold increase in the colonial population during the
same decades. Since the increase in American population was greater than
the increase in exports, there was a slight slippage in British exports per head
of colonial population—caused most likely by the growth of some industries
in the colonies. In Birmingham, at least, there was some uneasiness about
possible dangers in the development of an American iron and steel industry.
Most British merchants and manufacturers, however, were more than satisfied by North America's ever increasing importance as a major market for
British manufactures down to the 1770s.

It can be argued that every landlord, farmer, manufacturing worker, and
sailor benefited either directly or indirectly from the American market.
However, in the world before Adam Smith, the benefits that were perceived
tended to be only those that were direct and immediate. In this sense the
benefits of the growing colonial market were not spread evenly over the
British Isles. The most noticeable effects were to be perceived in the relatively
few ports that dominated the American trades (particularly London, Glasgow, Liverpool, and Bristol). The shipbuilding trades did not benefit as much
as might be expected, since the North American colonies themselves built
about one-third of the vessels known to *Lloyd's Register* around 1770.[61] A
much greater benefit was realized by the maritime supplies manufactures,
which were relatively weak in the colonies: the making of sails, cable, cordage, and anchors. The industries that drew most orders and benefits from
America tended to be concentrated in a few areas, particularly the West
Riding of Yorkshire, South Lancashire / Cheshire, and Birmingham and the
Black Country, though the luxury trades of London should not be forgotten
(tailors, dressmakers, coachmakers, watchmakers).[62] We are familiar with
all these places from the subscription lists to Wright's *American Negotiator*.
But, even if we add in Nottingham, Norwich, and a few other places we have
also met in Wright's lists and the petitions to Parliament, it remains evident
that only very circumscribed areas of the country and occupational groups
benefited much at first hand from the American connection.

61. Jacob M. Price, "A Note on the Value of Colonial Exports of Shipping," *Jour.
Econ. Hist.*, XXXVI (1976), 704–724, esp. 713–716; Joseph A. Goldenberg, "An
Analysis of Shipbuilding Sites in *Lloyd's Register* of 1776," *Mariner's Mirror*, LIX
(1973), 419–436.
62. Though most types of English cloth undoubtedly found their way to North
America, references to that from the West Riding are by far the most common in
merchants' correspondence. In Ireland, the more limited benefits of the imperial
connection were to a considerable degree concentrated in the linen manufacturing
areas around Belfast and in the southern agricultural areas serving the Cork provi-
sioning trade supplying victuals for both the West Indies plantations and vessels
sailing to all distant overseas destinations.

However limited in number, the ports and inland towns that did benefit from American trade prospered substantially during the first three quarters of the eighteenth century. During those years, their population, like their trade, grew more rapidly than that of Britain as a whole. Their residents could see evidence of both: at Liverpool, for example, in the celebrated new docks and, with all the towns, in new residential and commercial streets, churches, and theaters. In the bustling ports of Glasgow, Liverpool, and Bristol, the North American, West Indian, and African merchants were the leaders of the public as well as of the commercial life of the towns, furnishing many of the mayors, provosts, town councillors, and other municipal dignitaries, not to mention a number of local members of Parliament.[63]

In the much greater world of London, where public finance, monopoly companies, and the older European trades were at least as important as the newer open American trades, the situation was more complex. Leaving aside the court, administrative, legal, and fashionable world of the West End and Westminster, we can detect within the City of London proper three distinct clusters of eminence: *municipal* (mayors, aldermen, and comparable officials), *national* (including directors of the great chartered companies, government contractors, members of Parliament for places outside the capital), and *unacknowledged* (those whose eminence lacked formal recognition). Retailers, it should be remembered, had to be freemen (citizens) in order to trade in London, but wholesalers and merchants did not. It is among the latter that we find most of our unacknowledged worthies.

Between the third quarter of the seventeenth and the third quarter of the eighteenth century, the businessman's City of London had in many respects continued its evolution from *Gemeinschaft* (community) to *Gesellschaft* (market society). In the former period, leading merchants were frequently as prominent in the communal life of the City as in its trade. By the latter this limited communitarianism was less evident, and we find in the directories a very noticeable population of foreigners, Catholics, Jews, Scotsmen, Irishmen, provincial English and Welsh, even Americans, who were for various reasons not "free of the City" but who still were important in its commercial life. Of probably the fifty richest men in the City in 1780, only 12 percent

63. For contemporary awareness of the importance of the American trades to the outports, see William Enfield, *An Essay towards the History of Liverpool* . . . , 2d ed. (London, 1774); John Gibson, *The History of Glasgow* . . . (Glasgow, 1777); Andrew Brown, *History of Glasgow* . . . , 2 vols. (Glasgow, 1795, 1797). See also T. M. Devine, *The Tobacco Lords: A Study of the Tobacco Merchants of Glasgow and Their Trading Activities, c. 1740–90* (Edinburgh, 1975); W. E. Minchinton, ed., *The Trade of Bristol in the Eighteenth Century*, Bristol Record Society's Publications, XX (Bristol, 1957); Minchinton, ed., *Politics and the Port of Bristol in the Eighteenth Century: The Petitions of the Society of Merchant Venturers, 1698–1803*, Bristol Record Society's Publications, XXIII (Bristol, 1963).

were municipal worthies and 34 percent national worthies while 54 percent belong to our category of unacknowledged eminence.[64]

This general pattern was repeated in the American trades. In the seventeenth century we find an impressive number of American traders among the aldermen and common councilmen of London, but they become much scarcer in those circles as the eighteenth century progresses, in part because firms in those trades become fewer and larger, in part because the municipal life of London becomes more inward-looking. Among the national worthies we find slightly more American traders, most noticeably among government contractors and on the boards of the London Assurance and the Bank of England. (Both had American traders as their governors circa 1750.)[65] But many of the leading American merchants on the eve of the Revolution were Quakers, Scots, or even Americans and were unlikely to attract formal recognition of any sort. (The election of William Lee as alderman was quite exceptional.) But those identities did not impede their business careers. Quaker merchants trading to America were founding partners before 1776 of the London predecessors of both Barclays and Lloyds banks. The Barclays entertained the royal family on official visits to the City, and those other great Quakers, John and Capel Hanbury, were known to and consulted by cabinet ministers.[66] Even so, American merchants did not loom as large in the great London of 1770 as did the tobacco lords in the smaller contemporary Glasgow, for in the capital they had to compete for luster with financiers and the grandees of the European and Asian trades.

Burdens of Empire

If the benefits of empire trade, no matter how large, were in fact enjoyed only by limited sections of the population, the same cannot be said of the costs of empire. At the beginning we noted that, unlike the Victorian empire of 1857–1914, the mercantilist Georgian empire through most of the eighteenth century involved the British taxpayer in no heavy peacetime administrative expenses. Yet there were heavy defense costs. The post-1689 British state was forged in the fires of war. Thus, in the peacetime year of 1737 almost 82 percent of central government expenditure went to defense and

64. PRO, T 47/8, Register of persons paying the tax on male servants, 1780. The 50 were those paying for 4 or more.

65. On continuity and inbreeding among London aldermanic families, see Nicholas Rogers, "Money, Land, and Lineage: The Big Bourgeoisie of Hanoverian London," *Social History*, IV (1979), 437–454. Cf. also Henry Horwitz, " 'The Mess of the Middle Class' Revisited: The Case of the Big Bourgeoisie of Augustan London," *Continuity and Change*, II (1987), 263–296. The governors were William Hunt, Bank of England; John Hyde II, London Assurance.

66. Cf. Price, "Great Quaker Business Families," in Dunn and Dunn, eds., *World of William Penn*, 363–399.

Table 6. British Government Expenditures, 1737, 1764

Expenditure	1737		1764	
Civil government	£ 930,000	(18.1%)	£ 1,137,000	(10.6%)
Defense				
Army	835,000		2,234,000	
Navy	933,000		2,150,000	
Ordnance	327,000		279,000	
Total	2,095,000	(40.8%)	4,663,000	(43.6%)
Debt charges	2,105,000	(41.0%)	4,887,000	(45.7%)
Total net expenditure	£5,129,000	(99.9%)	£10,686,000	(99.9%)

Source: B. R. Mitchell and Phyllis Deane, *Abstract of British Historical Statistics* (Cambridge, 1962), 390.
Note: All sums are rounded to the nearest thousand; deviations in totals are due to rounding in source.

debt charges, that is, the costs of past wars, going back to 1689 (Table 6). After the great conflicts of 1739–1763 total government expenditure almost doubled, with the share allotted to defense and debt charges rising to more than 89 percent in 1764.

This mounting volume of expenditure was of necessity balanced by a steadily mounting burden of taxation. Peter Mathias and Patrick O'Brien have punctured the comfortable myth that somehow constitutional Britain in the eighteenth century enjoyed levels of national taxation lower than those of arbitrary France. Their comparative work reveals that "on a per capita basis, in Britain taxes were more than double the level attained in France at the beginning of the century (1715–30), [and] remained at about twice the level of those in France for most of the rest of the period up to the Revolution." It is particularly noteworthy that the burden of taxation borne circa 1760–1775 was unprecedentedly high both per capita and as a percentage of national income—though much higher levels were to be reached later, particularly during the Napoleonic Wars.[67]

This mounting burden of taxation was a constant, if not always acknowledged, presence in British politics throughout the century. Through indirect taxes on beer, wine, gin, tobacco, tea, and such, the burden of taxation fell

67. Peter Mathias and Patrick O'Brien, "Taxation in Britain and France, 1715–1810: A Comparison of the Social and Economic Incidence of Taxes Collected for the Central Government," *Journal of European Economic History*, V (1976), 601–650, esp. 610–611; Mathias, "Taxation and Industrialization in Britain, 1700–1870," in Mathias, *The Transformation of England* (New York, 1979), 116–130. See also John Brewer, *The Sinews of Power: War, Money, and the English State, 1688–1783* (New York, 1989), esp. chap. 4.

VI

upon the whole population, though the discretionary element in the consumption of such products made such taxes more acceptable to the puritanical streak in the British public mind. Direct taxes, particularly the land tax, were kept low in peacetime but allowed to rise in war, when they were felt as a particular burden by the landed classes. It was the irksomeness of this burden, when extended over many years, that helped create the political atmosphere and pressures that speeded the end of long wars in 1710–1713, 1760–1763, and 1780–1783. A significant, if not a major, part of the war expenditures of 1739–1763 was incurred on the American side of the Atlantic.[68] Whether expressed in debate or not, consciousness of fiscal burdens undoubtedly influenced the attitude toward the colonies of almost everyone in the British electorate, or political nation, who did not otherwise benefit from the American connection.

Those who did benefit, particularly businessmen, had, of course, a keener awareness of the importance and value of the American connection and of the need to maintain it. But how much could such persons influence what we now call the decision-making process? Such textbook tags as "commercial revolution," "industrial revolution," and "rise of the middle class" sometimes create the impression that the various middling classes had much more political weight than they in fact enjoyed through the greater part of the reigns of the four Georges. Commercial and industrial entrepreneurs and the like could not dictate policy. They could only try to influence decision making in one of four quite different ways: by participating in parliamentary politics, by negotiating or bargaining with those in authority, by quiet lobbying, and by open petitioning and related forms of legal public agitational activity.

Parliamentary Politics

The House of Commons after the Union with Scotland consisted of 558 members, including 405 burgesses representing English boroughs, 15 representing Scottish boroughs, and 12 sitting for Welsh boroughs, for a total borough representation of 432. Nevertheless, as is well known, most of the smaller boroughs had by the mid-eighteenth century fallen under the influence of individual borough patrons or the neighboring bigger landowners as a group, and they tended to elect as their members either local landed gentlemen or the friends, relations, and dependents of their patrons (including many of the noted army and navy officers). Businessmen in the smaller boroughs were seldom rich enough to bear the costs of campaigning and

68. Gwyn, "British Government Spending," *Jour. Imperial and Commonwealth Hist.*, VIII (1980), 74–84.

service in Parliament, though substantial merchants were more likely to be returned by larger boroughs and a few managed to buy their way in from particularly corrupt boroughs like Aylesbury. Even so, the number of merchants (including bankers and brewers) in the Commons was quite modest and was tending to decline through the first two-thirds of the eighteenth century. Thus the 73 merchants (and other businessmen) in Commons in the Parliament of 1715–1722 were reduced to only 51 in the Parliament of 1741–1747 but recovered to 64–68 in parliaments of 1754–1774. Most merchants in the Commons normally preferred to keep in the good graces of the government of the day, in part because they wanted to gain favors either for their constituencies or for themselves. (John Brooke reports that in the Parliament of 1754, 17 of them were government contractors, 27 in that of 1761, 14 in 1768, 14 in 1774, and 17 in 1780.) They were therefore very cautious and selective in choosing issues on which to take a conspicuous stand.[69]

Negotiating and Bargaining

If too few in numbers and too divided in interest to form a powerful battalion in the House of Commons, merchants and bankers as a class were not infrequently in a position to negotiate from strength with the government on particular issues. In wartime in particular the government most urgently needed to borrow money, to remit funds abroad, to purchase supplies, and to transport men and supplies overseas. For such services they, of necessity, had recourse to bankers, merchants, shipowners, and numerous specialists (from biscuit bakers to ropemakers to gunfounders). Under the pressure of war these people were usually in a position to obtain good terms for themselves. On large loans and refunding operations there could be important fringe benefits. Both the Bank of England and the South Sea Company were, for example, founded as part of such financial operations. To be sure, when charters came to be renewed, the government was often in a stronger position, particularly in peacetime, and could extract further loans and other services without necessarily making further concessions. However, even in wartime, there were limits to how much in the way of policy concessions even the biggest financiers could extract. The height of the hubris of the moneymen came in 1710, when a delegation of Bank of England directors led by Sir Gilbert Heathcote waited on Queen Anne and urged her not to dismiss Lord Treasurer Godolphin, lest the credit of the state suffer. The queen was polite, but Godolphin was dismissed a few weeks later. The

69. Sedgwick, *House of Commons, 1715–1754,* I, 155; Gerrit P. Judd IV, *Members of Parliament, 1734–1832* (New Haven, Conn., 1955), 89 (from Judd's "Net Total," I have deducted "Manufacturers and Nabobs" to get a category closer to Sedgwick's); Namier and Brooke, *House of Commons, 1754–1790,* I, 135–136.

directors had gone too far; their successors were to be more cautious. During the ministerial crisis of February 1746, the grands bourgeois did not take the initiative as in 1710, but some of the moneymen refused to commit themselves to continue their subscription to a pending government loan ("No Pelham, no money") and thus helped abort the formation of a Granville-Bath administration.[70]

Lobbying

A much more common way in which businessmen and others tried to influence policy was by rather deferential and quiet lobbying. This could be done in a more formal mode when members of Parliament, colonial agents, and individual merchants and other spokesmen for local corporations or interests appeared before the Board of Trade or the Treasury Board to argue the case of an interest or a policy.[71] Alternatively, such solicitation could take place in informal conversations with officers of state (particularly members of the Treasury Board or Board of Trade or secretaries of state) or lesser officials (undersecretaries of state or the secretaries and senior clerks at the Treasury or Board of Trade).[72] Such solicitation might even persuade the government to sponsor legislation desired by some local interest—such as the Walpolean measures permitting the exportation of Carolina rice to southern Europe or the importation of Iberian salt to New York.[73] Such successful solicitation, however, rarely involved fundamental government policy or important interests within Britain.

70. Sir Tresham Lever, *Godolphin: His Life and Times* (London, 1952), 238–240; Narcissus Luttrell, *A Brief Historical Relation of State Affairs* . . . (Oxford, 1857), VI, 594; Geoffrey Holmes, *British Politics in the Age of Anne* (London, 1967), 174; *Diary of the First Earl of Egmont (Viscount Percival)*, III, 1739–1747, Manuscripts of the Earl of Egmont, Historical Manuscripts Commission (London, 1923), 315; earl of Ilchester [G.S.H. Fox-Strangways], *Henry Fox, First Lord Holland: His Family and Relations*, 2 vols. (London, 1920), I, 125; *Remarks on a Letter to Sir John Barnard* . . . (London, 1746), 11–12.

71. The printed minutes of the Board of Trade (to 1782) and the Treasury (to 1745) contain numerous examples of merchants' and colonial agents' appearing and speaking at meetings of those boards. For an example of how such a meeting was conducted, cf. Jacob M. Price, "Glasgow, the Tobacco Trade, and the Scottish Customs, 1707–1730: Some Commercial, Administrative, and Political Implications of the Union," *Scottish Historical Review*, LXIII (1984), 16–19.

72. It is more difficult to find records of these informal conversations. Some are referred to in the correspondence between Sir James Lowther, bart. (1673–1755), member of Parliament for Cumberland, and his agent at Whitehaven (Lonsdale Papers, Cumbria Record Office, The Castle, Carlisle), the correspondence between William Gooch, lieutenant governor of Virginia, and his brother (copies at Colonial Williamsburg Foundation, Williamsburg, Va.), and the printed correspondence of Benjamin Franklin and other colonials in London.

73. Cf. n. 8, above.

Public Agitation

When all else failed, special interests might be forced into the open and attempt by publishing, petitioning, letter writing, and other overt political activities to influence government policy at even the highest level. Such political noisemaking was likely to be successful, however, only when the interests involved were able to form alliances with other elements having the weight of numbers in the House of Commons. Some examples of this are well known. For the highest reasons of state policy Bolingbroke, when secretary of state, wished to conclude a commercial treaty with France in 1711–1713. He tried in negotiating the treaty to obtain commercial benefits for important sectoral interests in Britain, but failed conspicuously to protect the interests of the linen and silk manufactures or to obtain anything for the port interests trading to the sugar and tobacco colonies. He also failed to convince the great woolen interest (embracing landlords, graziers, manufacturers, and traders) that what they might gain from an enlarged French market would compensate them for what they were likely to lose from a diminished Portuguese market. The woolen, linen, and silk interests and the port-colonial interest allied themselves with the Whig minority in the Commons to defeat the commercial treaty in 1713.[74] Similarly, in 1733 the merchants, manufacturers, retailers, and other traders opposed to Walpole's excise scheme for the tobacco and wine revenues were able to persuade enough usual supporters of the government to abstain or join the opposition, to undermine Walpole's majority and persuade him to abandon his bill.[75] In both cases the numerical core of the opposition came from the continuing antiministerial element in the House of Commons—Whigs in 1713, Tories and antiministerial Whigs in 1733—but the relatively few extra votes that the commercial interests were able to influence enabled these parliamentary minorities to do what the merchants and their allies wanted them to do.

It is, therefore, not too difficult to deduce why the mercantile pro-American interest had such mixed results in the decade leading up to the American

74. For the part of the colonial trades in the history of the commercial treaty of Utrecht, see Price, *France and the Chesapeake*, I, 522–530; Geoffrey Holmes and Clyve Jones, "Trade, the Scots, and the Parliamentary Crisis of 1713," *Parliamentary History*, I (1982), 47–77, esp. 65; D. C. Coleman, "Politics and Economics in the Age of Anne: The Case of the Anglo-French Trade Treaty of 1713," in Coleman and A. H. John, eds., *Trade, Government, and Economics in Pre-Industrial England* (London, 1976), 187–213.

75. Paul Langford, *The Excise Crisis: Society and Politics in the Age of Walpole* (Oxford, 1975); Price, "The Excise Affair Revisited," in Baxter, ed., *England's Rise to Greatness*, 257–321.

436

Revolution.[76] In 1766, when allied with the big battalions of the Rockingham ministry, they were able to help persuade the same Parliament that had passed the Stamp Act to repeal it. But, in January–March 1775, when allied with the much weaker parliamentary opposition, they were unable to accomplish anything.

Matters that came before Parliament can, on reflection, be divided between the politics of regime and the politics of interest—local, sectoral, and special. Most of Parliament's time might be devoted to questions of interest, but statesmen (or would-be statesmen) could never forget the primacy of questions of regime on which compromise was almost impossible. Since most peacetime colonial questions that came before ministry and Parliament between 1660 and 1760 involved compromisable matters of interest, they did not stir disruptive passions. However, when the debates over the Stamp Act raised a fundamental question of regime—to wit, the authority of Parliament—metropolitan-colonial relations entered a more dangerous phase. The politics of interest did not disappear. As late as 1772 the land speculator interest could help manipulate the fall of Hillsborough. But, less than a year later, in drafting and defending the Tea Act of 1773, the ministers consciously rejected the possibility of compromise and intruded into the bill "political reasons . . . of such weight, and strength," that is, of regime, as would ultimately provoke armed resistance.[77] At this level of principle, the American interest within Britain was politically impotent.

To conclude, then, Who in Georgian Britain cared about the colonies? A lot of people did, though they were very unevenly distributed geographically and socially and quite diverse in their approach to American questions. In the political sphere the better-organized of these interests, particularly the port merchants and the exporting manufacturers, could influence the minutiae of legislation much more successfully than they could questions of regime or the main lines of government policy. To affect the latter they needed strong allies in the House of Commons. These they had in 1713, 1733, and 1766, but not in 1775, not even before the start of fighting, even less so afterwards.

76. For the political role of the merchants, cf. Jack M. Sosin, *Agents and Merchants: British Colonial Policy and the Origins of the American Revolution, 1763–1775* (Lincoln, Nebr., 1965); Alison G. Olson, "The London Mercantile Lobby and the Coming of the American Revolution," *Journal of American History*, LXIX (1982–1983), 21–41.

77. Cf. the exchange between Dowdeswell and North, in Benjamin Woods Labaree, *The Boston Tea Party* (Oxford, 1964), 70–73.

VII

THE MARYLAND BANK STOCK CASE: BRITISH-AMERICAN FINANCIAL AND POLITICAL RELATIONS BEFORE AND AFTER THE AMERICAN REVOLUTION

The Background, 1715–83

A major scholarly contribution of Morris Radoff to the historiography of Maryland was his calendar of the Bank Stock Papers.[1] It is thus appropriate that this volume honoring Dr. Radoff should contain an article on the historical problem revealed by these papers. Maryland's complicated legal and diplomatic efforts in the generation after the peace of 1783 to recover the shares in the Bank of England purchased in the name of the colony before the Revolution reveal much of the changing nature of financial and political relations between the colony-state and Britain both before and after the Revolution.

The learned thirty-four-page introduction to Dr. Radoff's calendar of the Bank Stock Papers is the principal scholarly treatment of the subject thus far published. It is particularly unfortunate, therefore, that this volume has remained relatively unknown to persons working outside of Maryland history and has not been properly used by historians of British–American relations in the generation after 1783.[2] Radoff's calendar and introduction cover the Bank Stock Papers in the Maryland Hall of Records, Annapolis, and related items in the Maryland Historical Society, Baltimore. The present account will be based upon these same documents as well as upon related papers in the United States and England. The most valuable additional source in this country is the papers of Rufus King, heavily utilized by Bradford Perkins.[3] In London, the Foreign Office records in the Public Record Office contain much on the diplomatic side.[4] Substantial documentation on the legal side of the problem can be found in the records of the Court of Chancery and the Treasury Solicitor, also in the PRO.[5] Unfortunately, the private papers of Lord Eldon, the lord chancellor, and perhaps the British minister most closely concerned with the case, do not appear to have survived, nor do those of the legal firms involved. Minor additional references can be found in the archives of the Bank of England at Roehampton.

Every person or institution in the Thirteen Colonies that had business in London had to have qualified agents there to handle such business. A number of thoroughly researched and very useful studies have made us familiar with the work of the political agents of the colonial legislatures.[6] Colonial authorities also frequently had occasion for financial representatives in London to pay or to receive funds there. The Maryland colonial government had particular need of a financial agent in London in the eighteenth century. Like Virginia, it levied export duties on tobacco expressed in sterling and needed someone in London to collect the bills of exchange in which those duties were paid; it also needed agents to handle some of its financial relations with Lord Baltimore, as well as arms purchases and the reserve funds set up after 1733 to back Maryland's paper currency. Needless to say, all the larger merchants in London trading to Maryland would have liked to be named the colony's financial representative. Not only would the commissions earned by such a charge add to a firm's income but also the charge itself would give that firm large sums to handle, add to its liquidity, and mark it out in the eyes of both Londoners and Marylanders as a house of financial standing and importance. Even the sketchiest histories of the houses that got such commissions tell us a lot about who was who in the London-Maryland trade between the restoration of the proprietary (1715) and the Revolution.

When, after the accession of George I, the lordship of Maryland was restored to the house of Calvert, it was necessary for the proprietary and the colonial legislature to make certain new financial and administrative arrangements for the colony. One such measure was the act of August 1716 for "ascertaining the Gage & Tare of Tob[acc]o Hhds & . . . for laying Impositions on Tob[acc]o p[er] the Hhd. for the Support of Governm[en]t." Among other things, this act reestablished an export duty of 3d. sterling per hogshead on all tobacco exported from the colony, collected since the 1690s for the purchase of arms. The act provided that this tax, collected in the first instance by the naval officers of the several districts of the colony, was "to be lodged in the hands of such Merch[an]t or Merchants in London as the Upper & Lower Houses of the Assembly shall from time to time direct."[7] The first merchant named under the act was Captain John Hyde, who was already exercising that function, and, in partnership with his son Samuel, was to continue to perform it down to his death in 1732.[8]

It was not strange that this commission should go to the Hydes. John and Samuel Hyde were the greatest merchants in the Maryland trade from the

1690s to the 1740s. They were also the "bankers" to Lord Baltimore in the 1720s and probably earlier. Their correspondents in Maryland (to whom they extended considerable credit) included many of the leading planters and public figures. Challenging their grip on Maryland's London business would be difficult—but not impossible. In 1727–28, the Hydes were under attack in Maryland for selling to the French buyers in London in wholesale lots at low prices tobacco consigned in much smaller lots by numerous planters in the colony. The Hydes got quick cash by such sales, but it was felt that the consigning planters did not get the best price.[9] At a time when this attack was at its height, both houses of the legislature concurred in a resolution ordering that bills of exchange remitted to London on the province's account should henceforth be sent to William Hunt, a rising merchant there.[10] We do not know what proportion of the province's bill remittance business Hunt actually got; the Hydes in practice retained the business relating to the 3d. sterling duty for armaments.[11] Nevertheless, by the 1720s the province's financial business in London had clearly become an important political plum for which rival contenders fought, backed by supporting parties in the Maryland Assembly.

In 1733, the Maryland legislature for the first time authorized the issue of paper money or "bills of credit" (£90,000 worth). To support the credit of this new paper money and to provide for its redemption, the legislature at the same time levied a new tax of 1s. 3d. sterling per hogshead on all tobacco exported. The act further provided "That the Duty . . . so to be collected . . . by the several Naval Officers shall be, with all possible Speed, after Receipts thereof, remitted to Mr. Samuel Hyde, Mr. William Hunt, and Mr. Robert Cruikshank, Merchants in London, or any Two of them, or other Persons, or the Majority of them, who shall be intrusted or appointed Trustees in London. . . ." The sums remitted were to be invested by the trustees in shares or stock of the Bank of England, "to be entered in the Books of the Company [Bank], to be for the Use, and in Trust, for the Province of Maryland." The dividends accruing were to be invested in further shares. The "bills of credit" were to be redeemed in 1748 by bills of exchange drawn upon the London trustees, who, in the meantime, were to receive a two percent commission on sums handled.[12]

There thus came into existence both Maryland's paper money and the Bank stock trust in London that gave it backing. We do not know precisely which elements in Maryland supported Hyde, Hunt, or Cruikshank for a trustee's place, but there was nothing surprising about their being chosen. All three were prominent merchants, chosen by the London–Maryland trade for their committee of management.[13] Samuel Hyde, merchant and sometime East India Company director, of Rood Lane, mentioned earlier as the son and partner of Captain John Hyde, was now his heir and successor. Of Cruikshank we know little except that he was a merchant and sometime

6

Africa Company director of Poor Jury Lane (now Jewry Street), near Aldgate (subsequently of Magpie Alley, Fenchurch Street); his name is Scottish, characteristic of Aberdeenshire and adjacent eastern counties. William Hunt of Little Tower Street was much better known, though his origins are obscure. He had been sharing the colony's remittance business with Hyde since 1727. He was a director of the Royal Exchange Assurance and was almost the only Virginia or Maryland merchant of this century to become a director of the Bank of England. He served on the court of that company from 1728 till 1763, being also elected deputy governor for 1747–49 and governor, 1749–52. His control of Maryland's Bank stock no doubt enhanced his electoral importance in the Bank, but his being a Bank director made him a more than appropriate person to be a trustee. He owned land in Maryland and may have had family connections there.[14]

These trust arrangements of 1733 persisted until the London tobacco trade was shaken by several major stoppages in the mid-1740s. (These appear to have been associated with the wars and with changes in French buying policy, which redirected business away from London to Glasgow and other northwestern ports and created cash flow problems for some big London houses.) Among the merchants that went under ca. 1746 were Robert Cruikshank and Samuel Hyde. In the emergency, Lord Baltimore appointed Joseph Adams as substitute for Hyde and Cruikshank so that the Bank stock trust (now £15,000) could continue operations. (Adams was a very responsible Quaker merchant, prominent in the trade from the 1720s.) The legislature confirmed this substitution, and nothing was lost by the failures. Shortly afterwards, John Hanbury, another Quaker merchant of London, was added as the third Bank stock trustee.[15] After Samuel Hyde's failure, the other remittance business of the colony was handled primarily by Hunt, though a small share went to Joseph Adams during 1747–48 and thereafter to his son-in-law and executor, Silvanus Grove, a Quaker linen draper turned merchant, who was to become a figure of great wealth and reputation in the City.[16]

Grove, however, did not become one of the Bank stock trustees. After Adam's death in 1748, there were only two—Hunt and Hanbury. When John Hanbury died in 1758, his place was taken by his cousin and partner, Capel Hanbury. When Hunt died in 1767, he was succeeded by John's son, Osgood Hanbury. Though not active in the Bank of England like Hunt, the Quaker Hanburys were very important figures in the City of London. They were not only the biggest importers of tobacco in London in the 1750s but also contractors (with John Tomlinson) for all the government's remittance business to North America during the Seven Years' War. In addition, the Hanburys were the personal bankers to the last Lord Baltimore and thus of considerable political importance in Maryland, particularly in matters of patronage. This was shown when they were able to get their business and legal agent in Maryland, Daniel Wolstenholme, appointed to a number of coveted positions in the colony.[17]

The death of Capel Hanbury in 1769 coincided with a periodical renewal of the legal authority for Maryland's paper money. On this occasion, new trustees were not named by Lord Baltimore but were provided for by act of legislature as in 1733. Those so named were Osgood Hanbury, Silvanus Grove, and James Russell.[18] Grove, now an affluent Quaker merchant and perennial director of the London Assurance Company, was Adams's son-in-law and executor and had since Adams's death in 1748 handled part of the colony's financial business in London.[19] James Russell (1708–88) was rather more interesting. The son of a crown attorney (procurator fiscal) for Edinburgh, he had emigrated to Maryland ca. 1730 and a few years later married Ann, sister of Richard Lee (d. 1787), member and subsequently president of the council in Maryland. Russell was for many years a merchant in Prince George's County, Maryland, in correspondence with John Buchanan of London, but in the 1750s moved to London and set up there on his own account. With his Lee and other valuable connections in Maryland and northern Virginia and with a considerable amount of commercial drive, he replaced the Hanburys as the greatest London house in the Maryland (Western Shore) trade and as the biggest importer of tobacco in London. By the 1770s, his principal competition came from his son-in-law and former partner, William Molleson, another eastern Scot. Russell was severely embarrassed by the crash of 1772 but was still trading on a grand scale at the outbreak of the Revolution. He had extensive real estate interests in Maryland, the most important of which was a one-third interest in the Nottingham Iron Works in Baltimore County (worth about £30,000 sterling). His partners there were John Buchanan, his former London correspondent (one third), and the Ewers, West India merchants of London (the remaining third).[20]

The London Bank stock trust thus was not just a technical detail detached from the main stream of public life, but something deeply revelatory of the locus of power in colonial Maryland. Just as very powerful economic needs determined the issue of the paper money and the establishment of the trust funds for its redemption, so very real economic and political influence determined that only London merchants with strong connections or deep roots in the colony could hope to be named trustees for the Bank stock.

This was the situation on the eve of the Revolution. In 1773, the three London trustees held Bank stock with a face value of £27,500, worth £38,500 at the current market price of 140, plus £348:7:6 in cash.[21] By mid-1775, this had risen to £29,000 worth £41,180 at 142,[22] after which events precluded the normal operation of the trust. At first the revolutionary government of Maryland did nothing about the London trust. In no state did the Revolution produce a less radical government than in Maryland. After the excitements and alarms of 1775–76 and the removal of the dependents of the proprietor, Maryland was ruled by substantially the same sort of people who had ruled it before. Although there were sequestrations of real property and liquidation of debts, the new rulers were not unmindful of the sanctity conferred upon even enemy property by eighteenth-century law and custom. The first revolutionary governor was Thomas Johnson, whose own brother, the merchant Joshua Johnson, had remained in London until 1777 to wind up his affairs there.[23] The second revolutionary governor was Thomas Sim Lee, a nephew of Ann Lee, wife of James Russell, one of the London trustees.

At the outbreak of the war, there were three principal issues of paper money (bills of credit) in circulation in Maryland, all expressed in dollars: 1766 ($173,773 authorized), 1769 ($318,000), and 1773 ($480,000). Each was to circulate for twelve years, that of 1766 being due for redemption in 1777. The legislature at first did nothing about the 1777 redemption, but at the end of 1779 (at the same time as it was considering a bill confiscating British property) passed an act calling in the remaining issue of 1766 still outstanding to be exchanged for certificates of indebtedness of the state, or bills of exchange on the London trustees. As the existing trustees might refuse to perform their duties under the new law, the act named a panel of five Americans then in Europe, one of whom was to be selected by Benjamin Franklin, American minister in Paris, as a new and sole trustee.[24] On 4 January 1780, the revolutionary council of Maryland wrote to Franklin informing him of the act and asking him to write the existing London trustees (Hanbury, Grove, and Russell) and ask them "whether they will transact Business, sell out the Stock, [and] accept and pay the Bills drawn in Pursuance of the Act." If the London trustees agreed to accept these orders, the money realized by the sale of the stock was to be placed "in the Hands of some capital Banker in Amsterdam or Paris" upon whom the Maryland authorities could draw. If not, Franklin was to go ahead and appoint the new trustee from the five names sent him, though there could have been very little expectation the old trustees would hand over the stock. The Maryland Council also informed Franklin that a bill had passed the lower house in 1779 for the confiscation of all British property in the state (except mercantile debts), but that the Senate had not concurred "because they deemed a . . . Confiscation of British Property at this Time [NB] improper."[25] The restraint of the Senate was thought to deprive the trustees of any excuse for not paying; it was also a warning to them that their own property in the state was in peril should they refuse to honor the demands on them. When Russell received Franklin's letter of 20 May 1780, he and the other trustees applied to the attorney general (James Wallace) and the solicitor general to be (James Mansfield) for an opinion. The law officers eventually replied (28 August 1780) "that the Trustees could not with safety sell the Stock, or pay the Bills." The trustees accepted the advice and determined not to pay any bills drawn on them.[26] Before being notified of this, Franklin wrote to Governor Lee on 11 August 1780 that he had not yet received a reply from Russell and doubted that one would be forthcoming.[27]

Even before the receipt of Franklin's message, the Maryland legislature passed a new act in 1780 instructing the treasurer of the Western Shore to draw £35,000 sterling worth of bills of exchange on the London trustees and providing, in the event of their refusal to pay, for the seizure of their real property in the state as well as that of Henry Harford, the last proprietor, and the late Lord Baltimore, for the payment of the bills of exchange with normal penalties.[28] Thus authorized, the governor and council on 26 July 1780 drew a bill of exchange for £1500 on the trustees in London payable to Stephen Steward & Son, local merchants. They endorsed it to V. & P. French & Nephew of Bordeaux, who sent it for collection to their London correspondents, French & Hobson. Governor Lee also wrote privately to French's in Bordeaux that his uncle (Russell) faced confiscation should he refuse to honor the bill. Since French & Co. were also the Bordeaux correspondents of James Russell, the message as intended reached the trustees in London promptly. Nevertheless, they refused to pay the bill when presented on 26 September and only then wrote Franklin of the opinions they had received from the law officers.[29]

That winter, the Maryland legislature passed a more general act (1781) confiscating all British property in the state. By article vii of this measure, the iron furnace, forge, and related property belonging to James Russell & Co. in Baltimore County were to be sold to create a special fund "for making good and sinking" the bills of exchange drawn by the treasurer of the Western Shore under the aforementioned act of 1780.[30] Although all British property was confiscated by the 1781 measure, Russell and his heirs always argued that his property had been confiscated specifically because he had followed the instructions of the attorney general and solicitor general. He alone of the three trustees had extensive real estate holdings in Maryland and thus suffered under the act. He estimated the value of his one-third interest in the Nottingham Iron Works in Baltimore County (White Marsh Furnace and Long Caln Forge) at £13,709. After his death in 1788, his widow placed the value of his total losses at £69,729:13:2 sterling (including the value of debts paid into the state treasury in depreciated paper and £11,760 interest).[31] As early as January 1783, James Russell presented a petition to the Lords of the Treasury asking for the Bank stock as compensation, but that board's secretary, George Rose, simply marked it, "proper for the Consideration of Parliament, or of the Ministers in Case a Treaty being entered into with the Province."[32]

There was, of course, no treaty between George III and the province of Maryland. The war was concluded by the preliminary treaty of peace of November 1782, the interim armistice of January 1783, and the final treaty of September 1783 (proclaimed in January 1784). By article v of the preliminary and final treaties, Congress undertook to recommend to the several states the restoration of British property confiscated during the war; article vi prohibited further confiscations or persecution; while article iv unqualifiedly outlawed any legal impediments on either side to the recovery of bona fide prewar debts. Article iv provided some legal support for Maryland's claims to recover the Bank stock, but its impact was weakened by the fact that the several American states in the years following the treaty of peace failed to implement this article and even passed new laws making it more difficult for British creditors to sue in local courts for prewar debts. Virginia was particularly guilty in this respect, but Maryland was not entirely innocent.[33]

Samuel Chase and the Court of Chancery, 1783–97

As soon as news of the preliminary treaty of November 1782 reached Maryland, public figures there began to consider ways of recovering the state's Bank stock.[34] All during the war, the dividends earned by the stock had been reinvested by the trustees so that the £29,000 (face value) of 1775 had become £43,000 by April 1783.[35] In June 1783, even before the signing of the definitive peace treaty, the matter received serious consideration in the Maryland legislature. It was decided to send the lawyer and legislator Samuel Chase to London to recover Maryland's heritage. Chase had been a very active, somewhat demogogic but relatively moderate "patriot" politician before and during the early stages of the Revolution, serving inter alia as a Maryland delegate to the Continental Congress in 1774–78. His enemies had reasons to want him out of the way. His friends sought to reward his public services by granting him an exceptional 4 percent commision on the Bank stock recovered (which should have brought him well over £2000 as the stock was far above par), though others thought that any one of a number of Maryland merchants then in London could have handled the affair for only a 2 or even 1 percent commission. As authorized by an act of assembly, Chase received his commission from the Council on 5 June.[36]

Chase arrived in London on 7 September 1783 just after the final treaty of peace was signed in Paris (3 September). He found affairs rather more complicated than he had perhaps expected. The three trustees were now all old men with long memories and keen senses of grievance. He never did get to see Osgood Hanbury, who was ill in the country and died on 11 January. The amiable Quaker Silvanus Grove, who had conducted his affairs so prudently that he had lost little or nothing through revolutionary confiscations, was quite willing to turn over the trust fund as soon as the other trustees agreed. This left James Russell as the chief but very firm obstacle. His iron works had been sold during the war for the equivalent of £30,000 in prewar Maryland provincial currency, but Russell put their true value at at least £30,000 sterling allowing for the disturbed conditions under which the sales had been made. In addition to £10,000 for his one-third interest there, he estimated that other property of his confiscated during the war was worth £5-6,000 sterling. The rest of his estate was tied up in uncollected prewar debts in Maryland and Virginia, but the collection of these even in Maryland proved very difficult in the 1780s. He turned over his American business to the firm of De Drusina, Ritter, and Clerk, in which his grandsons James de Drusina and James Clerk were partners. James Clerk went out to Maryland in 1783 to collect Russell's debts. His appeal to the Maryland legislature in 1783 for the restoration of Russell's property procured nothing.

Chase, working through Richard Oswald, one of the British peace negotiators and formerly a London merchant, was in touch with the trustees from his arrival in September, but they were reluctant to deal with him until they had concerted a common position. They consulted counsel, including John Lee, attorney general under the Fox-North coalition, and Lloyd Kenyon, attorney general in the early months of the Pitt ministry, as well as the old and new solicitors general, James Mansfield and Richard Pepper Arden. Lee advised turning over the property to Chase, but Mansfield believed that Russell should retain at least the value of his confiscated property. The more anti-American Pittite law officers advised Russell to refuse any transfer until compensated. Grove and Hanbury's executors suggested turning over everything to Chase except £12,000, which would remain in trust until Russell's claims were settled. Russell said in February that he would agree to a transfer provided that he be given £12,000; a few days later, he suggested he would leave the £12,000 in trust provided that he receive the interest. A series of multilateral conferences were held on these points between February and June 1784, but without success. Chase did not have the power to allow anything to Russell, but probably could have agreed to a compromise leaving a portion in trust provided that Maryland did not have to surrender its claim to that portion. At every conference, however, Russell or his solicitor, Hutchinson, or his grandson, de Drusina, created some difficulty that prevented agreement on a compromise.

Chase was in a deep quandary. The simplest thing might have been to reach some private compromise with Russell, but Chase did not feel he had the powers to agree to any arrangement acceptable to Russell. He was reluctant to go to the government, for he realized that the Pitt ministry had other things on its mind during the early months of 1784 and was in no sense sympathetic to American claims. Eventually, on 26 March, Chase did see the foreign secretary, the marquess of Carmarthen, who told him that he could not take cognizance of the matter unless brought to his attention by the American minister (not yet arrived in London). He did, however, assure Chase that he would advise a settlement, sending word through Russell's son-in-law, Molleson, then an auditor of army accounts. (Russell chose not to take his advice.) The third alternative was to have recourse to the court of Chancery (as advised by Carmarthen), but Chase, a lawyer himself, must have foreseen the complications and delays this might entail and hung back. In the end, Russell forced his hand.[37]

Russell appears to have been frightened lest some legal way be found for Grove to transfer the stock to Chase without his concurrence. Alternatively, he was afraid that if he (Russell) died before Grove, the latter as sole surviving trustee could freely transfer the stock to Maryland without any compensation for Russell's estate. To prevent either of these from happening, Russell on 6 February filed a bill in Chancery against the Bank of England, thus beginning a cycle of more than twenty years of suits and countersuits in that court that would have impressed even Dickens. The suit asked that Grove and the Bank be enjoined from making any transfer to Chase, even if Russell should die, and that in the meantime Chase reveal his commission and produce accounts of the sale of Russell's property; the suit further asked that enough of the stock be sold to compensate Russell for the loss of his one-third interest in the iron works and the remainder be held in trust until it could be established what other property Russell had lost in Maryland and whether he would be free to recover his debts there.[38]

On 31 March, Bury Hutchinson, Russell's lawyer, finally notified Chase of the suit and sent him a subpoena to appear in court on 28 April. Chase's first reaction was to refuse to answer in court unless the Bank and Grove also appeared, and unless Russell agreed in advance that "if the Chancellor shall dismiss his Bill, or dissolve the injunction in the whole, or in part, that he will, if in the whole, immediately thereafter transfer all the stock" or, if in part, transfer all except that covered by the court's order. Chase had a series of conferences with Russell, Grove, Hutchinson, and John Maddocks, Russell's counsel, but they could agree on nothing. Maddocks seemed confident of getting from Chancery the sort of order Russell wanted. Chase felt under great pressure. If he left the country, he feared Russell would get his injunction. There was no hope of diplomatic help without an American minister in London. Yet, to go into court opened up the prospect that all sorts of other claimants would appear and the matter be prolonged indefinitely. Through Lord Buchan (David Steuart Erskine, eleventh earl of Buchan), he was introduced to his lordship's brother, Thomas Erskine, a prominent antiministerial lawyer (later famous as defense counsel in the sedition trials of the 1790s and lord chancellor in the Talents' ministry, 1806–7). Erskine advised him to answer Russell's bill, opining that Russell had no case unless he could prove that his property had been confiscated not as that of a British subject but as that of a Bank stock trustee. Chase accepted this advice and governed his conduct accordingly.[39]

A very expensive legal effort took shape. Russell retained three king's counsel, John Maddocks, John Lloyd, and James Mansfield (the last a former solicitor-general). In addition to Erskine, Chase consulted John Stanley, M.P., attorney general of the Leeward Islands, and Richard Pepper Arden, the new attorney general (and a close friend of Pitt). At a conference of counsel on both sides, Chase thought he had worked out a compromise with Maddocks, Russell's chief counsel, by which part of the stock would be transferred to Maryland, but Russell and his solicitor Hutchinson reneged. On the advice of Erskine and Stanley, Chase decided to take the initiative. He refused to answer Russell's bill but simply submitted a demurrer stating that the argument presented did not justify the remedy sought. Before this, however, he filed a bill initiating a suit of his own in Chancery, naming as defendants Russell, Grove, the Bank, the Ewers, and the trustees of the bankrupt John and Gilbert Buchanan (also interested in the ironworks).[40]

Meanwhile, the Ewers had decided to bestir themselves. Before the war Walter Ewer and his nephew John Ewer, West India merchants of 2 Little Love Lane, Aldermanbury, had held a one-third interest in the Nottingham ironworks along with James Russell and John Buchanan. Walter had died in 1779 leaving his residual estate to his nephews John and Walter (II). Walter (II) had died in 1782 leaving his entire estate to John's sons, John the younger and Walter (III). The Ewers had lost substantially by the confiscation of the ironworks but lacked James Russell's negotiating strength, his hold on the Bank stock. Lest their interests be disregarded in any settlement between Russell and Chase, they filed their own bill (6 May 1784) against all concerned (except Chase) alleging that the ironworks had been confiscated only because the Bank stock trustees failed to pay the bills of exchange; that the State of Maryland had settled the bills of exchange out of the proceeds of the sale of the ironworks and hence had no further claim in equity on the Bank stock that was now available to meet their claims as sufferers from the related confiscation.[41]

In early June, the matter finally received a hearing before Lord Thurlow, the lord chancellor. Thurlow ordered—pending a final settlement of the case—that the trustees (Russell, Grove, and Hanbury's executors) transfer Maryland's Bank stock to the custody of the accountant-general of the Court of Chancery, who was to receive the dividends and reinvest them in further Bank stock. Russell was thereby assured that if he died first Grove would not be able unilaterally to transfer the stock to Maryland. Maryland was also assured that if Grove died first, Russell would not be able to keep the stock or the dividends. Nothing else was settled.[42] Stock with a face value of £44,000 and £1,000 in cash was transferred to the accountant-general of the court on 25 June. As stock was then selling at 115 1/2, Maryland's claimed property in the hands of the court was now worth approximately £51,820.

Unable to reach any general or partial settlement with the other parties involved, Chase pushed for a final settlement of Maryland's claims by the Court of Chancery. When the case next came up for hearing before the lord chancellor in mid-July, Chase was represented by the attorney general, Richard Pepper Arden, acting in a private capacity. Arden for Chase moved that the court order its accountant general to retain part of the stock to cover the claims of Russell, the Ewers, and Buchanan's trustees, pending the settlement of those claims, and that the balance (estimated at £17,000 Bank stock at face value, approximately £19,635 at market value) be transferred to Chase for the state of Maryland. Lord Thurlow refused to make such an order, observing that "he must . . . be . . . fully satisfied of the pet[itioner's] Right to the Bank Stock . . . and that as it was stated, that the Stock was held in Trust in Virtue of laws made by the Legislature of the *Colony* of Maryland, and was now claimed on behalf of the *State* of Maryland, he was of Opinion that another Party was necessary, before he could give any Opinion on the Motion." Chase understood that the "Party meant, though not expressed by his Lordship, is the Attorney General of this Kingdom" acting for the crown. In other words, Thurlow brought the government into the question and returned to the point first expressed in the opinion of the law officers in 1780 that there was some question whether the state of Maryland in this case could automatically be taken to be the successor to the property rights of the *ci-devant* colony of Maryland. Lord Chancellor Thurlow was not just a judge but was also a cabinet minister, as he had been in 1780. He was undoubtedly fully aware that in 1784 as in 1780 beyond the legal niceties were questions of public import that might well have to be taken into consideration.

Chase could not have had many illusions about this. His counsel, Stanley, asked the attorney general (who had also been one of Chase's counsel) how he would answer if made a party to the case. Pepper Arden told him he would make the usual answer, claiming for the crown as much of the Bank stock as the lord chancellor might decide belonged to it. This meant that there was a chance at law that all the Bank stock would go to the crown, leaving both Maryland and Russell cut out completely. To prevent this, Chase wrote to the prime minister, William Pitt, explaining the case and basing Maryland's claims strongly on the peace treaty. (He was, of course, impeded by the absence of an American minister in London.) At the same time, he tried to persuade Russell that it was in both their interests to move for an early decision; if Russell would only moderate his claims as the Ewers had done, Chase would undertake to amend his bill to make the attorney general a party (for the crown) and move for a quick decision. When Russell proved adamant, Chase gave up and made plans to return to Maryland in late August 1784.[43]

However, even if Russell had proved more tractable, there was no assurance that the attorney general would, in fact, reply to Chase's bill. (Pitt never replied to Chase's letter.) If the British government regarded Maryland's claims as simply one detail of the broader question of debt claims on both sides, then the attorney general might simply refuse to make any answer to Chase's bill and thus prevent any decision being reached in Chancery until broader diplomatic questions had been settled between the United States and Great Britain. This indeed was to be the scenario for the next twenty years.

Russell's intentions in all this are far from clear. He was now over seventy-five years of age, and showed many of the crotchets and stubbornnesses of the elderly. He refused for example to file a claim with the British government for compensation for his confiscated real estate in Maryland lest such compensation weaken his claim to the Bank stock. Not until ten years after his death in 1788 was his family able to correct this slip and obtain the compensation to which they were entitled.[44]

Before Chase departed from London, he left detailed instructions with his solicitors, William and John Lyon of Gray's Inn. They were to preserve the status quo, leaving the stock in the hands of the accountant general of Chancery; they were not to amend Chase's bill to make the attorney general (for the crown) a party unless Russell agreed to moderate his demands as the Ewers and Buchanan's trustees had done. Chase wanted a further hearing delayed as long as possible so that he could report to the Assembly of Maryland and have a chance to concert new plans agreeable to his Maryland principals.[45]

Chase returned to America empty-handed, his expectations for a large commission lost in the labyrinthine ways of the Court of Chancery and international diplomacy. He tried unsuccessfully to get a further advance from the state of Maryland to cover his legal expenses and had to meet these out of the £500 originally advanced him and his own resources. The legislature did, however, pass an act in January 1785 approving of his actions and declaring the willingness of the state to have its claims decided by the lord chancellor. Chase was given full powers (under the direction of the governor and council) to pursue the state's case in that court and, if necessary, to make the attorney general of Great Britain a party to the suit.[46]

Chase was resourceful, but he could accomplish even less in Annapolis than in London. Sometime in 1785, he had his lawyers in London amend his bill to make the attorney general a party to the suit, but the attorney general failed to reply. Seeing that new initiatives would be needed, Chase obtained from the legislature in March 1786 a new act that requested the "governor and council . . . to receive from the agent . . . any proposals of measures by him to be executed concerning the said stock" and empowering them to authorize the carrying out of any such proposals they deemed for the advantage of the state.[47] Acting under this act, Chase wrote to the council on 7 July informing them that the attorney general had not put in his answer and that it was reliably reported "that the Bank Stock will not be recovered, so long as there is any Impediment thrown in the Way of the recovery of British

Debts by any One of the States." He asked to be given full authority to make any arrangement he thought best, provided only that the state received back £32,000 face value of stock (on which he would get his four percent commission). As the stock accumulating in the hands of the accountant general by then totaled about £49,135 face value, Chase would have had a margin of at least £17,135 with which to bargain with Russell and the Ewers. However, the governor and council declined to accept Chase's proposal. Instead they thought that Congress should be asked to instruct the American minister in London (John Adams) to intercede in the case.[48]

A few months later, Chase thought of an even more ingenious method of reopening the case. In 1774–76, Daniel Dulany had entered into two mortgages totaling £12,121:13:7 to Osgood Hanbury & Co. to cover debts owing to that firm by his late father, Walter Dulany. During the war, the lands covered by the mortgages were seized by the state and sold, without providing for the removal of the liens. Since the peace treaty of 1783 specifically confirmed prewar debts, the buyers of those lands did not have clear title until the mortgages could be removed. A plan was concocted that would serve the interest of the buyers of the Dulany lands as well as that of Chase and Osgood Hanbury's estate. Upon application by the Hanbury interests to Maryland for compensation on the mortgages, a law was passed by the Maryland legislature in January 1787 authorizing Chase, as agent for the Bank stock, to use £11,000 worth of that stock (at face value) to clear the mortgages held by Osgood Hanbury's estate on the former Dulany lands. The same act authorized Chase, with the approval of the governor and council, to make any composition for the Bank stock he deemed prudent.[49] Acting under the authority of this last clause and instructions from the government of Maryland, Chase in June 1787 made a provisional agreement with Russell's grandson, James Clerk (who represented his grandfather's interests in Maryland then), whereby Russell would get £6,000 sterling for his one-third interest in the ironworks and £4525 for his other real estate confiscated in Maryland, provided the owners of the other two-thirds of the ironworks accepted an equivalent offer and the Court of Chancery ordered the balance (over £30,000) paid to Maryland. This arrangement, though allegedly accepted by Russell prior to his death in 1788, was rejected thereafter by his widow.[50] Chase, however, was able to move forward under the other part of the act. On 26 May 1787, he assigned £11,000 (face value) of Maryland's claim on the Bank stock (plus £440 of the same for his own commission) to John Hanbury (Capel Hanbury's son), John Lloyd (Osgood Hanbury's brother-in-law), and David Barclay (Osgood's son-in-law), three Quaker eminences of London, the first two as surviving partners of Osgood Hanbury, the last of as one of his executors.[51]

The transfer of part of Maryland's claim to the Hanbury partners and executors in 1787 opened up an entirely new chapter in the Bank stock litigation, a chapter that was to fill the years 1787–97. In January 1788, the late Osgood Hanbury's partners (John Hanbury and John Lloyd) and executors (David Barclay, John Lloyd and Richard Gurney)[52] filed a bill in Chancery beginning a complicated new suit of *Barclay et al. v. Russell et al.* The defendants in this series of suits were James Russell (and his widow Ann), Silvanus Grove, the Ewers, the trustees of the bankrupt John Buchanan, Henry Harford (late lord proprietor of Maryland), Samuel Chase and His Majesty's attorney general. Barclay et al. asked the court to order the immediate transfer to the Hanbury estate of £11,400 worth of stock from the larger amount held in trust by the accountant general of the Court of Chancery.[53]

Responses were very slow in coming to this bill. Russell had not answered when he died on 1 August 1788, and the court had to be petitioned to make his executrix and widow, Ann Lee, a party to the suit.[54] Delays were also caused by the death of John Ewer the younger in 1788 and his father, John, in 1792.[55] Henry Harford further complicated matters by beginning his own suit against Barclay et al. in 1789, claiming that by the Revolution he had lost an estate in Maryland worth £477,854; of this, the crown commissioners under the compensation act of 1783 had recognized £230,000 but the Treasury had paid him only £70,000. Among the items that the commissioners had refused to recognize was Harford's claim for arrears of quit-rents and manor rents standing due at the time of the sale of his confiscated property. The commissioners claimed that these were still recoverable as ordinary debts under the treaty of 1783, but Harford had been unable to obtain this sort of justice in Maryland. He claimed further compensation out of the Bank stock, basing part of his claim on the argument that as proprietor he was the sole legitimate remnant of the prewar chartered government of Maryland.[56]

The months rolled by and the various parties to the dispute (including the attorney general) filed their answers to the suits of Barclay et al. (the Hanbury interest) and Henry Harford. Little new was revealed by these bills and answers. The stock kept accumulating in value and its face value came to £54,193 in November 1788 and £58,417 in November 1790. Even Ann Russell began to despair of litigation. Although she had rejected the composition Chase had offered in 1787, she departed from her husband's example and in 1789 filed a claim for compensation from the British government for her late husband's real estate confiscated in Maryland. The commissioners found in her favor, but the Treasury declined to pay anything until the Maryland Bank stock case was settled.

Another party to the suits was now, of course, the attorney general. His answers to the bills of Barclay et al. and Harford were most perfunctory. He denied any knowledge of the facts of the case but asked the court to preserve the rights of the crown.[57] However, when the case finally came up for a

18

hearing before Lord Chancellor Thurlow in Hilary term 1791, the attorney general, Sir Archibald Macdonald, "by the authority of the then Secretary of State [for Foreign Affairs, Lord Grenville] . . . waived the rights of the Crown to the Stock claimed by the Plaintiffs [Barclay et al.] in the said Suit but Lord Thurlow did not make any Decree therein."[58] Efforts in 1793 to revive the matter in Chancery—by Chase's attorney, Uriah Forrest, an American merchant in London, among others—led to hearings in February but came to nothing without the further cooperation of the attorney general.[59]

Not till 1797 could the Court of Chancery be stirred to consider the matter more seriously. On 27 June 1797, the entire case (Barclay v. Russell) was heard before the then lord chancellor, Lord Loughborough (who as Alexander Wedderburn had played a conspicuously anti-American role in North's time). Loughborough dismissed the petitioners' (the Hanbury interest) bill, giving his opinion "that the stock was by Law vested in the King [as the property of a defunct corporation], who had a right to dispose thereof in such manner as he should think proper, but upon the benefit of such legal right, the Petitioners [Barclay et al. for the Hanbury interest] . . . had morally and equitably a Claim on the said Bank stock in respect of the said Mortgages made to the said Osgood Hanbury and his partners." (In other words, the Hanbury interest had to depend upon royal charity, not upon any absolute right recognizable by the courts.) Even while making this order, however, Lord Loughborough suspended its operation, leaving the entire matter still inextricably tied up in Chancery.[60]

Thirteen years of litigation had gotten exactly nowhere; by November 1797, the accumulating stock had a face value of £78,742. It was then clear to all that this was a matter that could only be settled at the diplomatic level.

The Diplomatic Phase, 1797–1805

From the very first, there had been reason to doubt whether a diplomatic rather than a litigious approach to the Bank stock problem might not be best for Maryland. Before he left London in 1784, Chase, it will be remembered, wrote to the prime minister, William Pitt, discussing the political dimensions of the case, but did not receive an answer. When John Adams arrived in London in 1785 as the first American resident minister, things did not improve much. Thus, nothing came of the resolution of the Maryland Council in July 1786 that a memorial be sent to the Continental Congress requesting that the American minister in London solicit the aid of the British government in settling Maryland's claims.[61]

With the conclusion of Jay's Treaty of 1794, however, the objective political situation changed. Not only did British-American relations become much more relaxed, if not cordial, but instrumentalities were established for settling controversies still at issue between the two nations. The most important of these instrumentalities were two boards of arbitration commissioners provided for by the treaty. One sat in London, with an American majority, to consider claims of American citizens against the British government (for illegal seizure of ships, for example). The other sat in Philadelphia, with a British majority, to consider claims of British subjects for compensation for bona fide prewar debts from solvent debtors (confirmed by the treaty of 1783) rendered uncollectable by legislation of the United States or of any of the individual states.[62] While the British government was much more conciliatory after Jay's Treaty (its war with France gave it every reason to be tractable on minor matters), it was inevitable that the British ministers would delay any concessions on lesser matters such as the Maryland Bank stock until they found out how the greater matters in the hands of the arbitration commissioners were going.

It took several years before the two commissions were set up and before they started their operations. The one in London worked very well and produced substantial indemnity payments for American claimants; the other in Philadelphia worked less well. The American commissioners refused to accept the judgments of the British majority about what constituted legal impediments to the collection of debts and in the end walked out of the commission. This was a popular step in the eyes of their compatriots but greatly impeded the improvement of British-American relations and the settlement of other issues between the two countries.[63] No one has yet undertaken an historical study of the debt question as an issue in the *domestic* politics of the United States, ca. 1783-1805, and this great topic is far beyond the scope of this paper. However, one must keep in mind that the debt problem was not purely a diplomatic question and that its political sensitivity seriously circumscribed the freedom of negotiation of those representing the new nation.

On the British side, the burden of negotiation over the Bank stock fell primarily on the successive secretaries of state for foreign affairs: Lord Grenville (1791-1801), in the first Pitt government, Lord Hawkesbury in the Addington government (1801-4) and Lord Harrowby in the second Pitt government (1804-5). On the American side, the principal negotiators were the American ministers in London; particularly Thomas Pinckney (1792-96), Rufus King (1796-1803), and James Monroe (1803-7). In addition, one of the United States members of the London commission on American claims was a Marylander, William Pinkney, a political disciple of Samuel Chase. It was inevitable that Pinkney too should be drawn into the negotiations for Maryland.[64]

Even before the Jay Treaty was signed in November 1794, the Maryland authorities wrote Secretary of State Edmund Randolph asking that Jay, who was in London, intercede for Maryland.[65] These documents were forwarded to Jay, but neither he nor Thomas Pinckney did anything for Maryland. Rufus King was to be rather more active. King's instructions, like those to Jay, were to help advance Maryland's interests "not by any formal negotiation but by such occasional instances and good offices as circumstances will permit."

At first, King turned the matter over to William Pinkney, who went through all the papers and had a long discussion with the elder Lyon, one of Chase's solicitors in London. Lyon informed him that no purely legal means could extract a decision from Chancery, that a ruling was ready but was being held up by "Reasons of State," and that Lord Chancellor Loughborough had hinted to him that he would not be averse to a settlement out of court by the various parties concerned.[66] Pinkney could only go back to Rufus King and persuade him to intervene. This King did most delicately in a letter to Grenville in February 1797. Grenville responded in like spirit by referring all the papers on Maryland's claim to the attorney general, solicitor general, and advocate general.[67] The attorney general then, it should be noted, was Sir John Scott, who in 1801 was to become Lord Eldon and lord chancellor. The three law officers delayed until August before giving their opinion that the state of Maryland was the legal successor to the rights of the former colony of Maryland only so far as recognized by the peace treaty of 1783, and that the Bank stock, not being covered by the treaty, had reverted to the crown as the property of a defunct corporation. The crown was free to dispose of it at will and could grant it to the state of Maryland. However, if this were done for reasons of equity, the crown ought also to consider the equitable claims of Mrs. Russell, the Ewers, Henry Harford, the Hanbury estate, and others.[68] This was, of course, consistent with the judgment of Lord Chancellor Loughborough in June, dismissing the Hanbury (Barclay et al.) petition.

Rufus King did not wait for the law officers' report in August but pushed on as best he could. He heard that the Russells had been paid off by the Treasury for their claims and sent this information along to Grenville for the use of the law officers. What actually happened was that in March 1797, Mrs. Ann Russell, despairing of anything coming of the law suits, had appealed once more to the Treasury for the payment of her claim for compensation for her late husband's property confiscated in Maryland. The claim had been allowed in 1790 but not yet paid. The Treasury had referred this to the commissioners handling those claims who decided in April 1798 to pay Mrs. Russell her £10,560 citing Lord Loughborough's ruling of June 1797. Mrs. Russell (who died in 1800) and her son-in-law and advisor, William Molleson, decided not to withdraw their claims in Chancery on grounds that they were still entitled to the difference between the true value of their lost Maryland lands (even Chase had talked of £12,000) and the £10,560 allowed by the government. In a private letter to Grenville's undersecretary, George Hammond, on this matter, Attorney General Scott showed some sympathy to Mrs. Russell, as well as skepticism about King's information.

Rufus King pushed on during 1797 and entered into direct correspondence and conversation with the lord chancellor. For a time, he was most optimistic.[69] His intervention may have influenced Lord Loughborough to render his opinion of June 1797 rejecting the claims of Barclay et al. (and by inference all other claims) in favor of the crown's right to the Bank stock. The implementation of this ruling was, as already pointed out, suspended by Lord Loughborough, who explained privately to King that he had done this so that the king would retain the option, if he so chose from reasons of policy, to refuse the stock and consent to its tranfer to Maryland.[70] King immediately wrote to Grenville (who had been notified by the chancellor) asking for such a transfer, but to no effect.[71]

In this unsatisfactory way negotiations dragged on during the latter part of 1797 and all of 1798, 1799, and 1800. The Maryland legislature commended King's zeal and named him their trustee to receive all or part of the stock, but refused him permission to accept any "if the release . . . of the state's right to any part be insisted on as a condition precedent to the transfer of the residue."[72] Despite these highly restrictive instructions, King kept up his conversations and correspondence with Lord Loughborough and Lord Grenville; he even tried to approach Henry Dundas, secretary of state for war and president of the Board of Control for India, and something of an *éminence grise* in Pitt's government—all to no avail.[73] The delays in the starting of the debt commission at Philadelphia and its utter breakdown in 1799 gve the British government no particular motive for wanting to be generous about Maryland's Bank stock.

The chronology of the Bank stock solicitation merges from 1800 with that of the much bigger debt question. In December 1799, when the commission at Philadelphia operating under the sixth article of the treaty of 1794 ceased its meetings, the United States government proposed to the British "an Explanatory Article for the Regulation of its future Proceedings." In April 1800, the British government replied, turning down the proposed explanatory article, but offering "to accept a Sum of between One and Two millions [sterling] in satisfaction of the Debts contracted before the Peace of 1783, to abolish the American [debt] Commission, and take upon itself the distribution of the Money among the British Creditors." The London commission on American claims would have its operation suspended pending the settlement of British debt claims but would otherwise not be affected.[74]

This British suggestion did not come out of the blue. Since at least 1790, the merchants of London and Glasgow who held most of the prewar debt were organized into local committees to solicit the British government about their uncollected debts in America. The two spokesmen of the London committee who did most of the soliciting or lobbying were John Nutt, a prewar Carolina merchant, and William Molleson, a prewar Maryland merchant and James Russell's son-in-law. The London and Glasgow committees were in constant communication with Lord Grenville during the sitting of the Philadelphia commission and after its breakdown intensified their efforts. From the Glasgow committee in March 1800 came a reminder of an earlier suggestion made by them to Grenville during the negotiations of 1794 for a method of compounding for the sums still outstanding.[75] For the Glaswegians the problem was essentially Virginia. They had some success in federal courts there collecting debts secured by bonds and mortgages but none with book debts or simple notes of hand; nor could they go into federal court for sums under $500. The Glaswegians were thinking of compensation in the vicinity of £2.5 million and suggested that the British government might advance the money if the United States could not pay it all at once.[76]

In August 1800, the United States government refused to accept the British proposal for a lump sum payment to cancel all prewar debts of American citizens to British subjects, but offered instead a more modest "Sum in satisfaction of the Claims of the Creditors upon the American Government [under the treaties of 1783 and 1794]—leaving the Creditors to pursue the recovery of their Debts in the ordinary course of the Judiciary." In response to a further British inquiry, the American government made it clear that it did not want a comparable lump sum from Britain in return for American claims on Britain but wanted the London commission to continue.[77] The next year was spent in tedious negotiations (with the British government fending off the merchants' demands for a harder line) before both sides in August 1801 agreed upon the sum of £600,000 sterling to be paid by the American government to be quit of its immediate obligations to the British creditors under article vi of the treaty of 1794. (The creditors were free to continue suing in America under the ordinary course of law, but in most cases this would prove to be only an illusory right since the ordinary course of law included the statute of limitations.) The political changes of 1800–1801 made this agreement easier to reach. In Britain, the Addington government was more conciliatory, while the election of Jefferson at the end of 1800 convinced the British government that there were insurmountable political obstacles in the United States to recovery of prewar debts. Jefferson himself was one of the larger defaulting debtors in Virginia, the state with more than two-fifths of the upaid debts outstanding. That Jefferson's indebtedness had been publicized by Federalist newspapers during the election campaign could only have exacerbated his feelings on this issue. This goes far to explain the British government's willingness to accept a sum as low as £600,000, perhaps one quarter of the value of the debts still outstanding.[78]

The agreement reached in principle in August 1801 on the amount of compensation to British creditors settled only the most important of the issues left over by the treaty of 1794. During the ensuing months, Rufus King and Lord Hawkesbury continued their negotiations on several other lesser points before concluding what became the British-American convention of 8 January 1802.[79] One of these subordinate issues was, of course, Maryland's Bank stock. Some weeks before Grenville resigned, King had sent him a draft of the proposed new convention including a clause "that the King should release all claim to the Maryland Bank Stock, and that immediate measures should be taken to transfer it to the State." Ever sanguine, King foresaw no difficulty on the Bank stock, provided that agreement could be reached on the larger issue of debt compensation.[80] In March 1801, shortly after Hawkesbury's taking office as Grenville's successor, King sent him a similar draft of the convention, with a comparable clause on the Bank stock.[81] In August, after agreement had been reached on the amount of American compensation for the debts, King sent Undersecretary George Hammond another draft with a similar Bank stock clause; in the margin, King added, "All the late Min[iste]rs concurred in the propriety of this article, and it was firmly expected to have been accomplished a long time."[82] King was inclined to be oversanguine in this matter.

Rufus King also entered into conversations and correspondence with the new lord chancellor, Lord Eldon, who as Attorney General Sir John Scott had been familiar with the Maryland case in the late 1790s. Lord Eldon seemed deceptively agreeable but kept raising minor difficulties.[83] Finally, on 15 October 1801, King had a private conference with Hawkesbury and Eldon at which they worked out most of the clauses of what was to become the convention of January 1802. At the meeting, Eldon told King that Maryland's Bank stock claims could not be included in the convention:

The Chancellor, adverting to the Maryland Bank Stock, observed that after looking more fully into the question, he felt great difficulty in recommending that it should become the subject of a public Convention or Stipulation between the two countries. The claims of sundry Persons upon that Property, remained still to be decided in the Court of Chancery; and it would be contrary to the usage of this country for the King to enter into any stipulation, affecting or controlling the decisions of his Courts; that if any should be agreed to, it must be with a provisional reserve in favour of these claims; that an assurance from the King's Government that his Majesty's right, subject to such equitable claims as might be established, should be transferred to Maryland, and an Instruction to the Attorney General to bring these claims to a decision would answer all the purposes of a stipulation to the same effect.

On the next day, 16 October, King had a further conference with Hawkesbury alone at which he complained of the unconscionable delays on the Maryland Bank stock and the repeated wavering on the key point of whether or not the Court of Chancery had jurisdiction:

Upwards of sixteen years had elapsed since the State of Maryland had endeavoured to obtain a decision upon her claim to this Stock in the Court of Chancery of this country, to whose Jurisdiction she was willing to submit. Several years after the commencement of a suit for this purpose, the Chancellor discovered, that having no means of enforcing a Decree upon an independent State, he had no jurisdiction to try the merits of the Question before him. The Claim then became the subject of diplomatic representation, and a number of years having been spent in explaining, conferring, and exchanging Notes respecting the claim, it has been recently discovered that it was still depending in the Court of Chancery, and that it would be unusual and indecorous to make a matter of stipulation [that] which was in the possession of the Judiciary.[84]

Although King was greatly peeved by Eldon's tergiversations on the Bank stock, he realized, as he reported to Madison,[85] that he had obtained a significant concession on this: the attorney general would be instructed to bring the matter to a speedy decision; and the crown would yield all its rights in the stock to Maryland, subject only to the equitable claims of the other parties to the suits.

Going back to court was now less hopeless than it had been during the long litigations of 1784–97 because now, with the settlement of the debt issue, there no longer was a "Reason of State" to delay the course of justice. Who, though, were the "sundry Persons" whose "equitable claims" upon the Bank stock Lord Eldon had insisted must be heard in his court? The owners of the ironworks, the Russells, Ewers, and Buchanan's trustees, had been taken care of by the British government. The Hanbury interest was attached to that of Maryland. This left only two other significant claimant interests. One was Henry Harford, late proprietor of Maryland, who was not satisfied with the £70,000 compensation he had received from the British government and had been involved in the Bank stock litigation since 1789. The other was a group of émigrés and speculators in London, Bristol, and elsewhere who still held unredeemed prewar Maryland paper money, which they claimed was pledged against the Bank stock.

There had been three issues of paper money outstanding in Maryland at the start of the war: those of 1766, 1769, and 1773. That of 1766 was clearly based upon the Bank stock; those of 1769 and 1773 were convertible into sterling at redemption but had no clear lien on the Bank stock. All had been called in during the war, but many holders did not surrender them at the time of conversion, either because they had fled the province during the war, or because they did not want to accept in return the new revolutionary paper money of constantly deteriorating value. (When the issue of 1766 was called in, holders were also given the option of taking bills of exchange on the trustees in London, but there was little belief that such bills would be honored and only £1825:12:3 of such bills of exchange were issued on conversion of that issue.)[86] Maryland regarded these hoarded bills of credit as void, but they turned up, by one route or another, in Britain after the war, some in the hands of émigrés (most notably Daniel Dulany), others in the hands of merchants. In 1794, just before the signing of the Jay Treaty, some of the holders sent a memorial to Lord Grenville, asking that their interests be recognized in the negotiations.[87] In 1799, much the same group petitioned Grenville again, asking that, once the Court of Chancery had established the king's right to the Bank stock, their interests should be taken into consideration in discussions with the American minister on the disposal of that stock. On both occasions, the papers were referred to the chancellor, Lord Loughborough, who did not reply.[88] In 1802–3, the memorialists turned to the Privy Council and Treasury, without any greater success. Their holdings then were thought to come to only about £5000, while the face value of the Bank stock and other balances was £107,800 by the end of 1801.[89]

There was great disappointment in Maryland when word was received that the matter of the Bank stock would not be included in the British-American convention of January 1802 and that the whole matter would be sent back to the Court of Chancery. Chase and others pointed out that if the state had not been able to obtain redress when Britain was at war and trying to get redress from the United States for the prewar debts, Maryland could have little hope of justice now that Britain was at peace and the debt question settled. There was little understanding in Maryland of the weight of Lord Eldon's obduracy on this issue, nor did Chase and his friends give very much weight to ministerial assurances to Rufus King that the case would now proceed to an early decision. King was then being talked about as a possible Federalist candidate for the presidency in 1804, and his friends in Maryland were upset because anti-Federalists were spreading stories that he could have obtained more for Maryland from the British government if he had really tried. It was feared that King could never carry the state because of this issue.[90] Maryland's exasperation was ultimately expressed in a joint resolution of both houses of the legislature passed on 31 December 1802 authorizing the president of the United States to intercede for the state.[91]

The Maryland party in London tried to test the sincerity of the government by having the state's allies, Barclay et al. (the Hanbury interest) petition the Court of Chancery for a reopening of the case, which had been in abeyance since Lord Loughborough's suspended decree of June 1797. The petition was put down for a hearing in that court, but nothing was accomplished in the course of 1802.[92] The Hanbury executors tried a petition to the king in October 1802 without any more success.[93]

Rufus King, for his part, by correspondence and conversation sought all through 1802 to remind the foreign secretary, Lord Hawkesbury, of his assurances of a speedy settlement. These efforts had to be suspended during his trip to the continent (August-November 1802). The chancellor for his part remained true to his opinion as attorney general in 1797 that the stock rightly belonged to the king and must be transferred to his majesty before it could be disposed of as policy or equity might dictate; he so informed Lord Hawkesbury in July, but Hawkesbury did no more than refer the matter to the Treasury, where the relevant papers remained gathering dust on the desk of the Treasury solicitor.[94] On 13 November, the Treasury referred the whole matter to the law officers (attorney general and solicitor general) for an opinion on how a decision might be obtained in Chancery.[95] Rufus King, now returned to London, tried to hasten things along a little by writing privately to the prime minister and first lord of the Treasury, Henry Addington, on 7 December, as well as to Hawkesbury on the ninth.[96] This had some effect, for a few days later (15 December) Hawkesbury instructed the attorney general to take the necessary legal steps "for putting the Crown in possession of this property, in order that His Majesty may be enabled to dispose of it in such manner as He may think proper."[97]

Attorney General Spencer Perceval, the future prime minister, deputized the Treasury solicitor, Joseph White, to act for him in this matter. In March 1803, the latter petitioned Chancery asking that the decree of Lord Loughborough of 27 June 1797 (recognizing the king's title to the stock) "may no longer be suspended and that the Register [of Chancery] may be directed to draw up the same in order that any of the Parties dissatisfied therewith may have an opportunity of appealing against such Decree. . . ." After a hearing on 1 April 1803, Eldon dismissed the plaintiffs' petition in the case of *Barclay et al. v. Russell et al.* on the grounds that the old Maryland government was no more, "with liberty for His Majesty's Attorney General to apply to the Court in this Cause and in the Cause of Chase against Russell for a transfer of the said funds standing in the name of the Acc[ountan]t General of the Court in trust . . . and any of the Parties in . . . the said Cause[s] . . . are also to be at liberty to apply to this Court respecting their Claims. . . ."[98] Chase's solicitor, William Lyon, felt that this meant that the stock would be awarded to the crown, for, even without a knowledge of Eldon's privately expressed opinions, he felt that the lord chancellor would agree with his predecessor, Loughborough.[99]

Shortly afterwards, on 20 April, the attorney general moved "that the Accountant General may be directed to transfer the whole of the aforesaid Bank Stock . . . to such person as His Majesty by Warrant under his Royal Sign Manual be pleased to direct or appoint." King now perceived that such a transfer was the only route by which Maryland could get the Bank stock and on the twenty-second instructed Chase's solicitors, Lyon and Collyer, to concur. The motion was, however, opposed by Henry Harford and no order was made upon it. Though Harford filed a new bill against the attorney general and other parties to the suit, approaches were made to Rufus King, during the week 20-27 April, indicating that Harford would be satisfied with only a small part of the stock, perhaps £10,000 (face value). King, however, refused such a settlement, for he did not feel that he had powers from Maryland to make any payment to Harford.[100]

All these delays were particularly embarrassing to Rufus King, who was scheduled to return to the United States at the end of April 1803 and who wanted the stock question settled before he left. Hawkesbury smoothed King's departure by giving him a letter undertaking on behalf of the British government "that in the event of its being decided that the Title of this Stock has accrued, and belongs to His Majesty, His Majesty will cause the same to be transferred to the State of Maryland, together with the Accumulations which shall have accrued from the Re-investment of the Dividends. . . ."[101] King could report this in triumph to Madison and have the good news published in the press in the United States.[102]

King had in 1801 been given powers by the Maryland legislature to receive and transmit the stock.[103] With King departing from England in May and his successor as American minister, James Monroe, not arriving until July, there was also a gap in the management of Maryland's Bank stock affairs.[104] Once more this responsibility was entrusted both by the United States and Maryland to William Pinkney, the Marylander who was an American member of the London claims commission, now almost finished its work. Pinkney was himself planning to return to America in 1804 and naively thought he could finish the Bank stock business by then.[105]

As of 1 May 1803, the ever-accumulating trust fund totaled £187,567:12:0 at current values:

£98,518:2:9 Bank stock at 170	= £167,480:12:0 stg	
£15,290:17:9 Bank bonds at par	= £ 15,290:17:9	
£ 4,796:2:3 cash in Bank of England	= £ 4,796:7:3[106]	

At $4.44 per pound sterling, this was the equivalent of $833,625 in United States currency, a substantial sum for Maryland in those days. Nothing now seemed to stand in the way of the state's getting this save the claims of Henry Harford, their late proprietor. Rufus King did not think that he had authority to satisfy Harford, and Pinkney had no greater delegated powers. On 26 May 1803, Governor John F. Mercer sent him some very vague instructions in a private letter. If Maryland could get the balance immediately, Pinkney was authorized to leave part of the stock (equivalent in value to Russell's old claim) continuing in trust pending the settlement of any outstanding claims: "but if such arrangement cannot be made, the Executive of Maryland conceive themselves authorized in concurrence with the President of the United States and they are disposed to trust to your discretion the power of making this partial but absolute sacrifice, in preference to risking any longer the whole claim."[107] It is not surprising that Pinkney did not interpret these highly qualified words as authorizing him to make a settlement with Harford. Chase, however, had a clear grasp of the promise opened up by Hawkesbury's letter of 25 April, and on 11 July wrote Governor Mercer suggesting that Pinkney be specifically authorized to give up to £10,000 sterling "to any persons" on condition that the balance of the trust fund be paid to Maryland immediately.[108] The Council of Maryland made an order to this effect on 5 August with the added proviso that any such settlement must have the approval of President Jefferson.[109]

Pinkney, like King, was strongly convinced that Maryland's best chance was to concur in the transfer to the crown—rather than proceed by another Chancery procedure (an "Information") towards a definitive settlement of all claims, which might take several years and could be appealed to the House of Lords. However, to get such a transfer expeditiously, it was necessary to obtain the concurrence of Henry Harford, who had blocked the same in April 1803. Harford then had asked for £10,000 in Bank stock (worth perhaps £17,000), while the Maryland Council had since authorized a payment not to exceed £10,000 sterling cash.[110] Nevertheless, Pinkney pushed on with great firmness of purpose, ingenuity and political nerve. He decided to raise Maryland's offer from £10,000 to £11,000 cash, equivalent to £7,746:10 Bank stock at current prices, and persuaded the Hanbury executors (Barclay et al.), whose claim was based on an assignment from Maryland, to contribute £2253:10 in Bank stock from their claim to make up the £10,000 Bank stock demanded by Harford. With that gentleman taken care of, the government caused much less trouble. Pinkney used the assistance of the new American minister, Monroe, to obtain introductions to Lord Hawkesbury and the attorney general, Spencer Perceval, and, after a conference with the latter in November 1803, persuaded him to renew the government's efforts to obtain the transfer of the stock to the crown.[111] Appropriate notice for the attorney general was given on December 14 and this time there were no objections from Harford. On the sixteenth and twenty-first, Lord Eldon considered the matter yet again and ordered that, after deducting legal expenses all around, the balance of the trust be transferred from the accountant general of the Court of Chancery (its custodian since 1784) to a person to be named by the king by his sign manual (personal signature).[112]

Though the resumption of the war against France in May 1803 should have made the British ministers rather anxious to be done with this unending affair, many months were to elapse before the transfer ordered by Lord Eldon in December 1803 could be effected. It took until the end of February 1804 to get the eight sets of legal fees settled. Then the king's mental illness made it impossible to think of asking for his sign manual for several months.[113] Nor were matters hastened by the resignation of Addington and his replacement at the Treasury by William Pitt (10 May). In the new ministry, the earl of Harrowby replaced Hawkesbury at the Foreign Office. Meanwhile, another minor interest reappeared to delay matters a few months more.

The British owners of unredeemed prewar Maryland paper money had never formally entered the Chancery litigation, though they had frequently petitioned the government for compensation out of the Bank stock. They now renewed their applications and reminded the government of their unanswered memorials of 1802 and 1803.[114] The claim was called to the attention of the attorney general and solicitor general, who reported on 28 April 1804 that the paper money holders had "a Claim upon the Justice of the Crown, but which Claim cannot be sustained in any Court in Westm[inste]r Hall or otherwise than by Petition or Memorial." That is, the claim of the paper money holders was moral or political, but not legal.[115] Nevertheless, Lord Hawkesbury's undersecretary, Hammond, in conversations with Pinkney, tried to get Maryland to agree to pay off the paper money holders as part of the final settlement. Pinkney adamantly refused. He realized that the bona fide holdings of the paper money (in the hands of old merchants and émigrés) perhaps came to £8000 but could go much higher if any of the claims of speculators were recognized. Any such settlement was far beyond his authorization. The departure of Lord Hawkesbury from office facilitated things, but first he had to spend several months educating Lord Harrowby about the whole matter. In the end, Harrowby agreed to accept a simple letter from Pinkney assuring him that "justice" would be done by Maryland to the holders of the paper money. (In the end, they got nothing.)[116]

After every conceivable delay and the frequent postponement of Pinkney's departure for Maryland, on 29 July 1804 the king signed the warrant naming Joseph White, solicitor to the Treasury, as the person to whom the stock should be transferred, and who should hold it until otherwise instructed by royal warrant. Next, Pinkney had to get the attorney general to obtain from the Court of Chancery a final order (6 August) for the transfer to White. Its execution required a further warrant from the king, which was not signed until the thirteenth. Pinkney had by then left London to catch his homeward-bound ship between Gravesend and Deal but was summoned back to London because the warrant named only him to receive Maryland's share. He rushed back to London, effected the necessary transfers on the fourteenth and fifteenth and then proceeded posthaste to Falmouth in Cornwall, where the ship had agreed to wait. It cost him £200 for holding up the ship, but he was able to return to America with his family and the satisfaction of two jobs (the claims commission and the Bank stock) well done.[117] It is ironic that a matter under litigation in the Court of Chancery for more than twenty years should have had to be finished in such a breathless rush.

On 14 August 1804, the ledgers of the Bank of England show that stock with a face value of £100,940:0:1 (worth over £160,000 at the current price of ca. 160) was transferred from the accountant general of Chancery (in trust) to Joseph White, Esq., of Lincoln's Inn. The next day (15 August), White transferred £10,000 to Henry Harford of New Cavendish Street, Esq., and the balance of £90,940 to "William Pinkney of Baltimore in America Esq. . . . for the use & benefit of the State of Maryland." That same day, Pinkney transferred stock with a face value of £19,910 to David Barclay & Co. for the interest of the late firm of Osgood Hanbury & Co., and the balance of £71,030 to James Monroe, the American minister, who was to hold the same, pending instructions from Maryland.[118] In addition, the cash balance in the trust (from which the legal expenses had already been deducted) and some miscellaneous bank paper (analagous to modern bonds) in which part of the interest had been invested were also divided between Barclay et al. and Maryland in the same proportions. The Barclay share represented the £11,000 worth of stock (with accumulated dividends) transferred by Maryland to the estate and partners of Osgood Hanbury in 1787 in settlement of the Hanbury's mortgage on the Dulany lands.

An accounting of the Maryland Bank stock trust as of 15 August 1804 would appear to be roughly:[119]

Accumulation

	Face Value		Market Value
Bank Stock	£100,940: 0: 1	at 160	£161,504: 0: 2
Bank 5% annuities (1797)	8,314:16: 1	at par	8,314:16: 1
Bank 5% annuities (navy)	6,976: 1: 8	at par	6,976: 1: 8
Cash	5,865: 7: 5	at par	5,865: 7: 5
Cash spent on legal fees	3,487: 7: 6	—	3,487: 7: 6
Total accumulation	£125,583:12: 9		£186,147:12:10

Disposition

	Face Value		Market Value
To Henry Harford	£10,000 Bank stock	at 160	£16,000
To D. Barclay and J. Monroe			
Lloyd (Hanbury estate)	£19,910 Bank stock	at 160	£31,856
	1,825 5% ann. (1797)	at par	1,825
	1,531 5% ann. (navy)	at par	1,531
	1,237 cash	—	1,237
	£24,503		£36,449

	Face Value (Con'td.)		Market Value (Con'td.)
Chase's commission	£ 4,037 Bank stock	at 160	£ 6,459: 4: 0
Pinkney's expenses	£ 500 cash	—	£ 500
Legal expenses (Feb.)	£ 3,487: 7: 6		
(Aug.)	210: 0: 0		
	£ 3,697: 7: 6	—	£ 3,697: 7: 6
To Maryland	£ 66,993: 0: 1 Bank stock	at 160	£107,188:16: 2
	6,489:16: 1 5% ann. (1797)	at par	6,489:16: 1
	5,445: 1: 8 5% ann. (navy)	at par	5,445: 1: 8
	3,918: 7: 5 cash	—	3,918: 7: 5
	£ 82,846: 5: 3		£123,042: 1: 4
Total Disbursements	£125,583:12: 9		£186,147:12:10

Many of the items on the above account were only tentatively settled by Pinkney in August 1804. He had allowed Chase's four percent commission only on the Bank stock, leaving the rest of the commission (on the other items received) to be settled when Chase closed his accounts with the state and accounted for both the sums advanced him for expenses and the sums paid in London for legal expenses (his responsibility). Some years later, the settling of these accounts led to a lawsuit between Maryland and Samuel Chase.[120] More generously, Pinkney, who was indebted to Osgood Hanbury's son Sampson for much valuable assistance and advice, tentatively allowed the Hanbury executors (Barclay and Lloyd) their full claim, though he had doubts about part of it. They subsequently refunded a small part to Maryland when the state insisted that the Hanbury estate was entitled to the accumulation on the original £11,000 stock granted only from Chase's conveyance in 1787 and not from the act of legislature.[121]

The energy and acumen of Pinkney's efforts were genuinely appreciated. After the conveyance of August 1804, William Murdock, Chase's financial agent in London, wrote that Maryland would not have gotten a farthing had it not been for Pinkney. He suggested a reward of £4000. Monroe was equally generous in praise. In the event, the legislature awarded Pinkney $12,000 in consideration of his great and successful efforts.[122]

When Pinkney left England in August 1804, the securities and cash belonging to Maryland were left in the hands and name of the American minister in London, James Monroe. The Maryland authorities in April 1805 entrusted responsibility for the sale of the Bank stock and other assets in London and the remittance of the proceeds homeward to Joseph Hopper

Nicholson, a local Republican politician and friend and confidant of Jefferson's secretary of the Treasury, Gallatin.[123] To avoid loss of interest on the funds during the period of remittance, Nicholson, who was very knowledgeable on financial matters, advised the Maryland authorities to sell the stock and other assets in London and convert the proceeds there into American government bonds (even though they were higher in England than America), which could then be remitted. The details of carrying out this plan were entrusted to Monroe and George W. Erving, the United States consul in London and Nicholson's London correspondent.[124]

Monroe and Erving found out that trying to sell more than £100,000 worth of Bank shares quickly on the London stock exchange was likely to depress the market and lead to a loss by the state. Instead, on 8 August 1805, Monroe reached a private and quite favorable agreement with Francis Baring & Co., merchants and bankers of London and financial agents of the United States government. By this arrangement, Barings agreed to buy Maryland's securities at the following rates:

£67,421: 0: 1 face value Bank stock at 176 1/2	£118,998: 1: 3
£ 5,445: 1: 8 face value Bank 5% annuities (navy) at 89 1/2	4,873: 6: 9
£ 6,489:16: 1 face value Bank 5% annuities (1797) at par	6,489:16: 1
Total	£130,361: 4: 1

Barings agreed to pay for these securities in two months (8 October) in any combination of the following:

6% or deferred 6% U.S. stock [bonds] at 95
8% U.S. stock at 104
Bills of exchange with Barings' indorsement, payable in Washington, Baltimore, Philadelphia, or New York at sixty days sight on average (payable upon an average at sixty days after presentation) at the rate of 4s.6d. sterling to the dollar with a one percent premium.[125]

Between 8 and 11 October, in return for the £131,719:19:9 covered by the agreement of 8 August (the £130,361:4:1 shown above plus some cash received from Monroe and the Hanbury executors), Barings delivered to Monroe the following effects:[126]

U.S. 6% stock at 95	£ 5,560: 1: 4
U.S. deferred 6% stock at 95	49,645:18: 8
U.S. 8% stock at 104	14,367:12: 0
Total of U.S. stock [bonds]	69,573:12: 0
Bills of exchange on U.S. at 1% premium	62,146: 6: 9
Grand total	£131,719:18: 9

In addition, Monroe by then had in his custody £8632:17:4 cash representing dividends received during the past year or so. Barings expressed lack of interest in handling this owing to their heavy commitments on the main transaction. In the end, they agreed to furnish bills of exchange for this too, but at a 3 percent premium. The bills delivered on 14 October, like many of the others, were drawn on Robert Gilmor & Sons of Baltimore.[127] That liquidated the last of Maryland's trust fund in London.

The papers now available in the "Bank Stock Papers" in the Hall of Records do not contain a final accounting of the remittance business handled by Nicholson. A partial accounting from Barings contains some obvious errors corrected in a later account. Our own recalculation suggests the following semifinal account of the ultimate disposal of the Bank stock at current values:

To Maryland	£140,352:16: 1
To Hanbury Estate	36,449: 0: 0
To Henry Harford	16,000: 0: 0
To Samuel Chase (unsettled)	6,459: 4: 0
To William Pinkney ($12,000 + £500)	3,200: 0: 0
To legal expenses (London)	3,697: 7: 6
Total	£206,158: 7: 7

In the end, therefore, despite the resolution of the Maryland legislature in 1797 that Rufus King should accept nothing rather than give up Maryland's claim to the whole, the state received a shade under 70 percent of this "million dollar deal." Of course, in 1775 the trust fund had only been worth £41,180. Such are life's lessons and the wonders of compound interest.

Maryland had no immediate plans for the use of funds received and was embarrassed by the large proportion received in cash. Nicholson placed his cash balances temporarily in the Farmers Bank in Baltimore until he could convert them into United States bonds. He completed this work, turned over the bonds to the treasurer of the Western Shore and settled his accounts by 4 December 1806.[128] It would probably take a major research effort in the state accounts to determine exactly how the money received from the Bank stock trust was eventually spent, if the question could be answered at all. We do know that in 1812, $30,000 of Maryland's holdings of 6 percent U.S. bonds were lent to the Potomac Company.[129] In all likelihood, much of the balance eventually ended up in internal improvements of one sort or another. Whether they were profitable or not, that was a not ignoble end to the long history of the state's earlier investments in the stock of the Bank of England.

The long and complicated history of the Bank stock case is essentially the story of the "nationalization" of a local concern. In the colonial period, Maryland's property rights existed within the confines of English law and the protection of English courts. In the immediate postwar years Maryland, through Samuel Chase, sought to reassert some of these rights—those pertaining to the Bank stock—in the accustomed prewar way and came to grief. In the eyes of the British authorities, Maryland was part of the United

34

States and its claims could be considered only in the context of the general settlement of all British and American claims and counterclaims. Only when Maryland's cause was taken up seriously by the United States representatives in London, and only when British–American relations reached an appropriate conjuncture, could Maryland's claims find their equitable solution—a solution determined by the equity of diplomacy and not that of Chancery.

NOTES

1. Morris L. Radoff, *Calendar of Maryland State Papers, No. 2: The Bank Stock Papers,* Hall of Records Publication No. 5 (Annapolis, 1947), hereafter cited as *Cal.*

2. The principal modern works are Bradford Perkins, *The First Rapprochement: England and the United States 1795–1805* (Philadelphia, 1955); and Charles Ritcheson, *Aftermath of Revolution: British Policy toward the United States 1783–1795* (Dallas, 1969).

3. The most important of these have been published in Charles R. King, ed., *The Life and Correspondence of Rufus King,* 6 vols. (New York, 1894–1900); hereafter cited as *King.* The papers calendared by Radoff are much more complete than those found elsewhere because King and Monroe transferred many of their papers on the Bank stock to William Pinkney, who presented them to the State of Maryland; cf. HR [Hall of Records] Blue Book 2:90 (*Cal.*, no. 203), Pinkney to [Gov. Bowie], 3 Nov. 1804.

4. Particularly in FO [Foreign Office] 5/7, 20, 21, 27, 28, 31, 34, 37, 44.

5. Particularly PRO [Public Record Office] T.S.11/689/2186, ff. 1–52.

6. Including Michael G. Kammen, *A Rope of Sand: The Colonial Agents, British Politics, and the American Revolution* (Ithaca, 1968) and Jack M. Sosin, *Agents and Merchants: British Colonial Policy and the Origins of the American Revolution, 1763–1775* (Lincoln, Nebraska, 1965).

7. William Hand Browne et al., eds., *Archives of Maryland,* 72 vols. (Baltimore, 1883–), 30:627–32; hereafter cited as *Archives.*

8. Ibid., 459, 585; cf. also ibid. 449–50, 455–57, 462, 563, 575–76, 578–81, 584–87, 596–97; ibid., 33:14–15, 100.

9. On the Hydes, see Jacob M. Price, *France and the Chesapeake: A History of the French Tobacco Monopoly, 1674–1791, and of Its Relationship to the British and American Tobacco Trades,* 2 vols. (Ann Arbor, 1973), 1:514–15, 523, 533–534, 536, 586, 651–54, 657, 659, 662, 1007–8, 1016–17, 1058; Charles Albro Barker, *The Background of the Revolution in Maryland* (New Haven, 1940), pp. 74, 84, 88; *Archives* 37:585–86. John Hyde of Poplar, Middlesex (1655–1732), left three sons, Samuel, John, and Herbert, and four daughters, Anna Snelling, Ann Letten, Jane, and Althea. For his will, see PRO Prob. 11/656 (Prerogative Court of Canterbury [hereafter PCC] 11 Price).

10. *Archives* 36:51–52.

11. Ibid., 39:158; 25:514.

12. Ibid., 39:105–6.

13. Barker, *Background of the Revolution,* pp. 73, 88; cf. also *Archives* 38:441.

14. W. Marston Acres, "Directors of the Bank of England," *Notes & Queries* 179 (3 Aug. 1940):83. In 1727, Hunt acquired the Manor House, Woodford, Essex, where he died in 1767. His will (PCC 225 Legard) is in PRO Prob. 11/929; cf. also *Archives* 40:73, 161, 179, 182–83, 390–91, 401; ibid., 28:31, 50, 175–76, 211, 292, 297, 307, 319, 343, 348, 351–52, 354, 391, 408.

15. *Archives* 44:297–300, 355, 358, 694–95; ibid., 46:227–28. Cruikshank appears to have absconded, while Samuel Hyde settled with his creditors in England for 10s. in the £ before his death in 1748; see his will (PCC 178 Strahan) in PRO Prob. 11/762. His brothers John and Herbert continued to be active in London as directors of the London Assurance. The complete (1734–67) set of trustees' accounts in the Scharf Collection, Maryland Historical Society, shows that Cruikshank last signed the accounts in April 1743, and S. Hyde in June 1747. Adams and Hanbury first signed in October 1748.

16. *Archives* 44:652–53; 46:371, 387, 417–19; 52:293, 434, 436; 28:390, 464, 472–73; 31:46, 398, 413–14; 32:49; cf. J. Reaney Kelly, "Portraits by Sir Joshua Reynolds. Return to Tulip Hill," *Maryland Historical Magazine* 62 (1967):64–67.

17. In 1759, friends tried to get a trustee's place for William Anderson, Maryland merchant in London, who was connected to several prominent Eastern Shore families, *Archives* 31:475–76, 479–81, 506–7, 513, 517, 543, 545; 32:220; 55:liii, 24–25, 533–34; 56:xlii, 409, 413, 415; 61:290–91, 348–49; 6:15, 67, 120, 184–85, 240, 401, 423; 9:35, 38–43, 88–89, 128–29, 172, 263, 279, 338–39, 371, 435–38, 515–16, 544; 14:250–52, 255, 399, 407, 416, 482, 488–89; cf. also A. Audrey Locke, *The Hanbury Family*, 2 vols. (London, 1916), vol. 2, ch. 13, and PRO T.1/656/999, ff. 279–87.

18. *Archives* 62:133–44; see also William Kilty, *The Laws of Maryland*, 2 vols. (Annapolis, 1799, 1800), Acts 1769, ch. 14.

19. In 1766 Grove remarried. His second wife, Louise, was the daughter of Edward Hillersden, Hamburg merchant of London; see his will(PCC 24 Adderly) in PRO Prob. 11, and *Gentleman's Magazine* 70 (2) (1800):1010; cf. also n. 16.

20. Some correspondence of James Russell has survived at Coutts's Bank, London. For the Russell family, see James Paterson, *Scottish Surnames: Contribution to Genealogy* (Edinburgh, 1866), pp. 55–58. For the Maryland Lees, see Edmund Jennings Lee, *Lee of Virginia* (Philadelphia, 1895), pp. 96–101, 148–61, 304–6. I expect to publish a fully documented paper on James Russell in the *Maryland Historical Magazine* in July 1977.

21. *Archives* 64:54, 103. The trustees' accounts for 1767–73 are in Ms. 2018, Maryland Historical Society.

22. PRO C.12/446/3.

23. On him, cf. Jacob M. Price, "Joshua Johnson in London, 1771–1775," in *Statesmen, Scholars and Merchants: Essays in Eighteenth Century History,* Anne Whiteman et al. (Oxford, 1973), pp. 153–80; and Edward C. Papenfuse, *In Pursuit of Profit: The Annapolis Merchants in the Era of the American Revolution, 1763–1805* (Baltimore, 1975), passim.

24. Kilty, *Laws of Maryland,* Acts 1769, ch. 14; Acts 1773, ch. 26; Acts Nov. 1779, ch. 38.

25. *Archives* 43:50–51.

26. PRO T.1/582/154, ff. 131–32 (memorial of James Russell). Cf. also PRO C.12/2135/32. Franklin's letter of 20 May 1780 is quoted in Russell's answer of 3 June 1784 in PRO C.12/446/3.

27. HR Blue Book 2:43(*Cal.*, no. 1) Franklin to T. S. Lee, 11 Aug. 1780.

28. Kilty, *Laws of Maryland,* Acts June 1780, ch. 24, art. vi, provided that if the trustees paid the bills of exchange or transferred the stock, an equivalent amount of their own property in the state would be exempt from seizure.

29. *Archives* 45:131–33, 142, 144–45; PRO A.O.12/9, f. 16; cf. also n. 26.

30. Kilty, *Laws of Maryland,* Acts Oct. 1780, ch. 45; cf. also chs. 49 and 51. Subsequent legislation clarified procedures for selling the iron works, ibid., Acts May 1781, ch. 33; Nov. 1781, ch. 2; Apr. 1782, ch. 60.

31. PRO A.O.12/9, ff. 10–12 (claim of Ann Russell).

32. PRO T.1/582/154.

33. Cf. Ritcheson, *Aftermath of Revolution,* ch. 4; PRO T.S.11/689/2186, f. 105.

34. HR Blue Book 3:6 (*Cal.*, no. 2).

35. Bank of England Record Office, Roehampton: Bank Stock Ledger 55:840, 1010.

36. Kilty, *Laws of Maryland,* Acts Apr. 1783, ch. 35; HR Blue Book 3:1–4 (*Cal.*, nos. 3–7); cf. *Archives* 48:425–26; and Maryland Historical Society Ms. 1235 for Chase's bond of 13 June 1783. On Chase, subsequently a Supreme Court justice, cf. *Dictionary of American Biography* 4:34–37; David Curtis Skaggs, *Roots of Maryland Democracy, 1753–1776* (Westport, Conn., 1973); and Ronald Hoffman, *A Spirit of Dissension: Economics, Politics, and the Revolution in Maryland* (Baltimore, 1973).

37. HR Blue Book 3:25, 14 (*Cal.*, nos. 9, 12) Chase to Gov. Paca, 23 Feb., 31 Mar./1 Apr. 1784.

38. PRO C.12/2135/32 (*Russell v. Bank*), Russell's bill.

39. HR Blue Book 3:14, 23 (*Cal.*, nos. 12, 14), Chase to Gov. Paca, 1, 20 Apr. 1784; cf. also 13 (*Cal.* no. 11) for the subpoena of 28 March.

40. HR Blue Book 3:19 (*Cal.*, no. 15), Chase to Paca, 20 May 1784; PRO C.12/2135/32 (Chase's demurrer, 18 May 1784); C.12/446/3 (*Chase* v. *Russell* et al.: Chase's bill, 28 Apr. 1784).
41. PRO Prob. 11/1059 (PCC 494 Warburton) for W. Ewer's will, 1779; C. 12/1071/18 (*Ewers* v. *Russell* et al.: Ewers' bill, 6 May 1784); C.12/446/3 (*Chase* v. *Russell* et al., Ewer's answer, 17 July 1784); HR Blue Book 3:19 (*Cal.*, no. 15), Chase to Paca, 20 May 1784.
42. HR Blue Book 3:8 (*Cal.*, no. 17), Chase to Paca, 9 June 1784; 2:157 (*Cal.*, no. 18) for writ of execution of court signed by outgoing and new Master of the Rolls, 11 June 1784; cf. also PRO C.12/446/3 for Russell's answer of 3 June to Chase's bill.
43. HR Blue Book 3:9, 5, 16 (*Cal.*, nos. 19, 21, 26), Chase to Paca, 17, 22 July, 14 Aug. 1784; Blue Book 3:18 (*Cal.*, no. 23), Chase to Pitt, 3 Aug. 1784; PRO C.12/2135/32 (Answer of Bank, 26 Aug. 1784). There was a further hearing in Chancery on 28 July in which the lord chancellor allowed Chase's demurrer to Russell's bill, but the case was carried no further.
44. See below, pp. 20-1.
45. HR Blue Book 3:21 (*Cal.*, no. 24), Chase to W. and J. Lyon, 9 Aug. 1784.
46. Kilty, *Laws of Maryland*, Acts Nov. 1784, ch. 76; Kilty et al., *Laws of Maryland*, 7: Res., 1784, no. 2; HR Blue Book 3:24 (*Cal.*, no. 28), Chase to Paca, 21 Dec. 1784; cf. also Blue Book 2:100, 165 (*Cal.*, nos. 29, 31).
47. Kilty, *Laws of Maryland*, Acts Nov. 1785, ch. 88.
48. HR Blue Book 2:93 (*Cal.*, no. 32), Gov. Smallwood to Chase, 7 July 1786; *Archives* 71:120; Bank Record Office, Bank Stock Ledger 59:L, f. 36.
49. PRO T.S.11/689/2186, f. 2; Kilty, *Laws of Maryland*, Acts Nov. 1786, ch. 50.
50. HR Blue Book 2:29, 35 (*Cal.*, nos. 44, 63). For Chase's authorization to compromise (28 May 1787) and his own instructions to Uriah Forrest in London, see Maryland Historical Society Ms. 1195 (*Cal.*, nos. 36 and 39). Forrest was authorized to go to £22,525:10:2 for a settlement with the Russells, the Ewers and the Buchanans.
51. HR Blue Book 2:137 (*Cal.*, no. 33).
52. These are, of course, the great names of the London Quaker *haute bourgeoisie*. Barclay and Lloyd describe themselves as "bankers of London," Gurney as "banker of Norwich," and John Hanbury as "brewer of London."
53. PRO T.S.11/689/2186, ff. 2–7; C.12/2157/4, membrane 1.
54. PRO C. 12/2153/15 (14 Feb. 1789). For his will (probated 4 Sept. 1788), see PRO Prob. 11/1170 (PCC 455 Calvert).
55. PRO T.S.11/689/2186, ff. 11–21; C.12/1261/7.
56. PRO C.12/2158/1 and T.S.11/689/2186. ff. 53–71 for Harford's bill of 24 July 1789, with attached replies of other parties concerned, 1789–90.
57. See preceding and PRO C.12/2157/4, C.12/2153/15, T.S.11/689/2186, ff. 7–46, and Bank Record Office, Bank Stock Ledger 59:L, f. 46. On the Russell claims, see PRO T.29/62, pp. 122, 226; A.O.12/9, ff. 10–17; A.O.13/92, ff. 421–36; and for the related claims of the Buchanan trustees, see T.1/656/210, ff. 7–10.
58. PRO T.S.11/689/2186, f. 120(5). Chase was optimistic enough about a settlement in 1791 to obtain an act of the Maryland legislature empowering him to appoint trustees in London to receive and sell the Bank stock, Kilty, *Laws of Maryland*, Acts Nov. 1791, ch. 86.
59. HR Blue Book 2:21 (*Cal.*, no. 46); cf. also 2:29, 1, 70 (*Cal.*, nos. 44, 45, 49); PRO T.S.11/689/2186, ff. 123–24.
60. PRO T.S.11/689/2186, ff. 114–15, 120(5).
61. See n. 48 and Maryland Historical Society Ms. 1195 (*Cal.*, no. 37), Gov. Smallwood to J. Adams, 8 June 1787.
62. Cf. n. 2 and Samuel Flagg Bemis, *Jay's Treaty* (New York, 1923). For the work of the commissioners, see John Bassett Moore, ed., *International Adjudications: Modern Series*, 6 vols. (New York, 1929–33), esp. vol. 3 (Philadelphia commission), and vol. 4 (London commission).
63. Perkins, *The First Rapprochement*, pp. 116–19.
64. On Pinkney, see *Dictionary of American Biography*, and Henry Wheaton, *Some Account of the Life, Writings, and Speeches of William Pinkney* (New York, 1826).
65. HR Blue Book 2:25, 26 (*Cal.*, nos. 47, 48), T.S. Lee and Council to Randolph, 3 May, John Henry to same, 23 May 1794.

66. HR Blue Book 2:124 (*Cal.*, no. 50).
67. PRO FO 5/20, ff. 113–14 (R. King to Grenville, 10 Feb. 1797, printed in *King* 2:144–45); FO 95/370 (Grenville to law officers, 15 Feb., 28 July, 16 Nov. 1797); cf. also HR Blue Book 2:114, 171, 67, 30 (*Cal.*, nos. 51–54).
68. HR Blue Book 2:2 (*Cal.,* no. 70); PRO FO 83/2204, ff. 186–87.
69. HR Blue Book 2:173A, B, C (*Cal.*, nos. 59–61) R. King to Pickering, 7 July, to Loughborough, 19 June 1797 and enclosure; PRO T.29/70 p. 196 (Treasury minutes, 18 Mar. 1797); T.29/72, p. 369 (Treasury minutes, 7 Apr. 1798); FO 5/20, ff. 131–34, 237–40 (Mrs. Russell's memorial, 15 Feb. 1797, J. Wilmot's report, 30 Mar. 1797); FO 5/21, ff. 171–72 (J. Scott to Hammond, [July 1797]); cf. also HR Blue Book 2:173, 98, 89, 136 (*Cal.*, nos. 55–58). The last indicates that in Dec. 1796, Bank stock was selling at 143, making the £74,401 face value worth £106,393. Mrs. Russell appears to have been paid shortly after 7 Apr. 1798. The chancellor was in touch with Molleson, Mrs. Russell's son-in-law, in February–March 1798 and may have been instrumental in obtaining the payment for Mrs. Russell, PRO FO 5/24, f. 67 (King to [Hammond], 2 Feb. 1798). King was kept in touch with Molleson's intentions through Sampson Hanbury, HR Blue Book 2:12, 5, 4, 4A, 8, 9 (*Cal.*, nos. 73–78). The Ewers' and Buchanans' parallel claims were allowed £8,000 each by the commissioners and apparently paid by 1798. PRO A.O. 12/109, f. 51v; *King* 2:473 (King to Grenville, 1 Dec. 1798); New York Public Library, Mss. Div., Chalmers Papers: Maryland 2:32–35.
70. HR Blue Book 2:173B (*Cal.,* no. 62), R. King to Pickering, 15 July 1797.
71. PRO FO 5/21, ff. 149–50, 161 (King to Grenville, 19, 20 July 1797, printed in *King* 2:202–3); cf. also ff. 155–56 (King to Loughborough, 19 July 1797 and enclosure).
72. Kilty et al., *Laws of Maryland* 7: Res. 1797, nos. 17–21; HR Blue Book 2:23 (*Cal.*, no. 72); *King* 2:281–82. Some speculators in 1797 offered the state £100,000 current money for the Bank stock, then worth about £110,000 sterling or £188,333 current money. HR Blue Book 2:135 (*Cal.*, no. 63). For Chase's correspondence at this time, see HR Blue Book 2:134, 77, 133, 132 (*Cal.*, nos. 65–67, 71). Some in Maryland thought that after 1798 the British government wanted the state to reimburse the crown for the compensation paid to Russell et al; cf. Maryland Historical Society, Vertical File, Chase to J. McHenry, 19 Jan. 1799, Pickering to R. King, 6 Aug. 1799, with Chase's memorandum of 5 Aug. 1799.
73. *King* 2:265–66, 273–74, 323–24, 473, 566; 3:137, 271–74 (King to Pickering, 28 Dec. 1797 [also in HR Blue Book 2:48 and *Cal.*, no. 68 under date, 25 Dec.], 15 Mar., 21 Oct. 1799; to Loughborough, 19 Jan., 1 June 1798; to Grenville, 1 Dec. 1798; to Dundas, 11 July 1800); cf. also HR Blue Book 2:47 (*Cal.*, no 83) Chase to Gov Ogle, 20 Apr. 1799, which shows that by Nov. 1798 the stock had reached £83,148 face value, at 142 worth £118,070 sterling.
74. PRO FO 5/34, ff. 220–21 (retrospective notes sent by King to Addington in his of 3 Nov. 1801); cf. *King* 4:10.
75. PRO FO 5/31, ff. 96–99 (G. Hamilton et al. to Grenville, Glasgow, 29 Mar. 1800); cf. also ff. 41B–42, 53–62, 96–97, 111–34, 141–67; cf. also FO 5/28 ff. 202, 299, 303, 307; FO 5/34 ff. 259–62.
76. PRO FO 5/28, ff. 305–6 (Glasgow memorial, 23 Nov. 1799); FO 5/31, ff. 199–200 (G. Hamilton and R. Findlay to Grenville, 31 May 1800), ff. 207–8 (Grenville to Hamilton and Findlay, 3 June), ff. 214–15, 220–21 (Hamilton et al. to Grenville, 9, 13 June), ff. 234–37 (Molleson to G. Hammond, 3 July, with enclosure), f. 282 (answer of 10 July 1800).
77. PRO FO 5/34, ff. 220–21; cf. also for merchants' input FO 5/31, ff. 190, 192, 194, 196–97, 281, 284–94.
78. *King* 3:335–37, 502–4 (King to Sec. of State, 23 Jan., 24 Aug. 1801); 3: 501–2 (King to Hawkesbury, 20 Aug. 1801=FO 5/34, ff. 209–10); PRO FO 5/31, ff. 332–50, 406, 410–35 (Thomas Macdonald to Grenville, 10 Oct. 1800, with enclosure [important for political background in U.S.], to G. Hammond, 5, 11, Dec. 1800, with enclosure); FO 5/34, ff. 70–72 (King to Hawkesbury, 9 Mar, 1801, with enclosure), f. 94 (newspaper clipping on Jefferson's debts), ff. 138–39 (Macdonald to Hamilton, 4 May 1801), ff. 209–13 (for project).
79. Perkins, *First Rapprochement,* 130, 138–41; *King* 3:520, 527–34, 4:7–8, 10, 17–18, 31–32, 36–37, 44, 47–50, 54–56.
80. *King* 3:376 (King to Sec. of State, 23 Jan. 1801).
81. PRO FO 5/35, ff. 70–72, 79–81 (King to Hawkesbury, 9 Mar. 1801, with enclosures); cf. HR Blue Book 2:49 (*Cal.,* no. 89).

82. PRO FO 5/34, ff. 214-15 (King to Hammond, 22 Aug. 1801); cf. 209-10, to Hawkesbury, 20 Aug. 1801.

83. *King* 3:477-78, 514, 517-18 (to Eldon, 22 June, 10, 24 Sept.), p. 507 (to Sampson Hanbury, 29 Aug. 1801); PRO FO 5/34, ff. 226-27 (R. King to G. Hammond, 3 Sept. 1801); cf. also HR Blue Book 2:16, 17 (*Cal.*, nos. 90, 91).

84. *King* 3:530, 533-34 (King's "Note of conferences . . . ").

85. Ibid., 4:48 (King to Madison, 9 Jan. 1802).

86. HR Blue Book 2:29 (*Cal.*, no. 44), Chase's "Observations."

87. PRO FO 5/7, ff. 422-23 (memorial on behalf of Perry, Hay & Co. of Bristol; Robert Christie, Daniel Dulany, Robert Alexander [former member of Congress], and John Banytine of London; James Christie and Alexander Stenhouse of Fife, Scotland; James Miller and John Mason of Glasgow; and Hugh Dean of Shelburne, Nova Scotia, later of Nassau, Bahamas).

88. PRO FO 5/27, ff. 209-10 (memorial for same, plus Rev. Gilbert Buchanan of Woodmansterne, Surrey [probably son of John Buchanan] and Henry Riddle of Glasgow). The memorialists claimed that the issue of 1769 was also backed by Bank stock; cf. Northamptonshire Record Office, Fitzwilliam-Burke Mss. A. xxvi. 7 for memorandum describing Alexander as the chief manager of the note holders in the 1780s and 1790s.

89. New York Public Library, Mss. Div., Chalmers Papers, Maryland 2:28-46; PRO FO 5/40, ff. 15-17 (memorial of 3 Feb, 1803 to Treasury, enclosing [ff. 18-20] earlier petition to king in council); T.29/80, pp. 412-13. For value of trust, 1 Dec. 1801, see HR Blue Book 2:160 (*Cal.*, no. 93).

90. HR Blue Book 2:76 (*Cal.*, no. 99), R. King to Madison, 9 Jan. 1802; 2:131, 128 (*Cal.*, nos. 100, 111), S. Chase to Gov. Mercer, 13 Feb., 24 Dec. 1802; 3::22 (*Cal.*, no. 101), Mercer to Madison, 16 Feb. 1802; 2:112 (*Cal.*, no. 102), Madison to Mercer, 23 Feb. 1802; 2:130 (*Cal.*, no. 103), Chase to Mercer, 14 Apr. 1802. Cf. also 2:46, 129 (*Cal.*, nos. 92, 104); see esp. *King* 4:182-83 (W. Hindman to King, 21 Nov. 1802), and PRO FO 95/24 (from E. Thornton [No. 53], 28 Dec. 1802).

91. HR Blue Book 2:32 (Cal., no. 117); cf. also 2:123 (*Cal.*, no. 118).

92. PRO T.S.11/689/2186, ff. 112-13.

93. HR Blue Book 2:18, 3 (*Cal.*, nos. 106-112); PRO T.S.11/689/2186, ff. 116-22.

94. PRO FO 5/37, f. 141 (King to Hawkesbury, 30 July 1802); *King* 4:156-58 (to Madison, 10 Aug. 1802), also in HR Blue Book 2:127 (*Cal.*, no. 105); cf. also Blue Book 2:75, 51 (*Cal.*, nos. 107, 108).

95. PRO T.29/79, p. 490.

96. *King* 4:190-91 (to Addington, 7 Dec. 1802); PRO FO 5/37, f. 216 (King to Hawkesbury, 9 Dec. 1802).

97. PRO FO 95/374, p. 39, copies in HR Blue Book 2:116A, 11 (*Cal.*, nos. 109-10).

98. HR Blue Book 2:19, 159, 126 (*Cal.*, nos. 119-120, 139); PRO T.S. 11/689/2186, ff. 123-24 (White's petition), ff. 126-29 (full text of chancellor's order).

99. HR Blue Book 2:167A (*Cal.*, no. 121), W. Lyon to William Murdock (Chase's agent), 14 Apr. 1803.

100. PRO T.S.11/689/2186. ff. 72-80 for attorney-general's information of 20 Apr. 1803; ff. 133-36 for brief of 23 Apr. prepared by the solicitor general, Thomas Manners Sutton; ff. 110-11 for opinion (probably by crown law officers) of ca. 27 Apr. 1803; ff. 96-102 for material relating to Harford's claim; HR Blue Book 2:22, 117, 117a (*Cal.*, nos. 123, 125, 126), King to Lyon and Collyer, 22, 26 Apr. 1803; *King* 4:247-48.

101. PRO FO 5/40, ff. 13, 84, 124-27 (King to Hawkesbury, 1 Feb., 28 Mar., to G. Hammond, 24 Apr., with enclosed draft); FO 95/440 (Hawkesbury to R. King, 25 Apr. 1803); also in HR Blue Book 2:11A, 116 (*Cal.*, nos. 126-27); cf. also *King* 4:215-17.

102. HR Blue Book 2:115 (*Cal.*, no. 129), King to Madison, 1 May 1803, also in *King* 4:247-48.

103. Acts 1801, ch. 103 in HR Blue Book 2:24 (*Cal.*, no. 95).

104. PRO FO 5/40, ff. 173, 208 (King to G. Hammond, Cowes, 20 May, Monroe to Hawkesbury, 20 July 1803).

105. HR Blue Book 2:31, 119, 52, 103 (*Cal.*, nos. 133, 131, 136, 141), Madison to Pinkney, 3 May (2 letters) (also in PRO FO 5/40, ff. 225-26); Madison to Gov. Mercer, 19 May 1803; Pinkney to Mercer, 11 July 1803.

VII

106. HR Blue Book 2:115.
107. HR Blue Book 2:33 (*Cal.*, no. 137).
108. HR Blue Book 2:118, 125 (*Cal.*, nos. 140, 142), Chase to Mercer, Baltimore, 5, 11 July 1803.
109. HR Blue Book 2:108 (*Cal.*, no. 143). Cf. also 2:28A, 28, 35A (*Cal.*, nos. 147, 149, 150).
110. HR Blue Book 2:161, 162, 174 (*Cal.*, nos. 152, 151, 154) Pinkney to Mercer, 20 Sept. (2 letters), 22 Oct. 1803; cf. council order of 5 Aug. 1803 in Maryland Historical Society Ms. 1235.
111. PRO FO 5/40, ff. 221, 239 (Monroe to Hawkesbury, 29 Aug., 7 Sept, 1803); HR Sec. of State, no. 4 (*Cal.*, no. 156), Spencer Perceval to Monroe, 2 Nov. 1803; *King* 4:318-21 (C. Gore to R. King, 1 Nov. 1803); and HR Blue Book 2:90 (*Cal.*, no 164).
112. PRO T.S.11/689/2186, f. 132, contains notice to all parties of 14 Dec., sent by Treasury Solicitor Joseph White, acting for the attorney general, stating motion to be made on the twenty-first; ff. 137-40 contains minute of order to master from chancellor for settling legal expenses (also in HR Blue Book 2:109); ff. 141-52 contains chancellor's order of 21 Dec. On ff. 153-54 is a memorandum of ca. May 1804 indicating that the "Treas[ur]y have agreed to Transfer 10,000 Bank Stock to Mr. Hartford." Legal expenses were paid for Chase (£531:14:9), Barclay et al. (£741:13:2), Henry Harford (£523:13:3), the Ewers (£313:8:1), the Russells and Grove (£553:10:9), Buchanan's trustees (£359:13:2), the attorney general (£397:18:0), and the Bank of England (£65:16:4). Pinkney had to agree to assume all responsibility before Chase's solicitors, Lyon and Collyer, would agree to the transfer; HR Blue Book 2:35, 35B, 36 (*Cal.*, nos. 158, 159, 160); cf. also Blue Book 2:121 (*Cal.*, no. 162).
113. HR Blue Book 2:99 (*Cal.*, no. 164).
114. Cf. n. 89.
115. PRO FO 83/2204, f. 309 (J. Sargent to G. Hammond, 1 May 1804, encl. [ff. 311-12] opinion of 28 Apr.); also in T.S.11/689/2186, ff. 153-54; and FO 5/44. ff. 226-27.
116. HR Blue Book 2:95, 97, 106 (*Cal.*, nos. 202, 181, 199) Pinkney to Madison, 3 Nov., Harrowby to Pinkney, 14 Aug., Pinkney to Harrowby, 17 Aug. 1804; last also in PRO FO 5/44, f. 282. In 1806, Maryland provided for the redemption with interest of the bills of exchange and certificates issued in 1780 in exchange for the 1766 paper money called in. Nothing was done about outstanding paper money or "bills of credit," Kilty et al., *Laws of Maryland* 7: Res., 1806, nos. 8, 9; cf. also New York Public Library, Mss. Div., Chalmers Papers: Maryland, 2:52-59. The money holders were still seeking compensation in 1822.
117. HR Blue Book 2:95, 104 (*Cal.*, nos. 202, 175); PRO FO 5/44, ff. 242-43, 266, 272 (White to Huskisson, 2 Aug., Monroe to Harrowby, 11 Aug., Harrowby to Monroe, 13 Aug. 1804); T.S.11/689/2186, ff. 155-56, 158-61 (petition of White for attorney general, 3 Aug.), ff. 169-76 (Eldon's order of 6 Aug. 1804); cf. also FO 5/44, ff. 186, 224-25 (Monroe to Harrowby, 26 May, Pinkney to same, 2 July 1804); HR Blue Book 2:58, 55, 62 (*Cal.*, nos. 168, 176, 179); HR Sec. of State, no. 11 (*Cal.*, no. 177); cf. also S.M. Hamilton, ed., *The Writings of James Monroe*, 7 vols. (New York, 1898-1903), 4:233-34 (to Madison, 7 Aug. 1804).
118. Bank Record Office, Bank Stock Ledger 64:Q, f. 35; Ledger 67:T, f. 2350; Ledger 66:S, f. 1757.
119. HR Sec. of State, no. 12, Blue Book 2:102, 3:31 (*Cal.*, nos. 178, 193-94).
120. HR Sec. of State, nos. 11, 14 (*Cal.*, nos. 177, 190), Blue Book 2:59, 92, 95, 69, 72, 105, 42, 82, 85, 94, 172 (*Cal.*, nos. 191, 195, 202, 204, 209-10, 318-22).
121. HR Blue Book 2:39, 39A, 79, 95 (*Cal.*, nos. 185, 184, 187, 202); Sec. of State, nos. 11, 15, 21, 28 (*Cal.*, nos. 177, 197, 217, 226).
122. HR Blue Book 2:81, 113, 41, 54 (*Cal.*, nos. 196, 205, 211, 240), W. Murdock to Chase, 16 Aug. 1804; Madison to Pinkney, 16 Nov. 1804; General Assembly joint resolution of 19 Dec. 1804; Monroe to Gov. Bowie, 7 Aug. 1805; cf. also HR Sec. of State, nos. 19, 24, 25 (*Cal.*, nos. 215, 220, 222); Kilty et al., *Laws of Maryland* 7: Res. Nov. 1804, nos. 3-5.
123. HR Sec. of State, nos. 29, 33 (*Cal.*, nos. 223, 234) Gov. Bowie's certificate, 20 Apr. 1805, Gallatin to Monroe, 4 June 1805; cf. also Sec. of State, no. 26 and Blue Book 2:148 (*Cal.*, nos. 224, 221).
124. HR Blue Book 2:96, 146, 158/2 (*Cal.*, nos. 228-29), Nicholson to Gov. Bowie, 29 Apr., to Monroe, 22 May 1805; cf. also 2:66 (*Cal.*, no. 227).
125. HR. Sec. of State, nos. 41, 43, 58, 67, 70 (*Cal.*, nos. 244, 247, 281, 284), A. Baring to Erving, 8 Aug., Erving to A. Baring, 8 Aug., Sir Francis Baring & Co. to Monroe, 15, 29 Aug.

40

1805; cf. also Sec. of State, nos. 36–40, 46–57, 63–64 (*Cal.*, nos. 237–39, 241–42, 251–60, 263–64, 274–75); Blue Book 2:138/C–F, H, 84 (*Cal.*, nos. 261–62, 265–66, 278, 305).

126. HR Blue Book 2:144B, Sec. of State nos. 75–76 (*Cal.*, nos. 292–94); Francis Baring & Co. to Monroe, 8 Oct. 1805; cf. Blue Book 2:87 (*Cal.*, no 306) for an account by Nicholson.

127. HR Sec. of State nos. 72, 79, 80 (*Cal.*, nos. 287, 296, 299), Barings to Monroe, 3 Sept., Monroe to Barings, 12 Oct., Barings to Monroe, 14 Oct. 1805; cf. also nos. 69, 73, 81 (*Cal.*, nos. 283, 289, 302), and Blue Book 2:153, 153B (*Cal.*, nos. 279, 285).

128. HR Blue Book 2:155, 145, 156, 149, 150, 143, 158–1, 86, 147 (*Cal.*, nos. 308–16), Nicholson to Gov. Bowie, 30 Dec. 1805, 3, 11 Feb., 3 Mar., undated, 23, 26 Oct., 4, 6, Nov.; 2:154 (*Cal.*, no. 317), Resolution of General Assembly, 4 Dec. 1806 (also in Kilty et al., *Laws of Maryland* 7: Res. 1806, nos. 15–16).

129. Kilty et al., *Laws of Maryland* 7: Res. 1812, no. 6; cf. also. Res. 1813, no. 8.

INDEX

Abbreviations: Glas. = Glasgow; L. = London; m(s)/ = merchant(s) of; traditional abbreviations used for 13 colonies. Ampersand (&) used in formal company names or styles.

beer: I 32
Beer, George Louis: cited, I 33
Belfast:
 Lloyd's inspection at: IV 723
Bennassar, Bartolomé: cited, II 124
Bermuda, shipbuilding in: IV 712, 716, 718
Berner, R.C.: cited, IV 708
Beveridge, William Henry, baron: cited, I 21
Bezanson, Anne: cited, I 20, 21
Bideford, Devon: VI, 421
 Lloyd's inspection at: IV 723
bills of exchange: I 36; II 138, 141, 153, 166,
 168–9; V 294, 303–5, 307, 311–19,
 322–3, 332–3, 337
 long bills: V 317–18, 323
 in Chesapeake slave purchases: V 284–5
Birmingham: VI 408–410, 413–14, 428
 hardware trade: I 43
Black Country: VI 428
Bladen, Martin, M.P.: VI 400
Bladen, Thomas, M.P.: VI 400
Bladen, William: VI 400
Board of Control [for E. Indian affairs]:
 VII 21
Board of Trade: III 307–10; VI, 397, 399,
 400, 410, 434
Bolingbroke, Henry St. John, viscount:
 VI 435
bonds:
 for credit in slave trade: V 305, 310–11,
 314–15, 318–20, 324–5, 330, 332
 for other debts: I 37, 38
Bo'ness, West Lothian: VI 421
books, imported in colonies: I 35
Booth, Richard, m/L.: V 302
Bordeaux, slave trade: V 337
Boston, Mass.:
 entrepôt trade: II 149
 fish trade: II 141–3, 146, 149
 geographical setting: II 140–1
 growth: II 128–9, 143–4, 173
 maritime economy: II 142–9
 occupations: II 130–1, 134–7, 149
 population: II 136, 143, 176
 shipbuilding: II 142, 146–9
 shipping: II 146–7, 157
 social structure: II 136
 whaling: II 146
Botsford, Jay Barrett: cited, VI 395
Bourdieu & Chollet, ms/L.: II 159
Bowden, William, m/L.: VI 425
Bowie, Robert, governor of Md.: VII 34
Brazil:
 antecedents to slave plantation credit:
 V 297–8

sugar industry: V 299
Brazil wood (dyestuff): I 33
bread, colonial export: I 27, 28
breweries, in colonies, I 35
Bridenbaugh, Carl: cited, II 127–8, 155,
 176–7
Bristol: V 316, 318, 324; VI 406, 408, 413,
 421, 428–9
 Lloyd's inspection at: IV 723
 interest in American shipbuilding: IV 710
Britain, Great:
 data on colonial trade: III 307–25
 impact of North America on: VI 395–436
 government and debt claims: VII 9, 19,
 21–3
 and Maryland's Bank stock: VII 10, 18–25,
 33–4
 imports from American colonies: I 28–9
 market for colonial ships: IV 709–10
British Isles:
 market for colonial exports: I 27–8
British West Indies: V 328
 credit system: V 331
 see also West Indies
brokers: I 21
Brooke, John: cited, VI 433
Buchan, David Steuart Erskine, 11th earl of:
 VII 12
Buchanan, George, m/Glas.: V 313
Buchanan, Gilbert, m/L.: VII 13
 later clergyman: VII 38
Buchanan, James, & Co., ms/L.: V 325–6
Buchanan, John, m/L.: VII 13, 15, 17, 24,
 37–9
Buenos Aires:
 growth of: II 124
Burke, Edmund, M.P: VI 403

cabinet-makers: II 135
cables and cordage, ships': I 34
Cadiz: II 153
calicoes: I 32
Cambridge: VI 407
Cambridge, Mass.: II 133–4
Campbell, Archibald, inspector-general of
 exports, etc.: III 311–12
Canada: VI 402
 ships built in: IV 716
Canterbury: VI 407
capital:
 movements: I 37
 in export trades: I 38
 in slave trade: V 318, 336–9
 relation to land and labor: V 293–4
 'cargo trade': I 37

(English) to colonies: II 144–5

factors, British:
  in Chesapeake: II 166
  responsibility for slave credit sales:
    V 323–5, 333–4
Falmouth, Cornwall: VI 421
family studies: I 23
Farell & Jones, ms/Bristol: V 320–1
Farmers' Bank, Baltimore: VII 33
firms, size of: I 38
fiscal policy and colonial trade: I 34
fish, colonial exports: I 27–9, 36; II 141–6
fisheries, colonial: I 23
  employment in: II 136–7, 141, 186
flax: I 34
  seed, exported: I 27; II 158
flour, colonial export: I 27–8, 30, 36; II 145, 186
forest products: I 36
  export of: II 143, 161, 169; see also masts,
    pearl ash, pitch, potash, tar, wood
Forrest, Uriah, m/L.: VII 18, 36
Fort Duquesne: II 153
Fowey, Cornwall: VI 421–2
Fox, Henry, factor in Va.: V 304
France: VI 431, 435
  cereal market in: II 153, 159
  protectionism: I 30
  slave trade and credit: V 331–7, 339
  tobacco monopoly: I 34
  towns: II 125
Franklin, Benjamin: VII 8, 9, 35
Frederick, Prince of Wales: VI 398
Fredericksburg, Va.: II 164
French, V. & P., & Nephew, ms/Bordeaux:
  VII 9
French & Hobson, ms/L.: VII 9
frontier areas, settlement of: V 293, 295
fulling mills, colonial: I 35
fur trade: I 23, 27, 29; II 143
fur-using trades: II 136

Galenson, David: cited, I 35; V 299–300
Gallatin, Albert: VII 32
garrisons, military: II 134
George I: VII 4
George III: VI 416; VII 9
Georgetown, Md.: II 164
Georgia: VI 405
  ships built in: IV 716
  slavery in: I 36
  trade with Britain: III 322–5
  with Scotland: III 318–21
  trustees of: VI 401
Georgia Society: VI 398

Gilmor, Robert, & Sons, ms/Baltimore: VII 33
Glamann, Kristof: cited, I 24
Glasgow: V 316
  collector of: III 309–10
  firm size: I 38–9
  merchants: V 336; VI 430
  shipping: II 148
  trade of: VI 407–8, 411, 420–1, 428–9
Gloucester, Mass.: II 146
Godolphin, Sydney, earl of: VI 433
Goldenberg, Joseph A.: cited, IV 714–17, 718
Gooch, Sir William, lieutenant-governor of
  Va.: V 308–9
Gordon, Lord Adam: VI 399n
Grand Ohio Company: VI 403
Gregg Press, Ltd.: IV 714–15
Grenada: V 328
Grenville, George, prime minister: III 311
Grenville, William Wyndham Grenville,
  baron: VII 19–20, 22–3, 25
gristmills: II 151
Grove, Silvanus, m/L.: VII 6–8, 10–13, 17, 35
growth, economic, measuring of: I 18–19
Guinea, slave trade in: V 297–8
Gurney, Richard, of Norwich: VII 17, 36

haberdashery: I 35
Halifax, George Montagu Dunk, 2nd earl of:
  VI 400–1
Hamburg: VI 418
  price-currents: I 21
Hamilton, Henry: cited, I 20
Hammond, George, undersecretary: VII 21,
  23, 29
Hanbury, Capel, m/L.: VI 430; VII 6, 7, 16
Hanbury, John, m/L. (1700-58): VI 430
Hanbury, John, m. and brewer of L.
  (1751-1800): VII 6, 8, 13, 16–17, 20,
  24–5, 36
Hanbury, Osgood, m/L.: VII 6, 7, 10, 13,
  16–17, 30–1
Hanbury, Osgood, & Co., ms/L.: V 327;
  VII 16, 18, 30
Hanbury, Sampson, brewer of L.: VII 31
Harford, Henry, proprietor of Md.: VII 9, 17,
  20, 24, 26–8, 30, 33, 36, 38
Harper, Lawrence A.: cited, I 20–1, 33;
  III 308; IV 705
Harrowby, Dudley Ryder, lst earl of: VII 19, 29
Hartford, Conn.: II 176
hawkers: II 138
Hawkesbury, Robert Banks Jenkinson, baron
  (later 2nd earl of Liverpool): VII 19, 23,
  25–9
Heathcote, Sir Gilbert, bart., m/L.: VI 433

Lloyd's, Society of Underwriters at:
    IV 713–15, 719, 722–3
Lloyd's Register: IV 713–19, 721, 723
logwood: I 33, II 158
London: V 316, 324
    American firms in: II 169
    commission merchants: II 168–9
    discounting bills of exchange at: V 317–18
    firm size: I 38
    Lloyd's inspection at: IV 723
    merchants of: IV 412–16, 423–6, 428–30
    merchants in slave trade: V 302, 307–9
    price-currents: I 21
    ship prices at: IV 719
    subscribers to *American Negotiator*:
        VI 406–10
London Assurance Co.: VII 7, 34
Long Caln Forge, Md.: VII 9
Loughborough, Alexander Wedderburn, baron
    (later first earl of Rosslyn), chancellor:
    VII 18, 20, 21, 25, 26
Looe, Cornwall: VI 421–2
loyalists: I 37
Lyme Regis, Dorset: VI 421–2
Lynn, (King's), Norfolk:
    Lloyd's inspection at: IV 723
Lyon, William & John, solicitors: VII 15, 20,
    25
Lyon & Collier, solicitors: VII 26, 39

McCusker, John J.: work cited, I 18, 23, 36;
    III 308–9; IV 719–21
Macdonald, Sir Archibald, attorney-general:
    VII 18
Maddocks, John, K.C., lawyer: VII 12, 13
Madison, James: VII 24, 27
Madrid:
    growth of: II 124
mahogany: II 159
Main, Gloria: cited, I 23
Maine, fisheries: II 142
maize, colonial export: I 27; II 169
Manchester: VI 407–8
Manners-Sutton, Thomas, solicitor-general:
    VII 38
Mansfield, James, solicitor-general: VII 8, 11,
    12
manufactures:
    exported from Britain: I 43
    colonial: I 35
Marblehead, Mass.: II 142, 146, 148, 177
maritime occupations: II 136–7
Maryland: V 327, VI 400, 402, 405, 411
    Assembly: VII 4–10
    cereal exports: II 141, 163

credit law: V 307, 309
economy: I 25
shipbuilding: II 148, 168; IV 716, 724
ship sales: IV 711
slave trade: V 305
stores in: V 325–6
studies of: I 23
tobacco exports: II 163
towns in: II 128, 163–7
trade with Britain: III 322–25
trade with Scotland: III 318–21
warehouses, public: II 170; *see also*
    'Virginia and Maryland'
Maryport, Cumberland:
    Lloyd's inspection at: IV 723
Massachusetts:
    cereal imports: II 140-1
    external commerce: II 157
    fishing fleet: II 142, 146; IV 709
    population: II 143, 147
    ports: II 145–8
    ship registration: II 148
    shipbuilding: II 142, 146–8; IV 708–9
    shipping sales abroad: IV 711
Mason, John, m/Gl.: VII 38
masts, colonial export: I 27, 28, 30
    strategic value: I 34
Mathias, Peter: cited, VI 431
Mauduit, Israel, m/L.: VI 425
Mauduit, Jasper, m/L.: VI 425
Maxwell, George, m/Md.: V 313
'mechanics': II 134–5
Melcombe Regis, Dorset: VI 422
Menard, Russell R.: work cited, I 18, 23
Menzies, George: III 312
Mercer, John F., governor of Md.: VII 27, 28
merchants: accounts of: I 22
    defined: II 138–9
    networks: II 159–60
merchants (by region):
    British, debt claims: VII 6, 21, 22
    Chesapeake: II 166–9
    English: VI 408–16, 420–6, 428–30, 433–4
metal craftsmen: II 135
Meyer, Jean: cited V, 339
Middletown, Conn.: II 177
military officers, in House of Commons:
    VI 402
Miller, James, m/Glas.: VII 38
millinery: I 35
mills: II 151–2
Mitchell, B.R.: cited, I 20
molasses: I 35; II 150, 170
Molleson, William, m/L.: VII 7, 12, 20, 22,
    37

Parliament:
    House of Commons: III 312–13; VI 401–5,
        412–16, 432–3, 435-5
    House of Lords: III 312–3
Patapsco River: II 170
pearl ash:
    colonial export: I 27–8
peddlers: II 138
Pelham, Henry, prime minister: III 310;
    VI 398, 400
Pennsylvania: II 135, VI 405
    cereal exports: II 141
    external commerce: II 158
    migrants: II 171
    population: II 152
    settled areas: II 151, 154
    shipbuilding: IV 716, 724
    shipping exports: IV 711
    trade with Britain: III 322–5
    trade with Scotland: III 318–21
Penryn, Cornwall: VI 421
pepper: I 30
Perceval, Spencer: VII 26, 28
Perry, Micaiah, the elder: V 302
Perry, Hay & Co., m/Bristol: VII 38
Petersburg, Va.: II 164
Philadelphia: I 39
    commerce: II 151–7
    exports: II 144–5, 152–3
    hinterland: II 151
    imports: II 154
    merchants: II 152–3
    occupations: II 130–1, 134–7, 149, 152
    population: II 126, 143, 145, 157, 173, 176
    shipbuilding: II 148
    ship prices: IV 707, 719–20
    shipping: II 145, 154, 157
    social structure: II 136, 155
Pinckney, Thomas, American diplomat:
    VII 19
Pinckney, William, of Md.: VII 19, 20, 27–31,
    33, 34
pine:
    use in shipbuilding: II 142
pitch, exported: I 30
Pitt, William, the younger: VII 11, 13–14,
    18–19, 21, 29
plantation economies:
    credit in: V 293–339
plantation owners:
    absentee: V 329
Plymouth, Devon: VI 421
Polhill, Nathaniel, M.P., m/Southwark: VI 425
Poole, Dorset: VI 408, 421
    Lloyd's inspection at: IV 723

population:
    of Britain: VI 402
    of British colonies: II 175–7; VI 402, 419
    and economic development: I 25–6
    urban, classification of: II 130–7, 177; *see
        also* occupations
pork:
    colonial export: I 27–8; II 169
port books, naval officers': I 20–1
ports, North American: II 126–86
    function: II 139–40
Portsmouth, Hants: VI 408, 421–2
    Lloyd's inspection at: IV 723
Portsmouth, New Hampshire: II 177
Port Tobacco, Md.: II 164
Portugal:
    markets in: II 141
    ship sales in: II 142
Posthumus, Nicolaas W.: cited, I 21
potash(es): I 27
Potomac Company: VII 33
Poussou, J.P.: cited, II 127
Powell, John, & Co., ms/Bristol: V 320–1
Preston, Lancs: VI 408
price data: I 21–2
Princeton, N.J.: II 133–4
protectionism: I 30
Providence, R.I.: II 151, 170, 177
provisions, export of: I 36; II 161
public employment: II 133–4
Public Record Office:
    holdings on external trade: I 19
Pulteney, William Johnstone: V 328–9

Quakers: VI 423, 430; VII 6, 7, 10, 36
    in Newport: II 149

Radoff, Morris L.: cited, VII 3
Randolph, Edmund, U.S. secretary of state:
    VII 19
register-general of tobacco: III 309
religion and transatlantic ties: VI 422–6
retailers: II 138 and n.
Rhode Island:
    cereal imports: II 141
    shipbuilding: II 150
rice: II 159, 161–3, 186
    colonial export: I 27–30
    consumption: I 33
    cultivation: I 23
Richardson, David: cited, V 316, 337
Richmond, Va.: II 164
Riddle [Riddell], Henry, m/Glas.: VII 38
Rinchon, Father Dieudonné: cited, V 331
road, droving: II 152

Somerset: VI 413
South Carolina: *see* Carolina
South Sea Company: VI 433
Southwark, Surrey: VI 425
Spain:
　markets in: II 141
　ship sales in: II 142
　tobacco monopoly: I 34
Spotswood, Alexander, governor of Va.:
　V 320
Stamp Act: VI 436
Stanley, John, M.P.: VII 13–14
staple:
　model: I 24–6
Starke, Thomas, m/L.: V 304–5
Stenhouse, Alexander, of Fife: VII 38
Stephenson, Randolph & Cheston, ms/Bristol:
　V 320
Steward, Stephen, & Son, ms/Md.: VII 9
stores, in American colonies: I 37, 39;
　II 138n; V 325–6
storekeepers, country: II 138–9
sugar:
　Brazil: V 297–9
　consumption: I 32–3
　prices: V 301, 330
　production: I 36; V 306
　slave labor in production: V 297–8
　trade in: I 28–30; II 143, 158, 170; VI 421
tar:
　colonial export: I 27–8, 30
tea: I 30, 35
Tea Act: VI 436
Thomas, Sir Dalby: V 299, 301
Thomas, Robert Paul: cited, IV 706
Thomlinson, John, m/L.: VI 403
Thurlow, Edward Thurlow, baron, chancellor:
　VII 13–14, 18
tobacco:
　consumption: I 32
　cultivation: I 22, 30
　exports: II 143, 161, 163, 165–7, 186
　prices: I 21; III 317
　re-exports: II 167
　shipping used: II 148
　taxation: I 34; II 167
　trade (18th c.): I 25, 27–30, 38; VII 3–10
　varieties: II 167
　warehouses: II 166
Tobacco Act (1751): III 309
Tobago: V 328
Tomlinson, John, m/L.: VII 6
tonnage (ship), calculation of: IV 719
Topsham, Devon:
　Lloyd's inspection at: IV 723

towns:
　studies of: I 23
　underdevelopment in Chesapeake: II 164–9
trade:
　in England: VI 406–30
　networks: I 35–7; V 297
　regulation of, in colonies: I 34
traders:
　rural: II 166–7, 169
　varieties of: II 138–9
Treasurer of the Western Shore (Md.): VII 9,
　33
Treasury Board (London): III 307, 310–11;
　VI 434
Treaty of Fort Stanwix: VI 403
Treaty of Paris (1783): VII 9–10
Trecothick, Barlow, M.P., m/L.: VI 403, 412
Truro, Cornwall: VI 421–2
turpentine: I 27–8; II 143
Tynemouth, Northumberland:
　Lloyd's inspection at: IV 723

Ukraine, wheat from: I 24
United States:
　population: II 143
United States government:
　and Bank stock negotiations: VII 10,
　18–25, 33–4
　and British debts claims: VII 9, 21–3

Valladolid: II 124
Van de Voort, J.P.: cited, V 329
Virginia: I 21; VI 402, 405, 411
　credit law: V 308–10
　economy: I 25
　planter debt in: V 327
　population: II 163
　shipbuilding in: II 168; IV 710–11, 724
　shipping: II 172
　ships trading to: IV 719
　slave plantations: V 306
　slave trade: V 302, 305, 318–22
　stores in: V 325–6
　towns in: II 128, 163–7, 172
　trade with Britain: III 322–5
　trade with Scotland: III 318–21
'Virginia and Maryland', customs category:
　III 313
　data: III 314–15
Virginia Gazette: V 319–21, 327

wagons: II 155
Wallace, James, attorney-general: VII 8
Wallace & Co., ms/N.Y.: II 159
Wallace, Davidson & Johnson, ms/Md.: IV 717